CREATIVE TITLING with PREMIERE PRO

Sequence 01
00:01:00:08326
0:00:00000
Main Title
Sub Title
Credits 3
Credits 5
Video 2
Video 1
Audio 1
Audio 3

CREATIVE with TITLING PREMIERE PRO

SCREAM

SCREAM

SCREAM

SCREAM

SCREAM

First published in the United States in 2004 by
CMP Books
600 Harrison Street,
San Francisco CA 94107

This book was conceived by
ILEX, Cambridge, England

Publisher: Alastair Campbell
Executive Publisher: Sophie Collins
Creative Director: Peter Bridgewater
Editorial Director: Steve Luck
Editor: Stuart Andrews
Design Manager: Tony Seddon
Designer: Jonathan Raimes
Artwork Assistant: Joanna Clinch
Development Art Director: Graham Davis
Technical Art Editor: Nicholas Rowland

A CIP record for this book is available from the Library of Congress.

ISBN 1-57820-233-7

Printed and bound in China

For more information on this title please visit:
www.tpreus.web-linked.com

contents

Why use titles?

There are three fundamental types of titles in the world of digital video—excluding those of Mr or Ms Director (which is yours). These are opening titles, captions, and end titles. Their use is dependent on the genre of the production, necessity, and any obligations the producer might have.

A movie has a title because it identifies it. The bottom line of any commercial product, such as a movie, a video or a TV program, is that nobody could talk about it unless it had a title—a word or a string of words that identify it in any number of ways other than the blindingly obvious (the name of the product).

Still pictures can make a virtue of a lack of title, or play with the viewer's expectations. For example, an artist might entitle his or her artwork *Untitled*—because they believe the image speaks for itself, perhaps, or because the work is the result of abstract experimentation. Such debates sit uneasily in the more obviously commercial worlds of video, movies, and television, where the pictures move.

A good example of this is Fox's *Friends* television series, each episode of which is called *"The One With/Where...,"* alluding to the public's apparent inability to distinguish between one episode and another in such a prolific commercial production.

But beyond the simple practical necessity of slapping a label on a moving picture before it gets away, a title can in its own way manipulate the viewer's expectations just as much as the title of an abstract artwork can. There have been many examples of audiences' interest in a movie being sparked solely by fascination with the title, thanks to clever marketing and a title that sells itself. The same cannot be said of abstract artworks.

In an international market, movie titles are often changed due to the difficulties of idiomatic translation (the Chinese title of the Jack Nicholson movie *As Good As It Gets* translates back into English as *Mr Cat Poo*). However, many titles are changed deliberately to excite, or to hype. Plain old *California* became *Kalifornia* to signify a skewed or twisted take on a thriller; John Dahl's *Joy Ride* was made under the working title of *Squelch*—but bizarrely became the far more American-sounding *Roadkill* when it was released in the UK. The exception that proves the rule is *Return of the Jedi*, originally titled *Revenge of the Jedi*, but dulled down because George Lucas insisted that a Jedi would never seek revenge.

This example goes some way to explain the semantics of titling. *Payback, Starship Troopers,* and *Dawn of the Dead* all serve to spell out the nature of the movie. Conflict appeals, and two words set against each other are often used to create a mood, a feeling, or irony. *Fatal Attraction, Dead Alive,* and *Dead Calm* use the oxymoron to dramatic effect; *Minority Report, Paris Trout,* and *Event Horizon* use obscure terms to invite a desire for explanation; *Pitch Black, Primal Fear,,,,,* and *From Hell* use common word couplings that are transformed when isolated.

Single-word titles are common in arthouse movies (or ones that have pretentions to art). A minimal, often obscure title suggests it is a mere afterthought to the important part: the movie itself. That said, single-word titles can be no-nonsense stamps on a movie, successfully identifying it while creating anticipation at the same time. The word, though, has to be the *right* word. For every *Jaws, Cube,* and *Scream*, there's a *Bounce, Levity,* and *Careful*.

The more successful titles are a word in impressive isolation—usually accompanying a movie that "does what it says on the can." *Go* is probably the most cunning example yet. It creates enough dynamism to be enticing without purporting to be "about" anything. Once the can is opened, it becomes increasingly noticeable that the word is uttered throughout the course of the movie in all its possible interpretations.

There's also an all-out-war of individualism amongst the hundreds of movies produced every year. From shorter-than-short titles (*O* and *Pi*) to deliberate misspelling (*Pet Sematary, Beetlejuice*) to branded symbols (*Se7en, Swimf@n*), the race is on to BE NOTICED.

With reference again to well-known television series such as *Friends*, it is common within the genre to entitle each episode as it begins while no longer having to entitle the program itself (the series title sequence may follow some minutes into the episode). This is a device to identify individual programs within the series for listings magazines, reviewers, digital TV consoles and so on. The same goes for commercials, now recognized as works of art in their own right, and given (usually one-word) titles for reference in trade magazines and—if they're lucky—at awards ceremonies.

Puns, double-entendres, irony, and wordplay can enrich the package if used without trivializing the production. *The Matrix: Reloaded* refers both to guns and computer programs (and its sequel status); *Dressed to Kill* turns a throwaway phrase into something ominous; *Romance* isn't about romance, while *South Park: Bigger, Longer, and Uncut* needs no explanation unless you've missed the joke. If a title has been given enough thought, it indicates a production that has been given equally serious consideration. But a title must not betray a production, or promise what it can't deliver.

Basic. Instinct. Two words juxtaposed become evocative. Together they either say Sex or Murder, both of which sell films. The title, though, is hinting, but not promising, much in itself. This subtlety is complemented with a title sequence comprising a plain sans serif font against a wavering, lit background that is reminiscent of femme fatale film noir without setting to the audience with hammer and tongs (or an ice-pick) to labor the point.

An alternative to subtlety is found in Terror Firmer. Aside from a bad pun that means nothing in itself, it's also telling us that we're in for more dollar-guzzling sex and death. It sounds promising—and the film delivers in exactly the same cartoonish way as the title sequence suggests. And if it delivers on its promise, then it's as successful as any more sophisticated title sequence.

Titles like this aren't meant to go unnoticed and slip anonymously between covers on a DVD shelf. 1974's Ilsa, She Wolf Of The SS is absolutely a sign of the times (another 'nasty', SS Experiment Camp was made two years later) and pulls no punches in getting its audience. Again, it's selling sex and death.

The title Go even applies itself to the DVD menu design, as well as being explored on multiple levels within the movie itself. Sometimes even the most innocuous word can have a range of connotations that work on many levels beyond those of facile wordplay and dubious puns.

Opening titles

The opening title to any production is the first thing they'll see. An opening title isn't just the name of the production, it gives any credit that is necessary. Vanity and obligation are the two reasons for crediting anyone at the beginning of the titles, both of which will be discussed later. But there is another more practical reason for crediting "at the top"—and it's the same reason for a whizz-bang sucker-punch title sequence: to invite the audience in.

For the average audience, there's no real interest in viewing a title sequence—including the title itself. There's enough marketing around for an audience to know exactly what they're going to watch—they've read a review, it's the kind of thing they tend to go and see anyway, and once they're there, there's a full-screen ratings board certificate telling them exactly what the movie is called.

If it's broadcast, a viewer either goes out of their way to watch the program and knows the name already, or else they surf, stumble across a show, and either cross-reference what they see with listings, or simply don't bother. Does it really matter that they don't know the name of the program if they're enjoying it? If they like what they see, they'll refer to the listings.

But inviting the audience in is getting them onside and in the spirit of things to come. That's reason enough why honesty and thematics are so important. Because the audience knows that they have to sit through opening titles, they read them in search of anything that might be of interest, or that might anticipate what is to come—the second-guessing game. To the general audience, however, cinema is more of a catwalk than it is a business. The glamour aspect, though, applies only to the actors—the beautiful people who pretend to be someone else for money. The audience, by and large, is not interested in the people who built the catwalk (the technicians, gaffers and sound recordists, for example).

So, it's actors that can excite an audience and invite them in. Nevertheless, opening titles might get their attention only when they see that Julia Roberts or Tom Cruise is in it. Others, who read *Vanity Fair* and understand the etiquette and pecking order of the star system, might begin to show interest when they find out that Julia Roberts is actually second-billed to Shannen Doherty. And others who read into title sequences more than they read *Vanity Fair*, will be working out the screen-time ratio between the two stars if Shannen's first-billed credit is lower on the screen and in a smaller font than Julia's.

The latter creates exactly the same dilemma as poster designers were faced with on *Thelma and Louise*. How to accommodate two actors of the same star ranking with the same amount of screen-time? The answer in that case was to go with the alphabetical, but mount Susan Sarandon on the right-hand side higher than Geena Davis on the left. This brings us to some other important points: Westerners read text and images from left to right, many other cultures from right to left (and bottom to top).

Reading from left to right is something for later discussion, but let's look at alphabetical order now. Think of *Dallas*, *Melrose Place*—think of *Dynasty* if you must. With an entire cast-list of similarly ranked actors, diplomacy is applied by not only listing the cast in the opening titles alphabetically, but by clumsily fronting them with "starring (in alphabetical order)"—or "(in order of appearance)." These are older shows. The new generation of Spelling/Darren Star productions and their spin-offs considered the audience to have learned this, and the obligatory explanation became obsolete.

With light entertainment such as *Friends*, the same approach is used, but not signaled. This tactic is practiced only in television—specifically

OPPOSITE PAGE, TOP DOWN: *Some contractual obligations can force an "and" credit. These are the opening titles for* Tales Of The City. *The titles are played out from Olympia Dukakis (Oscar-winner) to Stanley Desantis (jobbing actor with a successful T-shirt business) in order of age and experience. Chloe Webb, on the other hand, is known for one part: Nancy Spungen in* Sid and Nancy. *She should, therefore, be lower on the list. The reason she gets the "and" is because* Sid and Nancy *has a huge cult following, and her role is much-acclaimed. She is a cult name and this sets her apart from the other actors.*

BOOGIE NIGHTS: *Alternatively, the way to deal with a big star in a bit part (Burt Reynolds) and a rising star with a lead part (Mark Wahlberg) is to eschew all opening titles altogether. In fact, even the title itself is almost absent from the movie as well, simply forming the canopy to the name of a nightclub in the first shot. Ultimately, and unusually, the leads are played out alphabetically after the Casting By credit as part of the closing titles.*

A ROOM WITH A VIEW: *It takes a certain kind of feature to be able to get away with the opening credits that* A Room With A View *wears on its lace cuff. It helps that it's born of a famous historical novel, and as the movie progresses and reveals itself, like the book, as having not a little humor, the captions working as chapters (e.g. "How Miss Bartlett's boiler was so tiresome") marry.*

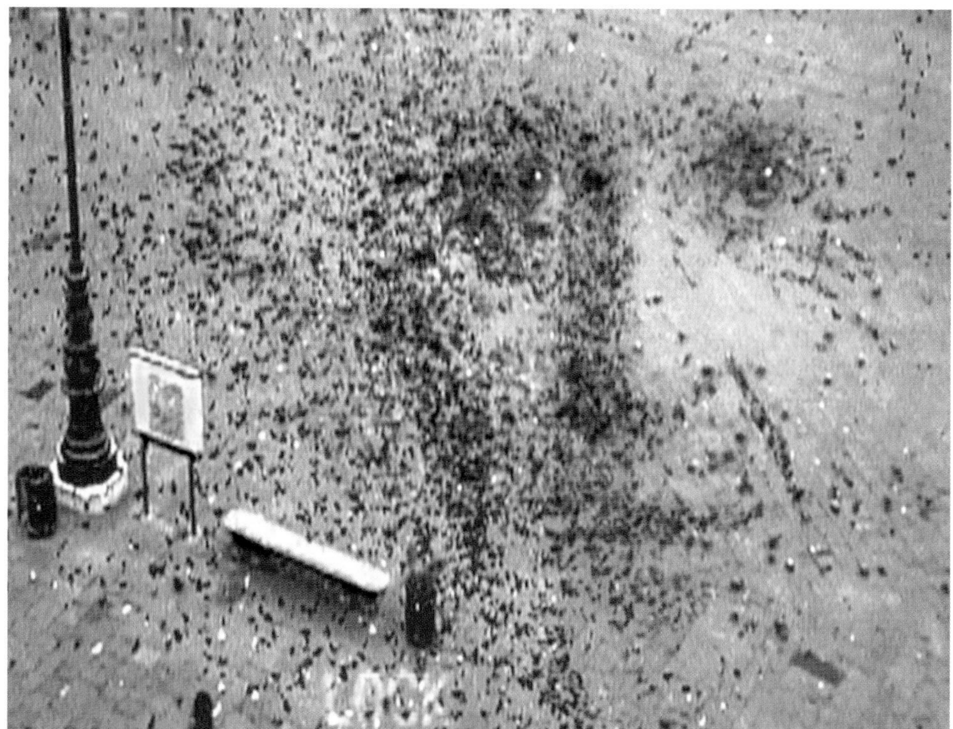

ABOVE: *You want flash? You want to be grabbed? Try the specifically shot opening titles for Ridley Scott's* Hannibal *where a flock of pigeons in a Florence square gather as the backdrop to the opening titles, to eventually form the face of—you guessed it—before taking wing. The entire sequence is shot as if it was on CCTV, perhaps by FBI agents searching for the whereabouts of Lecter (a nice touch). So what if it looks a little obvious, or like a desperate attempt to be clever. Was there a bit too much of the budget left over? Whatever the case, this is the kind of opening title that an audience likes and remembers simply because it's entertaining.*

American, and typically in soap operas; it's the by-product of a having a more general audience and, thereby, of catering to the lowest denominator of a mass viewership.

The other device that ran through the gate of Spelling/Star productions tackled the common concern of what to do with a part-time A-lister among a cast of full-time B-stars. The device was the simple use of the word "and." Arriving on the same frame as the celebrity actor's name and visage, the "and" works to isolate the name and increase its potency. Its placement at the end of the cast list is a paradox: rather like one of the onscreen divas making a deliberately late dramatic entrance at the party.

This device easily translated to cinema. While cameos are often uncredited—certainly in the opening titles—a star in a bit-part or minor supporting role can often receive an "and..." credit to emphasize their part. "And" was originally used in cinema as an opening title credit as part of "and introducing," usually for a young actor. Today's opening titles use it less, largely because it can be perceived as contractually patronizing, especially with actors coming from a theatre background before hitting the big screen.

If you are going along conventional lines such as these in your own work, it's probably best not to abuse the pre-credit "guest starring." Aside from the fact that it's not particularly amusing anymore (it's been done to death in wedding videos), it's actually one of those things that is pretty much dead and buried in contemporary television and cinema as well. It's about as out of touch as saying "X-rated."

My personal view is that the best wording, the best title, tends to be as minimalist as it gets. Any emphasis that you feel you should make can be far more subtly done with timing and placement on the screen.

Titles, straps, and graphics

Between the opening titles and the closing credits is the hallowed ground in which the drama plays out. This term is used loosely as every production—narrative, documentary, news item, etc—is dramatic. It has to be in order to attract an audience.

Titles, straps, captions, and graphics within this focal territory can be used in many ways. Straps, for example, might suggest documentary or news. But the fact is, titling within a production is not limited to any particular genre or medium.

If you're making a movie, you may wonder why on earth you would want to strap it with captions or introduce graphics within the production. But just like the "nu-skool" theory of the best effects being the least noticed effects, there are many captions that go unnoticed in feature movies.

These kind of graphical effects that you can create in Premiere Pro can be anything from emulating the movie convention of a camcorder Record screen, to captioning up a newsflash seen on a television in a bar scene, to faking a computer screen that might otherwise be a progressive-scanning nightmare to shoot.

The ones that most readily spring to mind within features are those that are used sparingly. They can be there to amuse (*Room With A View*), add zaniness (*Ferris Bueller's Day Off*), inform (*Shadow Of The Vampire*), allude to documentary (*Drop Dead Gorgeous*), provide a POV (*T2: Judgment Day*), add impact (*The Shining*), or simply be an unimaginative replacement for good storytelling (the rolling scene-setters from any of the *Star Wars* movies).

Okay, so the last example was not only controversial, it was blatantly untrue: it's not strictly an in-body caption. It's included here, though, because coming hard at the top of each of the features, it's not an open title in the sense that it's not an opening credit. The idea of filling in the gaps for an audience is an old trick from the days of movie serials. *Flash Gordon*, *Robin Hood*, et al, were all shown as a series of installments in theaters. To accommodate an audience that might not have seen the last episode, recaps were shown—and to some extent in contemporary soap operas, still are.

Star Wars rode on the back of such series and became episodic in the same way, making sense of the device. Interestingly, *The Texas Chain Saw Massacre* uses it as a way of invoking dread in an audience of what is to come. In this respect, precredit narrative rolls become an excellent device to manipulate an audience in the same way that opening titles can.

My Little Eye's *premise (*Big Brother *meets* Friday the 13th*) gave it the perfect opportunity to skip a few lines of dialog with this caption. A pre-credit sequence of logging into an audition site says it all without actually having to say it at all.*

The English language can throw up a few odd things with speech that does not translate particularly well to subtitles. While this frame from The Fourth Man *demonstrates the ease with which two lines of dialogue can fit into a frame, it also makes it very obvious that some things are better heard than seen. If you're translating a foreign language (in this case, Dutch), English is a tremendous language for providing at least ten ways of saying something—in slightly different ways.*

The most obvious use of captions in features is the subtitle. In these days of international movie-making and distribution—let alone multi-region DVD titles and those for the hard of hearing—subtitles now appear on most movies. Respecting the limits of the human eye and brain is the challenge of subtitling. Aside from the timing of the title, attention must be paid to placing the subtitle where it will not interfere with the image, yet without too much distance for the eye to travel to the text and back again to the image.

For legibility, sans-serif fonts with a multi-directional shadow work best in bringing the subtitle out from the background image—with no more than two lines of text at the same time. Couple this with the intricacies of translation and the importance of not running a title over into other scenes, and subtitling is practically a full-time occupation.

Strapping captions fall in and out of fashion. A strap is applied mainly to an interview and will denote who the person is (if they're not a celebrity) and what they do that's significant in terms of what they are talking about. Sometimes minimalist text is all the rage, and sometimes a sleeker, more corporate look is favored. This is block-building behind the caption text itself. The strap is usually prone to the application of some level of opacity to blend it with the image behind. If it's news or corporate video, a house style will be used—that is, a company color for the strap and a company font for the text. Consistency is also vital in the way that captions appear—as a crawl, fade, cut-in and fade, or page peel. Captions should not intrude on factual programs.

As for the information on the strap, keep it to two lines if possible. While news programs are good at objectively paring down a name and a title, corporate videos often provide so much information that it is distracting. Protecting a corporate image is usually to blame, particularly when there are specific management reporting lines within a company or there are several companies involved. Try to be firm with your client: nail the audience for the program and decide what would make sense for them.

For youth-orientated programs, the technique is much more relaxed and while consistency throughout the production is usually present and correct, fonts and transitions of a strap to screen can be as diverting as the program will bear. But remember that if your interview is saying something distressing or disturbing, the last thing you want is a Pudmonkey font racing all over the screen before exploding out of it.

Remember that locations often appear on straps, as well as people. This is something that has moved from factual programming into narrative situations. It is a device that tries to work as a "reality check," but usually looks hokey. The *X-Files* uses the technique with green computer type, and it works. *The Silence Of The Lambs* uses it occasionally and it doesn't. The reason is very much to do with theme. The *X-Files* is a very "techie" show using various locations; *The Silence Of The Lambs*, on the other hand, doesn't have any more locations than an average movie—and given that the location captions are there to explain where the characters are, it's inconsistent with an ending that cuts between two uncaptioned locations.

Go with the feel of your production. If it needs captions, use more than just one to make them part of the movie. And be consistent.

The introduction of the three Charlie's Angels in the first movie is enlivened by insert graphics. Staying within the style of the original television series, its faithfulness is endearing, and the kitsch kineticism that it adds sits well with the rest of the feature.

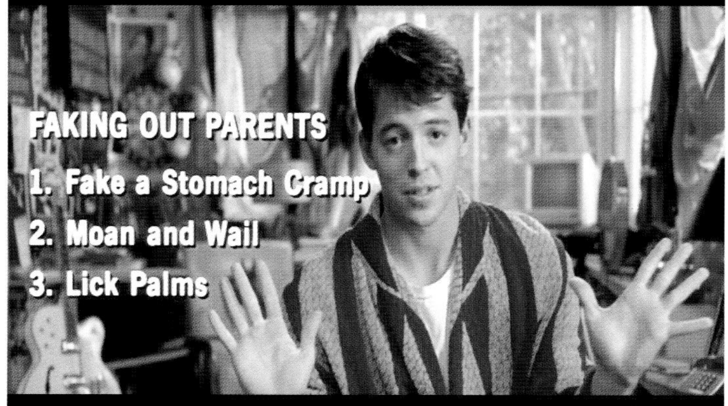

There is no reason for these Ferris Bueller captions to appear. Matthew Broderick is reading out the same list as a monologue—so why? The fact that it is nonsensical is exactly the reason why it works: it harmonizes with the movie's convention-crushing decision to break the "fourth wall" (talking directly to the audience), and adds to the slightly contrived and surreal auteurism seen throughout.

End titles and credits

End titles, movie credits... you either watch them or you don't. If you smoke, then you probably don't. Watching a DVD with friends? Then you probably won't. Obsessive fan? Then you almost certainly will.

Television watching offers a different experience to the cinema. Instead of getting up and leaving the room when the end titles roll, you're likely to sit there with the screen in front of you and still not read them. End titles are known as credits because they acknowledge the contribution of all involved—and register the producer's approval.

Conventionally, credits roll up the screen from the bottom. Just as the Western eye is trained to read from left to right, it also reads from top to bottom, so if you were reading descending titles you would be reading upward, one line at a time. There are end titles that buck the trend, which make for interesting if confusing experience at the end of a movie.

End titles usually start with the onscreen actors, if there are any. If it's a narrative piece and the credits do not begin with the actors, this will be because the original opening title sequence produced by the studio has been moved to the end of the movie. This technique is becoming a lot more common in features, largely because a new title sequence has been contracted out to a production or graphics company during the cutting of the movie. It therefore becomes an edit decision.

The order of the actors themselves falls predominantly into rank and file—although alphabetical and appearance order occasionally play out. Ongoing television series and soaps offer occasional exceptions. The UK's *EastEnders* soap opera credits actors in reverse order of appearance. In other words, whoever was last on screen takes top-billing. Again, it's the evergreen challenge of being fair to an equal-ranking cast.

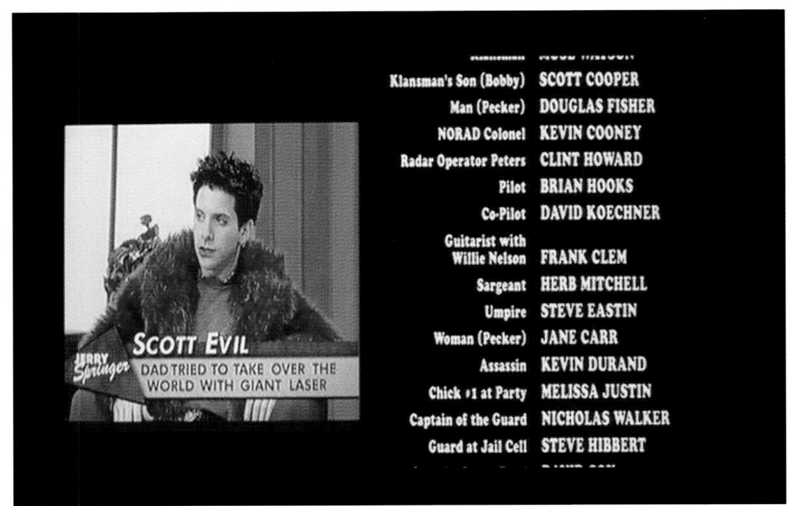

Aside from the actors, everybody else wants a credit. It's their pay-off for a job well done and, working with some directors, they probably deserve it. It's also evidence that they were involved, should anyone require it. In a business based on who you know and "Can you do it?" though, it's merely a qualification.

That said, while features have the time to list everyone involved, the same does not apply to television. Running times are limited in broadcast to give space to commercials or trail upcoming programs—and you can never afford to lose a viewer's attention. You would be hard pushed to find examples of a runner being credited after a television program, for instance. Nobody said the industry was fair and if you're not a key player, there won't be the screentime to acknowledge you. But if you want to buck the trend, the runners of this world will be indebted to you.

Corporate video production credits take an even more bare-bones approach to credits, often simply putting the company logo onscreen at the end. If your program is for internal viewing such as this, the names of those involved are redundant (not literally, we hope). Even more so if it's for an external audience—of investors, perhaps. Often a company contact name and number is all that's required.

End titles also offer the opportunity to get rid of all loose ends. They are:

Oscar speech acknowledgments

All those people without whom your production would not have been possible. Those who don't work in the industry appreciate this kind of payoff. It's good leverage to get what you want at the beginning ("I can give you a credit...") because to them the industry is glamorous and they have just become part of the glamour. It's also good PR to continue useful relationships: the caretaker who waited until 5 in the morning; your mother for allowing the world to witness your genius.

OPPOSITE: *If you're trying to squeeze in as many gags as possible, there's no reason at all not to continue over the closing credits.* The Spy Who Shagged Me's *end titles try to keep you in cinemas, they're not exactly asking you to read them...*

BELOW: *An ass-covering indemnity can be tailor-made for the production. Potential—and, as it happened, actual—accusations made against* True Lies *were covered with this reworded variation. Nevertheless, it doesn't stop it from being offensive, it just helps keep the distributors out of the law courts.*

BOTTOM: *While keeping you on the edge of your seat during the feature,* Wild Things *continues to keep you in it during the end titles where vital scenes "conveniently" hitherto unseen play out, making sense of the feature's deceptive plot.*

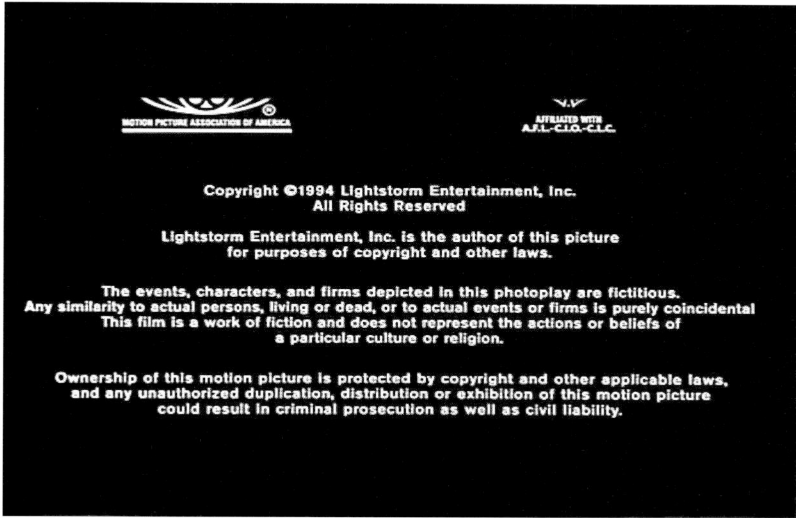

MOTION PICTURE ASSOCIATION OF AMERICA

AFFILIATED WITH A.F.L.-C.I.O.-C.L.C.

Copyright ©1994 Lightstorm Entertainment, Inc.
All Rights Reserved

Lightstorm Entertainment, Inc. is the author of this picture for purposes of copyright and other laws.

The events, characters, and firms depicted in this photoplay are fictitious. Any similarity to actual persons, living or dead, or to actual events or firms is purely coincidental This film is a work of fiction and does not represent the actions or beliefs of a particular culture or religion.

Ownership of this motion picture is protected by copyright and other applicable laws, and any unauthorized duplication, distribution or exhibition of this motion picture could result in criminal prosecution as well as civil liability.

Obligatories

These are the more heavy-duty acknowledgments: lenses by Arriflex, stock from Kodak, and so on. A lot of features actually feature the respective companies' logos as part of the deal. They stand out, brand the assisting company, and are a terrific way of striking a very lucrative deal.

Copyright

This is important. You can forget who you like in the two categories above. They will, after all, just hate you for the rest of your video-making life and never want to work with you again. Far worse is being sued for breach of copyright. Whether it's music, dialogue, a movie-clip, or the use of somebody's image, you will hopefully have got permission to use it. Whether you've paid or not paid, it's still probably in the release that credit has to be given. If you're contractually obliged to credit and you forget, you're in breach of copyright and eligible for a lawsuit.

Equally important, of course, is to mention your own copyright of all material. That includes the soundtrack and characters, and whatever else you might want to protect.

Disclaimers

"Any similarity to persons living or dead..." The litigation-heavy culture of the United States make this an essential part of any narrative feature. Yet while there may be cases of individuals finding likeness in characters or situations and taking legal action, the defense is not based on the disclaimer, indicating how worthless it is. Another indication is its lack of use in broadcast media.

Titles reflect your own pride in accomplishment. Bear in mind, though, that even in the Hollywood factory, a feature can always become an embarrassment or an executive battleground. In this case, there's always the industry-standard "Alan Smithee" credit to fall back on if you no longer want your real name associated with the production.

The role of audio

Ask any soundtrack composer and they'll always tell you that it's not about knowing when to use the music, it's knowing when not to. The opening and closing titles of a feature or a television show tend to be accompanied by music. It's convention, but in the case of TV, it calls viewers in from another room.

Music is an integral part of branding. Humans respond to music and rhythm and—even better for marketing—remember it and emulate it. People isolate movie and program theme music in a way that they do not with the moving image itself. They hum it, they buy a soundtrack, they download it to their mobile phones. One of the main reasons for pop promo videos is so that the brand image (the band or singer) is recalled when the music is isolated on the CD, record, or radio.

A movie theme has one-up over a standard promo: it recalls not just the brand, but the entire emotional experience of the feature. To jump to the end titles, briefly, the reason that so much of the music accompanying these becomes popular is that it does just this. It is the last thing to be heard on leaving the theatre, and the nature of memory (fading, romanticizing) latches onto this as a way of encapsulating what the viewer has just witnessed.

We've discussed how opening titles are incredibly important to get the audience "onside" from the start. Music is half the battle. It can stir, inspire, amuse, excite, scare. It can do all of these things in a matter of moments without even a glimpse of a moving image. Most of all, though, it can create anticipation, a desire to see what's to come. It sets the mood.

This can be a cynical and mathematical process. Some chords, themes, and arrangements can be guaranteed to evoke a particular response. Danny Elfman has learned this over time and created perhaps the greatest anticipatory opening theme with *Batman*. It was so influential that even he has drawn from it in later movies. If you couldn't afford Danny Elfman, you'd hire yourself a Danny Elfman soundalike (no names mentioned). And if you could afford him but he was busy, you'd get him to do the opening title music and then somebody else to fill in for the rest of the soundtrack (*The Gift*).

Creating a mood is essential for features, less so for broadcast television. Television usually requires a different response: familiarity. That is, if it's your favorite series, you want a sense of—literally—coming home to it. There are no television series that have a different opening theme every week. Although the British comedy series *Black Adder* offered amusing variations of its theme with each episode, the melody remained the same. One-off television shows and productions operate just as features do, without such a high budget.

Musical irony can be used within a movie, short, or video, or worked in at the end as a useful counterpoint to the drama, but it's not something that tends to be appropriate at its beginning—you need to start off on the right foot. End title music can be as ironic as you want it to be. On more cynical, commercial productions, it can showcase any number of bands on the "soundtrack" album (who are not actually heard in the movie).

Audio with titling, though, isn't limited to music. Movie-makers, especially auteurs such as David Lynch, create soundscapes as well as music. The introduction of sound effects to titling—or to music with titling—can produce some startling effects. If text fades onto the screen or drains away

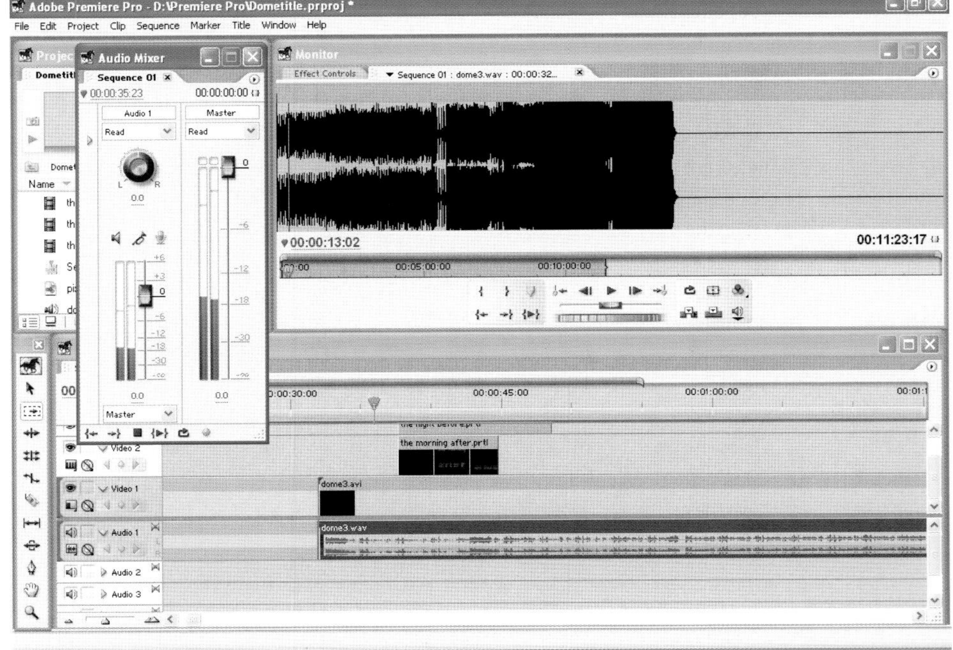

LEFT: *When a soundtrack is expanded, it becomes a unique visual tool in Pro. Guided by the peaks and troughs of the audio waveform, you can cut or perform transitions that are almost dictated by the patterns within it.*

off it, it is often best accompanied by sounds that suggest or evoke this kind of motion, so a cymbal crash or break-beat would not be appropriate, but something fluid or mechanical sounding perhaps would. The opening titles to Martin Scorsese's *Goodfellas* are just accelerating/decelerating crawls. But accompanied by the sound of screeching tires, they evoke a car chase.

You don't have to be so prosaic, though. Such effects can be emulated with musical instruments and incorporated into the main theme or left isolated. The dissonant musical effects that accompany the weekday captions in *The Shining* double the fear factor to the point that it would be hard to imagine any fear without them. Sound effects can also be used as in-jokes for the audience. You have to be patient to catch the sound of a scuttling facehugger at the end of *Aliens*.

We're so used to full-on musical soundtracks to titles (they at least entertain us while we sit through them) that when silence reigns it creates an effect of its own. There's not a single sound during the whole of the opening title sequence of Abel Ferrara's *Snake Eyes*. In the cinema the effect is uncomfortable; it makes the audience shifty, aware of themselves, of others around them. But translate this to television and an opening title sequence that did the same would either be talked over or the channel would be changed.

In short, the tunes are different, but the song remains the same: it's knowing when to use music, and when not to. Once again, the production that is thought through will have the greatest impact.

BELOW: *Sometimes music makes a title sequence iconic. This font is locked in time to the movie, and we'd want our money back if the music was changed. The two are inextricable.*

BOTTOM: *James Newton Howard's opening title sequence to* Signs *dictates the way that each credit is brought on screen. The quiet early stages of music accompany simple dissolves, while the later staccato horn stabs and bass drum beats bring credits crashing onto the screen. Each credit is classily composed with a thin serif font lit to look as though it's caught between the audience and a glaring torch beam, predictive of later scenes.*

SCREA

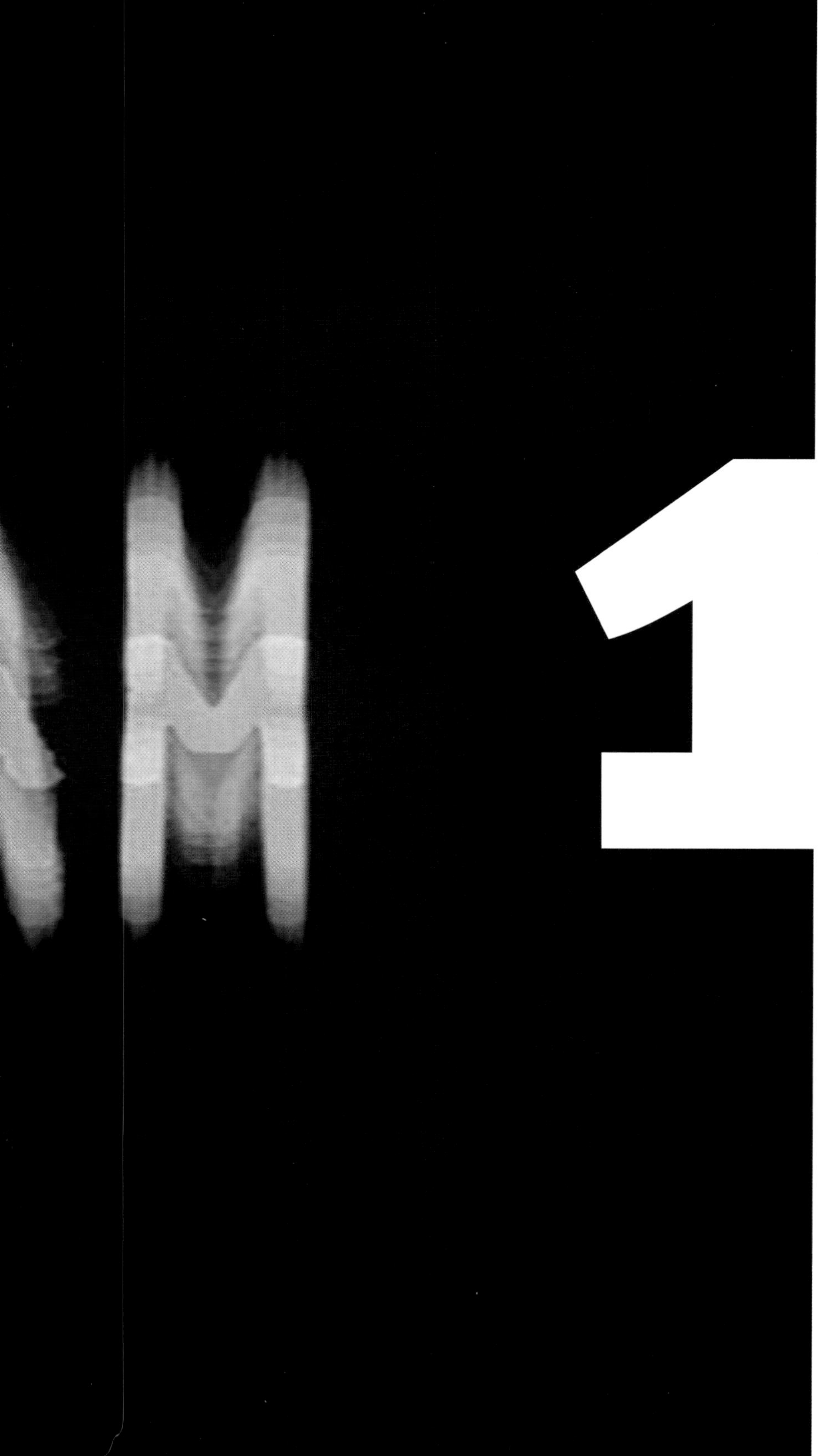

CHAPTER ONE

the art of title design

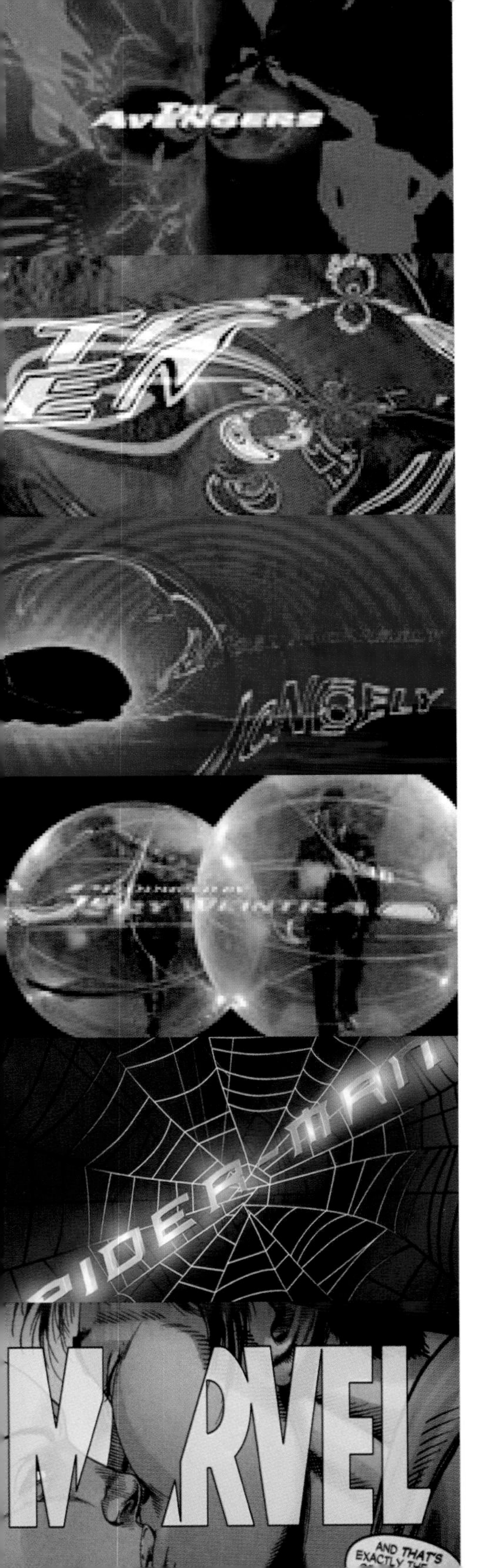

What is design?

And why should you care about it?

Design is the deliberate application of thought to the everyday environment. Poor design can take away practicality, turn the robust into the fragile, spoil purity, cheapen, and detract from purpose. Good design, on the other hand, can do completely the opposite. It can add depth, complement, enliven; it can turn the crass into the cool, the ugly into the beautiful, and the poor into the rich.

Good design of practical objects highlights their practicality and can make them easier to use and encourage us to use them. Engineers make functioning objects, but design engineers create things that work with the end user. However, a movie or a television show, as a leisure activity, offers little obvious practical value other than an emotional high or low (which may or may not be beneficial). It won't actually take you to the moon, and you can't clean the floor with it.

The Hollywood reality check is that movies are practically superfluous to life, no matter how important they might appear to be on Academy night. Good movie design is merely gilding the lily—or painting a white elephant. But you don't care about that: in your head you've been to the moon, and you've wiped the floor with your rivals. And back in the virtual edit suite of your desktop, good title design can add production value at little cost. Your only expenditure will be brain cells and time. This is a good trade.

Good design is also a question of branding. Branding is sealing your product with an identity that not only makes it stand out, but makes it a complete package: you know what strong brands stand for. Brands from Heinz to Batman are locked in the subconscious, but until *Heinz: The Movie* comes out, we'll stick with *Batman*. A stark, muscular logo doesn't need titling if it's familiar enough. Of course, familiar doesn't always mean *good* branding.

Superheroes require branding. Aside from the copyright issues, it's become a tradition in cinema that a superhero is not that super unless he has a logo and a whizz-bang—or imposing—title sequence behind him. Any product like this (one with a history outside the movie industry) has a duty to remain faithful to its original branding. The copyright pack are just as ferocious as the rabid fans.

Working within strict constraints, though, is a job for true creatives. Adapting the brand of one medium (a comic) to another (a movie title sequence) is a challenge all of its own if one wants to remain traditional yet contemporary.

Despite its notoriety as a Christmas Turkey that hardly gobbled the box office, *The Avengers* movie had just this issue to contend with. A surreal icon of 1960s British television needed a branding that made it cool again thirty years later. Contemporary technology allowed for a title sequence that embraced the 1960s (in terms of the font), but a software-powered spin made it contemporaneous. Added to this is the emulation of a specific theme of the movie (weather-control) in the animation of the text. This type of branding is good design: something that incorporates the look and feel of the production within. And even if the movie is bad, that still doesn't make it an awful title sequence.

Now that software and production houses abound, there is a tendency for titles to be a showreel for the designers themselves. There are even award ceremonies for title sequences. Some titles are respectable almost as small movies in their own right, but that doesn't mean that they brand the production appropriately. And that doesn't mean, therefore, that they are examples of good design in terms of the movie itself.

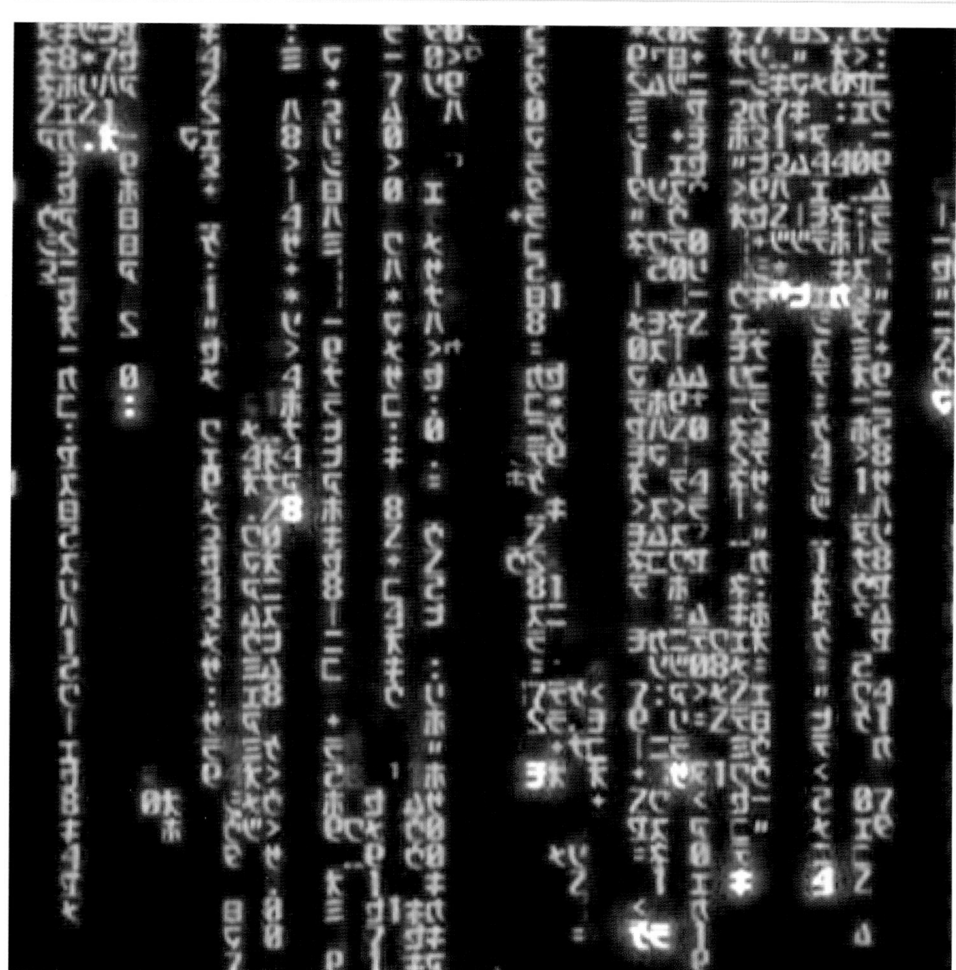

OPPOSITE PAGE, TOP DOWN:
If The Avengers *feature had been a success, doubtless it would have begun a franchise. It's also certain that the branding that this title sequence gave it would have been continued as a successful marriage of the modern and the retro.*

Comics are movies trying to escape from the page, providing such a rich source of branding with their look, their style, their wording, that they beg to be transferred to the screen. Spider-Man *has made an obvious choice of representation. If* Batman *has the Bat logo,* Spider-Man *has the web. What the animation does, though, is rather more witty, showing letters as flies that stick to the web in legible credit form.*

Marvel has also been smart in the pre-credit title sequence found on many of the recent blockbusters featuring Marvel characters. The logo is actually built through the flicking of classic Marvel comics—a cool trick for most viewers, but an extra dose of nostalgia for longtime fans.

LEFT: *What's this? Why, it's* The Matrix. *And how do we know this? Because* The Matrix *went from 0 to 60 (million dollars) in a weekend, creating a huge awareness of the style of the movie and the whole* The Matrix *brand. This was the single unique graphic that the makers had, and it soon became a backdrop to press events: it was on posters, magazines, DVD covers, screensavers. On its own it's pretty meaningless (granted, it's also code), but coupled with the trilogy juggernaut, it becomes a cool brand that says nothing else but the name of the movie.*

Movies want to be liked by the audience they are made for—and to get the audience they were made for they have to toe the line of genre design. In movies—and recently in television shows that try to emulate them—good, consistent marketing and title design does nothing more than enable us to the judge a book by its cover. In this respect, design may be exaggerated, but by and large, it tends to be honest. You pick a book from the shelves because the cover attracts you if you are its target audience: a yellow and pink title combined with a photo of a girl having a bad hair day will be sub-Bridget Jones holiday reading; a busy airbrushed artwork involving planets, fantastic landscapes, and futuristic hardware will be sci-fi; a photo-realistic watercolor of a swooning couple will be a mainstream branded romance. The conventions of movie publicity and title design aren't quite so stark and obvious, but ultimately they are all attractions for the target demographic.

Good and bad title design

There is no place for inconsistency in contemporary design with marketing and PR created hype (trailers, posters, T-shirts, websites) being the main driving-force behind a good opening weekend.

In bygone days, Tobe Hooper got away with titling his movie *The Texas Chain Saw Massacre*. The misspelling of "chainsaw" (one word) was corrected for the first sequel, and has been corrected for the original movie ever since on DVD covers and publicity. The title sequence, though, remains the same.

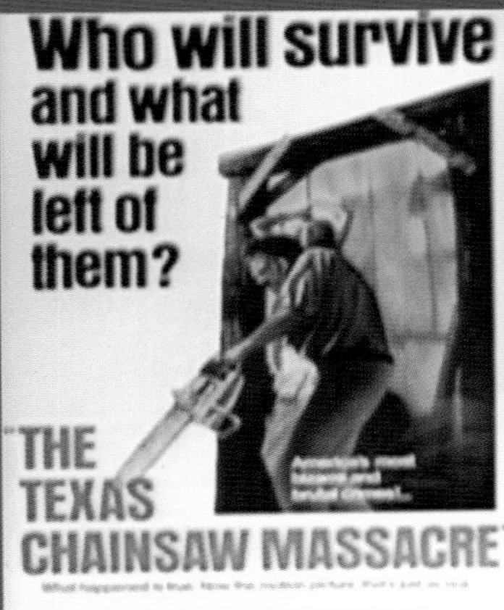

The Texas Chainsaw Massacre
Simple, no-budget, no-frills design, from the original title to the marketing campaign that followed, let the words speak for themselves. The use of speech marks to define the title in pre-1970's title sequences still lives a misplaced life in the *Chain Saw* newspaper campaign, but was soon to die a death later in the decade.

Even though title and promotional design is now a lot more market-tested and constructed, a title like *The Texas Chain Saw Massacre* doesn't need a blood-dripping font to create an effect: indeed, the basic block serif adds an irony to the sequence. Over the past 30 years with the movie passing through the hands of different distributors, the design has been subject to relatively little butchering, enabling it to become a design classic.

As an interesting aside, during the time that the movie was banned in the UK, the word "chainsaw" (correct spelling) also became outlawed in movie titles. This led to its imitators having to redesign or retitle altogether. In *Hollywood Chainsaw Hookers*, the word was replaced with an image of a chainsaw, which asked the audience to read it as a word—something that was a bit too unconventional to meet with much success.

If the name of a movie is a little less obvious, the choice of font can fill in the gaps for the potential audience. A font could say to the audience this is urban, sci-fi, horror, hip, or chick-flick. Of course, we're talking about publicity material here. The way that this relates to the title sequence itself is to establish some kind of consistency. If the publicity material emulates the title sequence (its design and mood), and the design for the title sequence is thematically based on the movie, then the integrity of the drama is preserved and you're a long way toward building a successful brand.

Hollow Man, an effects-heavy take on the old invisible man idea, has an expensive CGI DNA title sequence, which is thematically sound with cells forming and reforming on chromosomes to construct the text. It's rightly acclaimed and even won awards. However, the publicity material was entirely different: different font, different mood. The title sequence conveys the dangers of tampering with science and biology, but the mood of the publicity material suggested a somber ghost story. It isn't dishonest, just inconsistent—and with a little bet-hedging thrown in. Audiences can detect the latter and are confused by the message.

But ultimately, does an audience care about branding? No, they care about the movie (until they buy the merchandise). Do they care about the title sequence? No, they care about the movie. This is what "serviceable titles" are all about—simple, unpretentious titles that don't scream 'high concept' or beg deep critical insight, or which have a high graphical impact. These can be produced with minimal fuss but maximum impact. One example of this is the sheer black on white cut hard against white of Abel Ferrara's *Snake Eyes* sequence.

There's nothing complicated about adding textures to fonts—and there's nothing particularly clever about it either. Titles can be textured with steel (*RoboCop*), animated with blood (*Brain Dead*), even morphed from seminal fluid (*Ichi The Killer*). These examples are evidence enough that the more you try to be clever with the words themselves, the greater the potential you are creating for the effect to be cheap and trashy. It's very much a case of "Look at me—I'm a title," rather than "Let's set the scene for a drama."

Adding dimension to titling—not necessarily just in terms of perspective—can sometimes work with greater subtlety. Sci-fi movie *Total Recall* is all about the persistence and unreliability of memory, and the movie's fade-and-drain-away title sequence recalls precisely this. The same ghosting effect is used in *Body Snatchers*, tailored to leave a shadow of certain letters' former selves onscreen. This is a truly considered sequence, simple and thematic, yet striking and easy to achieve. In other words, it's a perfect example of good design.

Drawing on the movie for themes and mood predicts and forewarns an audience of what is to come. Clearly, there is a risk that some title designers may give too much away. The plain-and-practical titles for Brian Yuzna's *Society* are keyed over close-ups from the movie's pay-off finale—obscured with trail effects—but for a movie that relies on the surprise of its ending, it's hardly coy.

Mission Impossible does exactly the same thing, scenes from the upcoming movie played behind the opening titles with an animated burning fuse to help drive the action. Predictive scenes, though, become nonsensical in disjointed montage—and indeed, Brian DePalma's publicity juggernaut obviously took note of this with the European *Femme Fatale* trailer, which plays the entire movie at up to 1500% speed (including end credits) before challenging the audience with the caption "You didn't get it? Try again."

TOP: As the red *Body Snatchers* title drifts away from being the focal image, audience attention is seized by the more prominent white-filled cast and crew opening credits cutting on- and off-screen. Meanwhile, the *Body Snatchers* title is still being played with as it diminishes into the background. Black shadowed letters float in from space and "take over" the original red characters. With a driving soundtrack, it's a class act.

ABOVE: Aside from the thematic brilliance of the *Total Recall* titles draining away and leaving a temporary footprint in the sand, the choice of font, grand music and the background colors form a recollection of earlier, cinematic experiences. The animation even looks familiar as the lit, anticipatory curtain of a cinema.

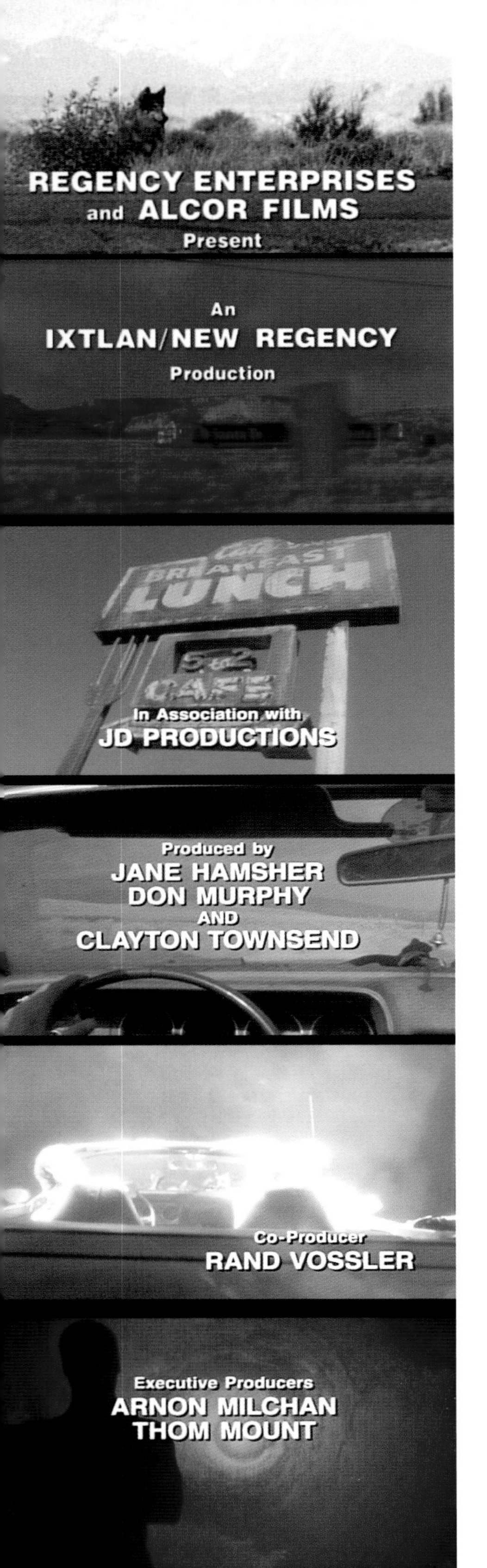

Constraints and convention

Constraints? Convention? How dull. In a guide to all things creative, this sort of discussion doesn't sound at all worth your while. But like all things, you can't get creative until you know exactly what constraints and conventions you have to work out of, or against.

Of course, most creativity is in the realm of the conventional. Convention sets a standard or a format that is recognizable as what it is. Titling conventions are appropriated for the medium, and run as follows.

TELEVISION

Unlike cinema, television programs are part of a seamless broadcast stream that is commercially driven—and opening title sequences often illustrate this. Sponsorship can brand the title to the point of ownership, the title itself becoming subsidiary to the sponsor's brand. Commercials themselves can dictate how the opening titles begin. To ensnare the audience, most American sitcoms and some popular drama series (*The X-Files*) cut hard after sponsorship to an opening "grabber" scene followed by the title sequence. Barely have the audience watched two minutes before the commercials begin. Once they're over, another hard cut takes us back into the beginning of the show, often with a five-second overlay caption to remind the audience which show is on.

Commerce aside, conventional titles within television break down as follows:

Light entertainment 20-40 second graphic culminating in title of show and host
Drama series (Producer); Title; actors; writer; (producer); director
Soap Title; (producer); actors (American); writer; (director)
Sport 20-40 second clip compilation culminating in title of show
Documentary Precredit introduction; title; presenter/narrator; producer; (director)
News Headline clips; 10-20 second graphic incorporating the title; presenter caption

FEATURE MOVIE

A movie already has your money as soon as you have bought your ticket. It's also helped itself to a little more in sponsorship (product placement, fast food, cars, computers, and the eternal Coca Cola/Pepsi tug of war) and will quite happily sell you the poster, the T-shirt, the soundtrack, the sunglasses, and eventually the DVD when you emerge. But while you sit in your seat, they're happy enough to let the titles play out without obvious commercial interruption.

Movies—as opposed to most television shows—usually have big enough budgets to afford proportionately "bigger" title sequences. At feature length, and without commercials, movies also give their makers more time to play with. And because of the bigger budget and the fact that television is a more disposable medium, movies tend to be held in higher regard than television, despite occasional exceptions such as *The Simpsons*, the title sequence of which is iconic. The associated pride (or vanity) makes the branding and the upfront credit important to the movie-makers—way above the wishes of an audience that would probably be happy to watch the movie without the list of names at the start. This is why titles either entertain or blend into the beginning of the movie. And this is why the conventions of movie opening titles exist.

Opening Titles

Distributor Logo; studio/production company pretitle sequence or underlay to opening titles: Producer; director; lead actors; title; supporting actors; casting; associate producer; costumes; music; effects; editor; production designer; director of photography; executive producer; writer; producer; director

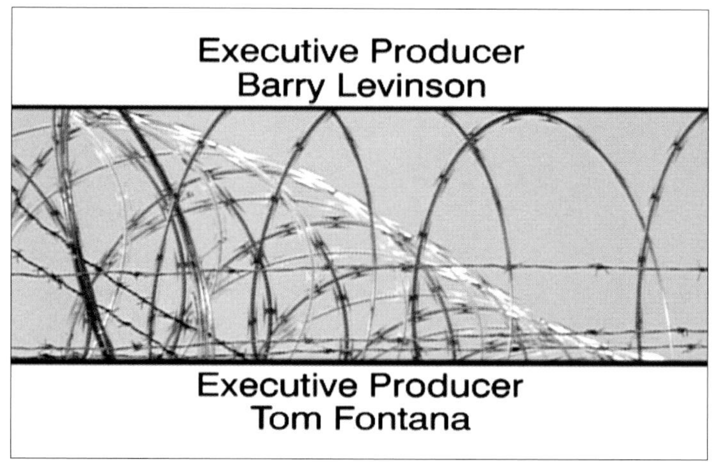

With

Bryan Callen	as Coushaine
Sean Dugan	as Kirk
Christine Toy Johnson	as Reporter
Chazz Menendez	as Skinhead
Leif Riddell	as Mack

Now it is time for vanity and more self-congratulation. We begin with "A [insert producer's name] production"; we follow up with "of a [insert director's name] film." They're the first words that you're likely to read. We end the list of opening title credits with "Produced by [insert producer's name]" and "Directed by [insert director's name]." You're likely to read these too because they'll hold slightly longer or they'll be placed more centrally or they'll have a different transition that brings them on. The audience will also know that the movie is about to begin because they have learned the convention.

The interesting factor in all of this is that it can be a surprise when we're not confronted up front with the movie-makers' vanity—when the convention breaks, in other words. A good example is *Scream*. The Dimension Movies logo manifests and disappears in the first 11 seconds. The title streaks on and practically leaps out of the screen in the next eight. The opening Drew Barrymore sequence lasts 13 minutes—long, as far as precredit sequences go.

When we reach the usual respite, the conventional underlay for the procedure of conventional titling, there is none. None in fact until the very end of the movie where the traditional titles precede the end credit roll.

This kind of (dis)order of titles is becoming more and more commonplace in features and elsewhere. The effect of putting a graphical opening title at the end is precisely that it was intended to head up the show, but was shunted to abut the end titles so as to not to impede the beginning. It suggests artistic integrity, in fact. What is unusual about the *Scream* example is that the opening titles (at the end), display the actors in slow-mo alternate take mode with their names overlaid. Not only does this borrow from the convention of introducing actors in American television series (*Beverly Hills 90210*), but it harks back to the days of theatrical curtain calls.

Why should this work? Because most of the actors were borrowed from American television series (including Tori Spelling), and the finale is pure grande guignol.

The audience knows the convention. They know it so subconsciously that they realize that, for example, UK satire *BrassEye*'s ridiculously extended, overgraphic titles are a pastiche of a news program and not merely a ridiculously extended, overgraphic sequence.

ABOVE LEFT: *A quality long-running television series like* Oz *relies on its* Executive Producers *to keep the whole thing together. When the actors change, and the producers, directors, and writers change, there has to be a lowest common denominator to oversee the global aspects of a series. This is why the two* EPs *are at the very top of the opening credits. Other than that, it's business as usual, the* EPs *followed by cast (most important first), then crew (least important first), culminating in the director credit.*

ABOVE RIGHT: *The closing titles to* Oz *have a typical extension to the cast list as their first credit screen. While the resident cast are at the top of the program, there will always be an organic support cast. These will often appear in this positioning because it's easier to shuffle things around at the end, rather than edit at the beginning. Indeed, an important issue with opening titles is that change is mitigated as much as possible.*

OPPOSITE PAGE: *Sure, it was Jane Hamsher and Don Murphy's first production, but because of this, they had to liaise with a lot of other backers who demand producer credits (i.e. two Executive Producers, two Associate Producers, and one Co-Producer, some of whom have different company names). The* Natural Born Killers *opening titles, therefore, have the job of presenting this without too much fuss and obstruction. Obligations can get in the way of getting to your titles. Cutting between pictures helps, distance between credits helps, and so does a Leonard Cohen soundtrack.*

Layout essentials

What do you need to create a title?

To represent a title for a production, the whole case must be put to you. That is, you need to see and fully understand the product before you can truthfully package it. If you've made your production yourself, you'll know it inside out—you may even be too close to it to get a balanced and objective perspective.

It's only once you've nailed your idea that you can work out the tools that you're going to need to construct it.

Pick out themes, write them down on paper, and see what you've got. Here's a random example: it's a story of jealousy, double-crossing, and corruption set in a subterranean parallel universe to the White House, where exactly the same activities are going on. The twist is that the President is an alien. Terrible example; it's probably a winner.

Once you've got your themes and synopsis down, think literally and laterally in design terms. Even word association can give you ideas.

Jealousy = green
Double-crossing = text duplication and motion
Corruption = distressed font
Subterranean universe = dark
Parallel universe = split the screen horizontally
White House = white embroidered font

You won't want to give the "Don't tell anyone the ending, it's the only one we've got!" twist away, so avoid a Stars and Stripes bedecked UFO for now.

The other consideration is where the director (yourself?) has planned for the titles to go. If you just have a black background at the top of the movie, you won't have to think about design issues on top of the opening images. This means you're starting with a blank canvas—something that can be a curse or a blessing. A curse, because if you decide that you *do* want background images for your title after all, you'll have to either get them shot or design them yourself from scratch—either from new material, or from source material on the video itself. Not having a blank canvas creates issues of its own. If you've got your heart set on that green font, for example, you may have to find ways of pulling the text away from the lush countryside background establishing shots you've also decided on.

Once you've got your ideas together, try to agree on the branding with whoever's marketing the project. If it's yourself, fine, but if there's another party designing it's important to negotiate fonts, images, mood, feel, and look. If there's a director involved, it'll probably have to be agreed with them too. Try a few still mock-ups if it's a complicated hierarchy or ambitious idea that you're going to realize. Even transitions can be storyboarded.

Before you begin, get hold of any important files: Fonts and images used by marketing, the distributor's logo—and most essentially, the credits themselves. The end titles are as complete as any credits get, duplicating all the names and job titles that appear in the opening titles. The ones that are required for the opening titles should be indicated as such. The reason for ensuring that you get this file is to eliminate any unnecessary typing errors (spelling, formatting, job titles). These need to come from the horse's mouth—the producer, director, or someone else in charge—and they need to be checked and double-checked before they get to you. You, after all, will be merely cutting and pasting. If you're compiling the list yourself, you need to get it right.The same goes for captions—only more so. Captions are there to be read and if they're wrong, you'll look amateur.

Once you've got all of your sources and your ideas are beginning to form, it's time for some forward planning.

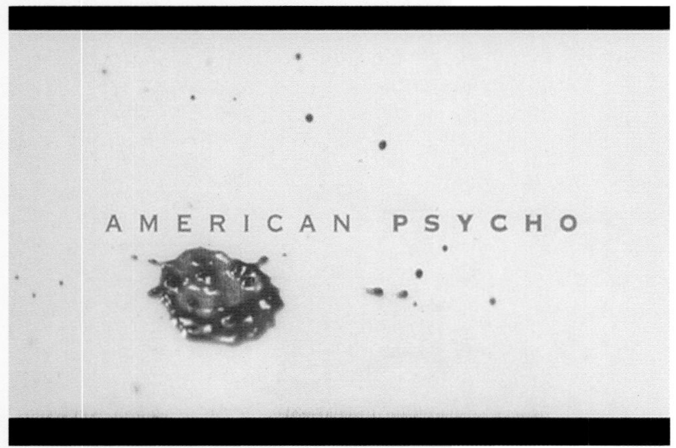

LEFT: *The* American Psycho *opening title sequence gets the font right. The anamorphic widescreen (**see Glossary, page 188**) gives the background the perfect ratio for a thematic business card. The font is making the same statement, right down to the Eighties' styling. There's the blood too, of course...*

Typefaces and fonts

Looking good is not just about dressing up—you need somewhere to go as well. Finding a font that supports the theme, motion, and mood of your title is important, but finding a font that won't let you down is essential. There are usually no more than three main fonts used in a feature, and perhaps only one or two in a broadcast television program. One is used for the title itself, another for the opening credits and another for the closing credits. Incorporated with the font is the method of transition—fades, rolls, crawls or an effect. Transitions themselves can affect the chosen font, especially when using effects. Before committing yourself to your choice, try out the font with the transition.

The big problem with fonts in the digital environment is that they're constructed out of pixels (picture elements). If the font was designed at a small size or low screen resolution, then the jagged edges of each pixel become obvious if you blow it up. Antialiasing smoothes the edges to a degree, but the algorithm is based on guesswork. Therefore a font with fine, complex glyphs at a low resolution cannot fulfil your ambitions.

ABOVE: *Choosing a plain font doesn't necessarily have to hinder your options.* The Cube *opening titles rely on the animation within the font as it manifests to make their point. Using stark whites and shadows, the cubic forms rise out of the white as three-dimensional shapes that eventually form the title. The animation then turns to the dark side to turn the shadows to highlight, and the highlight to shadow.*

Computer monitors are also bad at displaying what your title will actually look like once it makes its way onto the TV screen. Going so far as to export a few trial runs to DVD or tape for a TV preview can save you redoing a whole sequence later.

Not all fonts are created equal. Some—including most common Truetype fonts—contain sophisticated built-in hinting, which corrects the pixels in a letter that go awry during scaling, and adjusts the distance between it and neighbouring letters in a word. Others will not. There are many downloadable fonts on the Internet, but some will be low res, some may not have punctuation marks, some may support little or no hinting, and some might be available only as caps. Also, if you're importing a font, don't just think about Premiere Pro. If you're burning to DVD and want to create a menu using the same font, try it out and see if it works with the authoring software.

We'll discuss using Photoshop later . It has many options that you'll want to try out, but it pays to keep an eye on your "embroidery." That shadow might bring your text out from a busy background, but what is it saying? Using a bevel to smarten up your font? Nice, but more classic than Jurassic? Onscreen, everything is a signifier.

If color matters, check it against your background for flaring or broadcast legality using the vectorscope. The same goes for textures and any stroking you might have applied. They can be too busy on a background, just as a herringbone pattern plays havoc with broadcast. Textures can be unrecognizable through the text unless the letters are thick enough. Some fonts do not have a bold version, and you may need to apply a "faux bold" in the text editor.

With so many styles and permutations of fonts, it can take all of your time to make a simple decision. Perhaps that's why the simplest choice deployed boldly and imaginatively is often the most effective. Remember that people are familiar with typographical conventions without realizing it—a "caveman" style font won't suit a costume drama, however raw the emotion.

Using space, thinking ahead

Space. Hardly the final frontier here, but something to be conquered nevertheless. Space in a titling context is to do with all four dimensions: width, height, depth—and time.

To tackle the physical dimensions first: if you're working with Premiere Pro, the production that you're working with is unlikely to be anything more than 16:9 (1.78:1) ratio. This limits it to either 16:9 (Widescreen/HDTV) or 4:3 (Standard). Each offers entirely different spaces to work within—and for this reason, offer different choices and constraints.

Widescreen (anamorphic 2.35:1 or standard 1.85:1) in a cinema requires the audience to increase their interaction, and the nearer they are to the screen, the more they have to participate. They are required to move their head as well as their eyes in order to recognize the action. With subtitles, this is even more the case, and because Western subtitles operate on a horizontal axis, there is more room to incorporate captions. Subtitles in a viewer's own language demand to be read, and decreasing the amount of head movement needed to read a caption allows each one to be onscreen for less time. The result is that despite the width that widescreen permits for a caption, subtitles still tend to be distributed over two lines, opening up the amount of visible background image on each side of the lower frame. All this is particular to the cinematic experience.

Viewing 16:9 ratio in a domestic environment on a TV or computer screen reduces head and eye movement to a negligible amount, functioning effectively the same as 4:3 ratio. Because of this, captions become a bit more versatile with regard to using the space on each side, and the effect that this freedom has on titling is "looser" translations, larger fonts, or distribution over one line instead of two, easing the space for the background image.

Screen-safe parameters for titling are specifically relevant when it comes to a theater distributed feature being transferred to DVD or video. The slight variant in widescreen formats for both the mediums (1.85:1 versus 1.78:1) means that any caption bordering on the edge will be lost. Despite the hype about HDTV—i.e. widescreen television—there can still be a missing fraction on both sides of the screen with such movie transfers. A caption extending to both ends of the frame can be topped and tailed in telecine.

Worse still are the complications that pan and scan offer, where—in order to fit within standard television's 4:3 ratio—a widescreen feature is subject to refilming during telecine, tracking the portions of "interest" on the screen. In this case, of course, the subtitles have to be entirely stripped and reapplied or else the captions would move right and left across the screen during refilming.

The rule of lower-thirds pertains to titling, where the lower-third of the screen is the area allowed for captions. The psycho-physics of this relate to the tracking of the human eye. The eye is drawn to imagery (light, color, dynamics) before it is drawn to text—a picture is worth a thousand words. Because Westerners read top to bottom, left to right, we naturally look to an image placed top or left before we move to corresponding text beneath it or to the right of it.

If the associated text isn't where we expect it to be, we naturally hunt for image (or foreign dialogue) explanation—but it takes time. Time is not what captions are about: they are functional; they need to be read and then leave us to process the information with regard to the image.

LEFT: *For anamorphic 16:9, some title designers help exaggerate the space.* Dark City *uses a heavily kerned font to stretch across the vast width of the screen. Because it uses such width, the designer helps the audience by animating a light that reveals the characters from left to right and right to left in portions. Cut to...*

BELOW: *...our glide into a hotel bathroom and the swinging light that wakes our protagonist up with a start. So not only has the title illumination animation been useful to the audience, it's also predictive to the point of almost being the first part of the opening scene.*

ABOVE RIGHT: *With 1:33 digital video (here, in a subtitled version of* Baise-moi*), the lower-thirds rule applies, never exceeding two lines of text. It leaves plenty of room to see the action around the caption.*

RIGHT: *If a line does run on and is likely to be a sentence covering three lines, a character with dialogue takes enough time to utter the dialogue in order to let the subtitle run over two or three separate captions without cluttering the image.*

Time, then, is a vital dimension in which titlers work. With titles, it relates to the time it takes viewers to process the information they contain—usually about one-third of a second per word. This is discussed in more detail on page 28.

In the movie *Scream*, however, the title of the movie is held onscreen for eight seconds—long enough to allow for reinterpretation. (Is it merely the title, or has "Scream" become an instruction to the audience?) This demonstrates the difference between the main title and a caption. It goes beyond information and explanation: a title *isn't* functional, as we know the name of the movie before we pay to see it (unless we're in the wrong theatre). It's about branding. That's not to say that a one-word title can justify 20 or 30 seconds of screentime—there are limits to human tolerance. But as long as it's holding our interest, the title can command more sustained screentime than anything else bar the stars.

The frame has become a battleground.

BELOW: *At 1:66 ratio, captions don't necessarily have more breathing space—i.e. more image viewing space—but they allow for larger-sized fonts, and for lines that might have taken two screens to take just one. This might seem as though it saves the viewing time of a potential second subtitle, but in real time the longer caption requires a longer time onscreen.*

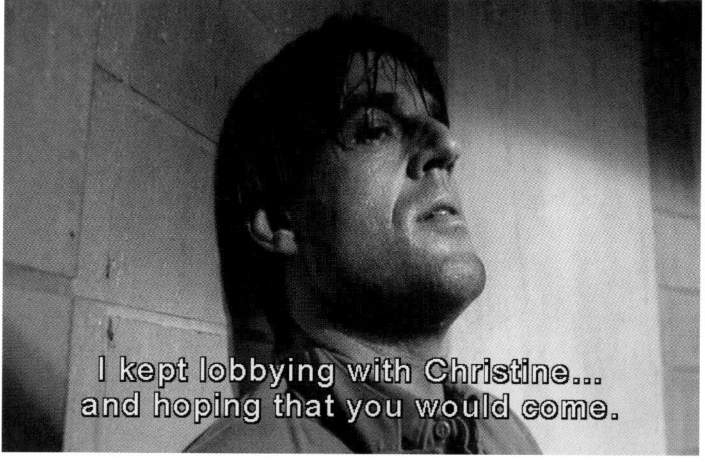

The importance of timing

The key to great comedy is...timing, and so is the secret of better titles. To a general audience, titles, credits, and captions get in the way of the action—a necessary evil, as the production machine has to fulfill its legal obligations.

For this reason, good titling is never protracted. It fulfills its obligations by not interfering with or obstructing flow, movement, and pace—while hopefully also generating visual interest and entertainment appropriate to the main content.

In most cases, then, the shorter the titles, the better. This is governed by the time it takes an audience to read any title (including a caption, subtitle, and so on). Conversational speech tends to be conducted at roughly 2.5 words every second. This is due to the three stages of articulation, processing, and comprehension. The average reader, on the other hand, can read out loud at around three words every second. Somewhere between the two is the average movie-viewer who, while not articulating the titles, captions, or credits while sitting in their seat, is attempting to process the information and understand it.

The calculation of how long to leave text onscreen for, though, is not simply a case of multiplying the number of words by a safe 0.33 seconds each. The only time that this really applies is with more than about 14 words onscreen at one time. When confronted with such a bulk of text, a viewer will accelerate their reading and processing rate at the expense of full comprehension. They will take in the overall gist rather than risk the loss of the final words. If the text still remains on the screen after the viewer has finished reading it, they will automatically begin reading it again for more detailed understanding.

With shorter titles or captions, this acceleration or panic-reading isn't triggered, and a more leisurely process can be adopted. When less than 14 words are onscreen at the same time, it's always best to add another half a second or so to compensate for this.

This two-second credit roll from the "I Love Mallory" sequence in Natural Born Killers *is probably the only credit roll in cinema history that you're not meant to view at leisure. To continue the parody of television conventions, even the Sixties-style font plays horrifically against an oversaturated NTSC background image.*

With a title of only one or two words, you don't need to worry so much about the precise calculations. Nevertheless, a title or caption lasting less than a second will merely be an irritation or an almost subliminal image. No text should last for less than a second and a half, and—again, for one or two words—last for longer than sheer boredom allows.

If you genuinely have a choice of timings at your disposal, then count yourself lucky. Captions and subtitles are the two areas where the shots or dialogue will dictate the length of time available to ensure the text makes sense with the image. If the image doesn't allow for the amount of time required to read the text, then one of them has to be changed.

The eye will retain an image once it has gone for about a quarter of a second. This should be the minimum amount of time between one title or caption and the next. While most opening titles opt for a short and practical "make them legible, get them over with" gap between individual titles, a few opt for a dramatically long gap (sometimes ten, sometimes 50 seconds) between consecutive titles. This tends to be when the titles are keyed onto the opening shots of the movie, and the gap therefore minimizes distraction from the unfurling action behind. Conversely, if the opening titles appear against a plain background, it makes sense (for the sake of holding your audience's attention) that they adopt a brisker pace and are kept to the minimum of timing requirements.

End titles (usually against a plain background), are an anomaly, and take a more leisurely approach. There are two types of movie-goers: credit-watchers and non-credit-watchers. This is usually down to the fact that unless the movie-makers have added outtakes at the end (*Charlie's Angels*) or a trailer for a sequel (*The Matrix: Reloaded*), there is really nothing else for the audience to see . But many remain, out of

Premiere Pro gives you complete control over the motion, speed, and duration of every element in your title. It's up to you to make sure that everyone gets their time in the sun, but not at the cost of boring the audience to death.

respect to the team of perhaps hundreds who have contributed to the production. Some factors will increase an audience's inclination to linger in their seats while the credits roll. For example, if the movie has inspired an individual to want to know more about how it was made (for example, where it was shot, whether J-Lo had a body double, and so on), or if it has an appealing soundtrack. The importance of audio, especially music, during end-titles is largely responsible for the phenomenon of after-movie loiterers, but it is not an exact science when it comes to whether or not they actually read the text.

With a television program, there's normally another one right around the ad-break corner, so holding onto the channel's audience is the greater imperative. For this reason, title timing rules are often broken. The fast, illegible credit roll in *Natural Born Killers*' "I Love Mallory" sequence satirizes television's need to move swiftly from one item to the next, whether it is an advertisement or the next must-see or must-flee show. The other technique used in real television is to box-panel the end-titles of the program—making the titles unreadable—and trail the next show while the credits are still rolling.

Cynicism aside, abiding by these general rules will lead to an interference and annoyance-free viewing experience. When actually creating your titles in Premiere Pro, letting intuition, your script, your legal obligations, and above all, your images dictate your moves while you sit in front of the timeline will relieve you of a lot of the responsibility of getting rigid calculations right. Everybody involved will want to see their names up on screen, but nobody will want to see that at the expense of turning your production into a drawn-out vanity display.

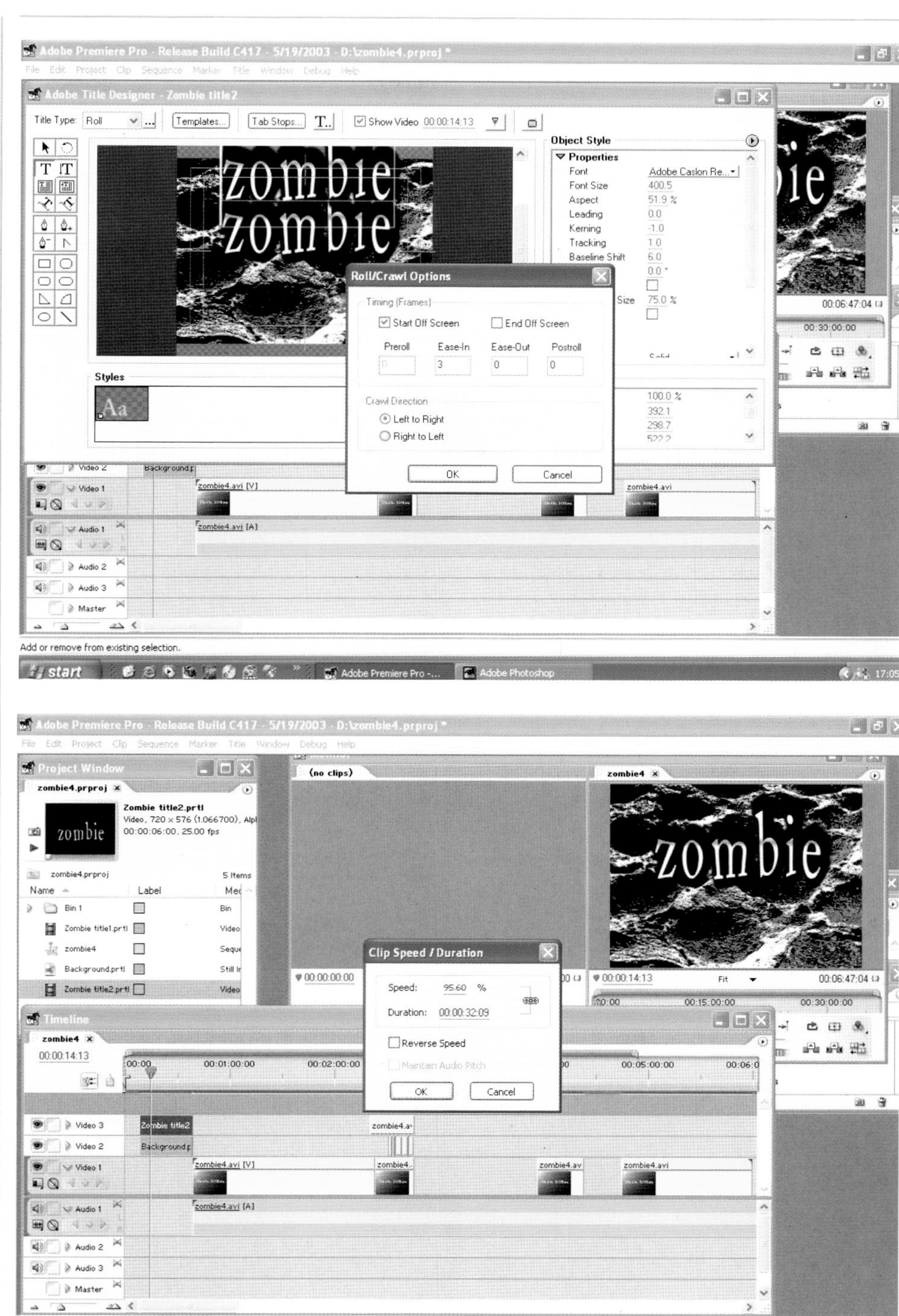

Motion and transition

There are very few titles or captions that hard cut into screen vision. To understand this is to understand cinema language. The staple diet of editing is the hard cut. It usually takes us from one camera angle to another within the same location. Sometimes, it takes us from one location to the next. An alternative is a fade. A fade between two shots has entered the vernacular to convey the passing of time.

The hard cut is hard on the eye. How the viewer resolves a hard cut without distraction is by recognizing the rearrangement of the same characters, the same furniture, the same background music, the continuation of the same dialogue and so on. All these pieces of the puzzle let the viewer know that the hard cut has taken us to another angle—a different perspective, in other words. We travel in daily life from one place to another in the same location or to an entirely different one and this allows us to make sense of our wider environment.

French New Wave cinema introduced the jump-cut as the 1950s rolled into the 1960s. This post-modern approach threw out everything we'd been taught to recognize and gave us hard cuts from the same or similar angles and perspectives. It was jarring and unesthetic. Once it became established as a dialect within the language of the moving picture, it became seen as a more "realistic" representation of life on the screen. In time, however, the technique became less regarded as an imitation of life. After all, it was only editing out a few frames of recognizable travel.

But the relevance of the hard cut in titling is that text (until recently) has not normally existed in a three-dimensional space as people or physical objects do. If we shot text in a 180° reverse-shot, the letters would appear backward. Because text exists to be read, any jarring and unesthetic manipulation of it, such as a jump-cut, is likely to cause some distraction. Transitions, then—effects which bridge the movement from one location or angle to another—have become an essential element of any series of titles in a movie or video. In order for the brain to process the information stored in the text, it can't be distracted by sudden changes unless it's given more time. And a lot of time is something that opening titles and captions don't have the luxury of having.

When applied to titles, the fade doesn't have any pretentions to emulate the passing of time. What it does do, though, is emulate the natural process of image-fade from the retina to be replaced by the next. In titling, if the fade from one title, color, or image to the next is extended so the transition is slower, you can give the brain more time to process the information.

A fade, though, doesn't have to be followed by another fade. As long as there's a consistency to the way the text appears, the viewer's eye and brain will soon catch on. A single hard cut followed by a fade might be jarring on its own, but a sequence of the same becomes a recognizable pattern. The door to making deliberate, jarring changes work to maximum effect, however, is best unlocked with audio.

Audio is the key element in turning sudden distractions to your advantage. Just as transitions can be described by music or sound effects, so a hard cut on a beat can drive a title sequence forward and give it momentum. It's not appropriate in every case: because captions tend simply to support a background image, any further information is too diverting—such as hard cuts and cymbal crashes. But when there's little else but titles onscreen, an audience is only too grateful that there is an audio soundtrack, let alone one that's cut to the beat. Distraction is, after all, entertainment.

Of course, the digital world has made some changes to our concept of space by creating the phenomenon of virtual space. Today, text can exist in a three-dimensional space in a computer. X, Y, and Z axes enable us to give substance and weight to letter forms, let them cast shadows from a pseudo light source, and even composite them as part of a background scene. To be legible, though, they still have to spend a specific amount of time in the two-dimensional plane that we recognize them from.

This, then, gives us a new rule. As long as the text manifests at some point in that two-dimensional plane long enough to be read and understood, any motion that it takes to get there is forgivable—if not always embraced as entertainment. The eye hungers for bigger, brighter, faster, and so on. Faster requires motion; motion requires time—and time is exactly what the fourth dimension gives you. Time comes as standard with video.

The movement of end titles in narrative features usually takes the form of a traditional roll. In broadcast, because there are so many genres of programming, rolls are used in addition to crawls and hard cut text screens. Captions are equally unfettered. Serious news may simply use a fade on/fade off, whereas comedy shows might fly them around like a deflating balloon.

Opening titles give you the chance to use your computer's abilities, especially in the narrative arena where it is understood that such titles can constitute a movie of their own. As long as the title or credits are legible for at least three seconds, they can be moved around as much as your concept permits.

It's time to go crazy.

Both the 28 Days Later *teaser and trailer rely on their text tagline to propel them through to the "The days are numbered" ending. For each noted day, the status of the virus ("Exposure," "Infection," "Epidemic," "Evacuation," "Devastation") is delivered on screen in different ways: crawls L to R and R to L, a DVE zoom, throbbing, resonance. Aside from this upping the interest level for an audience, each motion works with the audio. Breathing, sirens, radio frequencies, and helicopter blades make sense of their movement.*

Day 3
INFECTION

The first scene in Hannibal *is first heard as voice-over for the producer/distributor credits before the whole frame comes into vision, zooming larger until it fills the screen and eclipses the director credit. More than this, there is a slow camera track within the shot, which makes the simple DVE (DIgital Video Effect) zoom even more effective. Again, it's a matte with an effect that Premiere Pro is perfectly suited to if you've got the shot.*

Title designer Michael Riley (III) must have had a "eureka!" moment to notice that everyone in Gattaca*'s opening credits had at least one of the letters of "GATTACA" in their name. Making use of this, each title blurs onto the screen with only the siGnifiCAnT letters fading through sharply. The theme of the movie (perfect genes in an imperfect body) make the entire design a classic.*

Once the bandaged letters of The Mummy *have hit the screen with a reverse DVE zoom over a background image of an Egyptian statue, the bandages peel away to reveal a shining gold font with allusions to hieroglyphics. It's a good, clean graphic effect and the transition (DVE zoom) and the motion (peel) keep things lightly entertaining enough—very much hand-in-hand with the movie. This kind of transition and motion is easy in Premiere Pro.*

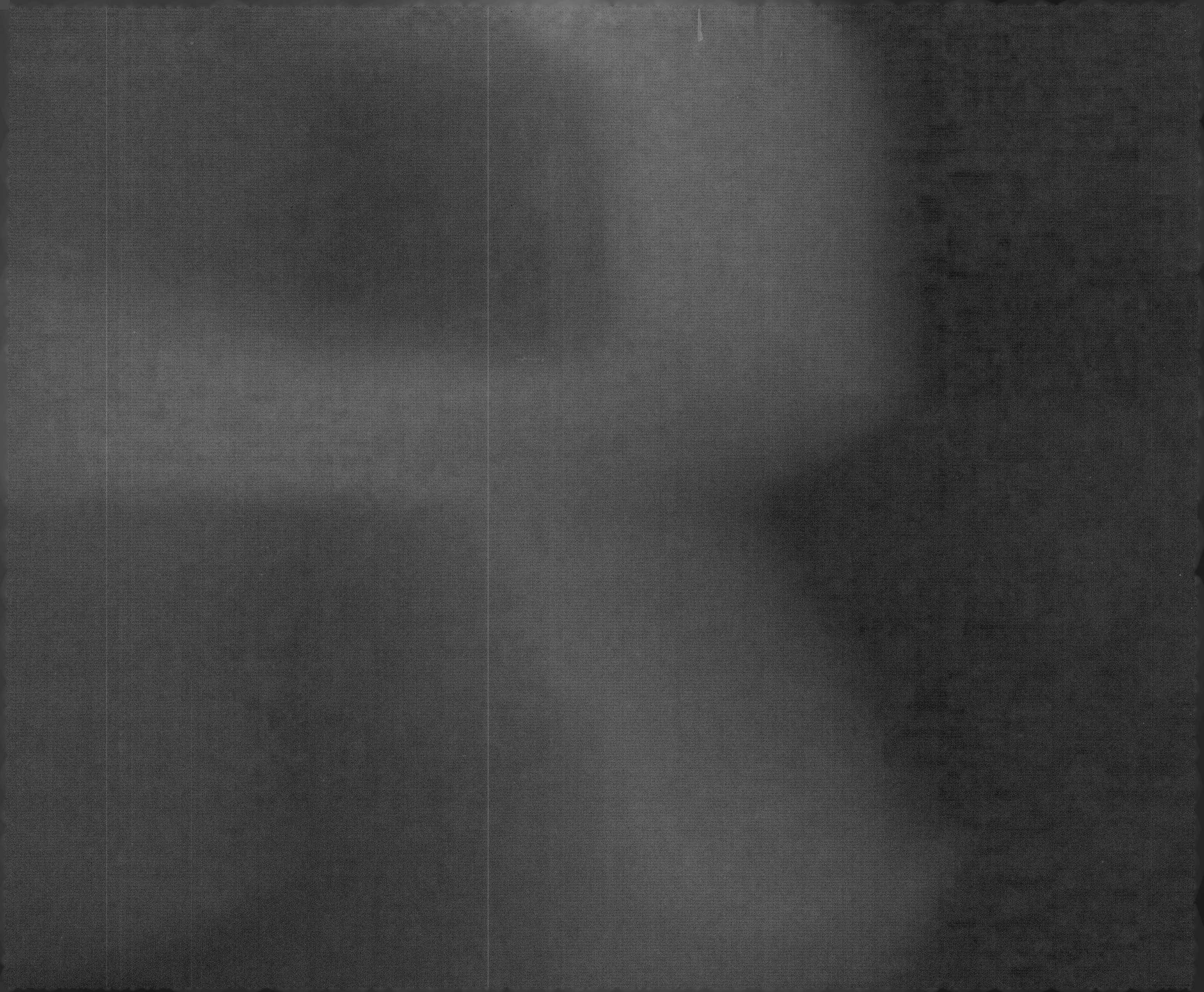

CHAPTER TWO

2

creating a title in Premiere Pro

Organizing your material

Working with titles in your *Timeline* needs careful preparation. Do you have all your source material organized? And how is the final video going to be seen: is it intended for broadcast, or home consumption? It's all about housekeeping...

Ideally when you begin working on titles, you'll have a completed AVI of the production that you're working to. The more complete the movie or program, the more you will have a chance of:

Synopsizing
Referencing themes
Sourcing images and textures
Sourcing audio
Exacting timing
Working your font, color, effects, transition, and motion against a nailed background
Having finalized interviews (no edits and subsequent overlay) for captioning

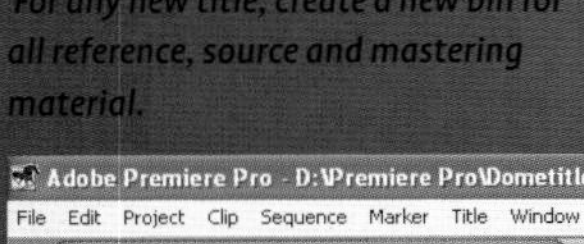

For any new title, create a new bin for all reference, source and mastering material.

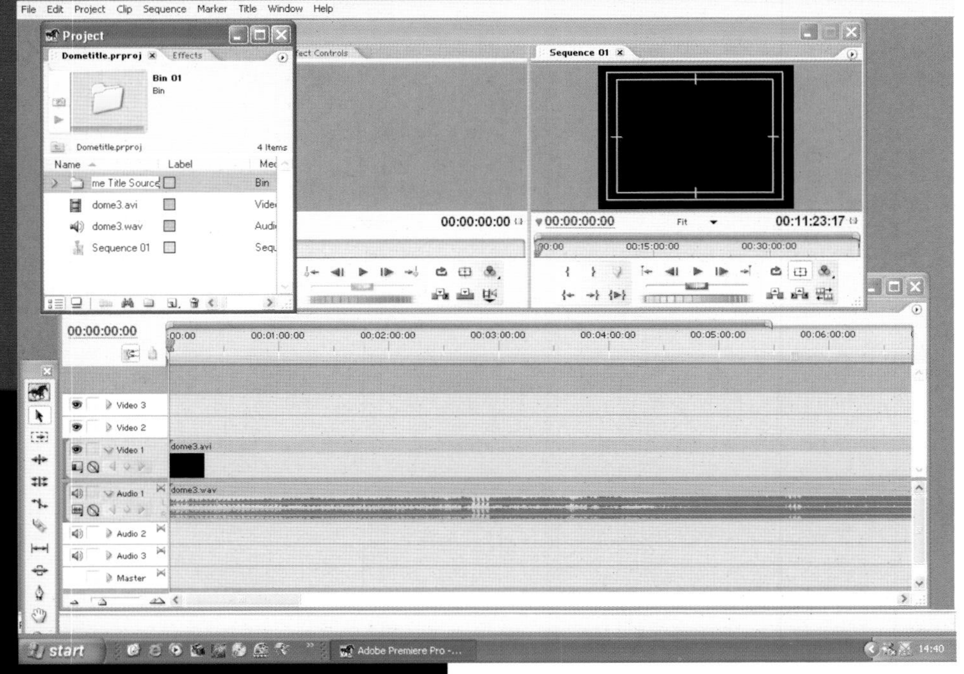

In essence, it's knowing what you're up against. Alongside the finished (untitled) production, you should have a complete, agreed file of all the credits, name captions, and job titles, which have been spell-checked and put in the appropriate order. If you're working alongside a marketing strategy, have the requisite font on file with any other images that you're obliged to use.

Your basic setup will be to import the production and place the video on Video 1 and the audio on Audio 1. If your time constraints are part of the movie—the AVI (the video file) is blacked (see Glossary, page 188) at the top for your use, or you're overlaying onto the top of the movie—abut it to the front of the *Timeline*. If there's a length of audio before the pictures begin, abut the start of the audio up to the top of the *Timeline*. If your production's for broadcast, get 30 seconds of bars and tone and a 10 second counter leader up first before you drop in the movie. These can be found under *File > New*. The secret to eliminating frustration in an edit is good housekeeping. If you keep your housekeeping simple, you'll know where you're going—and where you've just been.

If your work is not dictated by audio or visual timing and it's entirely up to you what you do at the front end of the AVI, leave it loose. Give yourself a good minute's worth of space before both audio and video begin.

If you've got a font that you need to use either in Premiere Pro or Photoshop, save it to c:WINDOWS/Fonts to be accessible from both. If you're importing images or using a separately supplied audio soundtrack, make sure that you copy and save them to your project's chosen scratch-disk and clip folder for easy extraction. This will stop you from having to find your sources every time you start up the project.

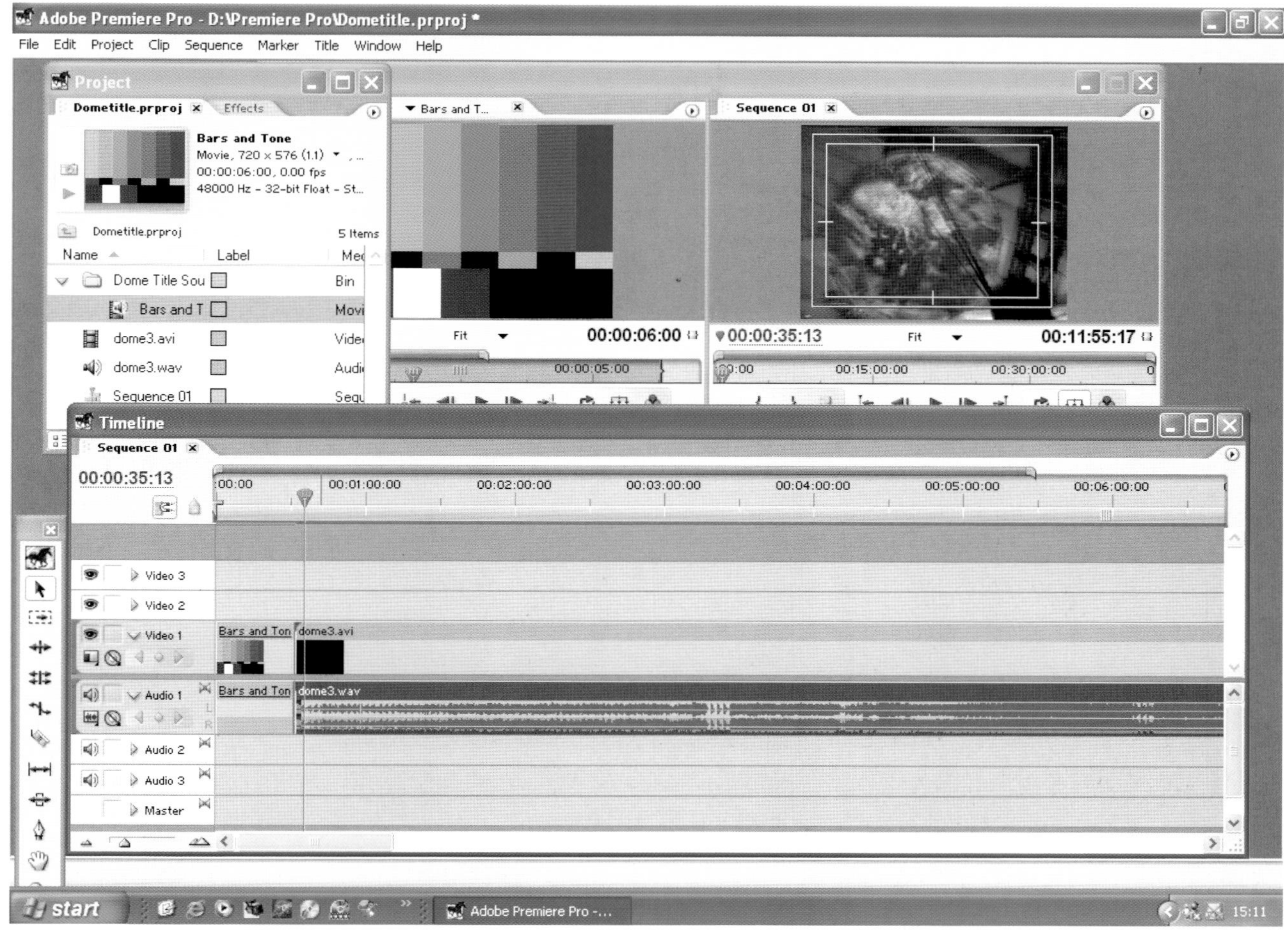

You should add 30 seconds of bars and tone before the production—and you should do this before you even get into Title Designer. *This keeps your* Timeline *prepared and professional.*

Bins are a great way to manage your titling project from the start. While your production audio and video remain the base of your work, a new bin can contain all of your source footage, audio, and upcoming title layers. Right-click in your *Project* window to make a new bin, then name it and import everything you're going to need into it. If you're starting from scratch and working against black or a color matte, using a counter leader or bars and tone, make sure you put these in here too because Premiere creates them as clips in your *Project* window.

If you're working from your PC monitor, make sure that you click the *Screen Margin* icon. Screen safety is possibly the most important thing when applying titles and graphics to a production. Premiere Pro, like any other video-editing application, will be as true to your image ratio and viewing area as possible, but traditional CRTs (including television screens) will not. Even if you're thinking of high-definition television as your viewing medium (you may have no control over how people see your work), the cut-off point for the image on the television will still be somewhere around your screen-safe area and it will all depend on the make and specification of the TV. There can also be some slight bending in the corners of CRT screens. Premiere Pro's screen safety option will let you know when your title is safely on- and offscreen.

Opening the title generator

Premiere Pro's *Title Designer* is located under *File* > *New* > ***Title***. Once *Title Designer* is open, maximize it to ensure that you're getting the easiest navigation and the highest resolution.

SHORTCUTS

*This drop-down menu lets you decide on the motion of your text (*Still, Roll, *or* Crawl*). If you're opting for* Roll *or* Crawl*, the adjacent button will highlight to click the* Roll/Crawl options menu*.*

The Templates *shortcut brings up Premiere Pro's preset templates for an array of themed title designs or for any that you've designed and saved previously. Use if you really want to save yourself a bit of time and brain-power.*

The Tab-stops *shortcut is especially useful for end titles, or where you require any list of job titles and names aligned with consistency.*

The Fonts *shortcut is far more useful than any other font access on the page, as it displays the characters rather than just naming them.*

The Show Video *checkbox either lets you work with a standard Adobe transparency checkerboard, or permit your video as a backdrop to work against. To scrub through the video, your timecode can be dragged either left or right to reverse or forward your movie, or double-clicked to let you input the timecode of choice.*

The associated Sync to Timeline *button will automatically take your video to your edit point on the* Timeline*. It's of selective use—and if you don't use it often, you're likely to forget it's there and never use it at all.*

The Output to External Monitor *button does exactly that. If you've got a monitor connected for the purposes of exact observation, it'll output your title preview full-screen.*

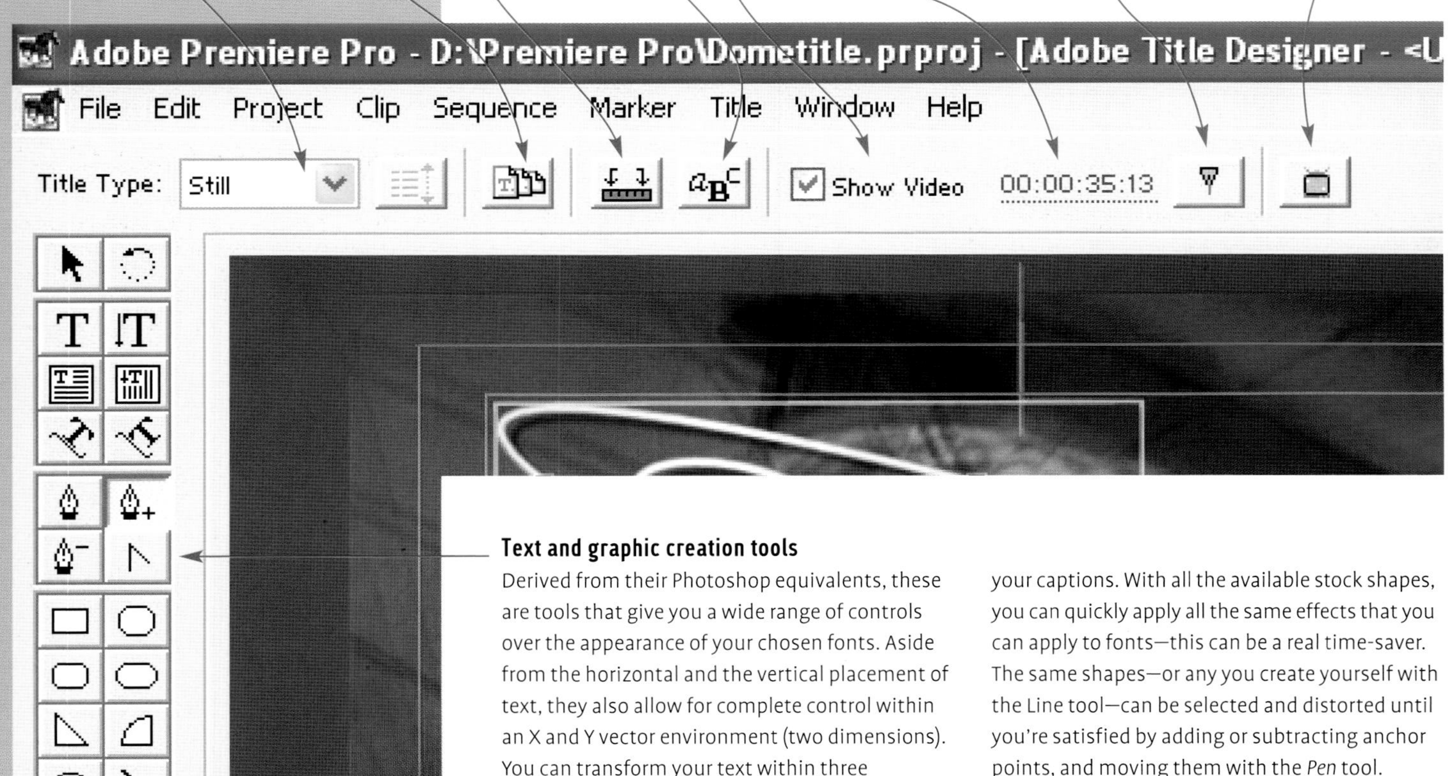

Text and graphic creation tools

Derived from their Photoshop equivalents, these are tools that give you a wide range of controls over the appearance of your chosen fonts. Aside from the horizontal and the vertical placement of text, they also allow for complete control within an X and Y vector environment (two dimensions). You can transform your text within three dimensions over time once the title has been placed on your *Timeline*.

The graphics tools might be basic, but they're perfect for creating straps and shapes for your captions. With all the available stock shapes, you can quickly apply all the same effects that you can apply to fonts—this can be a real time-saver. The same shapes—or any you create yourself with the Line tool—can be selected and distorted until you're satisfied by adding or subtracting anchor points, and moving them with the *Pen* tool.

But if you intend to do anything more sophisticated and intricate with your text and graphics, then look to Photoshop for much greater versatility and subtlety (*see page 144*).

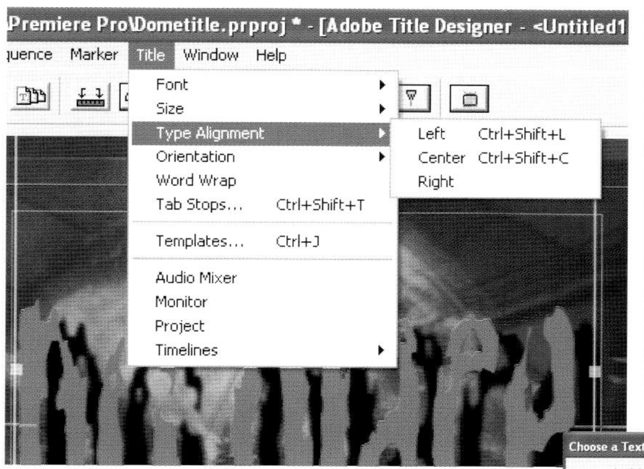

OBJECT STYLE

Everything you could ever want to do (within reason) to your objects or text can be done in the menu, right. While you can drag anchor points within your Preview *screen to change the overall size of your graphic, the* Object Style *menu will give you a massive range options for the look of every font you have. The left/right - /+ draggables (nodes) alter the x and y axes of either the graphic, or the space between. Like your blue timecode shortcut, double-clicking will enable you to input the measure of your choice precisely, which is very handy when matching different title designs.*

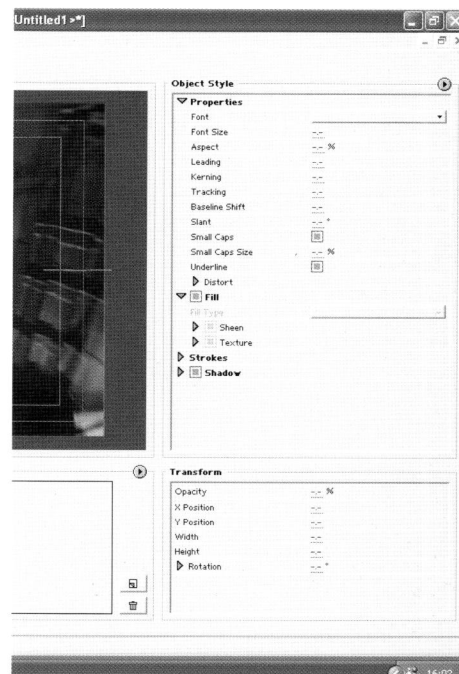

Choosing colors for Fill *or* Shadow*, by spectrum or dropper,* Opacity*,* Texture*,* Sheen*, and* Stroke*, can also be done from this menu. The only one here that sends you off in a different direction is the* Texture *option. Textures are, by default, .tga files (Targa Graphics Adapter)—a video capture file format. Premiere Pro includes a number of them as presets, but you can import your own images for use—it will take most graphic file formats (bitmaps, jpegs, et al). Although .tgas are not very high-resolution, they do support both 24-bit true color and 8-bit grayscale images.*

LONG CUTS

Your long cuts are the drop-down title menu above the shortcuts. The functions that are particular to this menu are Type Alignment *(left, center, right) and* Word Wrap *(justification). Other than this, the only real reason to access it is when you're working full-screen in* Title Designer*, it can bring up different windows (*Audio Mixer*, your* Timeline *monitor, and any* project *or* Timeline *you have on the go).*

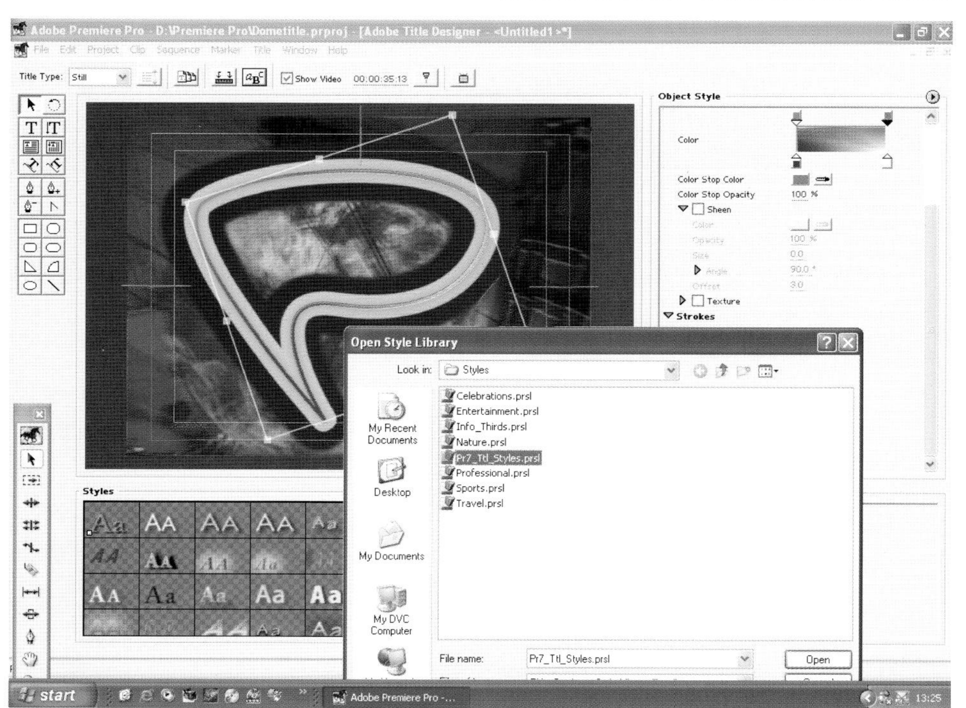

TRANSFORM

The Transform *menu (again in blue, again draggable/ clickable) is the mathematical equivalent of dragging your anchor points. If you are matching other titles or objects—or those on the same screen with different moves—this is where you can set precise numerical values. There's also yet another* Opacity *option, which will effect your entire graphic.*

STYLES

Like your preset textures, your font styles are found in a separate area. The small arrow button on the top right lets you access them from a drop-down menu, and you can load a style library in .prsl (Premiere Style Library) format and choose as you will. These styles act like templates for quick application to your text or object, and require clicking on them to alter their appearance. Most will change your options in the Object Style *menu, but more of that later.*

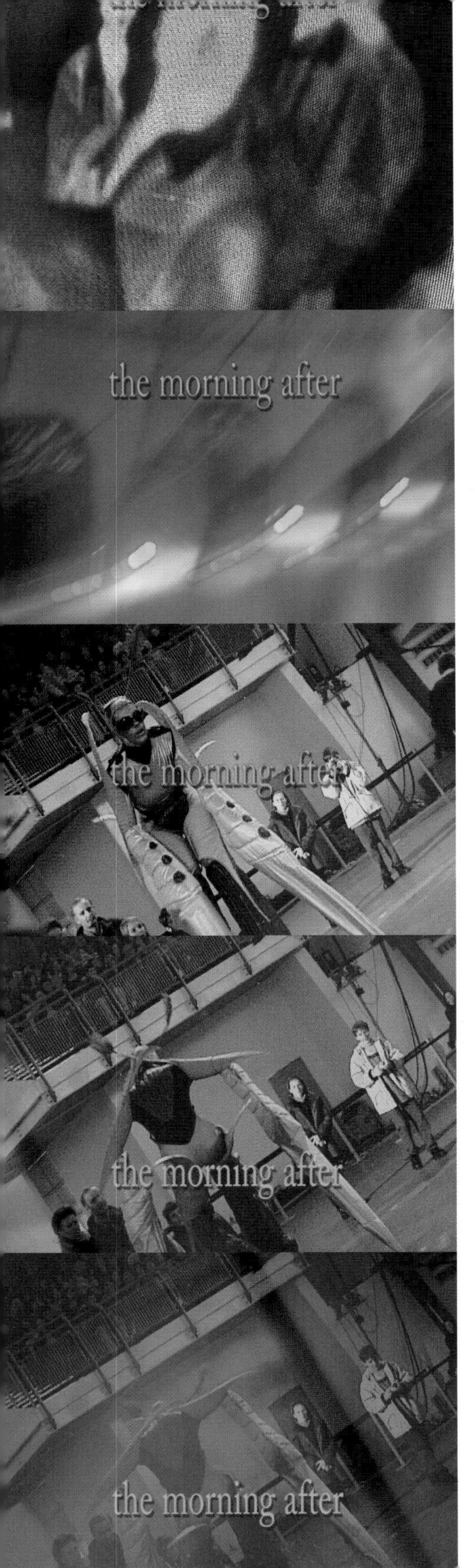

Different styles of title

In the dimension of time, a title can do two things: it can move, or not move. When moving in two dimensions on an x/y axis, a title can move on the screen in two standard ways: it can move vertically—roll, or horizontally—crawl.

In *Title Designer* your text can be moved to exactly where you want it to be on the screen. If you choose the *Still* option from the drop-down menu, it will stay in that position for the duration of the still on the *Timeline*. And until you do anything about it on the *Timeline*, it'll just be a jump-cut.

Both *Roll* and *Crawl* rely on more information than just your selection from the drop-down menu, though. If you decide that you want to roll your title, select *Roll* and then use the shortcut for *Roll/Crawl* options. Checking the *Start Off Screen* box will let your title do exactly that—the same with *End Off Screen*.

Titles can sometime look a little strange rolling on and off screen at speed, which is why there is also an option for *Ease-In* and *Ease-Out*.

Easing is a way of telling the title to gradually pick up speed when entering vision and slow down when leaving, and the boxes that contain zero by default require a numerical value which indicates how severe the change will be between slow and normal playback speeds. The lower the number, the quicker the acceleration—blink and you'll miss it. The higher the number, the slower the acceleration—and you may not even notice it. Playing with speed and movement is one of the pleasures of titling.

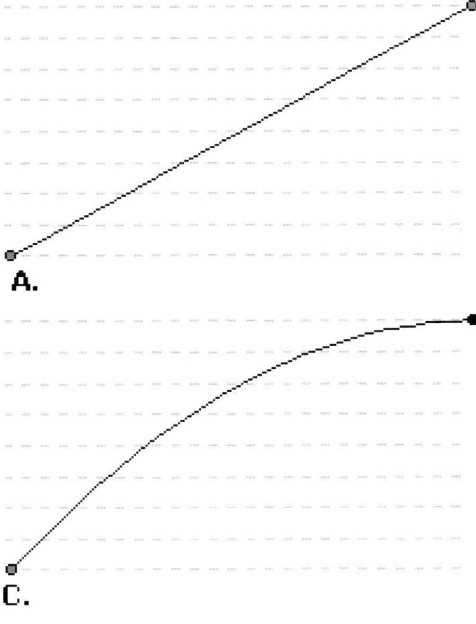

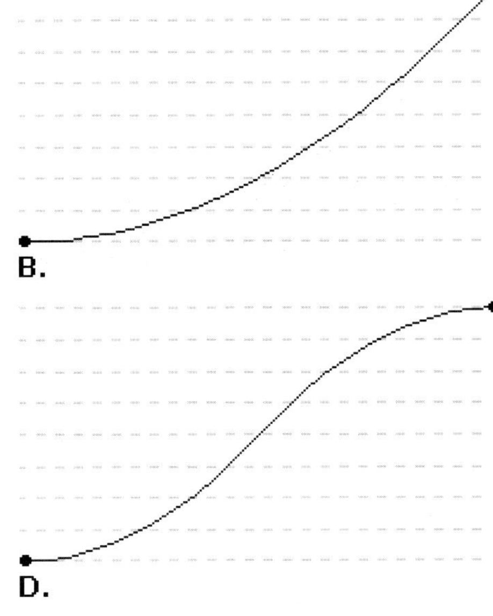

A: No ease applied
B. Ease-Out *applied*
C. Ease-In *applied*
D. Ease-In *and* Ease-Out *applied*

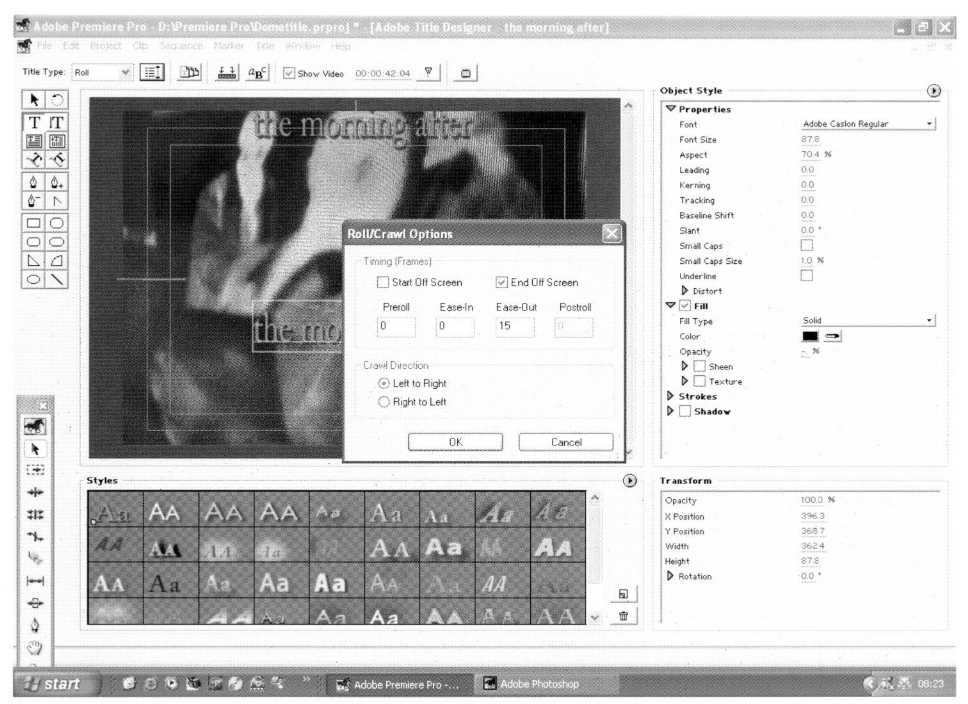

We've discussed how standard the roll from the bottom of the screen to the top is, but if you want your roll to be reversed, you'll have to do it when you've got your title on the *Timeline* (right click, then select *Speed > Duration >* ***Reverse Speed***). The issue with this is that if you do decide that this is what you want, don't get confused going back into your *Roll/Crawl* options to find that your *Start Off Screen* checkbox is still checked when your title is actually ending off screen. The above options window shows the result of a reverse roll.

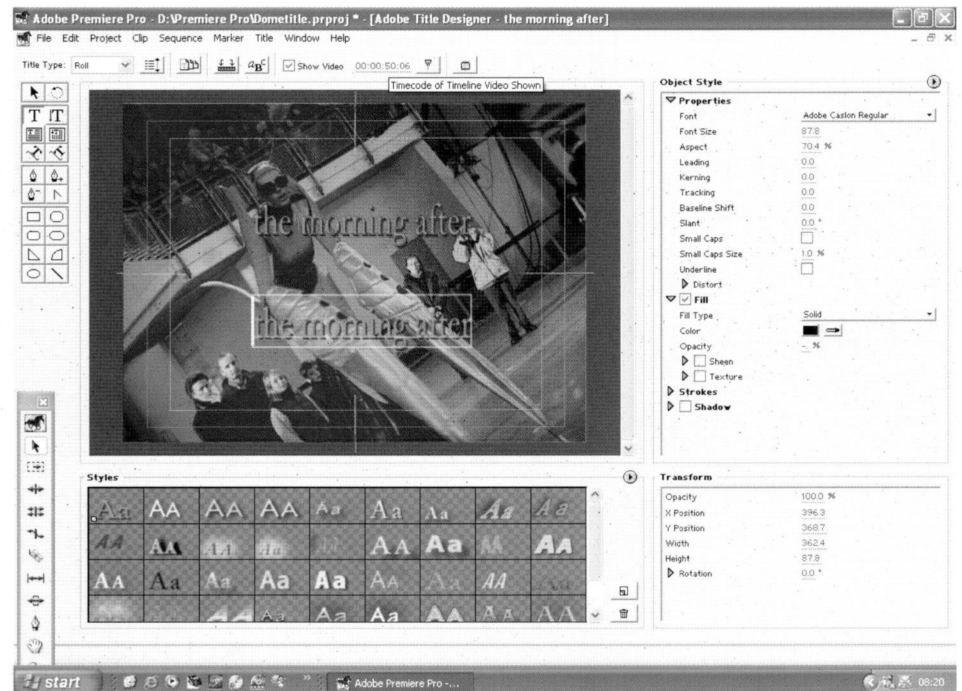

If you are concerned about your audience not reading a title until it has 50% *Opacity* through a fade (and by then it's hurtling toward the top of the screen), this can be resolved by combining a **still** with a roll (or a crawl). Scroll through your timecode until your preview shows the end text position of your move. Keep the text in place and select *Still* from the drop-down menu. Save as a different file and then you can just drop it on your *Timeline* at the end of the move as an invisible edit that keeps your text hanging in its resolution position, letting you do whatever you want with it.

Frankly, though, this title sucks. No themes, no ideas, no creativity—and worse, a default font...

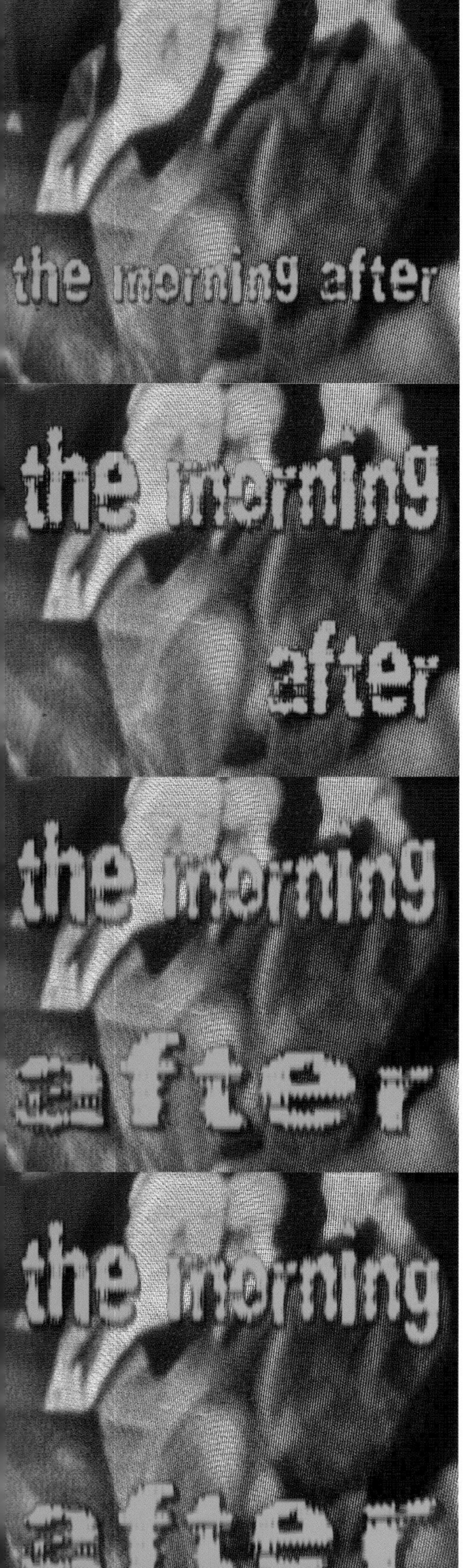

Using fonts

Fonts can say so much about your production. They say whether it's cool, scary, or romantic, whether it's hard news or a fluff piece. In Premiere Pro, you can either type your text, select it, and then apply a font, or apply the font before you start. Use the shortcut menu to look at your options. If you're separating your text to work as different sections, decide whether you're going to use the same font or find a compatible or contrasting one. If you don't have a font that appeals or works with the background, download one.

You can do a lot of things with your fonts—and with your objects. The *Object Style* menu is broken down into various expandable sub-menus. The one that deals with your text size, shape, and its positioning is...

Properties

A screen is of a certain size only and your text may best suit your background image by being presented in a different way. This is the main concern of the *Properties* submenu. When working with it, it's essential that you are displaying your screen safety margins. Properties can either be applied to portions of highlighted text, or to individual characters.

Font

To change the size of your font, you can either drag the text box or change the size specifically in the *Font Size* box.

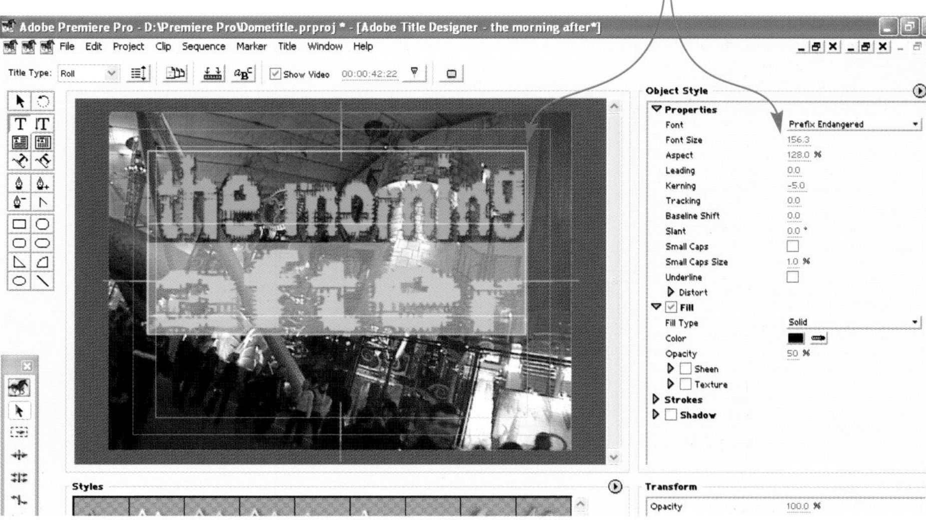

LEFT: *The title's for a movie about the UK's Millennium Dome. The project, now sitting idle on a peninsula in London, perhaps requires a distressed feel to the font. As it's a subject of so much fading newsprint, I've gone for a font that has a yesterday's news look to it. Prefix is perfect.*

Aspect

Your *Aspect* relies on a percentage. This is the percentage scaling of the text horizontally, while maintaining a fixed height of the font. It also gives a good idea of the kind of resolution that your font can withstand. If your percentage is under 100% and the title is broadspread across your screen, you'll have better resolution than if stretching it to fit the screen takes it well over 100%.

Emphasis is required on the word "after" if I want this title to work. It needs to be big, bold, and brave to do the job, so I've carriage-returned the text to split it and upped the Aspect *of the word to fit the frame.*

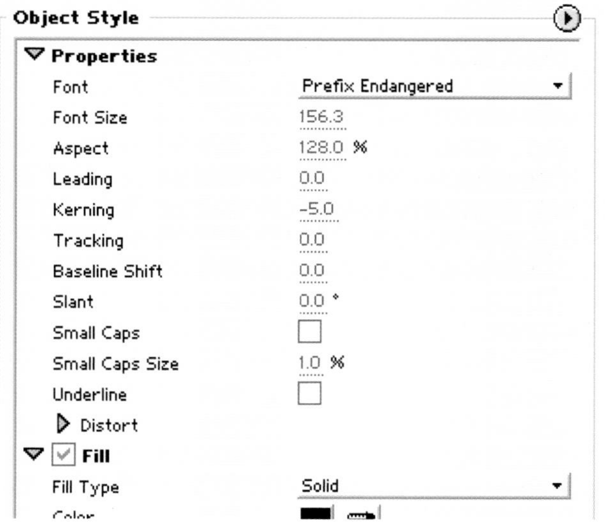

Leading

Leading is the distance in points between different lines of text or objects within the same *Title Designer* project. If you've hit return at any point when typing your text, *Leading* will alter the space between the lines. This applies to any alignment of text—horizontal, vertical, or path-led.

Splitting the text isn't enough. Not only does the text have to command the frame, but I want to let the next part of the title breathe, between the first line and the second. Opening up the gap between lines, by increasing the Leading*, covers both of these.*

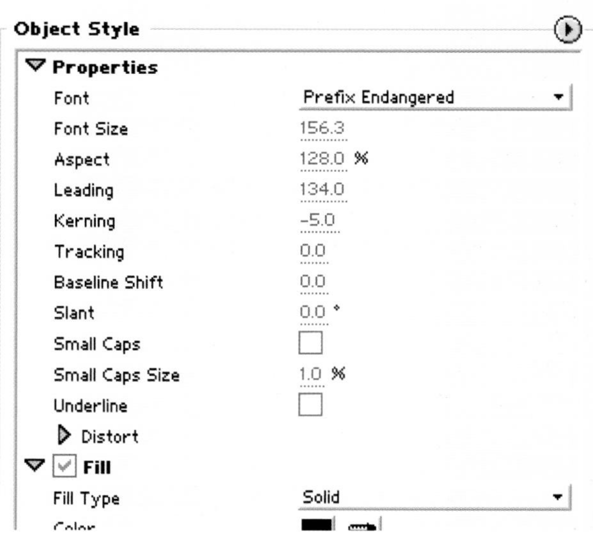

Kerning

Kerning, again measured in points, is the inter-character distance. Widening the spaces between letters (e.g. A L I E N) can indeed alienate it from conventional reading while still preserving legibility. Alternatively, narrowing the space can conjoin letters. On occasion, this might work well, but it risks turning text into illegible patterns. This is also the point where inputting values becomes meaningless: put simply, the space between some letters can look right, and sometimes it needs to be put right. The reason is that we read the English language left to right, and the spaces in between are vital to our understanding of where one word stops and another begins. This is particularly important in titles where quick understanding is essential.

This is just as important in the case of numbers. We read “1961” as “nineteen sixty-one” and it becomes a year. If we read “196 1,” it’s “one hundred and ninety-six” and a “one.” It’s vital when experimenting with the design of text and numerals to remember that comprehension is vital when you are dealing with moving images.

Video is a visual (and aural) medium, not a text-based one, so any text that does appear onscreen will be minutely analyzed. So, kerning

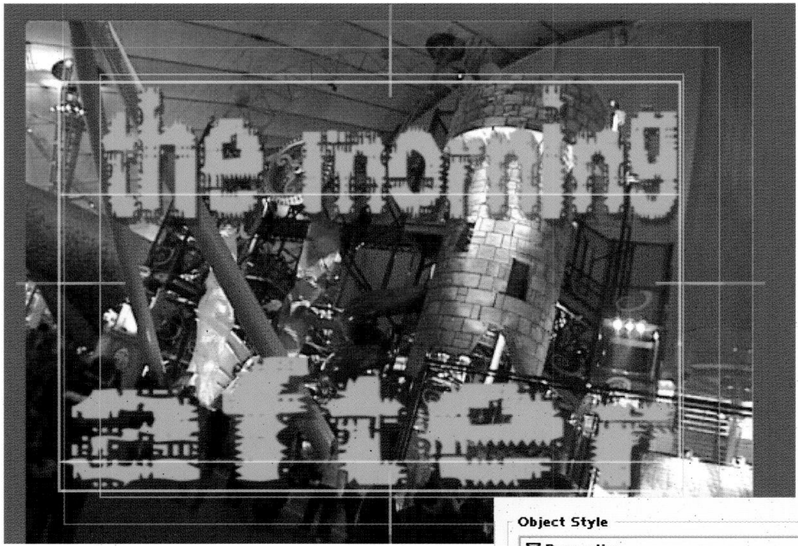

Object Style

Properties

Font	Prefix Endangered
Font Size	156.3
Aspect	128.0 %
Leading	134.0
Kerning	10.0
Tracking	0.0
Baseline Shift	0.0
Slant	0.0 °
Small Caps	☐
Small Caps Size	1.0 %
Underline	☐

Distort

Fill

Fill Type	Solid

Applying Aspect has really shown up quite a difference in distance between the “a” and the “f,” and the “e” and the “r.” Placing the cursor in each respective space, kerning then pulls them apart to make them less esthetically troublesome.

123456789

ABCDEFGH

abcdefgh

your text is just as important when dealing with video as it is on the printed page. If a title is onscreen for several seconds, it attracts a great deal of scrutiny, and certain letterforms within words can appear in not-so-splendid isolation unless you kern them. Also, shunting letters too closely together will highlight gaps elsewhere.

Backgrounds can highlight these problems even more if there’s a sudden change in contrast in the space between characters. If your background is moving, you’ll have to try even harder to make sure that your text remains easily legible. If you’re introducing motion (DVE zooms, etc), always keep an eye out for any problem areas in terms of font sizing and character spacing.

All fonts are different, but if you think of each letter as appearing within an imaginary rectangle (think of an LED display), then you can imagine that the gap between an “M” and a “B,” for example, will be different to that between a “p” and an “l.” In practice, all font families and page layout programs, for example, are designed to compensate for these inconsistencies, but video-editing suites are not primarily intended as typographical design tools, so you may have to fix a lot of these problems manually by kerning.

For all the reasons above, kerning is at its most useful when used esthetically rather than mathematically. Position your cursor in the space between the characters that need adjusting and add or subtract points as appropriate. Kerning can also be used to change the whole or parts of your text when the text is highlighted.

The Kerning *has now affected the width of the text beyond screen-safe, so the whole word now has to be reapplied with* Aspect *in order to reign it in while maintaining the inter-character ratios.*

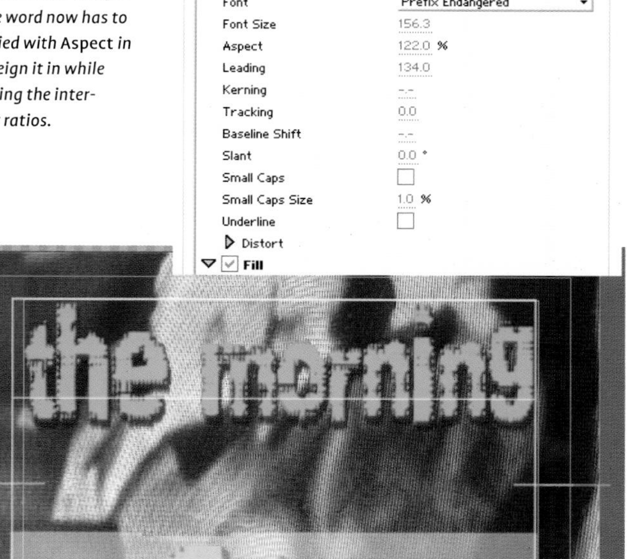

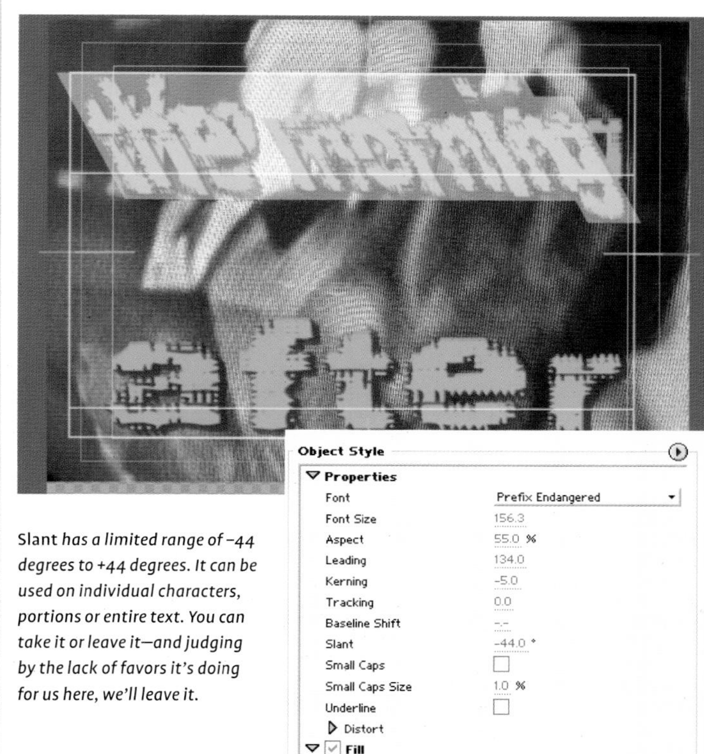

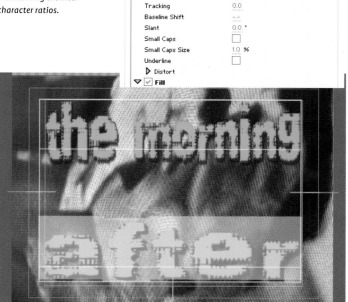

Slant *has a limited range of −44 degrees to +44 degrees. It can be used on individual characters, portions or entire text. You can take it or leave it—and judging by the lack of favors it's doing for us here, we'll leave it.*

Baseline shift

Baseline Shift *can be used to move each character vertically in relation to the text's baseline. Hanging noncap characters (g, p, q, etc) can be raised or lowered from the baseline by points so that they don't intrude on other text beneath or above. For a more distressed look, this can be time well spent. Highlighting all of the text and shifting the baseline will raise or lower the whole line or lines of text.*

Prefix's hanging characters have, of course, the same baseline as all the other letters. In order to break up the level and evoke the feeling of "the morning after," I've shifted the "g" downward relative to the baseline.

Slant

The degree of Slant *for your characters can be changed right here. The baseline will remain in place while the top pixels will travel the farthest distance from the vertical. A negative value will take the top pixels to the left, and a positive value to the right. This is perhaps most useful for copying text as a reflection of itself.*

Small caps

SMALL CAPS? Small checkbox. There are fonts, however, that are resilient to any pixel transformation that Premiere Pro wants to make. *Small Caps* can sometimes make your text seem classy or, with individual characters, help distress the look of the entire text. Remember that a small cap will still be greater in height and width than a non-cap, so you might want to reconsider your kerning.

Small Caps defaults at 1% larger than your current font size. Change it as you will.

Creating a new test text screen in Title Designer *makes it easier to see the difference in effect between what we've done already and a version in small caps at 94%. Subjectively, it seems more legible ("after" looks more like "after" than "alter", as it did before) and, like all caps, it fills the screen better. But there's something a bit self-important and structured about it, and it doesn't fulfil the thematic and screen requirements.*

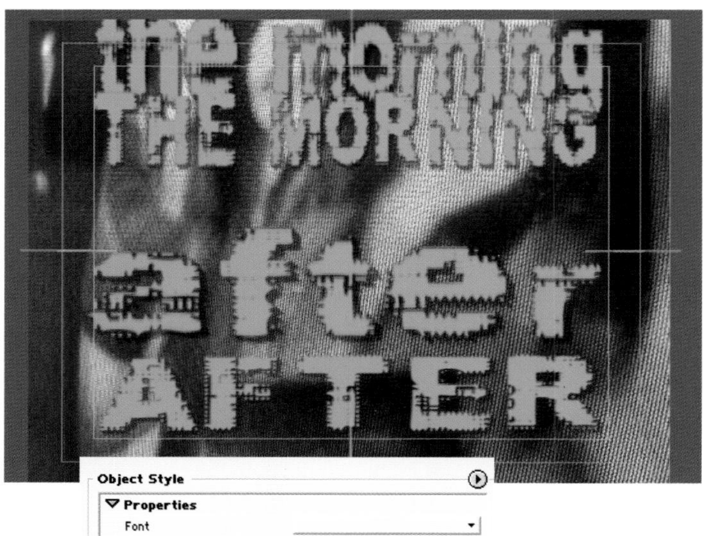

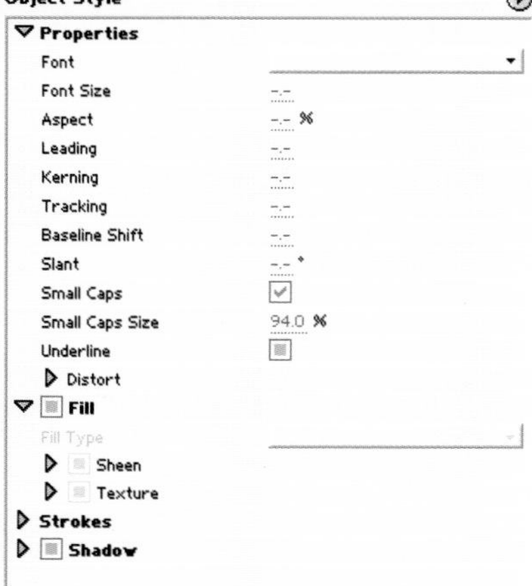

Underline

Check one more box and you've got a <u>REALLY HORRIBLE EFFECT</u>. Underlining text is not a good thing to do in titling unless there's a truly good reason. It's unlikely that you're trying to emphasize anything in the world of titling, unless you're captioning subtitles. And then you'd probably use italics.

An audience recognizes underlining more along the lines of *"Could do better. <u>SEE ME!!</u>"* It talks down to your audience; it shouts. If you need to create a line to work graphically with your text, it's better to create it as an object. And if you're looking to emphasize your text, there are more interesting ways in store...

Some things just don't help your text...

Object Style
Properties
Font
Font Size
Aspect
Leading
Kerning
Tracking
Baseline Shift
Slant
Small Caps
Small Caps Size
Underline
Distort
Fill
Fill Type
Sheen
Texture
Strokes
Shadow

Distort

Distorting your characters is done by the manipulation of pixels, like *Slant*. The difference is that *Distort* works on the central x or y-axes as a mirror image. Input or drag up the distortion percentage (up to 100%) on the x-axis and your characters either wear flares as a negative value or take on a sky-scraper-from-a-helicopter look as a positive value. On the y-axis, a negative value makes it appear as though the character is being spewed out and—on the positive side—as though they're being stuffed into a cone.

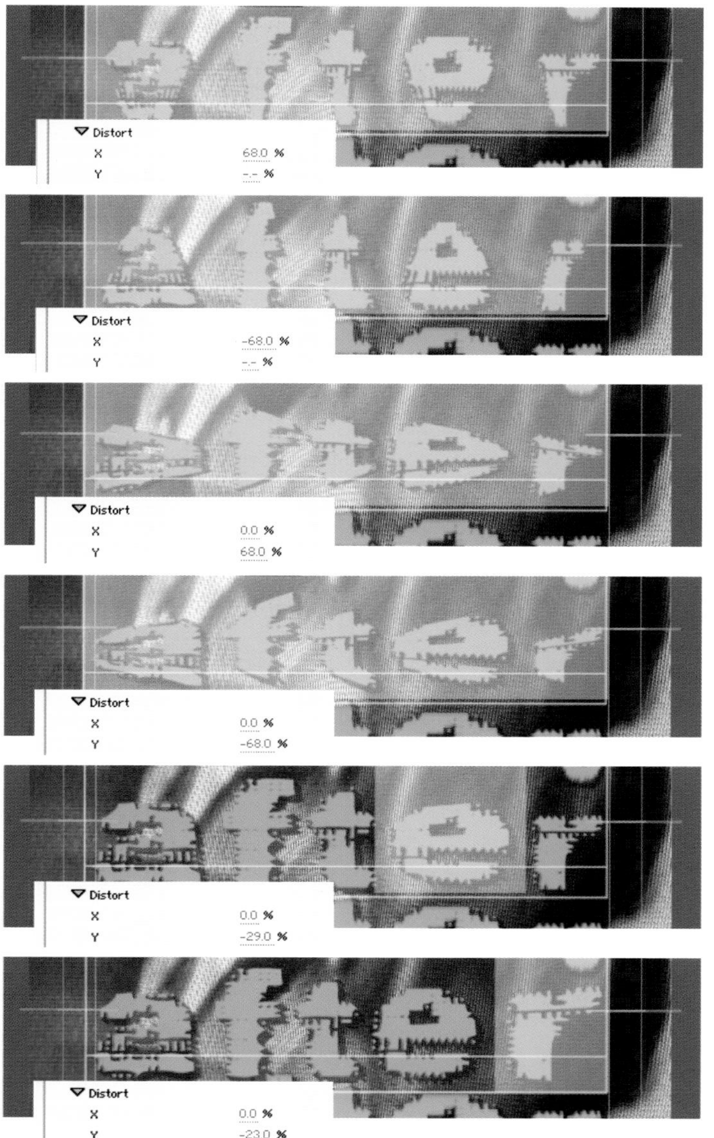

LEFT, TOP DOWN: *Distorting on the x-axis by +68 degrees would be fine if this were* Twister 2: Bad Wind.

Distorting on the x-axis by −68 degrees makes Prefix seem like a tormented Goodies *re-run.*

Distorting on the y-axis by +68 degrees sucks.

Distorting on the y-axis by −68 degrees blows.

You can continue positioning your text and objects in the *Transform* menu. Any changes you carry out using *Transform* tools apply to the entire page, not just to selected characters, lines, or objects. Vectors *X* and *Y* can be dragged left or right or input with a value to position it onscreen. Like tabs, these are most useful when matching the position of different titles or caption across different screens. 0.0/0.0 X/Y refers to the vector at the top left of the screen, and 770.0/576.0 (PAL, 4:3) represent the pixels in the bottom right.

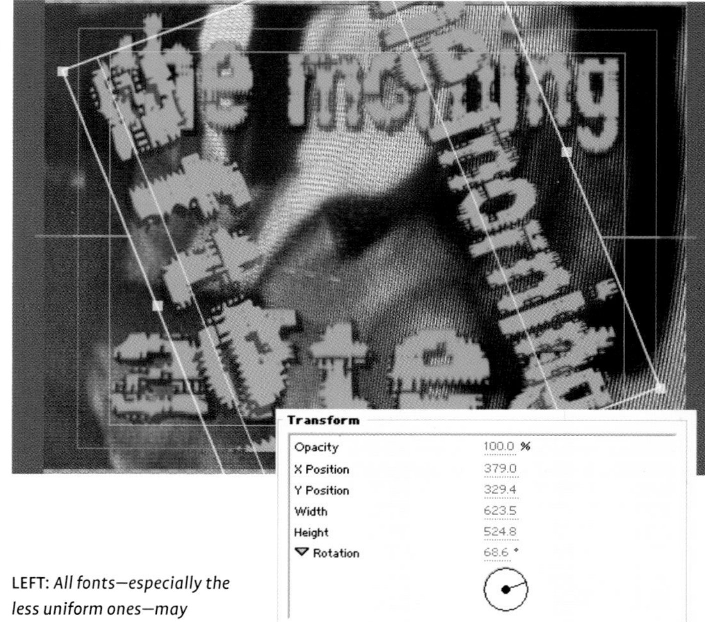

LEFT: *All fonts—especially the less uniform ones—may require some tweaking to meet your own requirements. The "a," "e," and "r" here have been distorted slightly along both x-and y- axes to break the mould of the font. The "r", though, became visually diminished and seemed lost as the final letter. Selecting just this character and enlarging the font gives the word greater unity and, as a result, much greater impact.*

Likewise, *Rotation* by degrees (above) applies to the whole of your page, and the amount can either be input as a value, dragged, or expanded to bring up the *Rotation* clock. This is useful for objects, or for text if you want to create a "rubberstamp" effect on your screen.

So now you've chosen the font and the text is positioned, but something is still lacking...

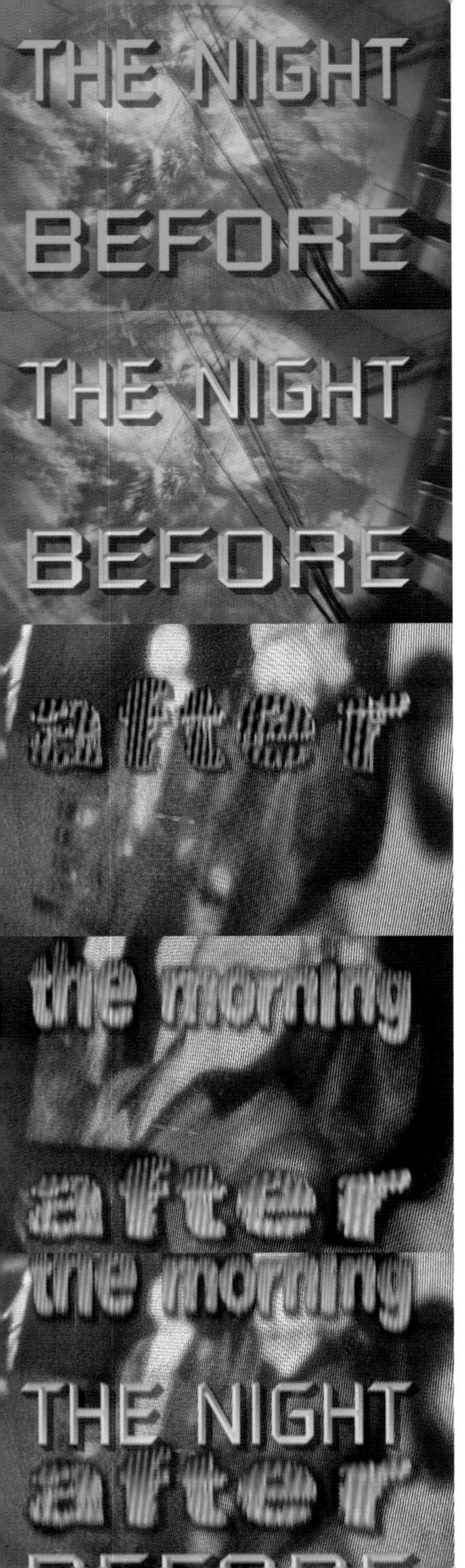

Coloring fonts

Color has its own language, but the meanings change in different contexts. Green might mean "Go," but a magazine designer will tell you that it evokes the least emotional response. Red can signify danger, but a television producer will tell you to wear it to get in the picture. In titling, color is no less context-heavy.

Look at your background. What's happening out there beyond the title? Is it busy? Is your text going to stand out if it's plain—or will it win the beauty pageant? If you've got a black background, is white your best option? But what if red is one of your recurring themes?

It's easy to experiment with color in *Title Designer*. Like everything in the creative digital arts, everything is set in stone, but written on the sand. If you change anything and you don't like it, then either *Edit* > ***Undo*** or right-click on the value and reset it.

In the *Object Style* menu, your font will also have the *Fill* checkbox checked. Default also gives you *Solid* as your *Fill Type*, font-willing. Your fill will be color-based and there are two ways to select the color that you want. The first is to double-click on any small color-box in sight. This will bring up the *Color Picker*, offering a meager choice of 16.7 million colors. The other way is to use the *Eyedropper* tool. Clicking this once will allow you to sample any color that you might want to match, whether it's from another character, object, background, or moving image.

There are various types of *Fill* in Premiere Pro, all available from the drop-down menu. Apart from choosing colors, the other thing that they have in common is enabling you to select *Opacity*. Alter this by percentage to make your text or objects more or less transparent against the background. A solid fill is only the start, though. Go further down the drop-down menu and the following options will give you some useful results.

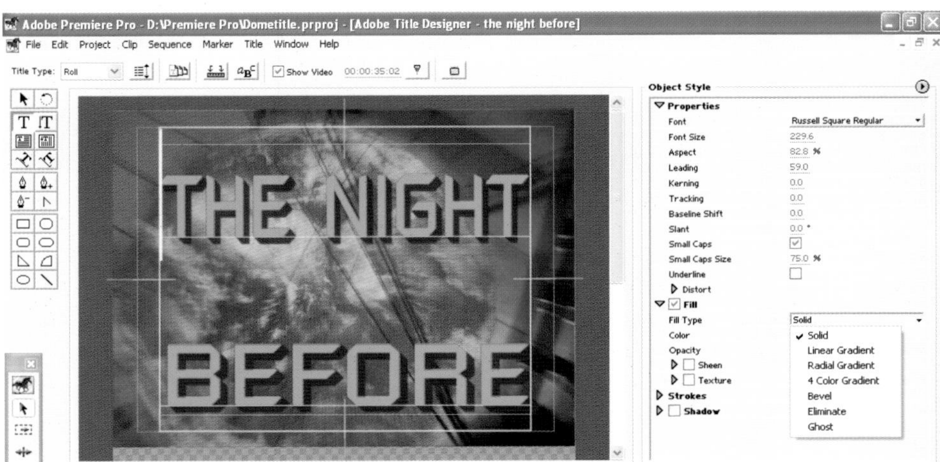

Still in default blue, everything looks a little...well...blue. This is the second part of the title sequence. The font has been chosen as a modern emulation of how sci-fi shows in the 1970s believed the future would look (retro-futuristic). In small caps, it's as neat as an invitation to the dome for the millennium night itself would have been . It has been positioned identically to the other part of the title. The only difference is in the motion: a standard roll rather than a reverse roll.

Linear Gradient

Selecting this brings up a color slider that allows you to choose two colors, which the fill in your selected text or objects can graduate between. Once you've double-clicked on the two color-boxes to pick your colors, the slider lets you adjust the balance between one color and the other—i.e. whereabouts in the text or object that the graduation begins, and over what distance within the glyph (or individual letter form).

Choosing two colors, though, isn't the end of the story. For good measure, the *Color Stop Color* option lets you pick a couple more to graduate through on the way. Clicking either of the color-boxes will activate it, indicated by the black arrow immediately above. Once selected,

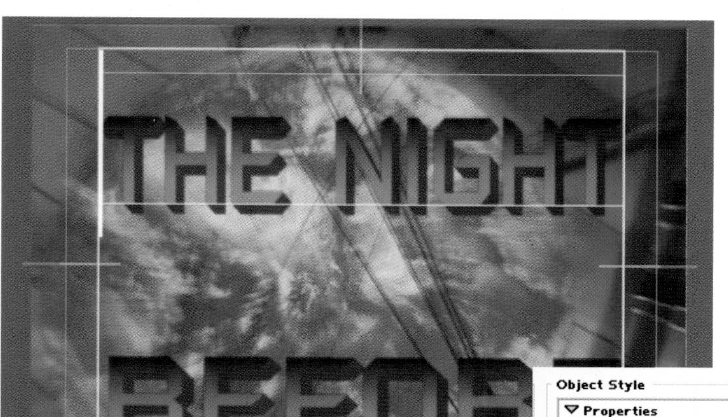

click on the *Color Stop* box and pick a color for that part of the gradient to stop through.

If you don't want more than two colors, just leave it: it will default to your chosen two on the slider anyway. If you do pick an additional one, make sure that you then make the *Color Stop Opacity* lower, as 100% can override your first chosen color .

Your gradient, by default, is horizontal, but this can be changed with the *Angle* value—click on the triangle to see the expanded *Angle* clock.

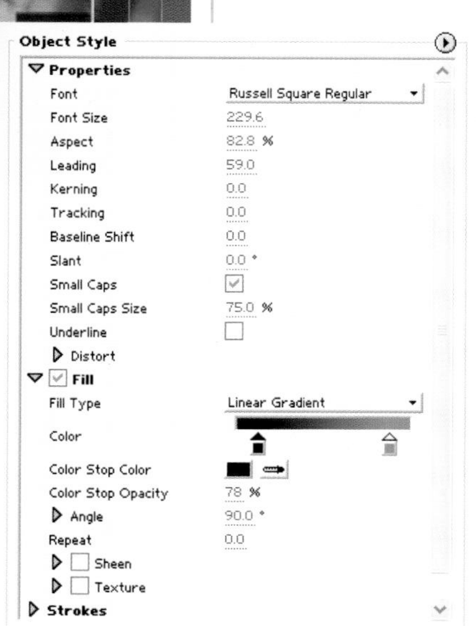

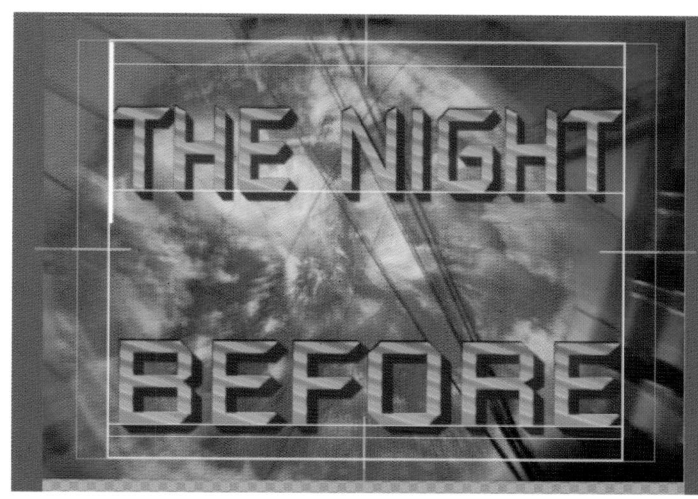

And once you've done all of this, you might be so happy with your results that the idea of repeating the same pattern over and over again within your text is irresistible. Add a value to the Repeat *box to indicate just how many times you want your pattern to run through the glyph. In this case, it's obviously a monumental style disaster.*

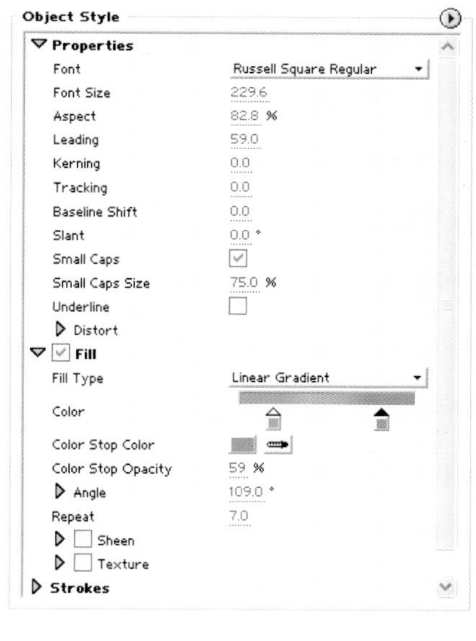

4 Color Gradient

A *4 Color Gradient* allows a color value to be input for each corner of the glyph. The association of the gradient is therefore from each color to the next horizontally and vertically. The benefit of four colors (each with *Color Stop*) has its limitations, though. The slider doesn't facilitate the degree of gradient over pixel distance to the vertical relationships—it acts as two fixed horizontal linear gradients—and there's no ability to change the angle, so it promises more than it delivers.

That said, it is a very useful tool for adding subtleties of different shades within your glyph.

Radial Gradient

The *Radial Gradient* functions exactly the same as a *Linear Gradient*, but graduates in a circular pattern from the center of each character. The only difference to be wary of is that because of the nature of letters and objects, they tend to be thin and intricate and the results aren't always that obvious unless your color sliders are in the right spot. That said, the gradient is emitting from a central source, so a more subtle application can be more effective than a very evident one. Varying the sliders, though, should give you the effect you want to see—or at worst a series of options that you don't.

Repeat also applies to radial gradients. Just as the application of a gradient can be subtle, so can the use of a repeat. This creates a single repetition, and corrupts a predictable, uniform gradient into a slightly more random one.

The larger and bolder the text, the more the gradients reveal themselves. With a 4 Color Gradient, all colors will be very much more apparent, which is why shades or subtle color changes can appear a bit more dignified.

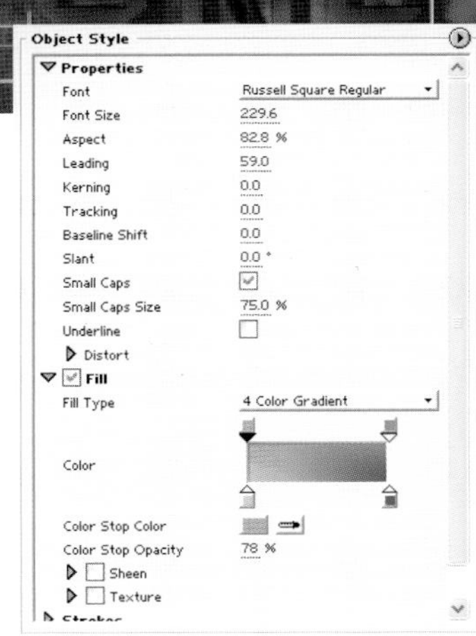

Bevel

Bevel can add that Roman-esque touch to your glyph, as if you've been itching to apply it for two thousand years. It relies on the input of the text color and of the highlight color, which is added to all inner and outer edges of the font. How the two interact together—i.e. their strength and prominence—depends on *Size*, *Opacity* and *Color Balance*.

Balance is the fight for attention between the two colors and *Size* is the width of your bevel measured in pixels.

Of course, a bevel in the real world is three-dimensional. On a flat screen, however, it's only an illusion. Beveling without lighting doesn't offer much in the way of three-dimensional illusion. Checking the *Lit* box, though, does. This filter performs the trick by shifting the bevel a few pixels in a given direction, and softening and hardening the bevel highlights and shadows. You have the option of changing the direction of the light source—again, input degrees or expand to use the clock—and changing the *Light Magnitude*. The higher the magnitude, the harsher your bevel will be (i.e. the harder the color separation lines and therefore the bigger the contrast change between them). Conversely, if the angles are simply too great, the *Tube* checkbox immediately beneath will smooth them off for you. Some thinner fonts can gain an interesting iron bar effect with this.

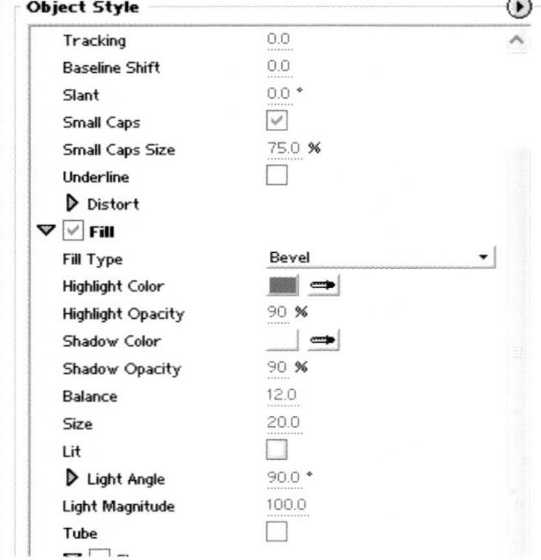

The font's contemporaneous feel has been changed with a bevel. It still retains the modern feel, yet suggests a Pathe news bulletin, complementing the newspaper print of the other title portion.

Keeping the flavor of old news, adding some lighting has the very desirable effect of giving the title a perfectly suitable "Night of a Thousand Stars" revue touch...

Eliminate and Ghost

The final two types of fill work in a particular way. Selecting *Eliminate* has the instantaneous effect of getting rid of all of your work. Luckily, it's an effect, not a reality. What Premiere Pro does is to leave any fill or shadow unrendered in order that a stroke may be applied. Hiding your fill and shadow has the effect of just leaving he stroke. Strokes are basically outlines to your text, and by checking the box and adding, you can apply up to 12 outlines on the outer perimeter of your glyphs (*Outer Strokes*) or inside their perimeters (*Inner Strokes*).

Ghost will enable you to do exactly the same, the only difference being that *Ghost* leaves any shadow that you've created (or that's already part of the font) rendered.

Within *Strokes*, there are a number of options that you can apply to each outline. There are three different stroke types. *Depth* creates a stroke with the illusion of being three-dimensional—i.e. it applies strokes along only certain edges, just like a shadow. *Edge*, on the other hand, creates strokes around the perimeter of your glyph. *Drop Face* is a very useful tool, and duplicates your glyph as another layer that you can offset against the original and to which you can apply different filters and values.

Once you've applied a stroke and selected its type, you can use the expandable menus to apply all the usual suspects to it—the *Fill Type*, the *Highlight Color* and its *Opacity*, the *Shadow Color* and its *Opacity*, the *Balance* between the two, whether you want it *Lit*, and so on. You can even apply *Sheen* and *Texture* to your strokes. It can, in fact, become an endless game that either leaves you the winner of a unique effect, or which will simply lose you sleep and time.

Of all your stroke options, there are some that are particular to the type that you've created. Getting the *Size* right for your stroke matters, as some combinations of values won't be visible unless your stroke is big enough. You won't, though, find *Size* available for the *Drop Face* type, as it isn't relevant to duplication. Instead, *Magnitude* enables you to specify the height of the stroke. The *Angle* to offset your stroke also isn't applicable to an *Edge* stroke as, logically, there is no offset angle for a complete glyph outline.

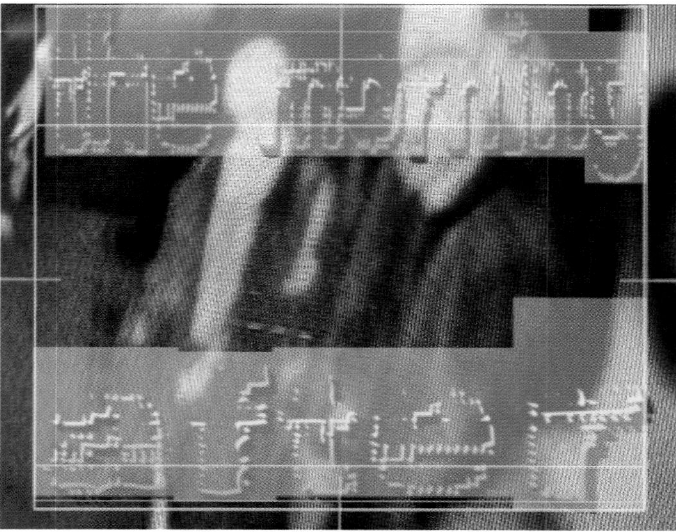

Back to the other part of the title sequence. The transition that I'd like to use will bring it out of the background image of a pixelated CCTV monitor. To make this work, the title has to be far more subtle than the original solid fill. Using Ghost *as a fill and adding a couple of* Depth *strokes with a* Radial Gradient *between colors from the background image has helped. A sheen sampled from the background helps to lift it, and a shadow to work with the depth of the stroke. It might, though, just be a little too subtle for this font and when juxtaposed with the other part of the sequence...*

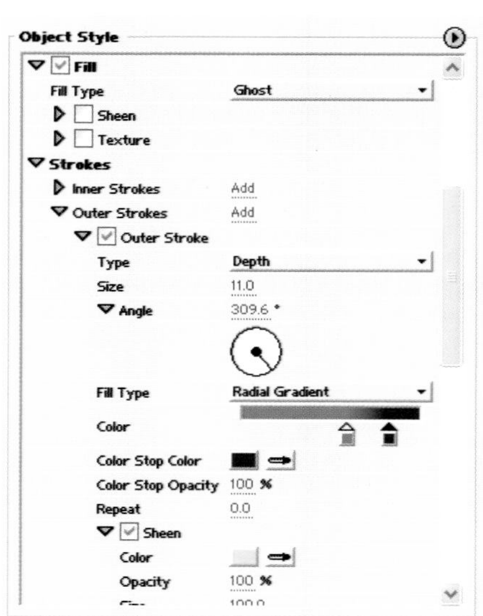

Sheen

Sheen exists to make your glyphs look shiny, but given the right *Color, Size, Angle, Opacity,* and a more central *Offset*, they can also fill text and objects just as a *Linear Gradient* can, but between 0% *Opacity* and your color of choice. In effect, they can be a second layer of gradient and work with it to highlight, or to lowlight.

Texture

Check the box and you can apply any texture to your glyph. Textures in Premiere Pro are, by default, .tga (targa) files. You can, though, use any conventional graphics file that you might have on disk by redirecting Premiere Pro away from its preset textures. The texture doesn't work like a matte; instead the image will be inserted into each separate glyph. If you think that your text is likely to be flipped or rotated, there are checkboxes to make sure that the texture adheres to the same rules of motion you've applied.

The *Scaling* features define how you want the texture to be stretched to your glyph. The *Texture* option simply uses the natural size of the graphic and doesn't alter it at all. This means that if your glyph is smaller than your graphic, you'll see only a portion of the graphic. *Clipped Face* applies to the use of inner strokes. If you've used them, then choosing this option will apply your strokes over the top of the graphic—i.e. you'll lose that part of your graphic to the strokes. The *Face* option stretches the texture to fit your glyph exactly—instead of losing anything to strokes. And *Extended Character* takes outer strokes into the application of the texture, stretching it to your outermost stroke.

Of course, your graphics are all within your glyph's two dimensions, and Premiere Pro enables all of these options to be applied on either or both X (Object X) and Y (Object Y) axes. The scaling of both X and Y of the graphic can be altered with the *Horizontal* and *Vertical* percentage drag/click values, and the *Tile X* and *Y* options allow for the image to be repeated horizontally and/or vertically if your glyphs are too large for the graphic applied and scaling blows your resolution to bits. If you don't choose to tile,and your glyphs are simply too large for the texture,the graphic will be replaced where it ends by an alpha matte, which will let the background image through.

You can move your texture to where you want it on your glyph with the *Alignment* options. These are defined by X and Y positioning. The stretching options are the same as those for Scaling, but if you're keeping your texture large enough not to be tiled, then the *Rule X* and *Rule Y* will position it respectively to either the *Left*, *Center*, or *Right*, or the *Top*, *Center*, or *Bottom* for roughness. Any offset that you need from here can be tweaked with the *X* and *Y Offset*. Just drag or click to adjust the values in pixels.

The expandable *Blending* menu is the last concern with regard to your texture. The *Mix* drag/click value is set by default to 1.0%. This is the mix between the *Color* (-100%) of your *Fill Type* and the *Texture* (100%). Somewhere between the two is a perfectly esthetic balance. The *Fill Key* checkbox lets the render take the opacity of the original *Fill Type* into consideration, and the *Texture Key* checkbox does the same for the opacity of the texture.

The *Alpha Scale* drag/click value is the percentage of mix to your background. At 100%, you're working with just your mix of texture and fill. At 0%, your texture will have disappeared. Of course, mattes come in different keys, and the *Composite Rule* drop-down menu permits red, blue, and green mattes, as well as having none at all.

The *Invert Composite* is really a panic button. If your texture doesn't appear to be happening at all yet, then that may well be because your texture has an inverted alpha range. If this is the case, the checkbox will turn your blank into a solid.

Because the text needs to mix out of the CCTV image, the texture applied is an exported frame from the background image in Premiere Pro. This has then been scaled by 400% on the horizontal and vertical to emphasize the pixels and pull it away from the background. Because the texture is now four times the screen size, Extended Character *is hardly crucial to cope with the small outer strokes applied. Even so, trying out different combinations of clipping and nonclipping has defined these settings as the most appealing for the texture.*

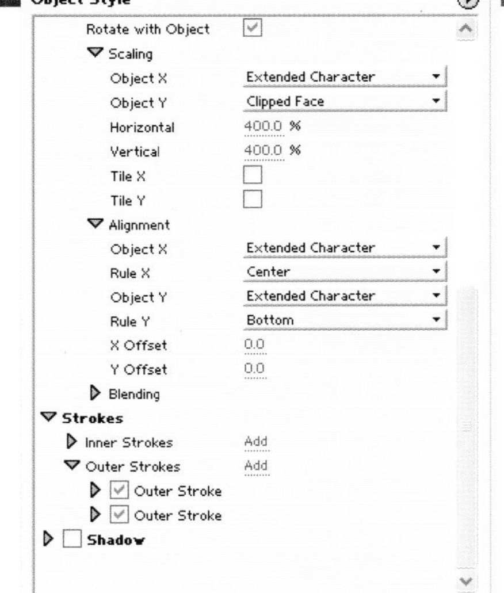

Adding a eyedropped Sheen *from the background highlights and, for a* Shadow, *the background lowlights, picks out the text. The* Opacity *of the key has been raised in favor of more control on the* Timeline, *where the title will be mixed through.*

Shadow

The drop-down menu for applying *Shadow* to your glyph, gives you exactly the same options that you'd find in Photoshop. *Color, Opacity*, the *Angle of Preference, Distance, Size,* and *Spread* all come into play to help your text or graphic distance itself from the background and come to life. The problem with *Shadow* is that we've all seen it applied badly, or clumsily. It can simply look cheap. On the other hand, if a shadow is cast for a reason—i.e. it helps a usually three-dimensional glyph become part of a three-dimensional space—then it makes sense to use it. In this case, it's the background that makes the shadow work—it provides a plausible source of light to cast the shadow.

Inserting logos

It's part of the nature of commercial work that you may have to work with graphics and fonts supplied by a separate marketing department. Your job is always to get them at as high a resolution as humanly possible. This will afford you the maximum amount of versatility when it comes to putting those graphics into the fourth dimension.

When receiving graphics from another source, it would be ideal for your purposes if they are broken down into separate elements—if this is possible. These elements may include a background, the font, a logo, and all of the text required. Inserting logos is easy in Premiere Pro, mostly because it makes it easy.

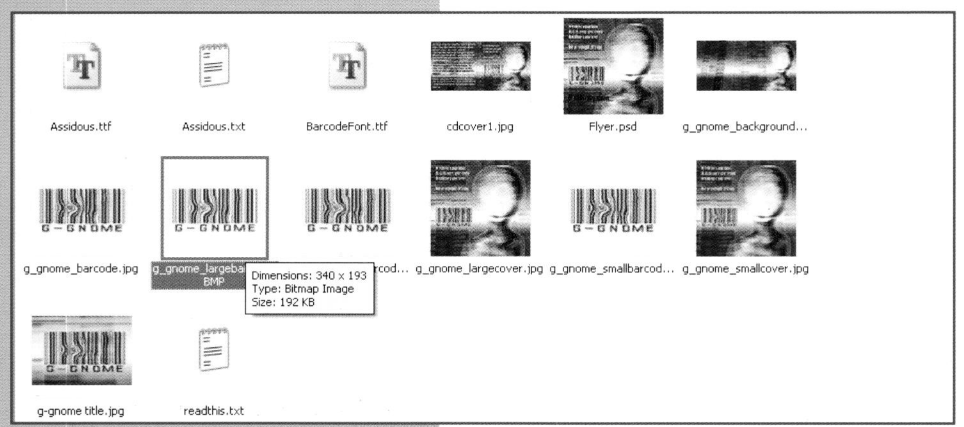

The example here is a teaser trailer cut with AVID Symphony with some hastily applied teaser graphics that currently look like this. They don't do much. They're stills that are placed within the body of the end of the trailer, and which are all subject to the same slight zoom. But there's much more that can be done with them given a little effort.

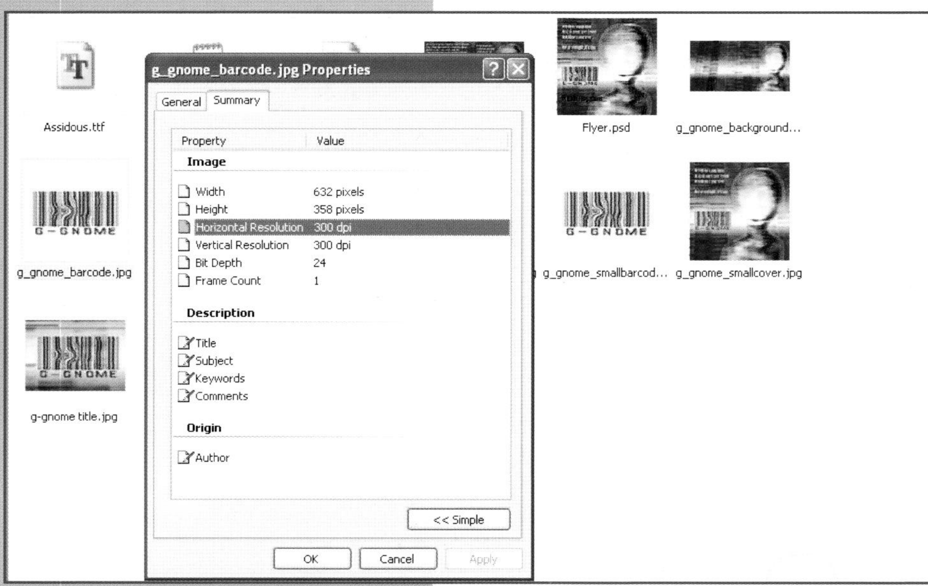

1

I've gone back to the source—to the designer, who has provided a number of options to work with. Some of these images have been created for the Internet and so have not been required to have a resolution greater than 72 dpi. Others are of higher resolution, intended for print.

2

The file names are misleading. "Largebarcode" sounds like the one that I want, especially if I diminish it as a title, but right-clicking on each to find the *Properties* > ***Summary*** of the graphics indicates that the only ones of use for video (i.e. they have a resolution of 300 dpi or more) are a jpeg image of the logo and a flyer saved as a PSD Photoshop file. Fortunately, the crucial Assiduous font is attached and somehow, out of these three elements, I can re-create what the client is looking for.

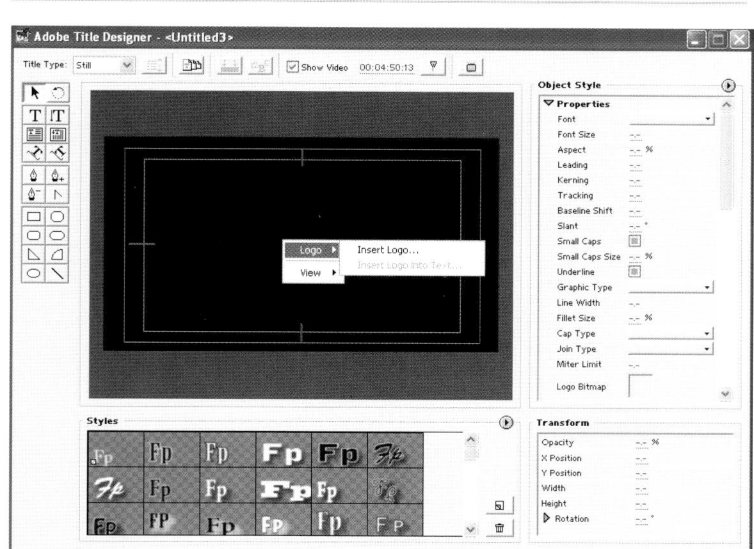

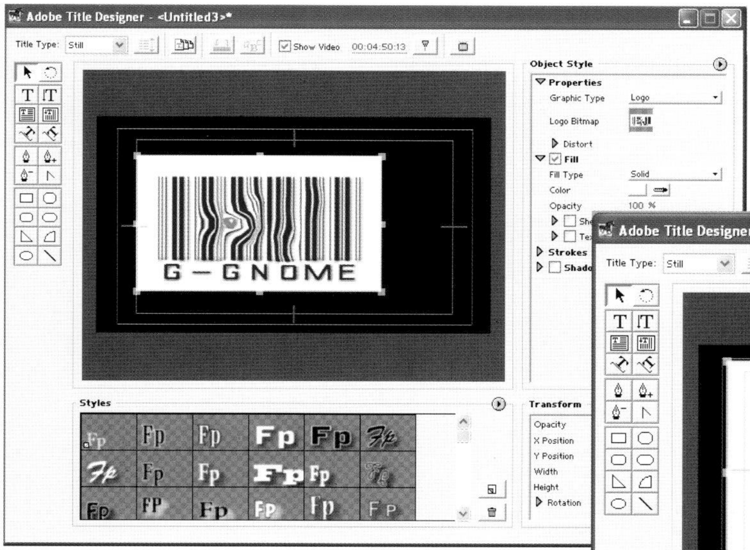

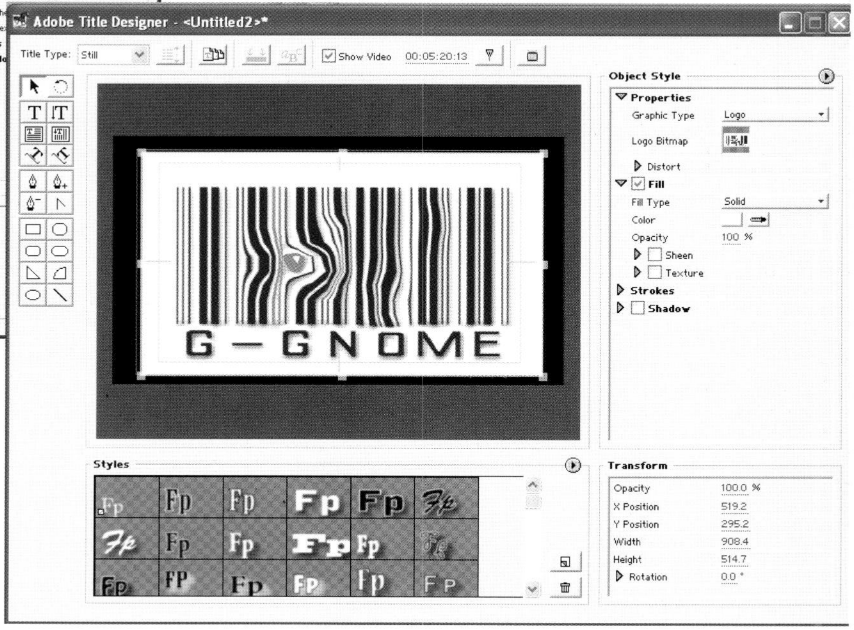

3 With a black matte in place synched with *Title Designer*, and using the arrow cursor, right-click on the title screen to bring up the *Logo* > ***Insert Logo*** command.

4 Importing the logo gives an indication of its screen presence: in this case, it's large enough to work with.

5 What it doesn't do, though, is fill the 16:9 aspect ratio that the video is cut to. Dragging both X and Y to the limits of the blue screen-safety lines will ensure that everything hits the mark. In the edit, it's better to go too big than too small. Let's presume that I'll have to rescale once the logo's on the *Timeline* so that the actual logo (rather than the white border) fits onscreen.

Indeed, the problem is going to be the white background to the glyph. It's too glaring and unforgiving for video—it was obviously intended for print, where it would have worked very well. I'm also aiming to replace the white with a different background, and can't progress until this background is found among the images supplied in Photoshop.

Working with your style library

Premiere Pro's Style Library can be found underneath the monitor in Title Designer. There are twenty-three of them available by default—but there are a whole lot more of them if you explore farther.

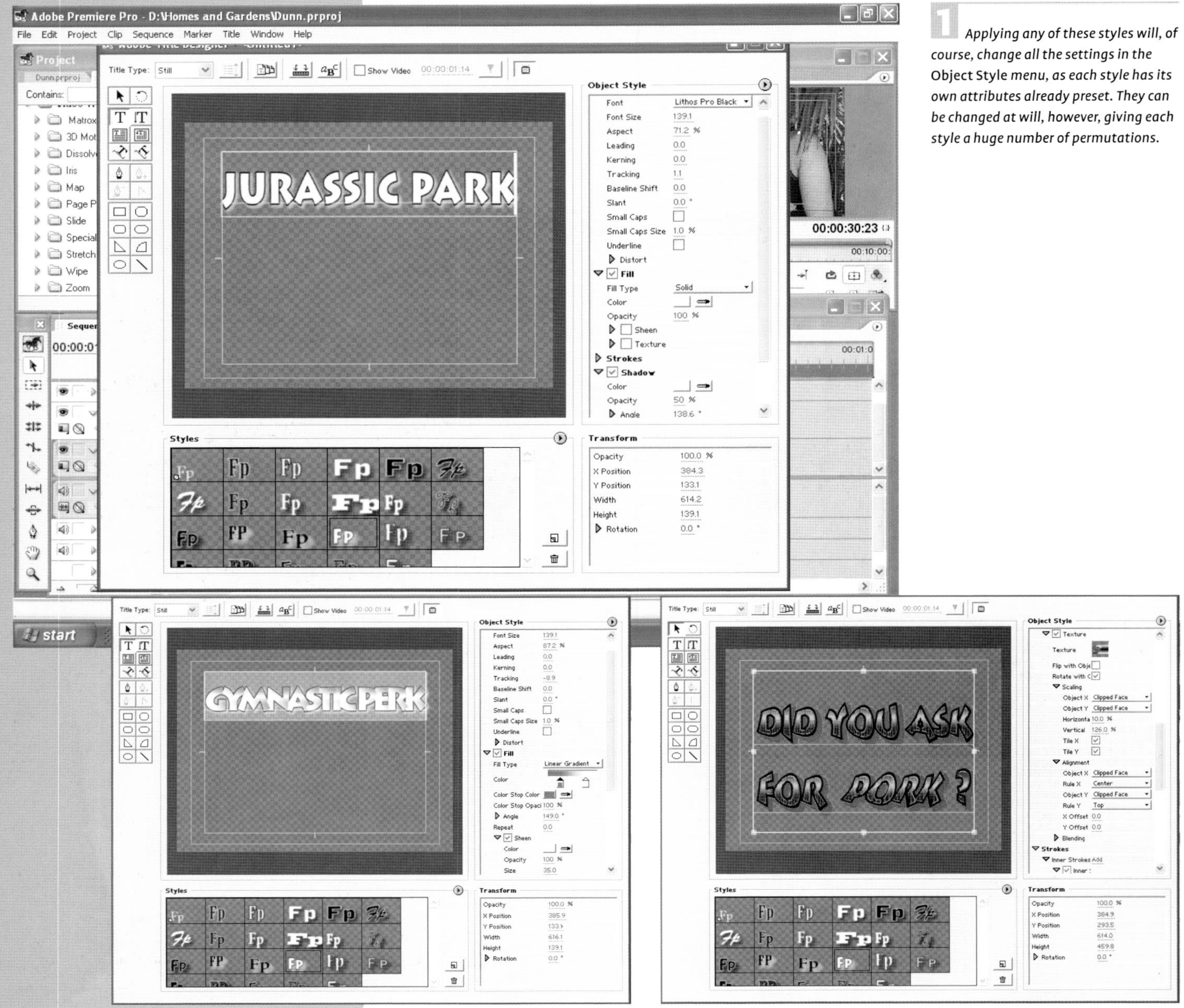

1 *Applying any of these styles will, of course, change all the settings in the Object Style menu, as each style has its own attributes already preset. They can be changed at will, however, giving each style a huge number of permutations.*

2 *In the same way, the* Styles Display *window demonstrates the kind of effect that you can achieve by using an arbitrary font—but this doesn't mean to say that you have to use that particular font. Any font that you choose will take on the same style attributes by default until you change them in the* Object Style *menu.*

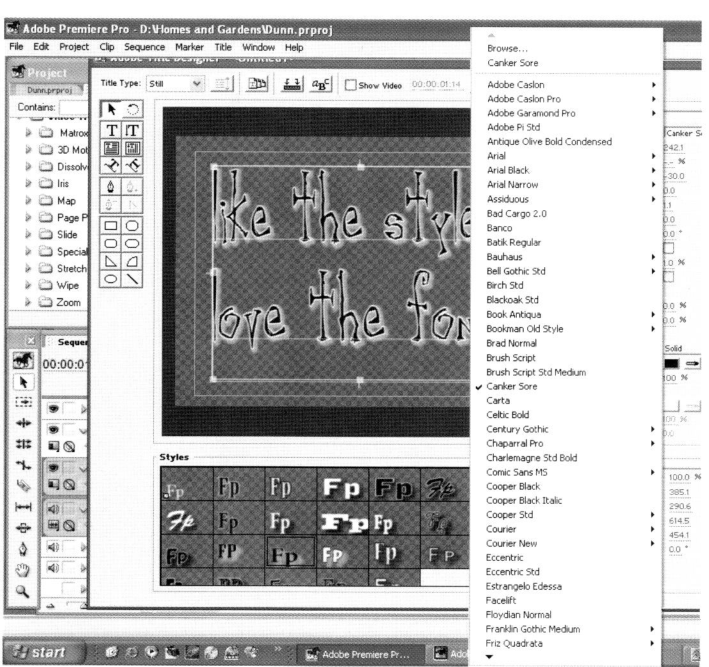

3 *The small arrow to the right of the Styles window signals a drop-down menu that applies to the styles, the most important option being* Load Style Library. *The presets available in Premiere Pro's style file are those that are fundamentally a breakdown of the styles used within each Template—which goes some way to explaining the odd choice of genres. The 4MB specific "PR7" prsl file, though, contains most of them, so it's worth loading up from the start if you're using styles.*

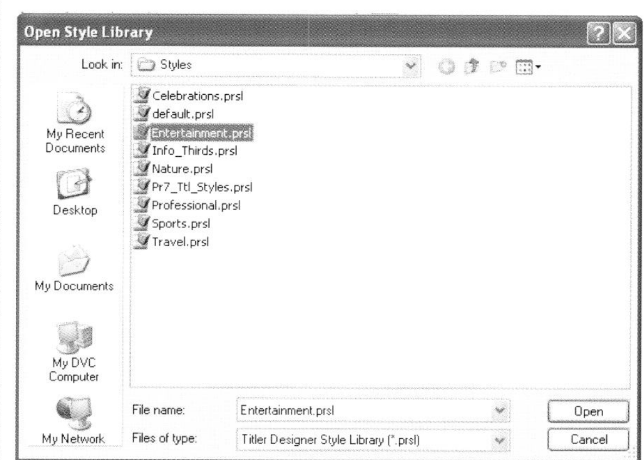

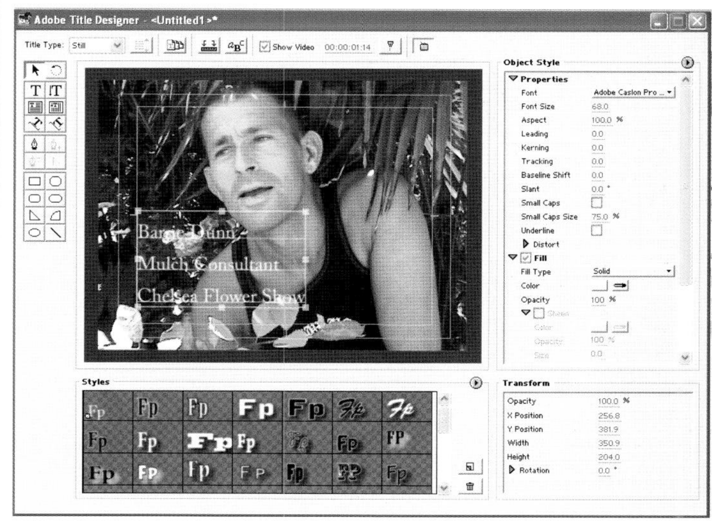

4 *Getting practical, typing your desired text in and then clicking through the styles will show you different ways of presenting it. If you don't know what you're looking for, remember to look at the style and not the font. This interview would be very easy to caption just as it is by default. It's a corporate job and would therefore give the clients less to have issue with. In this case, though, I'd rather be creative to divert attention away from the interviewee a little. The interviewer on the audio track is asking a serious question of him, so the smile is slightly too broad to kick off the interview with. I could have covered it up in overlay, but I felt that this would have detracted from the honesty of the interview. Clearly, we all make highly subjective choices.*

Barrie Dunn

Mulch Consultant

Chelsea Flower Show

BARRIE DUNN
MULCH CONSULTANT
CHELSEA FLOWER SHOW

BARRIE DUNN
Mulch Consultant
Chelsea Flower Show

BARRIE DUNN
Mulch Consultant
Chelsea Flower Show

BARRIE DUNN
Mulch Consultant
Chelsea Flower Show

BARRIE DUNN
Mulch Consultant
Chelsea Flower Show

5 *In this case, the corporate style called for a lower-third with a three line-caption. This sample is a good indication of what style I can use in order for the caption to be legible. Its onscreen time will be three seconds with a one second mix on either side. As said, the style is everything and I'm looking at the changes in the* Object Style *menu as I click through the different styles to see what attributes each has. This seemingly inappropriate* Mission Impossible *style is the one that I've settled for. I think, thematically, that it's the one with which, in the titles, I can best emulate the sun filtering through the palms on the video track.*

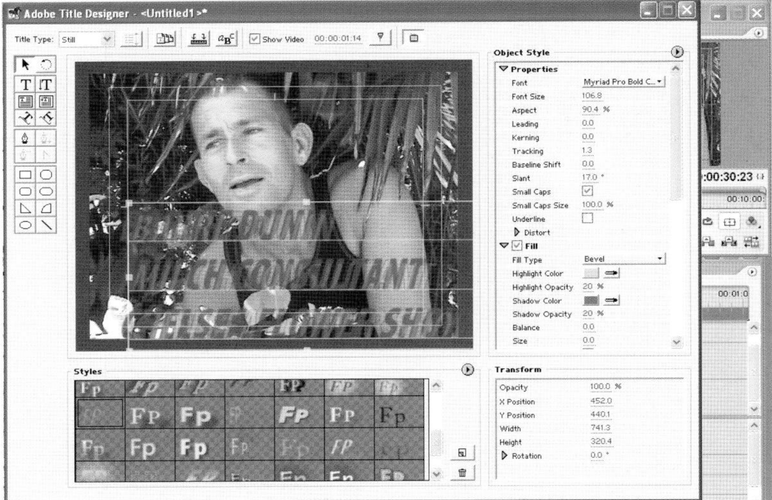

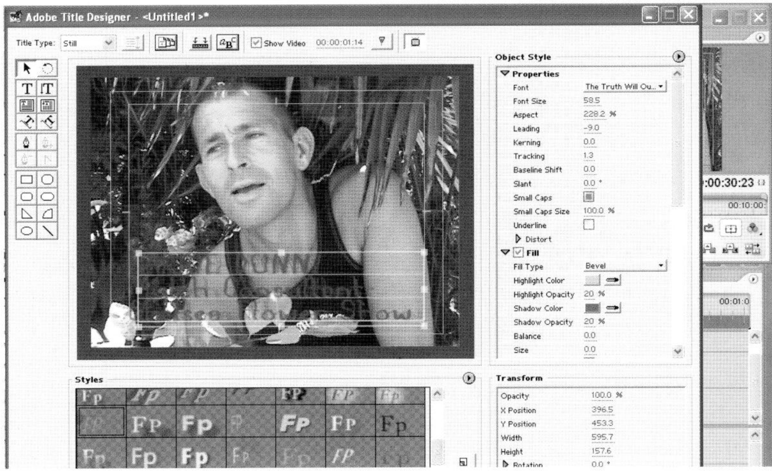

6 *The fun begins with the* Object Style *menu. There's quite a lot of text, and in order for the caption to apply to lower-thirds, the font and leading have to be corrected whilst keeping it within screen-safety at the same time. Getting rid of the* Slant *helps, as does getting the bottom two lines out of* Small Caps. *Even though it's corporate, I'm using a font that's supposed to be a pseudo-X-Files rip-off. Given attention, it could become a bit more* Little Shop of Horrors...

7 *Looking at the* Object Style *attributes for* Fill, *it becomes apparent that what seems the dominant text is actually the shadow, while the shadow has become the main font. Treating the* Fill *as shadow becomes an interesting job. Unchecking the* Shadow *box, it's easier to work with the font outline in question. If we also uncheck the* Show Video *box, it becomes clear that the font fill (as a Bevel) is stroked, which gives the text its outline. Without it, the fill acts as the dappled highlights that I want. It makes perfect sense then, to take the* Fill *(*Highlight *and* Color*) as dropper samples from the highlights of the video, then add* Sheen *to brighten it up.*

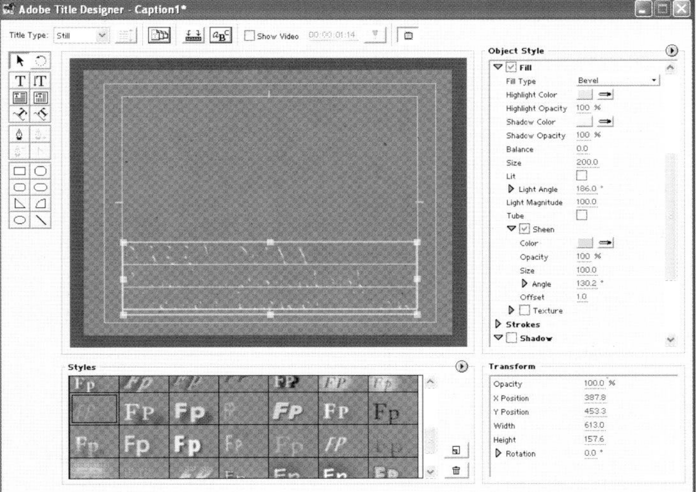

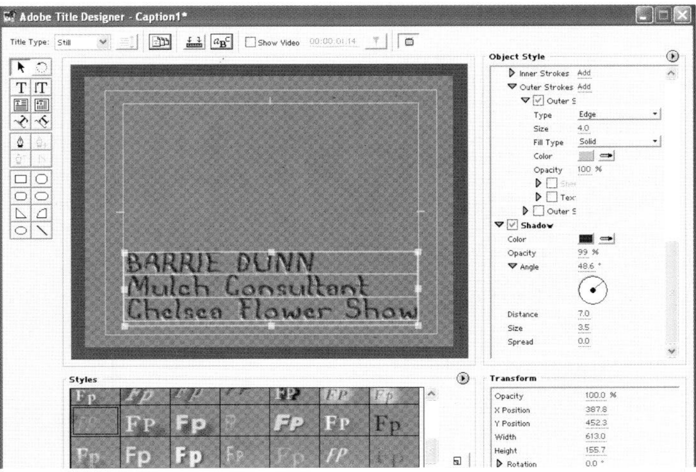

8 *Checking the* Outer Stroke *back into action, I've again sampled part of the video track's foliage for the color, changed the size so it's not so much of an outline, and then increased the* Opacity*. Doing the same with the* Shadow *(dominant text) for a green almost close to black, and changing the* Angle, Distance, Size, *and* Spread *has hardened the text and given it much greater weight and body.*

9 *Bringing the interview back into vision, it's unsurprising—given that the color samples are from the image—that the text is very well camouflaged. This may not sound like a good thing, but it's actually going to work in favor of the caption...*

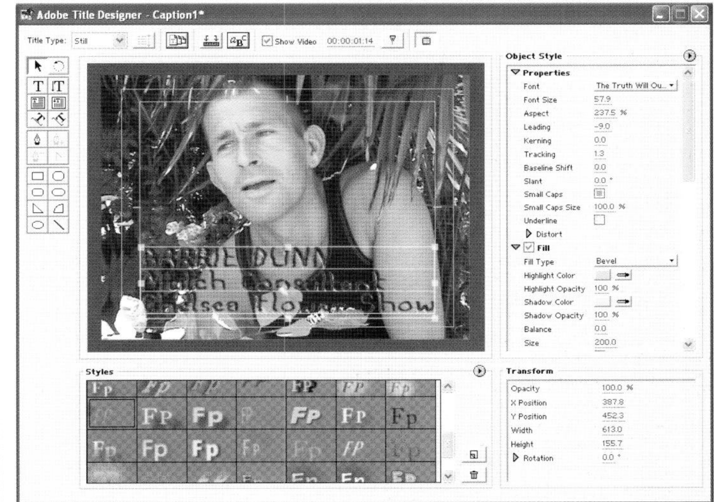

Templates and presets

Why should any preset deserve a place in a book on Creative Titling? Because you can change them. If it's not a question of lacking bravery, it's one of lacking time. What presets can do is give you a quality title tailored to your requirements with very little effort—and the good thing about creativity is that it doesn't have to mean sweat.

There's a whole host of presets available in Premiere Pro under some oddly specific themes. You might come to the conclusion that if you don't have a family, work in an office, holiday in the Bahamas, or play golf in your spare time, then the presets are not going to be too useful. You might be wrong...

Templates may be there to save time and effort, but you can make them as time-consuming and inconvenient as you wish. If you acquaint yourself with them, they can be a good basis to start a title without starting from scratch—if you've an inkling as to what your title is going to be about.

In Premiere Pro, anything represented as checkerboard under *Presets* is a matte. While this is apparent under the *Matte* options (here, a pseudo letterbox effect), the upper third and many lower third templates particularly rely on them for captioning with your video running behind. The other templates tend to require the input of text against a prerendered background.

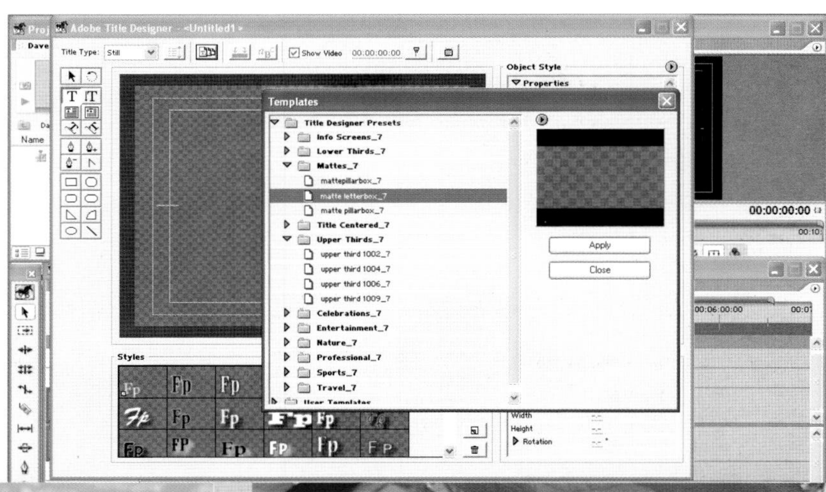

WATER SPORTS SUB TITLE

WATER SPORTS

1 *To go some way to prove that templates can be used creatively, I've chosen one that's a million miles away from the wedding title we're going to create. Moving the arrow cursor around indicates how many parts of the template there are. Clicking on each indicates all the values that it has in the* Object Style *menu. Again, the checkerboard is for a matte, but it has probably been designed for video to move through rather than for a still.*

2 *The secret of personalizing any of the templates is in the right-click options. The first thing is to get rid of the water aspect of things in this preset. Right-clicking on the background to bring up* Logo > **Insert Logo** *will enable you to introduce a graphics file of choice.*

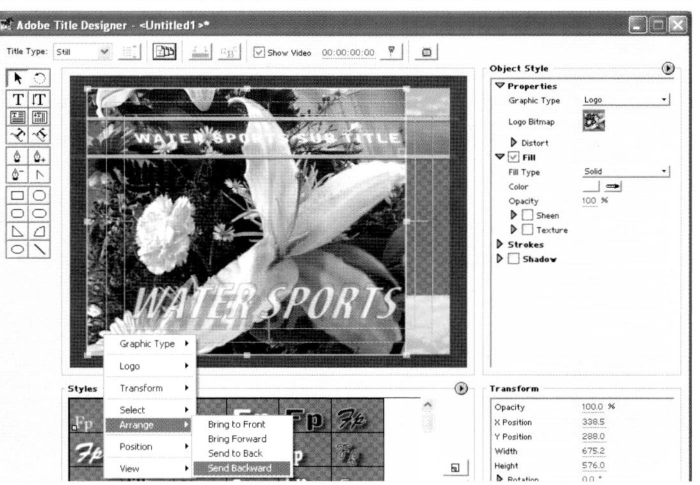

3 *Premiere Pro treats the image as the dominant layer, which makes the template worthless unless the image is diminished. Alternatively, a right-click will give you an option of either transforming the* Opacity *of the image, or arranging it toward the back of the template.* Title Designer *doesn't make it clear which layer is which, so either keep clicking on the* Send Backward *option until it's in the right place, or—at the risk of never finding it again—*Send to Back *and then* Bring Forward *to the right layer.*

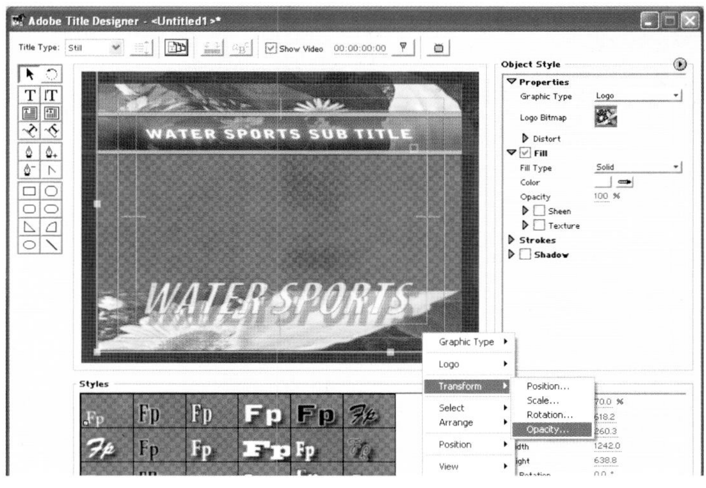

4 *Once it's on the right layer, resizing the image can provide a better background. The* Transform *options also enable you to change the* X/Y Position, Scale *(watch for pixelation),* Rotation *(the angle of the image), and* Opacity*. By default, the* Opacity *is based on the original template layer. Here, the layer was a light-blue water texture, with the* Opacity *taken down to 70% to lighten the flower image.*

5

The top "subtitle" strap, as a rectangle, is a little corporate. To change that, right-clicking and selecting Graphic Type *gives you options that are slightly more appropriate, but still harshly geometric. I could delete it entirely, but there are other things that can be done with it just to break up the screen. I've chosen an* Ellipse *and enlarged it. What could we make with this?*

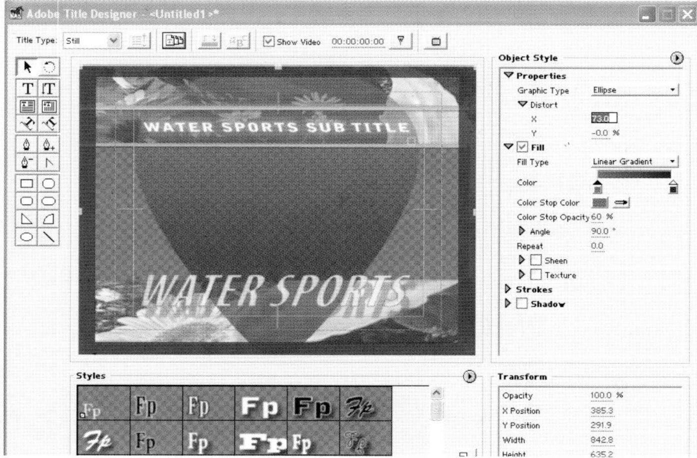

6

Distorting the X *axis value in the* Object Style > **Properties** *menu creates a shape that is neither heart nor diamond ring, but alludes to both—especially when stretched out of screen safety to bleed off the frame.*

7

Pulling down the Graphic Type *menu once again, the newly created shape can be turned into an* Open Bezier. *This removes the fill for an altogether more subtle break-up of the frame.*

8

But it's too subtle—especially for CRT playout. The bezier Properties *menu allows for the* Line Width *to be adjusted, and all the usual suspects in the* Fill *menu allow for the* Fill Type, Color, Color Stop Color *and* Opacity *to be changed to suit within the bezier itself. This time a* Repeat *has been used to create a slightly ribboned effect to pander to the use of the flower image. Weddings, eh?*

9 *Tailoring a* Sheen *and a* Shadow *helps the bezier lift itself a little from a background that's actually only half there…*

10 *…so I've introduced the missing part—the happy couple—as a* Logo *in exactly the same way as the flowers. The bridge and groom were exported as a frame from the video and given a romantic air of mystery in Photoshop.*

11 *Time to get rid of the horrible thin bezier rectangles that have been hanging around for far too long. Instead of just highlighting and deleting them, they've proved their use by their ability to be dragged into a useful position. Changing both* Color *and* Fill Type*, they can now be employed as a framing device for the bride and groom, creating a more suitable cinematic mood to a still title.*

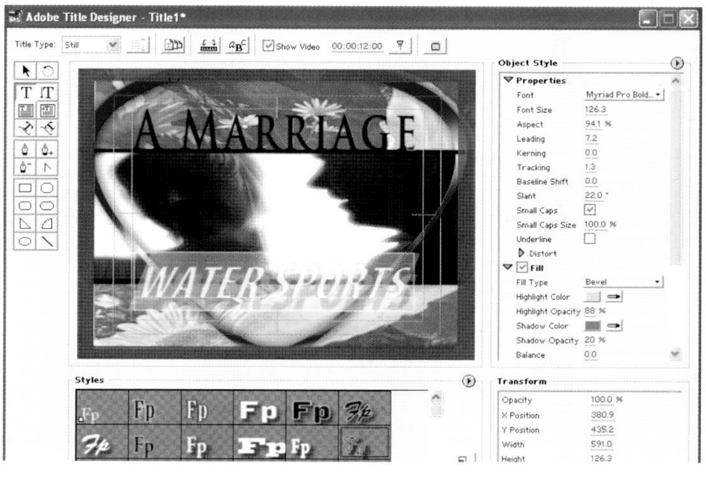

12 *And this just leaves the text, font, and all applicable* Object Styles *at your disposal. As with all text boxes and objects, more can be added (or deleted) when you require as another layer to the template. Don't worry—we'll come back to this one later.*

Creating user templates

Templates are always useful. As time-savers, they can provide a quick resource for an easy, tried-and-tested title format. As reference, they can show a client the kind of thing that you can offer. As in-project title attributes, they can save a lot of confusing copying and pasting.

User templates created in *Title Designer* can be any title that you've created at all. Using templates can just be a matter of changing text, or it can be dragging beziers to fill a 16:9 ratio instead of 4:3. Any title is still editable before export, and if you want to make sure that you can reuse it long after you've created and exported a production, you simply have to make sure that that editable title is available and at your fingertips.

1 *This project is the documentation of the making of a music promo. Shot in various locations over different days, the idea is to caption each location and date in the same house style. The music is Irish folk-punk and the caption design has been tailored to suit. The animated heading is in place and this will be used for all captions. What I want is a design beneath it, which I can adapt for each separate location and date.*

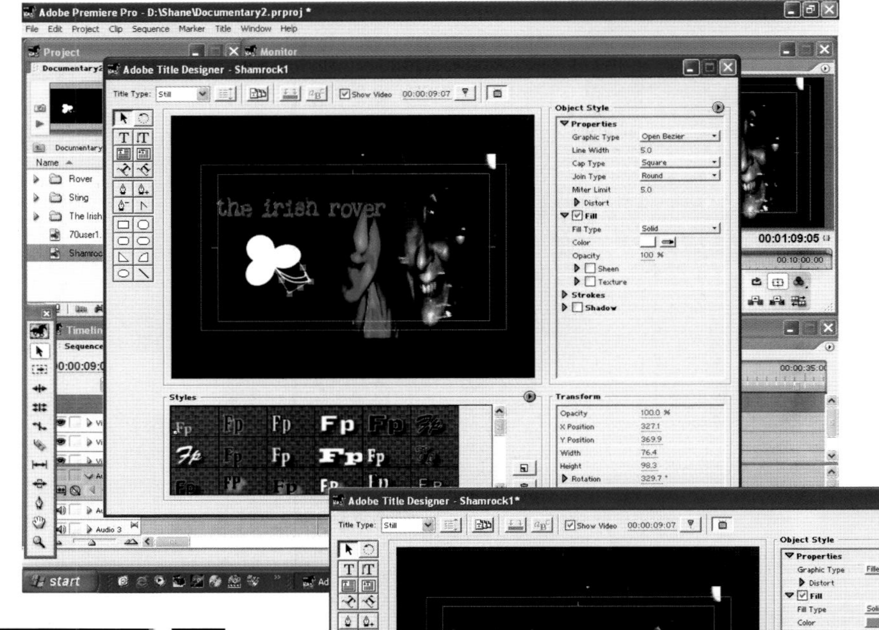

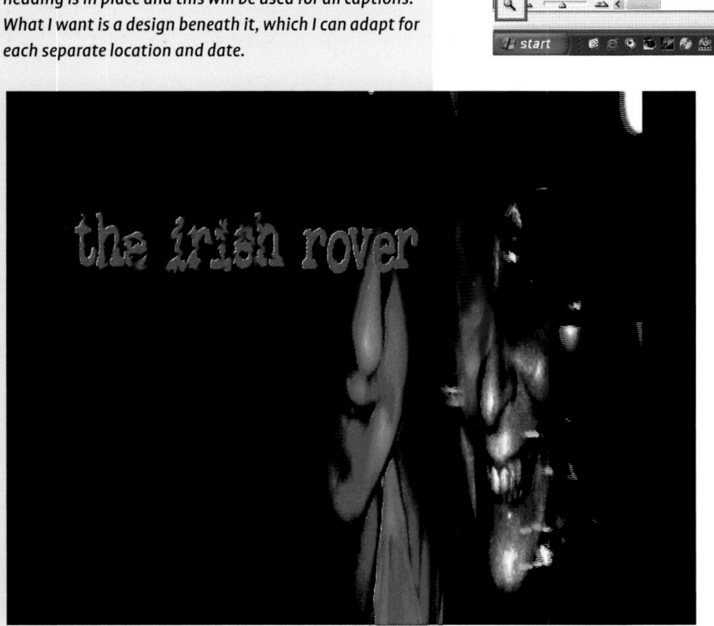

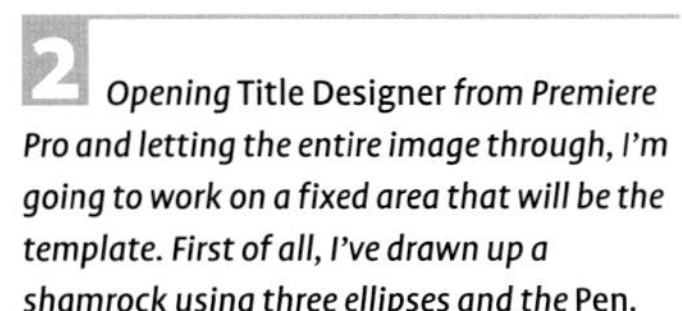

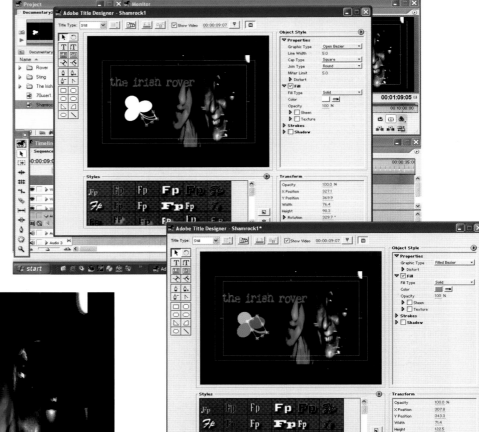

2 *Opening Title Designer from Premiere Pro and letting the entire image through, I'm going to work on a fixed area that will be the template. First of all, I've drawn up a shamrock using three ellipses and the Pen.*

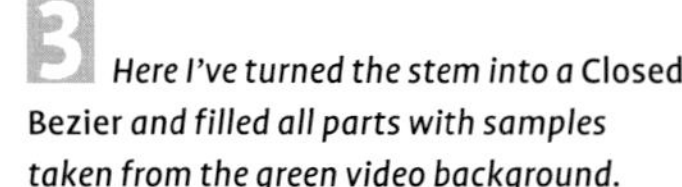

3 *Here I've turned the stem into a Closed Bezier and filled all parts with samples taken from the green video background.*

4 *To finish off the graphic, I've added a slight sheen to each "leaf" and right-clicked on the stem to Arrange >* **Send to Back** *to neaten up the image. It's far too graphical for punk—it's very much sham-rock—but I'm confident that it won't be by the time I've finished with the title.*

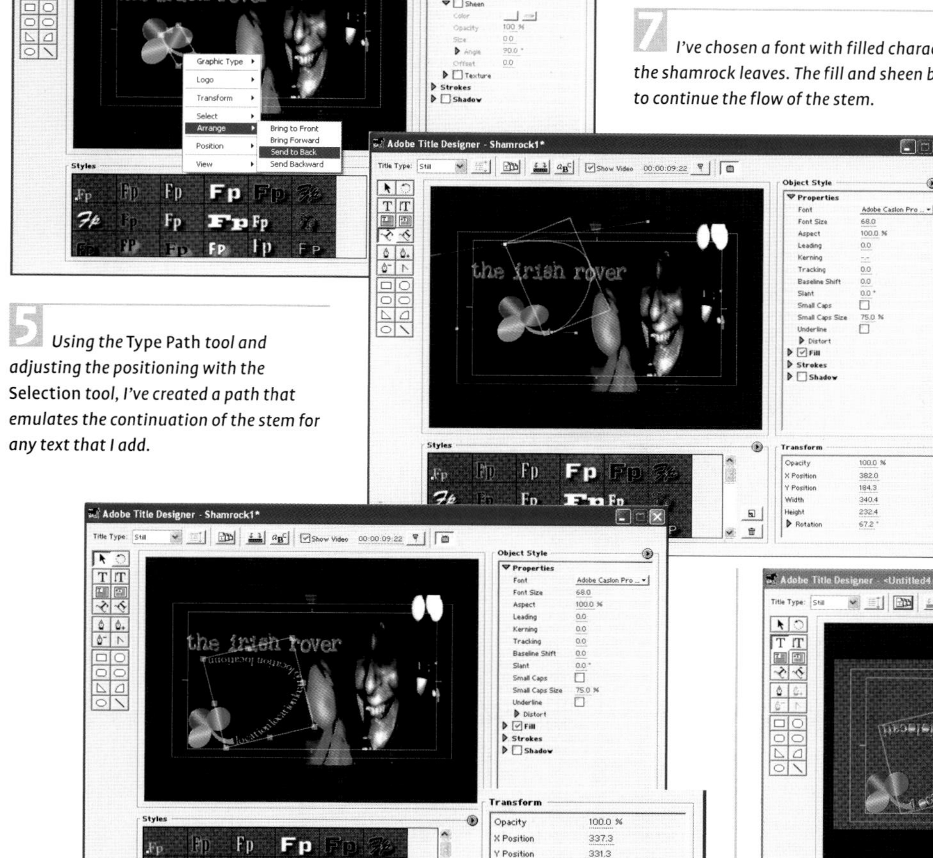

5 *Using the* Type Path *tool and adjusting the positioning with the* Selection *tool, I've created a path that emulates the continuation of the stem for any text that I add.*

7 *I've chosen a font with filled characters that imitate the shamrock leaves. The fill and sheen both copy the leaves to continue the flow of the stem.*

8 *Having done all of the things that you need to, it's the saving process that makes a title a user template. By default, the title is saved to your project so that it can be dragged straight onto the* Timeline. *Best practice, though, whatever your clip archiving habits, is to save the title again. With the title open in* Title Designer, Save As *whatever you'll remember it as, but this time to the* Templates *folder. This can be found under* Adobe > Premiere Pro > Presets > **Templates**, *where both* Styles *and* Textures *can be saved and stored for later use.*

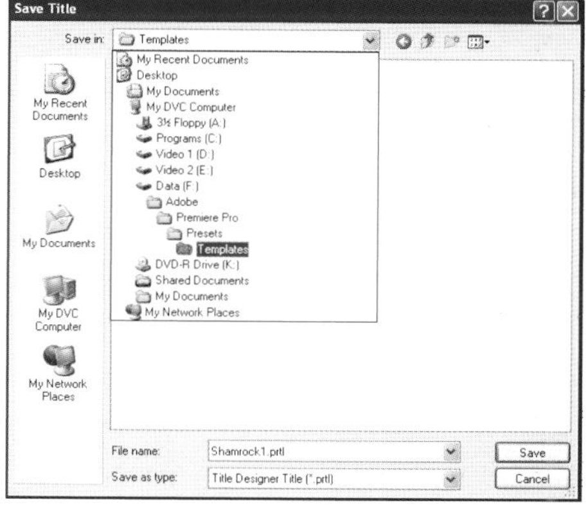

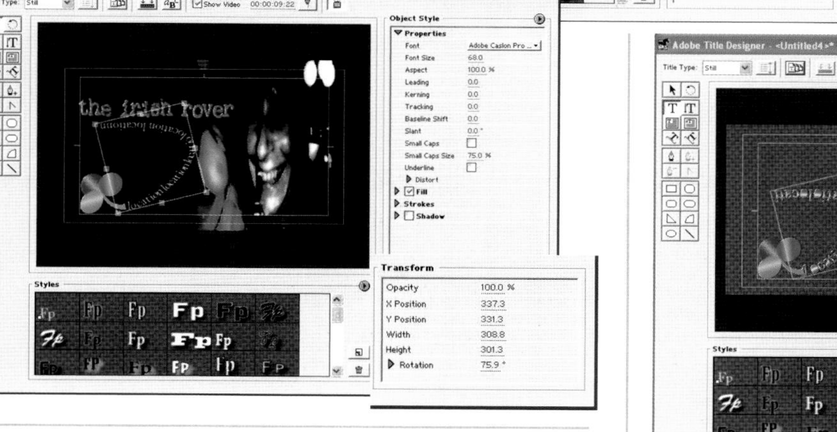

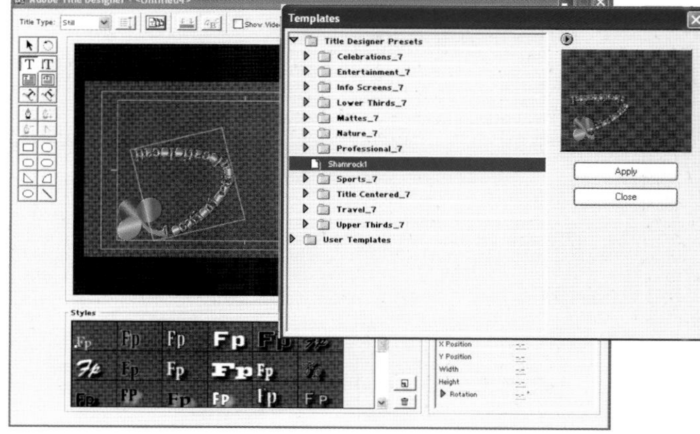

6 *Now that the path has been created, it's obvious that the template will always be in the wrong place on-screen. This either means correcting* X *and* Y *every time in Premiere Pro, or correcting at source. The latter is always preferable and I've dragged all elements to the template into their resting place. Having a bit of sample text at maximum length is an essential part of hitting the right marks.*

9 *After that, the template will always be ready for use and editing at the click of* Title Designer's Templates *shortcut button.*

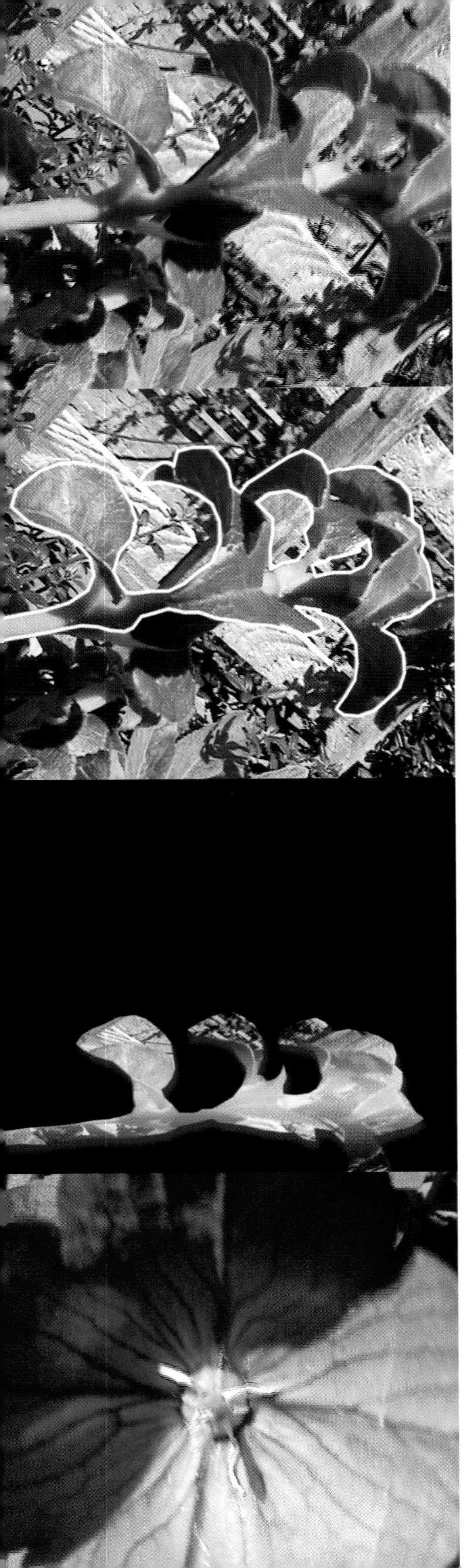

Using the graphic tools

The graphics tools in Premiere Pro are not the most sophisticated, but if you are willing to push against their limitations you can cover your titling needs without the expense of a separate graphics application.

One thing they can do, for example, is provide a quick and easy way to make your title much more professional looking with the click and drag of a couple of buttons.

1 *Going back to the earlier gardening promo (pages 54–57), I'm giving the interviewee's title caption a background that is a little more appropriate to the branding of the video. On the shoot, I ensured that both setups—interviewee and B-roll—were shot. Dragging some potential overlay into Premiere Pro, I've located a branch that I'm going to use as a caption logo. Keeping the* Edit Line *in place at the chosen frame, it's time to get more creative.*

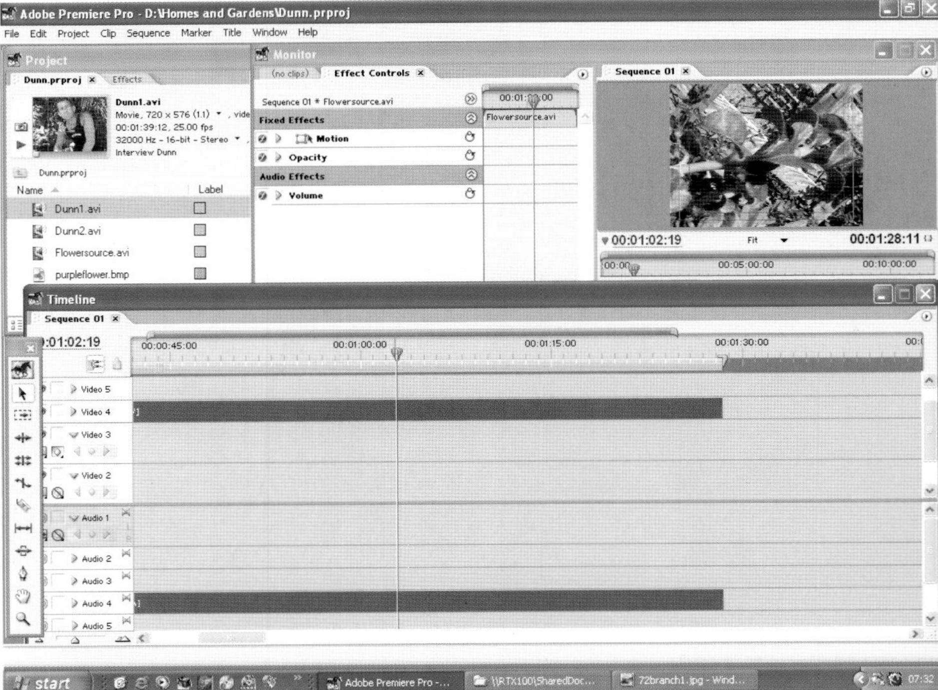

2 *Ensuring that* Show Video *is optioned guarantees that the image at the* Edit Line *is the frame of reference. Selecting the* Pen *tool, I've gone all the way around the outline of the branch in question, clicking anchor points in place. The final point at the left-hand stem of the branch is made at an angle that will be flush once the branch is rotated to a horizontal. Clicking the anchor point where I started turns the* Graphic Type *into a* Closed Bezier *in the* Properties *menu. It has to be closed if the graphic is in need of a* Fill*—which this one certainly will be.*

4 *By default, the* Closed Bezier *fills in white. To rectify this and replace it with the original reference, hitting* Window > **Timeline** *brings me back into Premiere Pro with the ability to Export the same frame that the* Edit Line *has remained positioned on. Save this in the same project to import it immediately into the project.*

3 *The limitations of* Title Designer *mean that what I'm doing here is not masking, but simply drawing. Losing the* Show Video *option shows just my very unlifelike-looking outline. But at least the outline is placed on a matte—which will be useful, as we will see.*

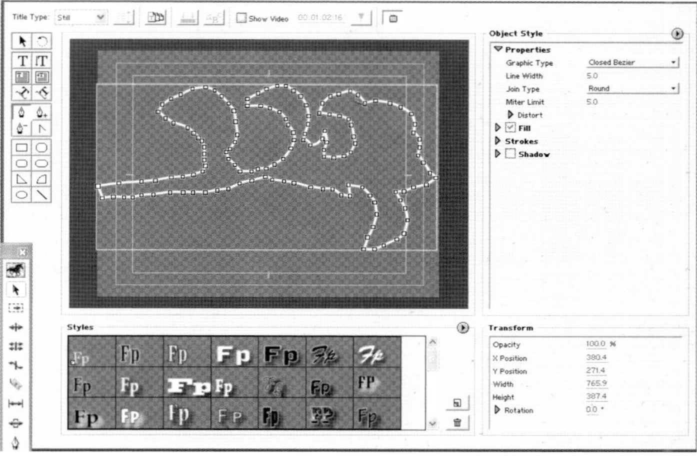

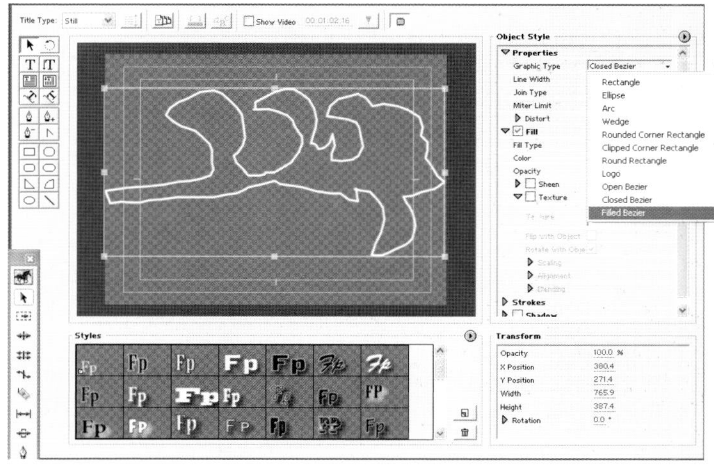

5 *Back to* Title Designer. *The bezier needs to be filled with the reference bitmap that I've just saved off. Choosing* Filled Bezier *in the* Properties > Graphic Style *menu will activate the* Fill *menu.*

6 *Overriding the* Fill Type *by checking* Texture*, I've clicked the box and found the reference bitmap of the entire frame. As a* Filled Bezier *matte, though,* Title Designer *understands this as filling just the bezier with the frame. Without acknowledging the* Scaling *and* Alignment *options, the texture is applied as a full frame behind the matte, in perfect positioning to fill it with the original branch.*

7 *Because I want the reference texture to be constantly applied to the bezier, no matter what manipulation the branch goes through, checking both* Flip *and* Rotate With Object *becomes essential. Firstly, though, manipulation is limited to getting the branch into the lower third of the frame as a background to the interviewee's caption. Simply dragging the handles forces a perspective on the branch. Adding a shadow compensates for the flatness of the cutout.*

8 *Bringing in the video allows for positioning the sorting out of any color clash. Because the caption is going to be overlaid, any camouflage can be combated with the* Opacity *and* Sheen *controls. Using the dropper to sample a light green from the video image, I've applied a* Sheen *that lifts the branch away from the background.*

9 *The caption and logo still need a strap to brand the caption graphically and to pick out the title more legibly. With the video showing through, selecting the* Rectangle *tool and dragging it out so it fits the safety margins creates a lower-third caption area with a default white fill.*

10 *Not wishing to go for too corporate a feel, I've gone back to the B-roll and located a close-up of a purple flower. Exporting this as a frame will give me a texture that I can apply to the strap.*

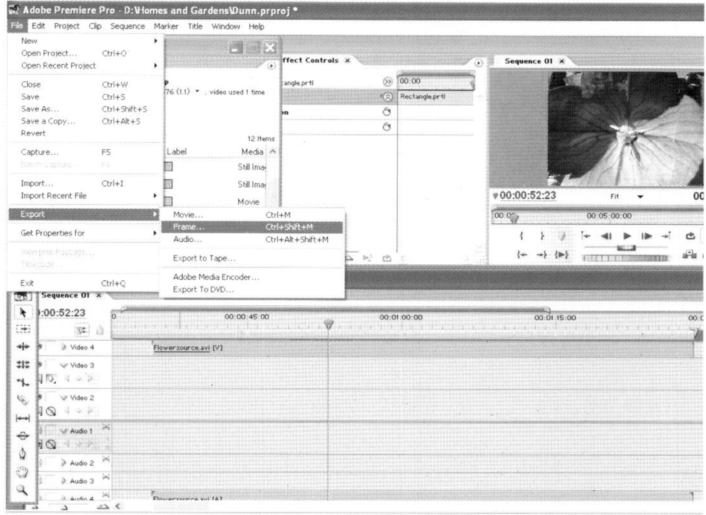

11 *Selecting the texture for the rectangle, I've again ensured that it both flips and rotates with the object for any future effects or transitions.*

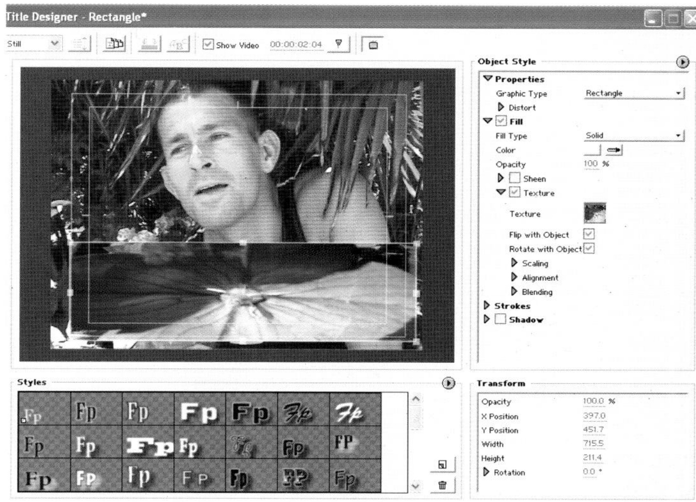

12 *The complementary color to the green caption and branch is red, but lightening a red will just give me a rather sickly pink. What the purple flower does is permit a less heady lilac to be picked as a compatible texture brightener. The Sheen applied is offset to cover the slightly darker area of the flower toward the top left of the texture.*

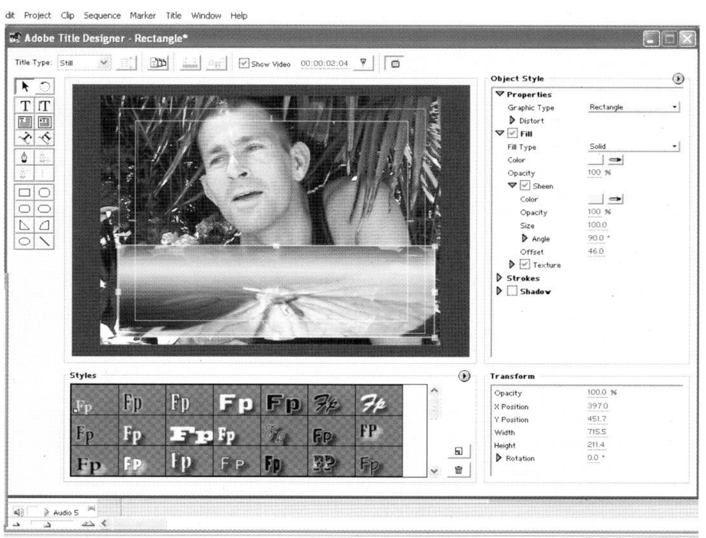

13 *In composite, on the Timeline, the clips need to be dragged in order of layer placement. The caption is on top of the branch, which is on top of the flower strap. However, they do not entirely succeed in my aim of compensating for the interviewee's inappropriate expression at the beginning of the interview sequence. That is a job saved for the Timeline itself.*

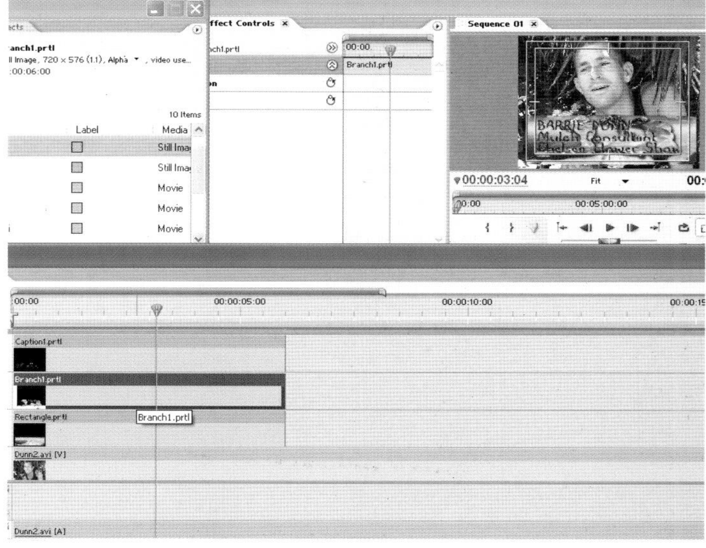

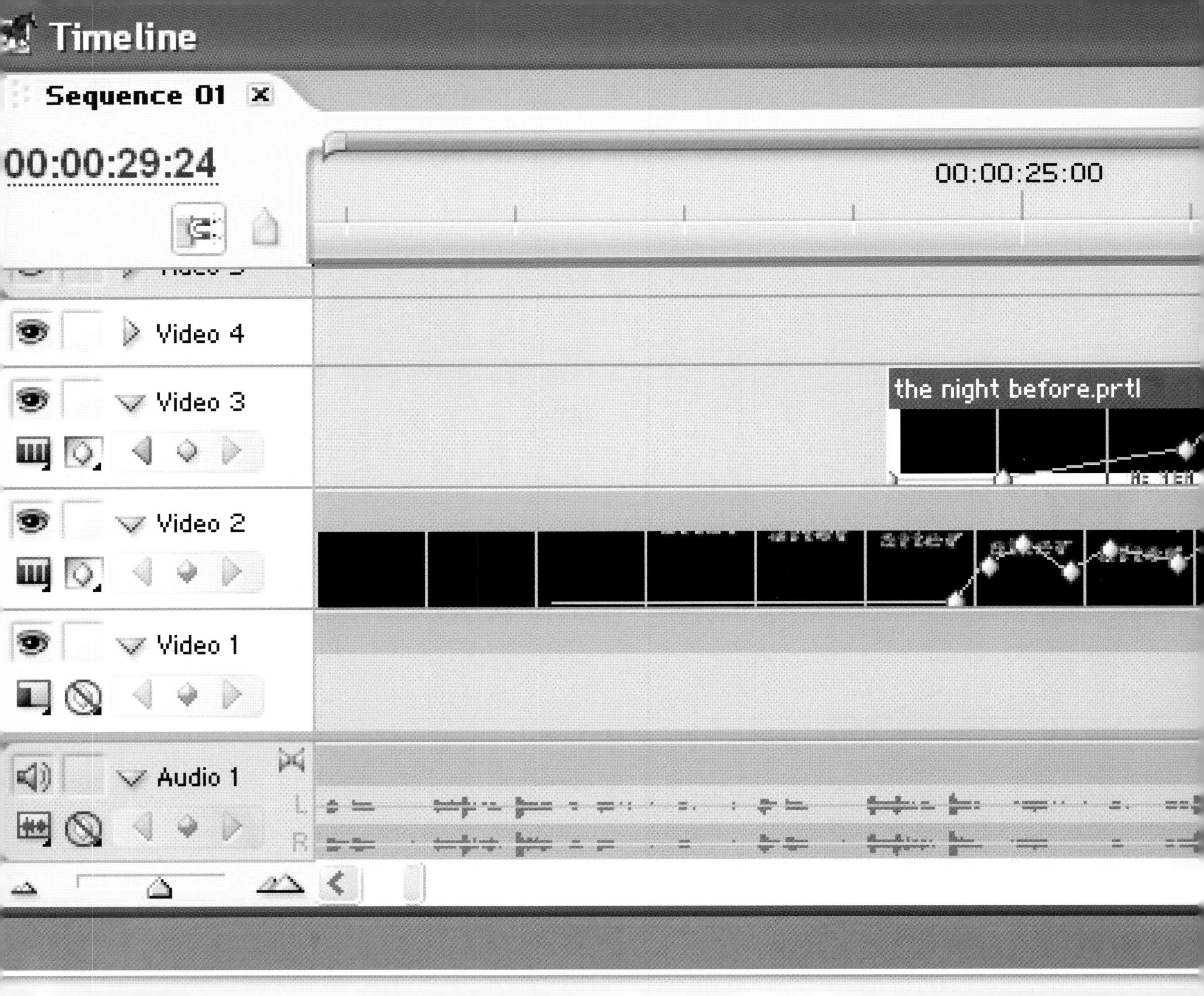

Timeline

Sequence 01

00:00:29:24

00:00:25:00

Video 4

Video 3

the night before.prtl

Video 2

Video 1

Audio 1

L

R

CHAPTER THREE

working your title on the timeline

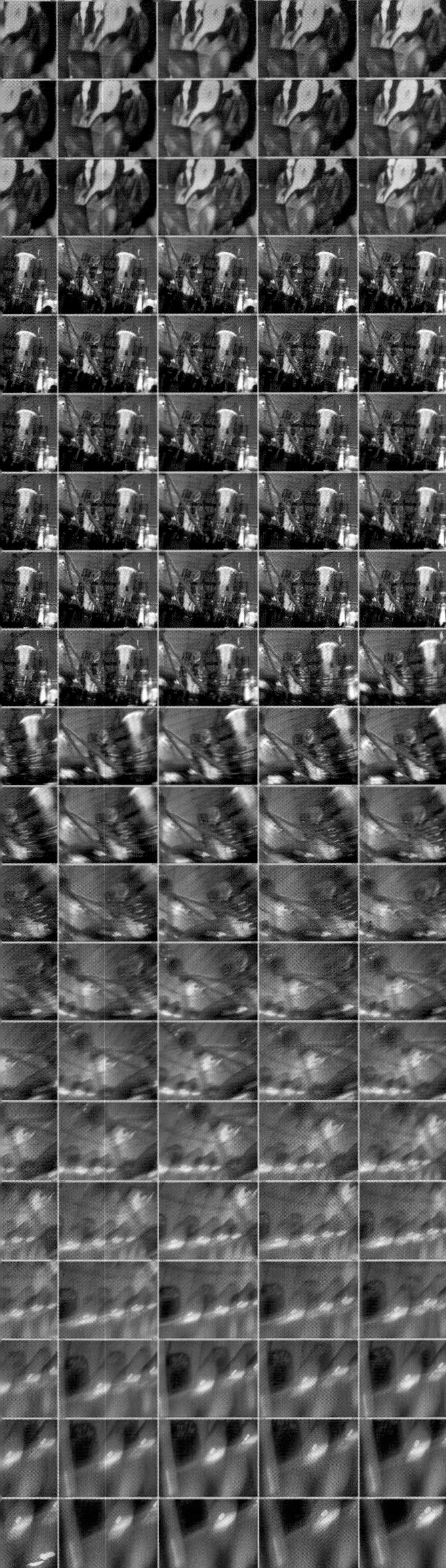

Titles and the timeline

Once you take your title out of the realm of pure design and place it on the *Timeline*, there are many practical things to consider, and many simple steps you can take to make your work easier and free up all that pent-up creativity.

The titles that you've created will automatically be placed into your Premiere Pro project. Depending on whether you've imported your movie as a file or as clips, you'll either have a neat project clips window or you'll have a whole load of different files and formats. For good housekeeping, get your clips into sensible bins to avoid repetitious expansion of your window. If you have just got to set titles against a finished movie, you may find that the icon list is more helpful when using layers of graphics and titles.

Bins can be created by either right-clicking your mouse inside the project clips window; through the drop-down menu *File* > *New* > ***Bin***; using the file icon at the bottom of the window; or by using the shortcut CTRL+ /. Label them sensibly, putting your original movie and soundtrack into one, graphics into another, titles into another, and so on. If there are clips lying around needing a home, just drag them onto the bin in the window.

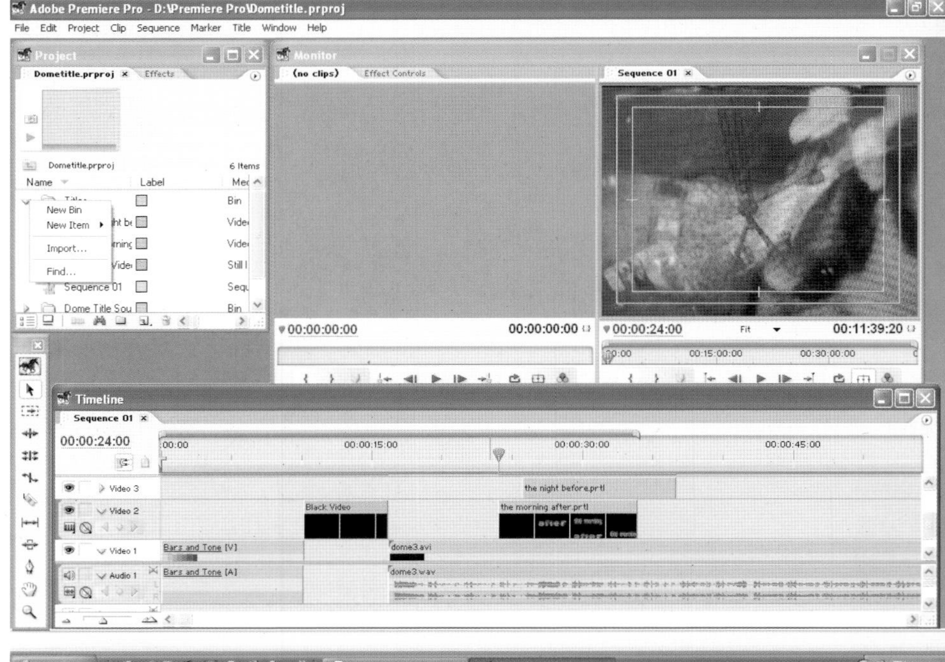

From then on, your titles behave just like clips and can be dragged and placed on the *Timeline*. By default, though, your titles are black alpha mattes, which means that the black that you see behind your text is read as transparent. What you can't do with mattes is put them underneath an image, or the text won't be read at all. This is why titles always have to be placed on a video track higher in number than that of your background.

In turn, different titles on different tracks will superimpose each other in the order of their placement on the tracks. A title on *Video 4* will automatically ride over a title on *Video 3* if the two of them meet on screen.

If your titles are to appear on a black background, don't think that the black alpha matte is good enough on its own. It's not. The transparency is not a true black, despite what your eye might see. Get some black laid down by selecting *File > New >* ***Black Video***, then drag it onto a low video track and put the alpha matte above it. Alternatively, if you want another color as a background instead of black, follow the same menu, but choose *Color Matte* to bring up the *Color Picker*.

With your titles on the *Timeline*, it's pretty much essential to be able to see what's going on with them, frame by frame. Use each title video track's *Display* button to bring up your options, then check the *Show Frame* box. This can be especially useful should your roll or crawl be subject to any unusual still default.

Likewise, you need to ensure that the *Screensafe* icon below the *Monitor* window is clicked. If you've worked your title in *Title Designer* to your screensafe margins, your titles on the *Timeline* should translate perfectly to within the inner frame.

Treat any sequence just like you would a script or story. The beginning is when and how your titles appear on screen. The middle is how they work on screen. The end is when and how your titles disappear offscreen.

1 *I've three criteria to meet for the beginning, the middle and the end of the sequence. The entire background sequence that I want the title to fill is eight seconds long, from the center of the CCTV mix to the end of the pan. Within each of those criteria, there are two types of positioning issues. There's the relationship of the text to the background, and the relationship of one part of the text to the other.*

At the beginning, I want at least the "after"—if not "the morning" as well—to appear out of the three-second CCTV image. Putting the title in this position is easy enough.

2 *In the middle of the sequence, while the "the morning after" title is rolling down and "the night before" is rolling up, I want the "after" to have a relationship with the passing "before," and the same with "the night" and "the morning"... somehow.*

3 *At the end, I want the remaining word—"before"—to streak off screen with the pan.*

Like most scripts, starting at the beginning is not necessarily the way to go. With a title like this, the real story tends to be in the middle.

Adding and manipulating keyframes

Aside from its new attitude towards A/B roll (it does not make a firm distinction), Premiere Pro's major change lies in its ability to work with keyframes. Because titles become governed—to an extent—by clip rules when they're on the *Timeline*, keyframes have the same degree of potency.

Keyframes are an essential part of video because of one thing: the fourth dimension, time. Whereas a painting has only one frame, a PAL video has, potentially, 25 keyframes every second, and an NTSC video, 30 keyframes every second. What each of these offer is the ability to change the video at every frame.

Because titles respond to manipulation to almost the same degree as clips, they are just as susceptible to keyframing. In your editing workspace, each title on each track has, by default, two ghost keyframes: the first frame of your clip, and the last frame of your clip. As ghost keyframes, they don't really exist. A change in any clip or title can happen only if given two different values, and the change will take place between those two points. The values for your first keyframe and your last are either zero, 100% or any other non-affected value.

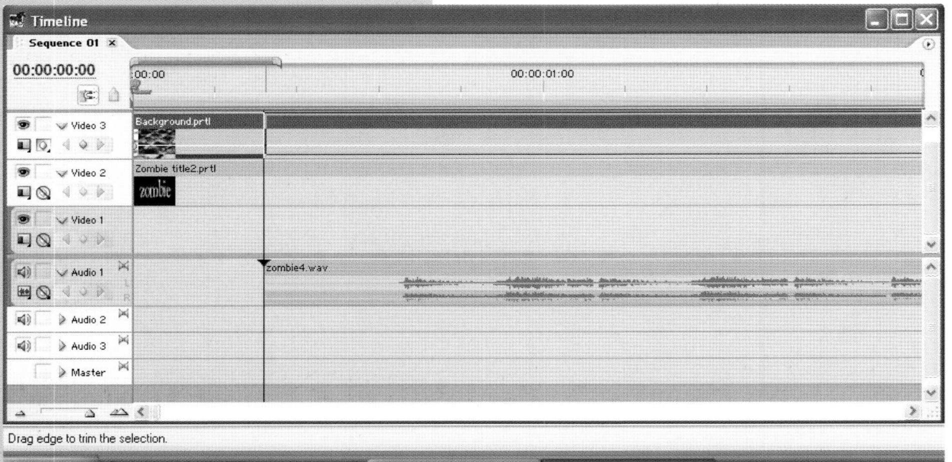

Any title that has an altered value given to either of these two points will change between them, creating an altering (two different values) or altered (the same different value) state. If it is an altering state, the change will take place, by default, over the duration of the clip at a velocity that is the length of the clip divided by the difference in value—i.e. with 0 acceleration.

Of course, this isn't always what you want. You might want a movement to decelerate just as you applied your ease out—or you might want a color change to start at the middle of your title and not at the beginning. For these reasons, adding and changing keyframes becomes an essential part of manipulating your title.

When in your dual-monitor editing workspace, your title (when clicked on the *Timeline*) will appear in the right monitor and its associated *Effects Control Window* (*ECW*) in the left monitor. The *ECW* contains a mini-timeline just for that clip. Scrubbing the *Edit Line* left and right will take you through it from the first frame to the last in the right monitor. The reason your first and last frames are "ghost" keyframes is that they are not identified on the *ECW* timeline—because they don't actually exist. If you expect to add one keyframe and the title to change from the beginning to that point, it won't. Instead, it will change the whole of your clip to that value. If you want your title to change up to that point, you'll have to add a keyframe at the very beginning. Likewise, your end frame.

Any effect or motion that you might add has the ability to change over time from the non-altered state.

1 Add/Remove Keyframe

To set a keyframe, position the *ECW* edit point at the frame that you want and click. To remove one, hit it with the edit point using the adjacent next/previous keyframe arrows, and click the button again. Adding and removing is easy, but so is getting yourself confused. If you have added keyframes all over the *ECW* and it's a mess, don't worry. You can fix it in a second.

If you really loathe what you've done, the drop-down menu from the top right arrow in the ECW *has an option to delete all effects with all keyframes (aside from those for standard motion and opacity controls).*

4

All of these options are available as cut-and-paste editables when right-clicking a highlighted keyframe. You can also find a few more options thrown in for good measure.

The options in the lower two sections change the speed of motion/effect alteration from constant velocity. Using Premiere Pro's set algorithms, these are the key to accelerating or decelerating the motion/effect upon arrival at, or departure from, that keyframe. The options that you select are then visually represented in your *ECW* as an alternative to the normal in/out diamond keyframe. It's important to remember when using these that between two keyframes, there's only a certain amount of time to redistribute. Therefore, a *Fast Out* from one point will automatically give you a *Slow In* to the next keyframe.

Well, that's the theory. Here's the practice...

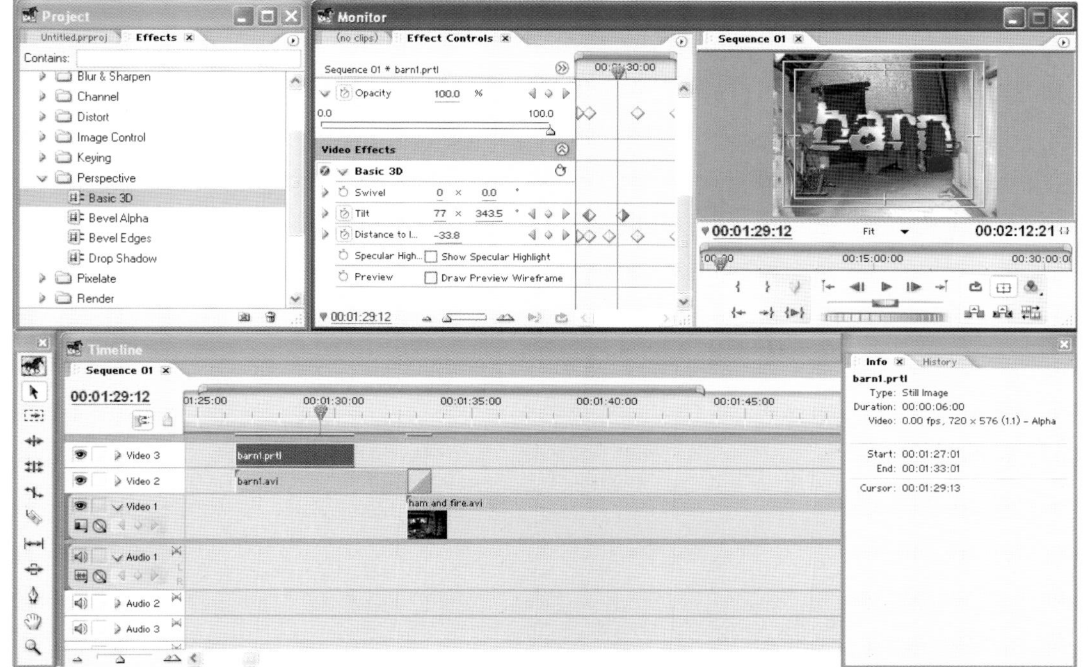

2 Reset Clock

Reset to the default values with the icon to the right of the main effect or motion. If you don't select a particular keyframe, this will reset all of those that you've added for that effect or motion. If an effect has a number of different sub-values, resetting one specific keyframe will also automatically add another default keyframe to any other parts of the effect which you've changed at precisely that point on the *ECW* timeline.

3 Toggle Animation Clock

If you want to delete all of your keyframes for an effect or motion, toggle the clockface on the left of the effect to "no hands." You will get a continuation warning...

Effect Toggle

...alternatively, the *Effect* toggle to the left of each effect will just turn it off if you want to see the clip without that adornment.

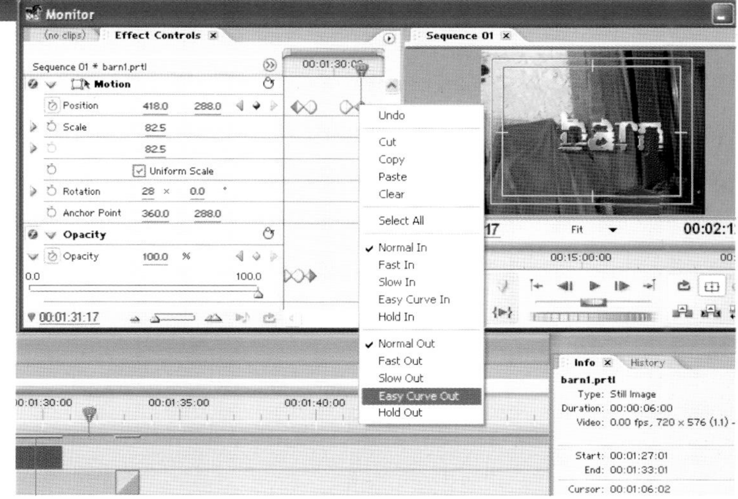

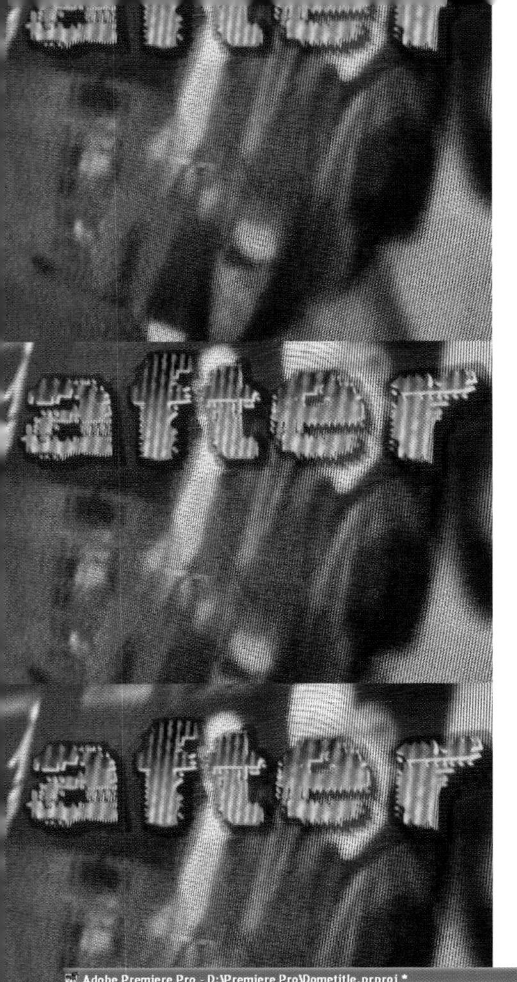

Activating and manipulating opacity rubber bands

Opacity is the amount of image that is permitted to breathe through the base black signal. At 0%, no image is permitted, and at 100% a full image is permitted. Between these two values, there's an entire spectrum of possibilities to allow for complete control over a mixing transition between two—or more—clips or sources.

Whereas a cut is noticeable over two frames (A on; A off/B on), a transition allows for gradual change over a stipulated number of frames (A; A/B; B/A; B). A change in opacity between two clips or sources can therefore fulfill three fundamental requirements for video: a fade up, an interaction between two clips and a fade (to black).

Fades and mixes become just as vital—if not more so—with titling. Because words take longer for the brain to process than images, any slight distraction wastes a proportion of the amount of time a title is given before it outstays its welcome. A hard cut is just such a distraction.

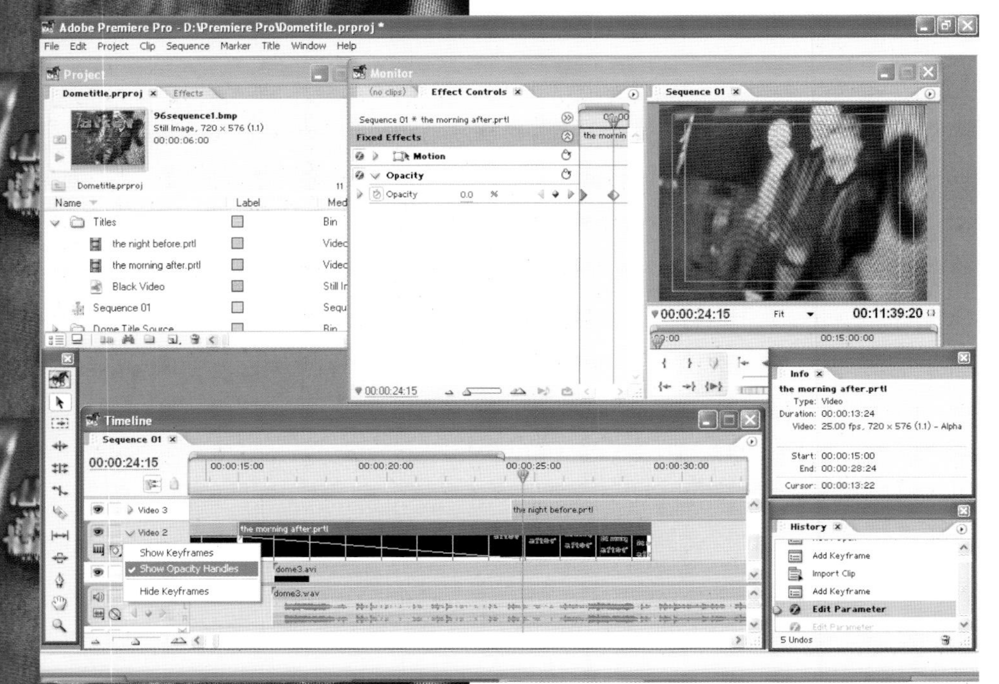

Mixing or fading not only eliminates this distraction, but offers a few more 'permissible' frames for the title—and depending on the strength of background image versus title, those few frames can mean the difference between comprehension and confusion. Indeed, white-on-black titles are just about legible at 50% opacity, but black-on-white titles can reach 5% opacity and still be visible.

Opacity can be altered with three methods. The first is through preset video transitions (e.g. *Dissolve*). The ways in which each handles opacity are slightly different, using algorithms applied to the chrominance or luminance of the image.

The second method of changing opacity for your title is by tweaking the *Opacity* handle rubberbands on the *Timeline*.

And the third method is using the ever-present *Opacity* effect in the *ECW*.

Three methods? This goes someway towards showing just how important opacity is to an edit.

1 *Because "the morning after" title needs to begin its journey through the frame at the point of the background mix, the title needs to be absent up until that point. Although it may seem reasonable just to add a keyframe at this point and lower the* Opacity *to 0%, all this will do is cause the title to fade from any visibility it has in the frame from the start of the roll. Observing the effects on the* Timeline *with the* Show Opacity Handles *option, the ghost keyframe at the start of the clip is apparent and set to 100%. This gives an idea of how essential it is in these situations to ensure that you add a keyframe at the start of the clip—in this case, reducing it also to 0%.*

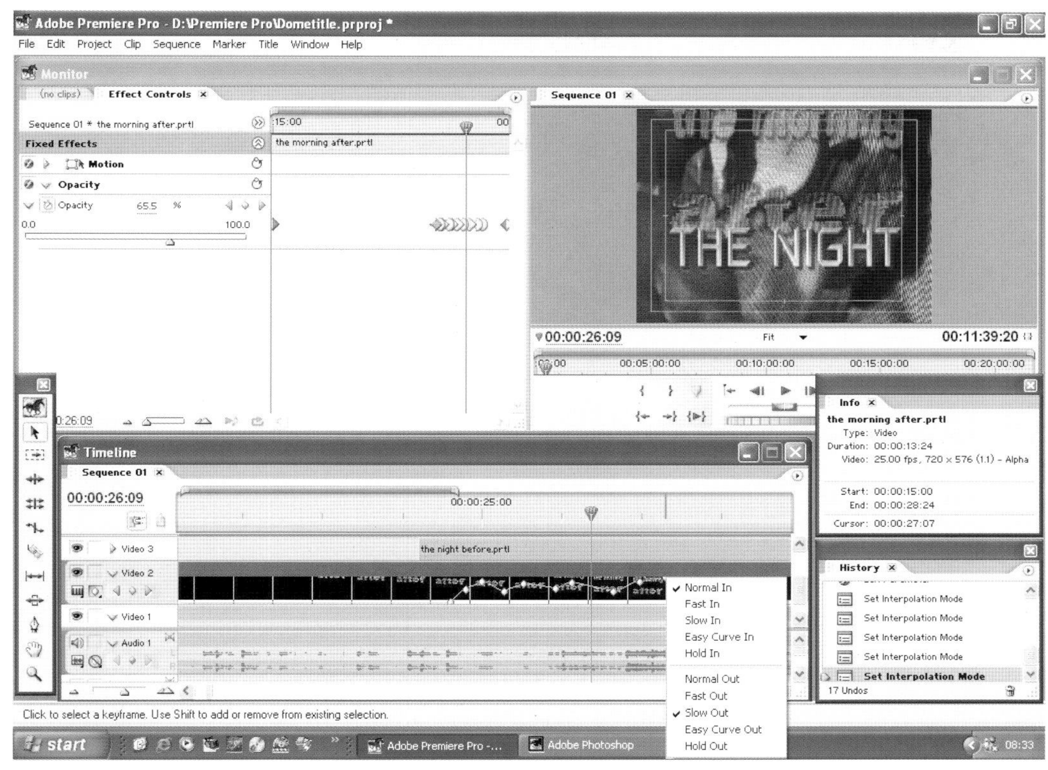

2 *After the point that the title is required to mix through, a number of keyframes have been added with variant* Opacity *values, in order to create the "zoning in and out" of the CCTV footage. These are all represented on the* Timeline *with the yellow* Opacity *rubberband, and all of the keyframes can be dragged up, down, left, and right once they are there to achieve visual exactness. Right-clicking on each keyframe has added to the movement of the effect with a* Fast In, *a few* Easy Curves, *and a* Slow Out *to break up the uniformity of the motion.*

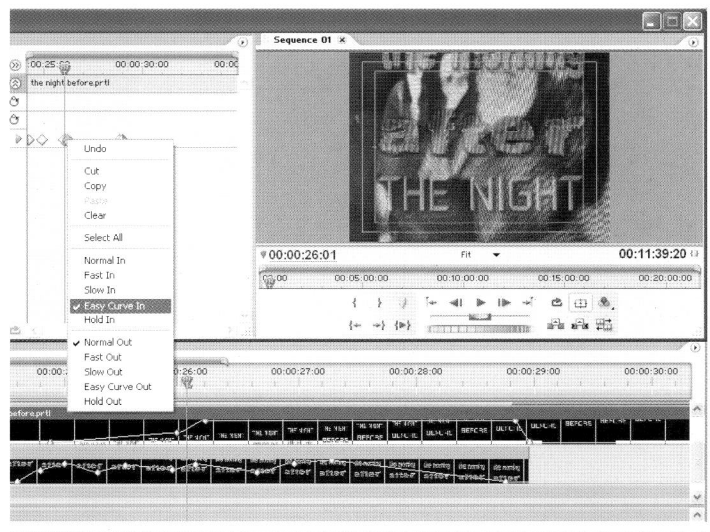

3 *Despite easing in, the roll up of "the night before" title is too instantly diverting from reading "the morning after." Adding increasing opacity with an* Easy Curve In *from the second keyframe helps this sudden intrusion into frame.*

4 *The point at where the background begins to pan is the point that I want to play with the residue "before" title. For this reason, I need to be able to isolate that title frame. To enable this, two things need to be done: firstly, the opacity of the original title frame in its desired final position needs to get out quickly without a fuss and without any noticeable jump-cutting off the screen. The opacity is therefore dropped quickly to 0% with a subtle* Fast Out *and* Fast In. *Secondly, I need to duplicate the original title in its final position as a freeze frame...*

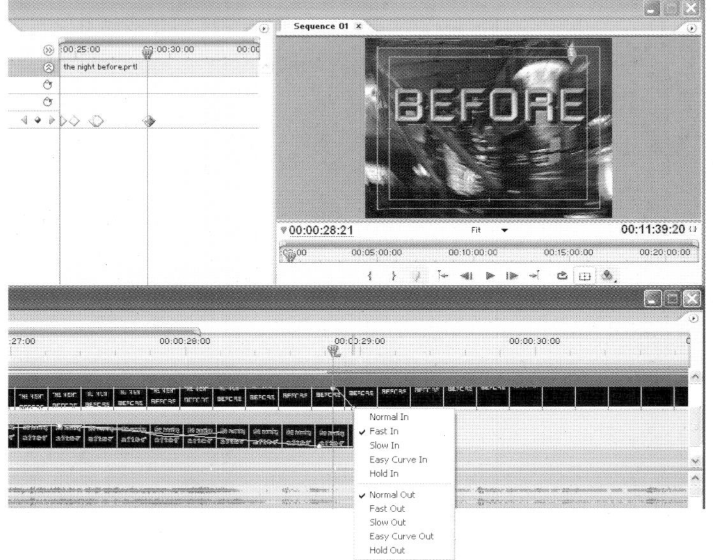

Adding freeze-frames

If your title is in motion and you want it to stop it in its tracks—or the other way around—there are various ways that you can do it. The first is, quite simply, to have your title not end on- or offscreen and add sufficient pre- or post-roll. This, however, won't help you if you wish to freeze your title in the middle of a move. It also won't help if you want to apply different values and filters to that part of the title.

The second way is to right-click on the title clip and instruct a frame-hold. Again, though, this will give you that specified freeze only for the duration of the clip, making any move null and very void. The way to maintain some kind of control in this instance is to superimpose a duplicate title as a still image.

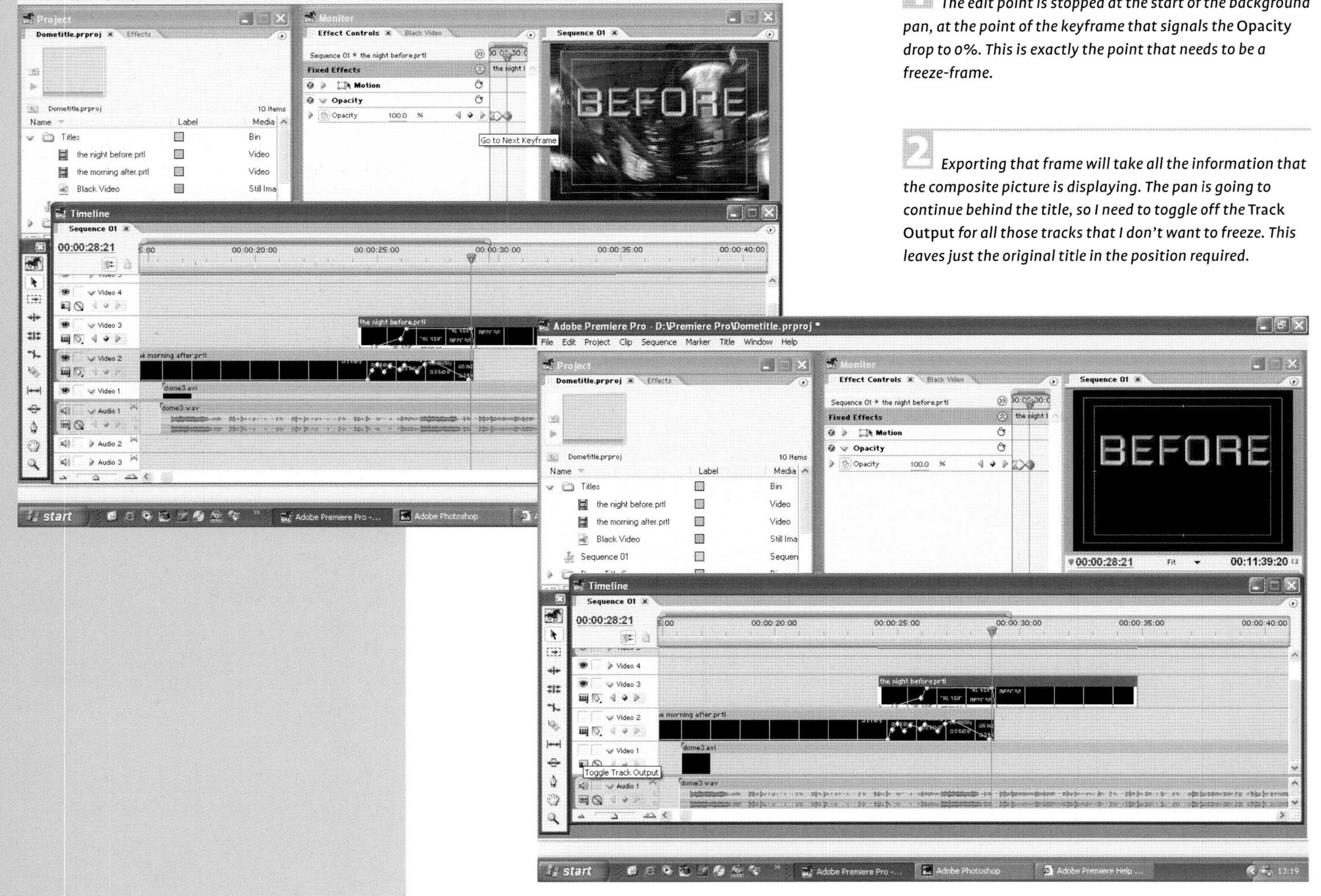

1 *The edit point is stopped at the start of the background pan, at the point of the keyframe that signals the* Opacity *drop to 0%. This is exactly the point that needs to be a freeze-frame.*

2 *Exporting that frame will take all the information that the composite picture is displaying. The pan is going to continue behind the title, so I need to toggle off the* Track Output *for all those tracks that I don't want to freeze. This leaves just the original title in the position required.*

3 *Through the* File *menu, export the frame as a Bitmap, Targa, or Tiff. Check the* Export > Frame > **Settings** *box to* Add to Project When Finished *and save it where it suits.*

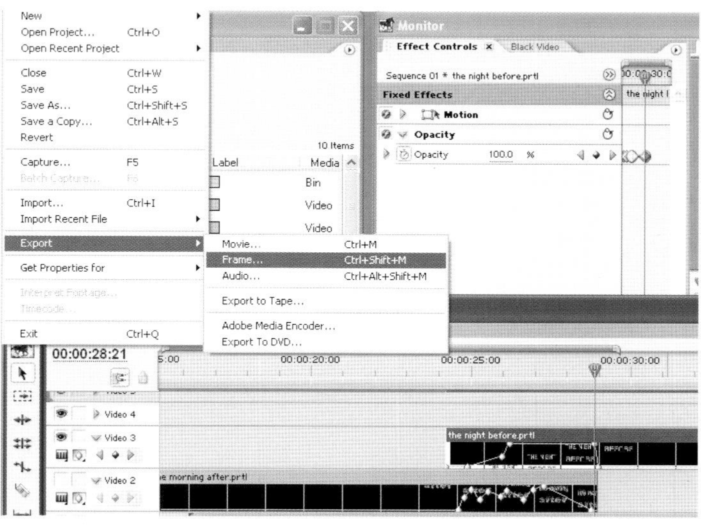

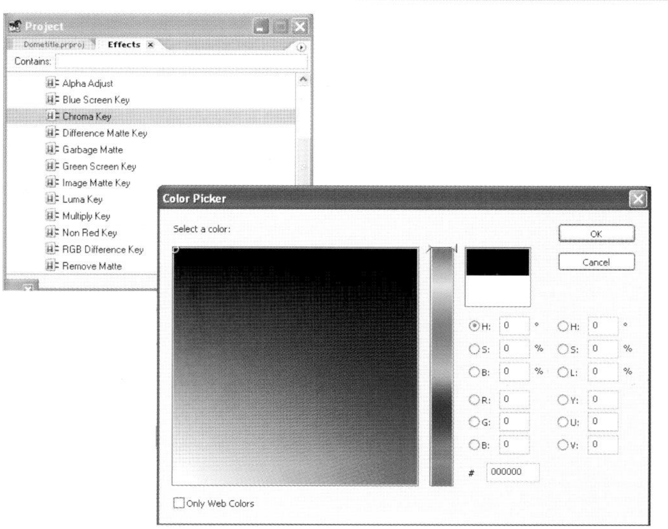

5 *From your* Effects *window, choose* Keying *from* Video Effects *and drag the* Chroma Key *icon onto the clip. The* ECW *will display the key, and its drop-down menu will bring up white as the default white color key. Click on the white to access the* Color Picker *and change the key to black.*

4 *Toggle any* Track Output *that you turned off, back on again, and drag the title or graphic from your bin to your* Edit Line, *which should still be in place. Put the freeze-frame on a superimposition track higher than the title that you've taken it from—and you'll quickly notice that the black alpha matte has been turned into a graphics file-friendly black video.*

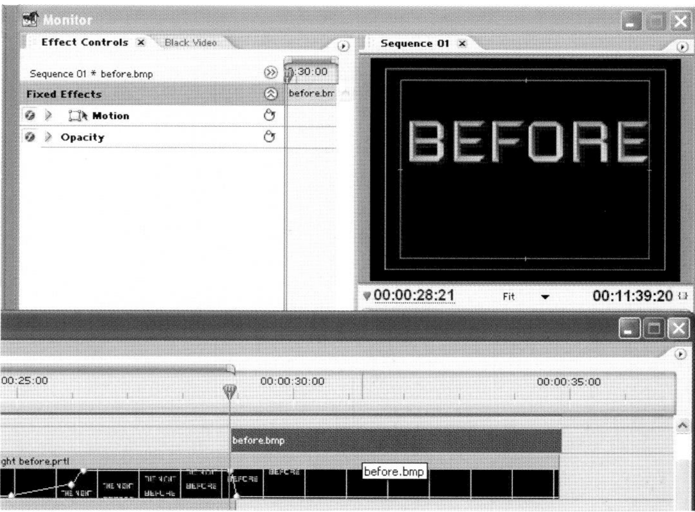

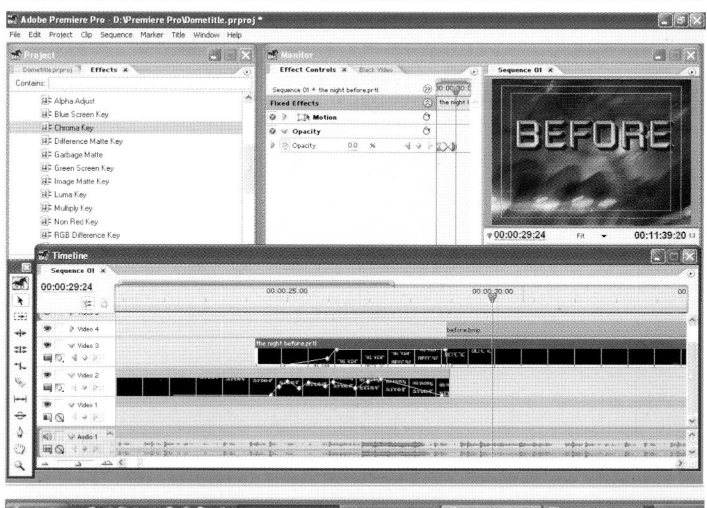

6 *Accepting the change makes black the new key, and the background should shine back through again. The 'before' here is now a still that runs over the original title, fading to zero* Opacity *exactly behind its duplicate frame, and before it has a chance to roll any farther and reveal itself.*

Color correction

Correcting color can become an essential legal process for broadcast—or a never-ending quest for some aesthetic Nirvana. As its name suggests, Premiere Pro's built-in *Color Corrector* is there to correct the chrominance (hue, saturation) and luminance (brightness) of images with problems.

Images with problems don't just exist in broadcast, although broadcast media have strict guidelines for limits of chroma and luma. The bottom line is that pushing color and brightness can lead to your final images showing crushed blacks, flaring whites, color bleeding—and this will be ten times worse if they're trying to cope with an effect on top.

Color correction for titles can be applied at any time. However, if you're adding effects or transitions on the *Timeline*—particularly if you are keying—any adjustment is better done sooner rather than later.

As soon I take the wedding flowers to the Timeline, *they wilt a bit. This is because of the opacity that I used in* Title Designer *to let the template blue glow through. As a separate layer, they're now without the benefit of that slight illumination.*

1 *As this is fundamentally a still, I could quite feasibly export the frame as a jpeg and take it into* Photoshop *for a bit of cross-application doctoring. Video, though, is very particular about color in a way that graphics applications don't necessarily have to be, and* Premiere Pro *has all the tools to make the image color video-friendly.*

2 *The* Color Correction *workspace can be accessed from the* Window *drop-down menu, and the controls for color correction drop down from the* Video Effects *window—mainly under* Image Control.

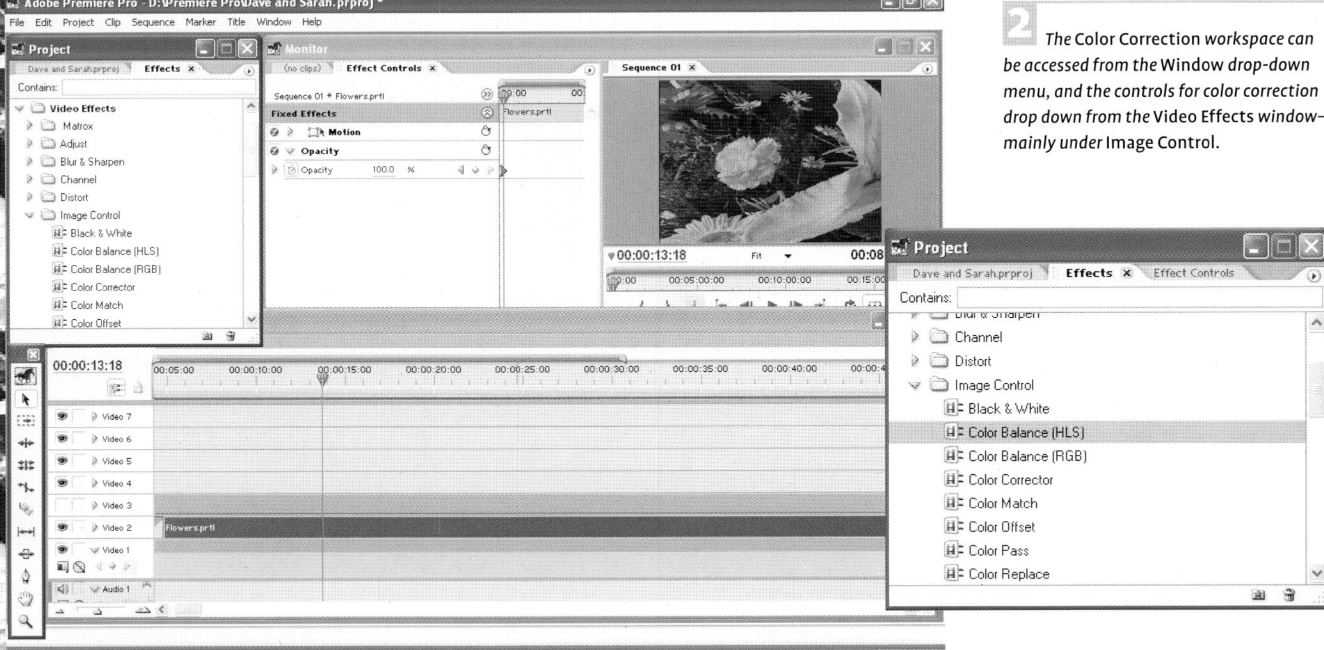

3 *The issue with the flowers and the reason why they're not particularly great quality is the fact that they were saved off from the template without changing their* Opacity *back to 100%. Re-entering* Title Designer *and changing this is the first step to managing and improving the quality of the title sequence. Right-clicking on the flowers allows both for the* Opacity *to be brought back up from 70 to 100% (*Transform > **Opacity***), and for the image to be arranged at the front of the title. This is enough for me to be able to save it as the new flowers image into the project.*

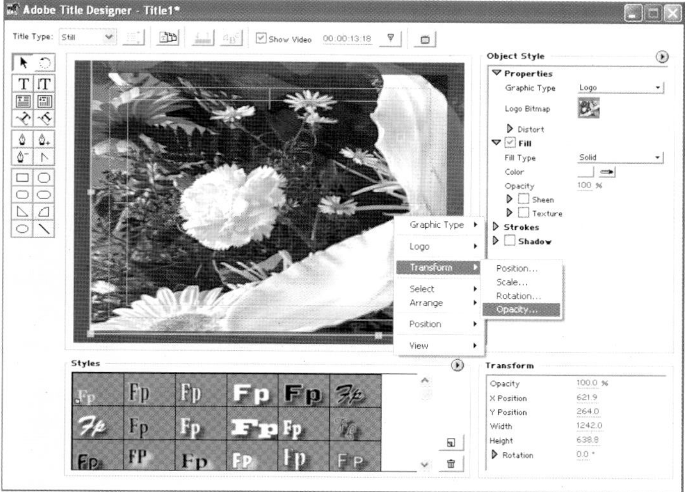

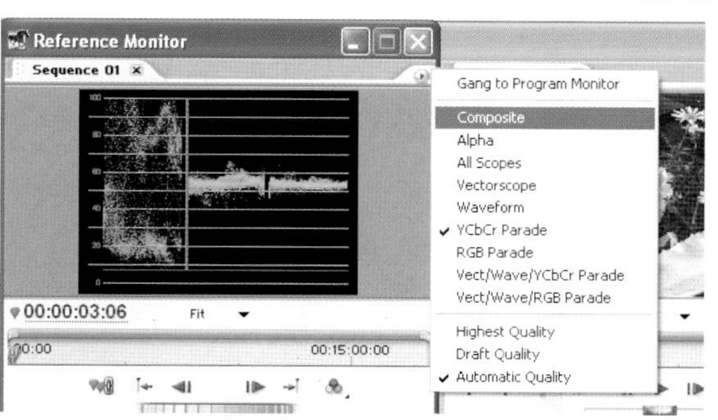

4 *Depending on your setup (external monitor or computer screen) and your intended final program output (broadcast or non; digital or analog), refer to the appropriate monitor type to track your changes in the right-hand drop-down menu of the* Reference Monitor.

As this video is really intended for private viewing and sharing, I won't have to worry too much about being broadcast friendly—unless something embarrassing at the event makes it onto the News. This means I can simply work with a *Composite* reference. Premiere Pro, however, does contain its own *Video Limiter*, in which luminance and chrominance can sensibly work. It can be found with many other settings when the *Color Corrector* is dragged onto the clip.

5 *Just as video relies on chrominance and luminance, so the* Color Balance *is divided to apply to both. While RGB refers to the filtration of color in the image, HLS refers to the* Hue, Light, *and* Saturation*—the luminance. Black and white, on the other hand, has values that are tonal, relying on the density and intensity of* Shadows *and* Highlights*. All of these values can be adjusted in the* Color Corrector *menu. As your titles have been specifically designed, they shouldn't need it. Your background images might need it, or you simply want to change it. Be aware, though, that arbitrary changes to a good picture can just make it look like you haven't white-balanced...*

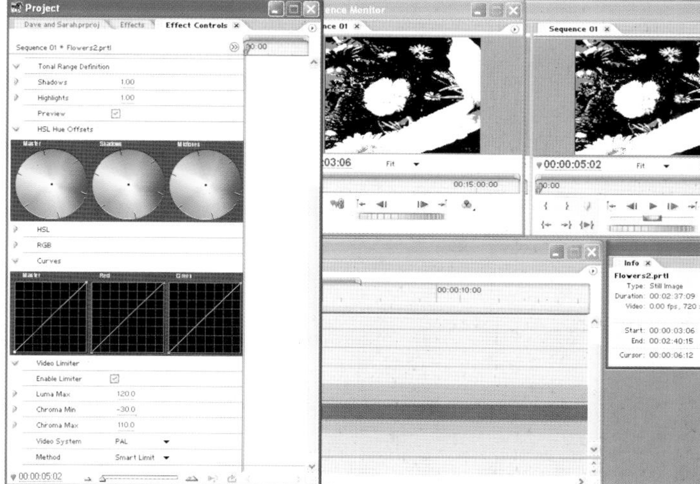

6 *If you're not using a separate monitor, checking the* Split Screen Preview *box is going to be very useful, given that you have an even distribution of color and image across the horizontal. Under the* Tonal Range Definition *drop-down, check the* Preview *box to see your changes to the amount of shadow and highlight present in your picture. These allocate the coverage of pixels given to each, so you can see how they will be affected by any other changes that you make.*

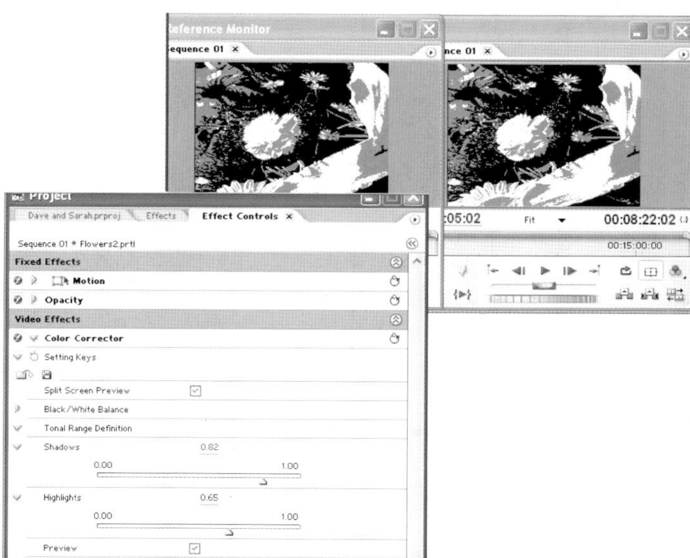

7 *The* HSL Hue Offsets *apply to the hue, saturation, and luminance of the image within the* Shadows, Midtones, *and* Highlights *(as dictated by the* Tonal Range*).* *Using color wheels, click colors to the outside (high saturation) or the center (low saturation) to make adjustments. Clicking the center of the wheels will reset them.*

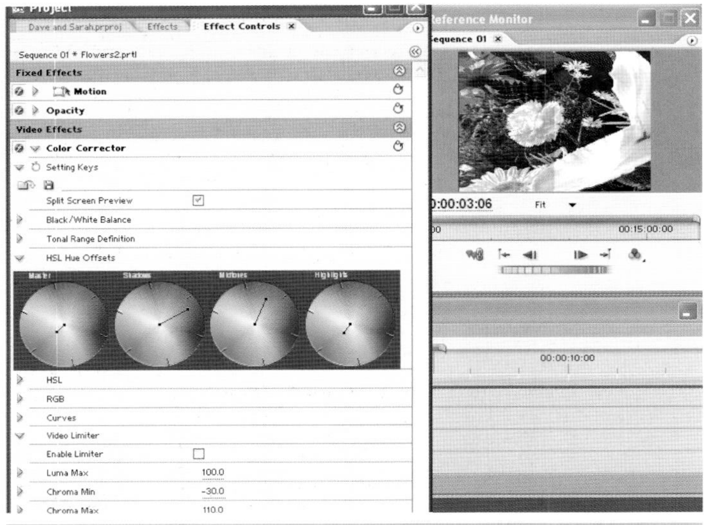

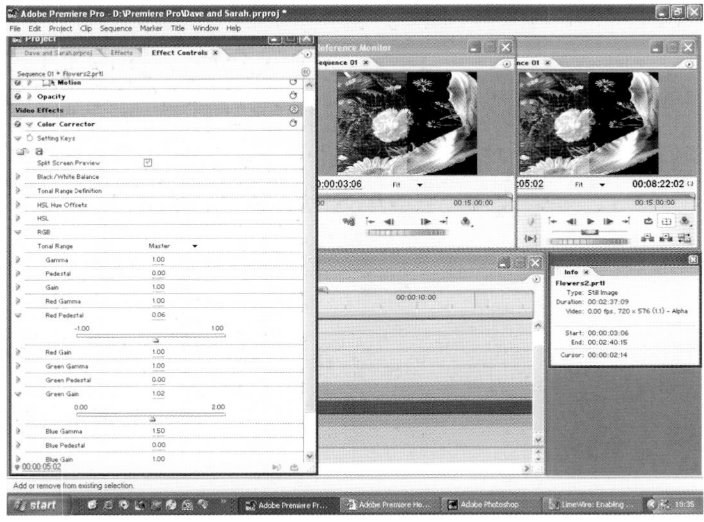

9 *For total control over your Rs, Gs and Bs, each one can have their* Gamma, Pedestal *or* Gain *within each* Tonal Range *adjusted, again through a choice of input values or sliders.*

8 *The* HSL *option is an alternative to the color wheels. Selecting the* Tonal Range (Master, Shadow, Midtones, Highlights), *enables you to adjust the* Saturation, Brightness, Contrast, Gamma *(midtone brightness),* Pedestal *(used with* Gain *to adjust master brightness), and* RGB Gain *(color brightness) by sliding scale. If you're going for unusually vibrant images, it's always advisable to keep your waveform monitor or your limiter on.*

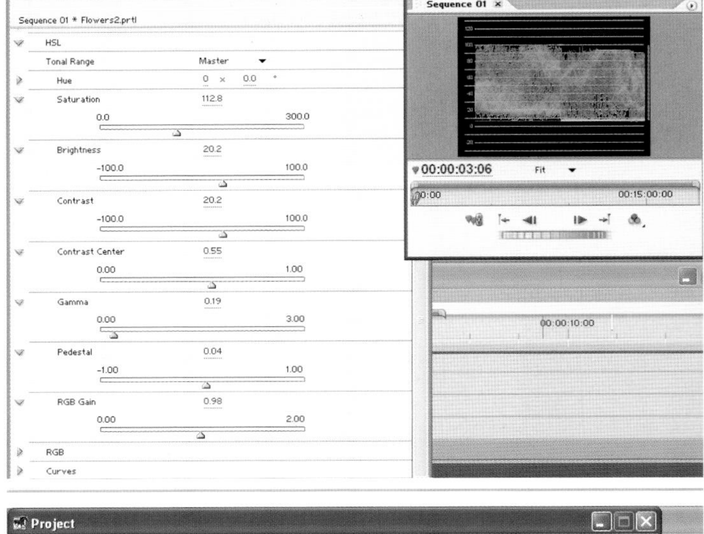

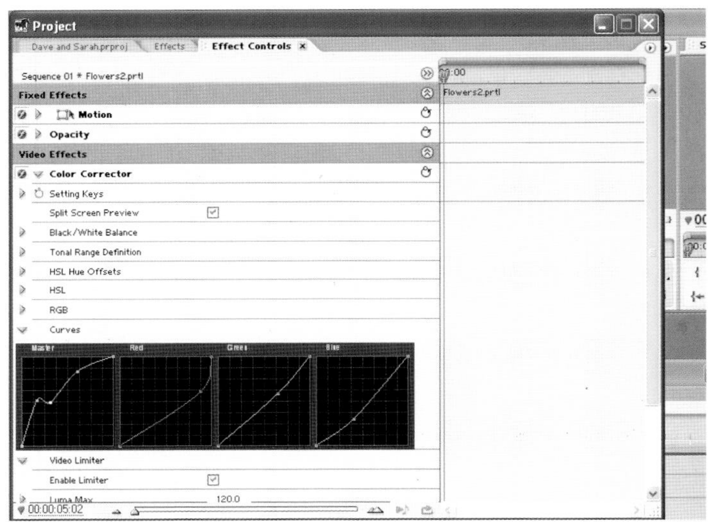

10 *Grabbing part of one of the* RGB Curves *can fine-tune the output of your color channels graphically. You can add up to 16 adjustment points on each scale.*

11 *Finally, the* Video Limiter*—as mentioned—will keep your images safe from over-shrieking. It's vital in broadcast and sensible elsewhere. Working either with PAL or NTSC varies the rules applied when it comes to black limits or changing your luminance limits. If you are using the* Limiter*, set the* Luma Max*,* Chroma Min/Max *by a* Method*. Reducing luma or chroma by* Method *will clip one or the other within the limits that you've specified. Otherwise, the* Smart Limit *sets defaults.*

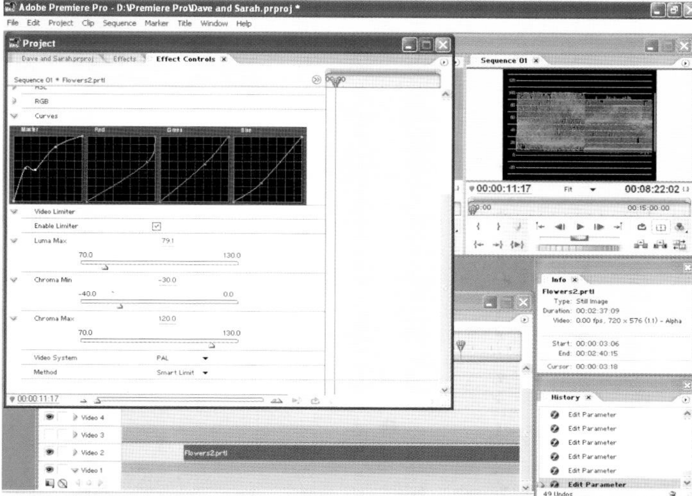

12 *I'm reasonably happy with the color effect that I've added to the flowers for the purpose I have in mind. They're safe, and I'm hoping that they bear up when I add a transition later. The happy couple photo, superimposed on the flowers, is quite monochrome. I'm going to give it a bit of help to work better with the flowers. This is easily done with a* Color Match*. Dragging it onto the clip from the* ECW*, and then opening the* Color Correction *window in turn, opens up all the options for matching color. The choices are to match the hue, saturation, and luminance (HSL), the chrominance (RGB), or the graphic Curves from another source.*

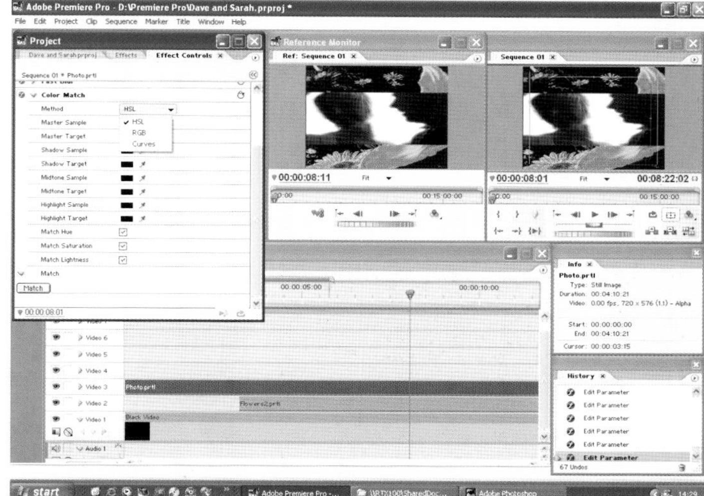

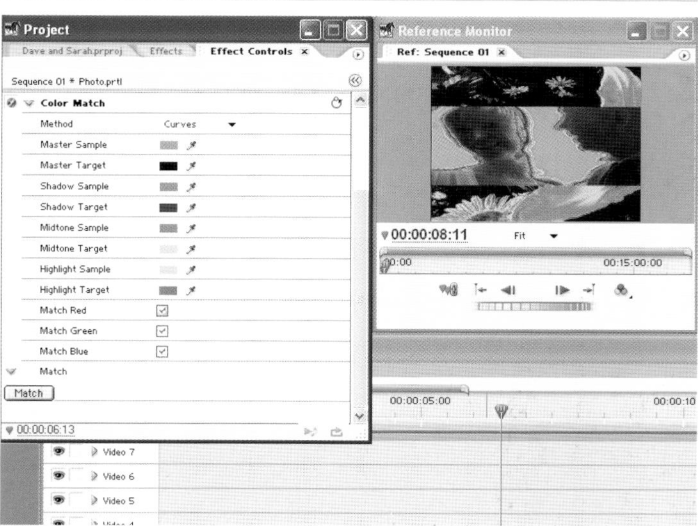

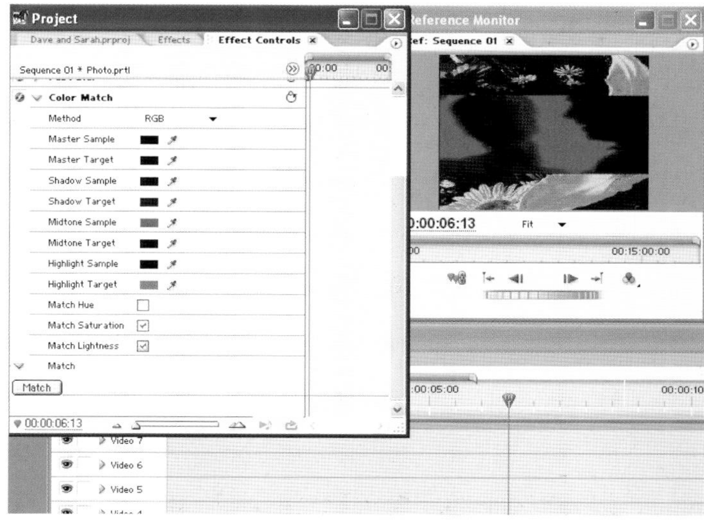

13 *Color matching works by dragging the dropper to the source for a sample, and then dragging to the edit screen to specify the target. Clicking* Match *seals the deal. You can achieve some interesting color matches this way...*

14 *...but I've decided, by accident (the worst and best way for any title designer), that actually this vivid red works wonders with the stretched widescreen of the image. Not only have I used the dropper, I've also matched the* Saturation *and* Lightness *of the flowers.*

15

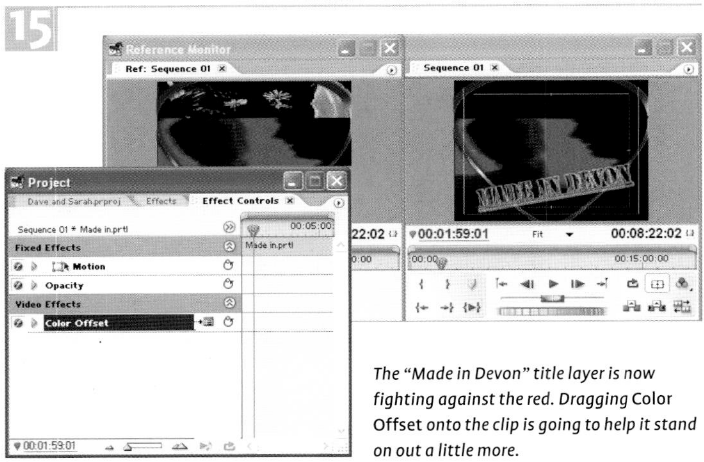

The "Made in Devon" title layer is now fighting against the red. Dragging Color Offset *onto the clip is going to help it stand on out a little more.*

16

Clicking the Setup *icon will get you into the* Settings *screen where each color channel can be offset by a percentage. Aside from incremental shifting of color, offsetting a channel can be a quick way of entirely extracting R,G, or B from your image or title. By offsetting by 100% here, I've completely taken the green from the title to leave the residue as a more vivacious purple. Be wary of this if your title is a roll or a crawl, and make sure that you offset in a perpendicular direction...*

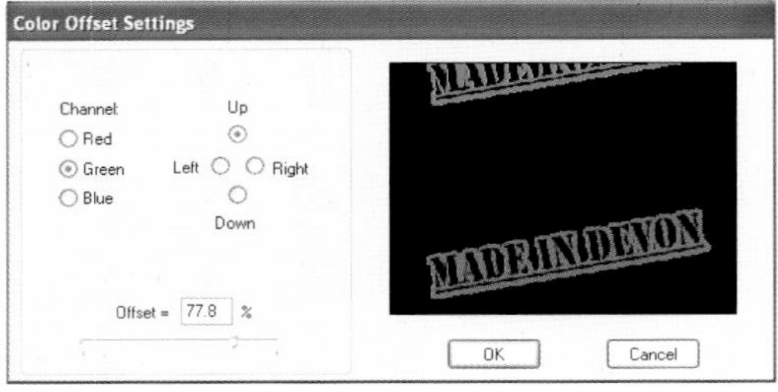

17

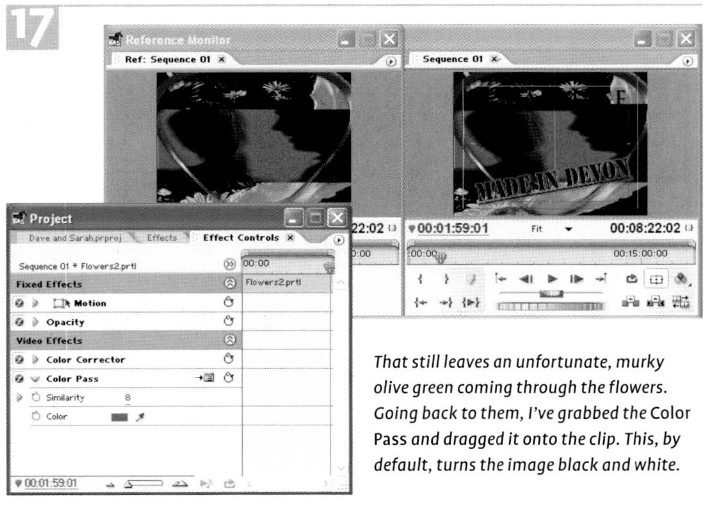

That still leaves an unfortunate, murky olive green coming through the flowers. Going back to them, I've grabbed the Color Pass *and dragged it onto the clip. This, by default, turns the image black and white.*

18

In the Color Pass Settings *dialog, I've taken a sample of the murky green by clicking on the offensive color in the* Clip Sample *window. Upping the* Similarity *value on the slider to incorporate all shades of the green, the color is preserved in favor of anything else, as shown in the* Output Sample *window...*

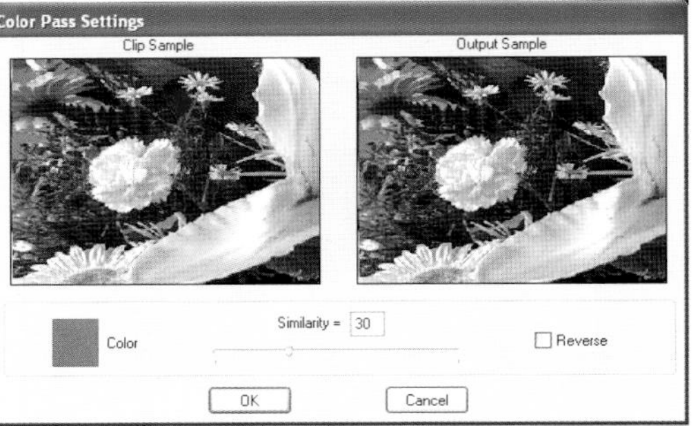

19

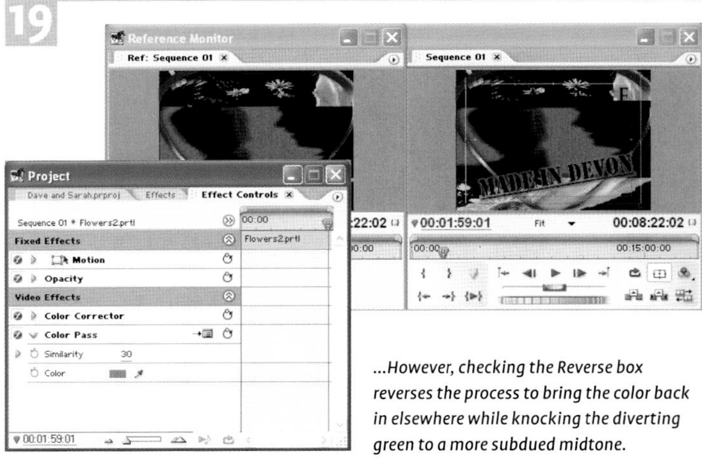

...However, checking the Reverse *box reverses the process to bring the color back in elsewhere while knocking the diverting green to a more subdued midtone.*

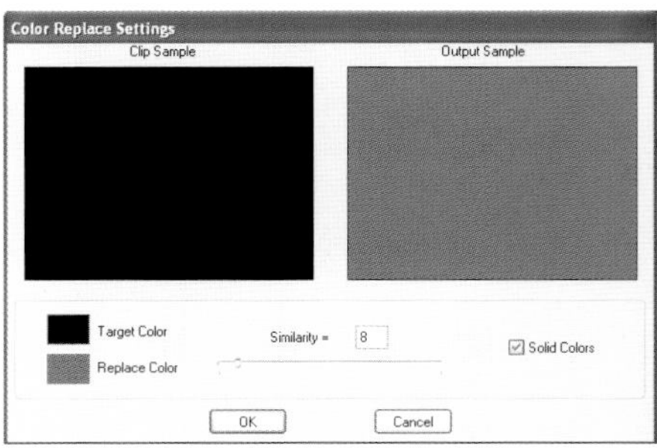

20

The "A Marriage" title has become lost in the undergrowth of the flowers background. To change this, the Color Replace *effect can quickly change any color to another. Using the* Solid Colors *option is essential when replacing black, because without it, all grey levels are maintained (i.e. you get nothing but black). I've dragged the dropper to the "Made in Devon" title to take a color sample, and the effect is coherent and legible.*

21 *The extent of color correction is nearly complete. Looking at the layers together, if there's anything I would change it would be that the flowers seem a little dark, but I don't want the blackness levels to change. In order to alter this, a* Gamma Correction *dragged to the image can lighten (or darken) the midtones—the flowers themselves.*

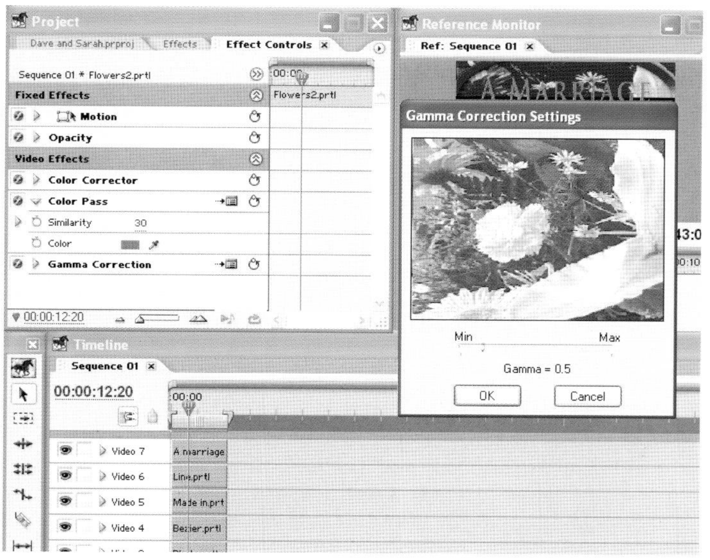

22

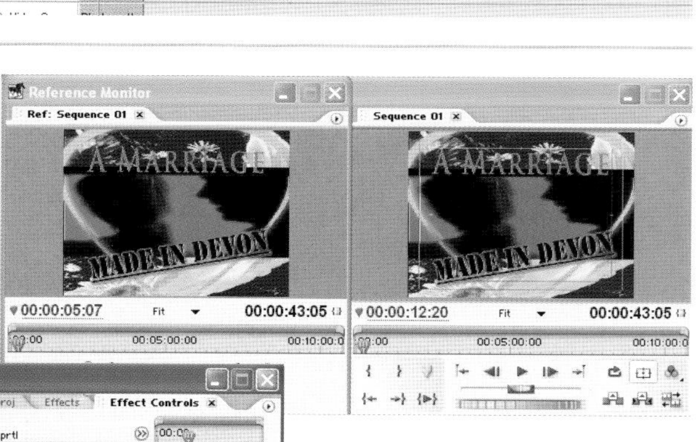

Finally, the bezier. It's almost lost now in the riot of lilacs and blues. By default, there is no Tint *to the layer. If I drag* Tint *to the clip and drop the look at menu, black is black and white is white. Using the dropper tool, however, I can take samples to tint both the blacks and the whites from the completed title. Using a high* Amount to Tint *value, I've almost entirely changed the color of the bezier, but the new colors help the object to embrace the rest of the image. For the moment, my work is done.*

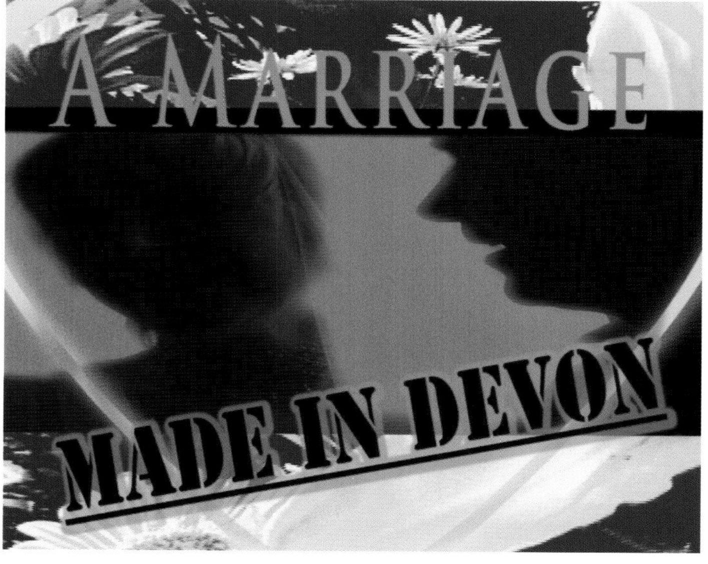

jonny quality

is always

sean moody

and often

louisa dupret

Making your motion versatile: separating words and creating multiple layers

Layers are another element that Premiere Pro shares with Photoshop. Whether it's clothing in changing climates or changing titles on a *Timeline*, versatility can make all the difference between hot, cool, and frozen. In Premiere Pro, Layers are essential if you want to create certain effects or relationships onscreen.

Layers in Premiere Pro can be lines, words, letters, images, photographs—whatever it takes to bring the title to life. This can be as simple or as complex as it needs to be to make the title work. The fact is that because all titles created in *Title Designer* originate as alpha mattes, compositing them on the *Timeline* is done by default.

All that's required in *Title Designer* is that you think ahead about what you'll need when you are compositing each layer on the *Timeline*.

1 *Some end titles for a music video here. There are only a few, so it's no effort to give a bit of bounce and vitality to them. The bounce will be movement, the credits will be free-roaming text. The background will be black...for now.*

2 *Starting off in* Title Designer, *the background is a black matte, which means the text can simply be inputted and saved. Because the titles are going to be so short, I don't plan to let them be dull. Therefore, the first layer is going to be various letters from the name of the band...*

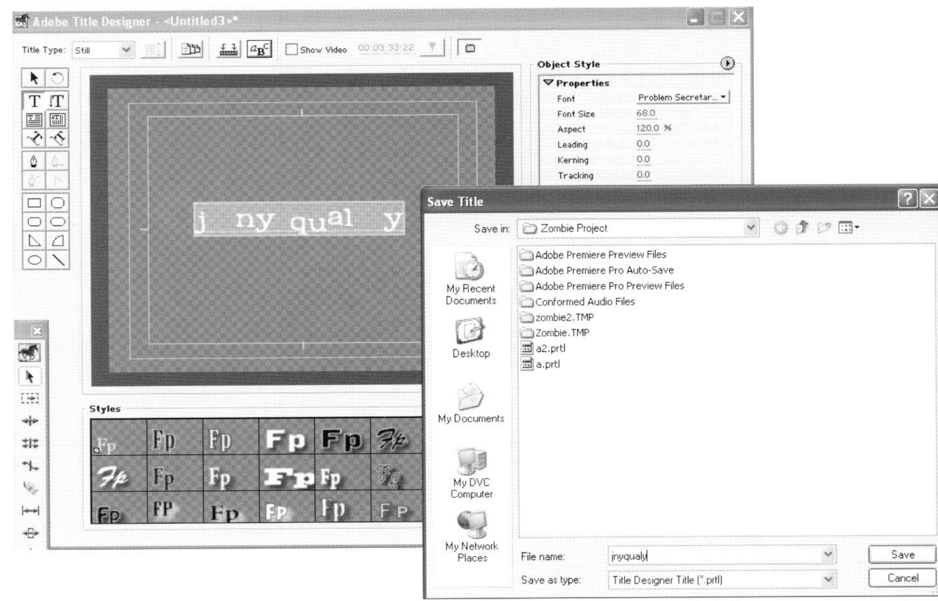

3 *...and the second layer consists of the remaining letters, worked within the same text box. There's nothing complicated about the letters. They're white on black for the moment, to keep things simple, and the only change to the font has been an increase of* Aspect *value to 120%.*

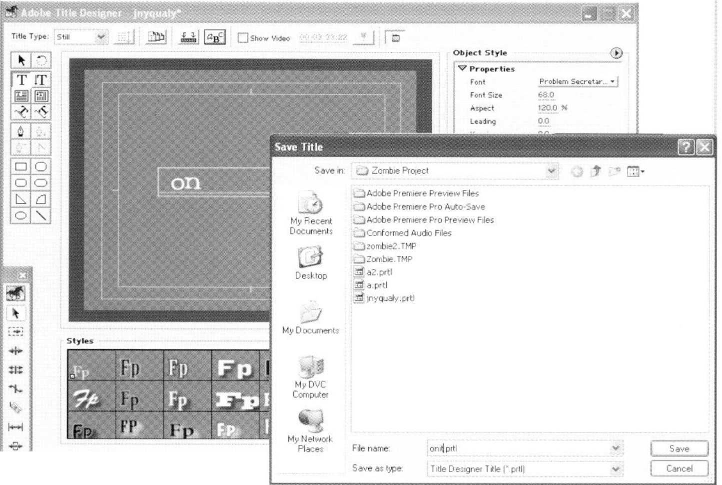

4 *I've gone along in the same vein for each title that will appear, dividing each into two separate layers. When each layer of each pair is on top of the other on the* Timeline*, they form the title cards needed—albeit a bit loosely. A touch of kerning and a repositioning sorts them out so they are both legible and sensible—but more importantly, it proves that they can work together.*

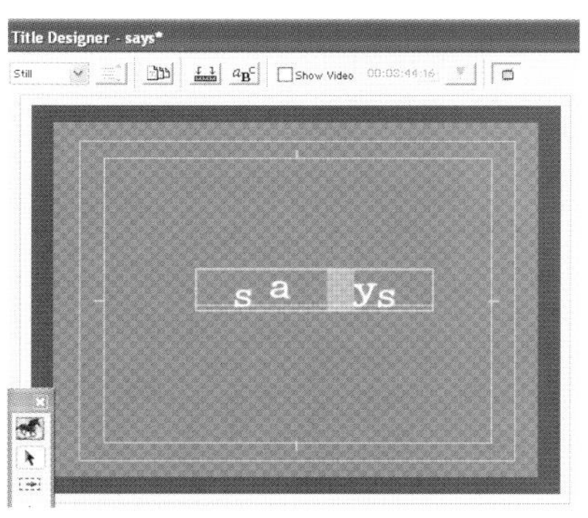

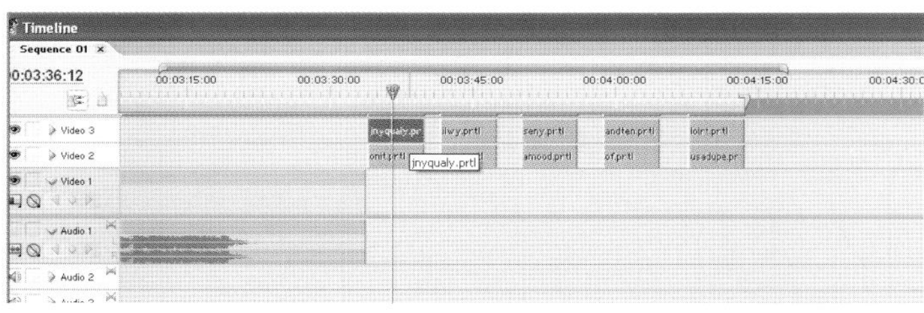

5 *Current logic puts the titles in their pairs like this. What this will have the effect of, though, is simply five title cards cut on screen. I want transition and movement with all layers together.*

6 *The* Timeline*, restructured to help all the interaction, now looks like this. It's almost no help at all, visually. This is precisely why organization, visualization, and good housekeeping skills can be so important during titling. Each layer has been dragged to a length that stretches over the time, in order that they all have plenty of room to maneuver. Whether it comes to changes in* Opacity *or* Motion*, each layer will have space to have its say in its own time.*

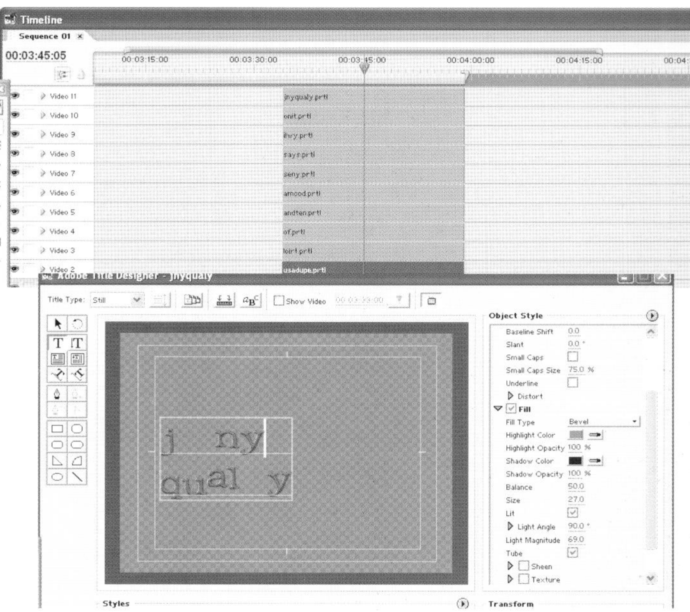

7 *Once I can be sure that it all appears to be working, I have the time to go back into* Title Design *and start to get the look to the text layers that I want. While I'm simply adding a black* Outer Stroke *to one layer of each title, a* Bevel *with* Tube *and* Lit *switched on highlights the rest of the glyphs.*

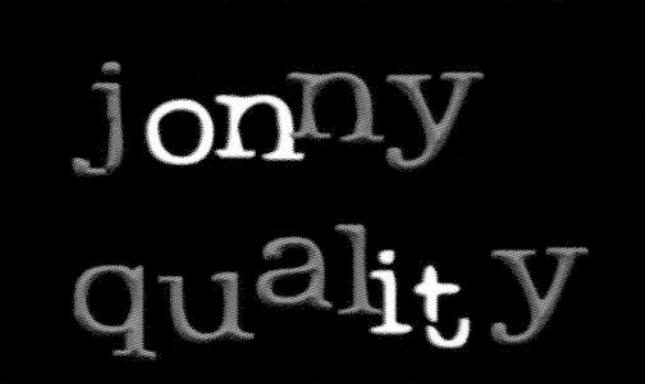

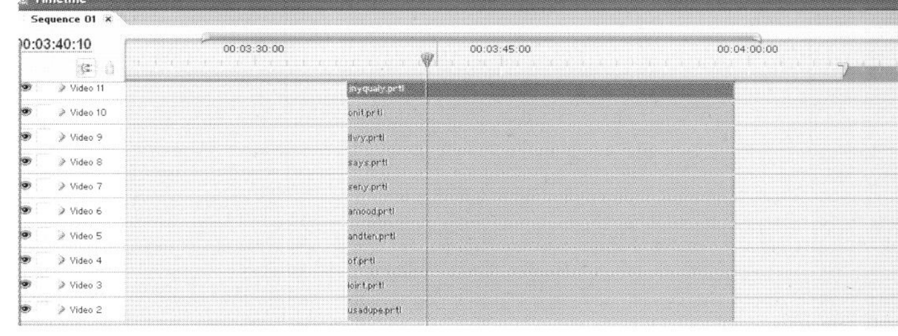

8 *The first pairing of layers is tested for size and quality within size, using the* Scale *and* Position *in the* ECW*, and the title is now ready for action* *(see page 96)**.*

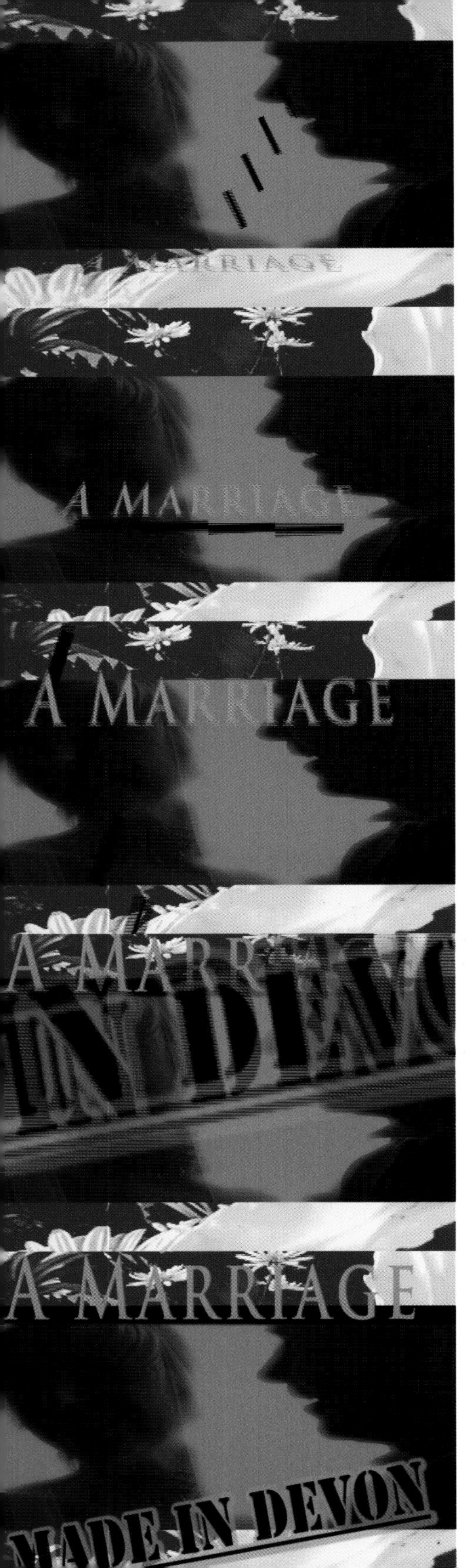

Working with layers: transitions

Titles are more legible when they're stills. They're also a lot less interesting. A transition may lift it out of the doldrums.

When you're working with layers, it makes sense that some kind of transition between them is going to make it a lot more pleasing than hard cuts—especially when the layers form a composite picture. Like video effects, though, badly chosen transitions can really trash your title sequence...

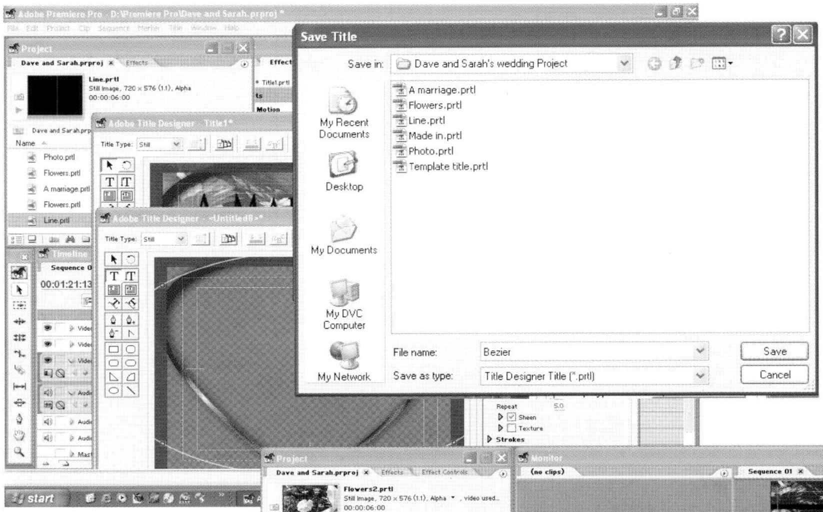

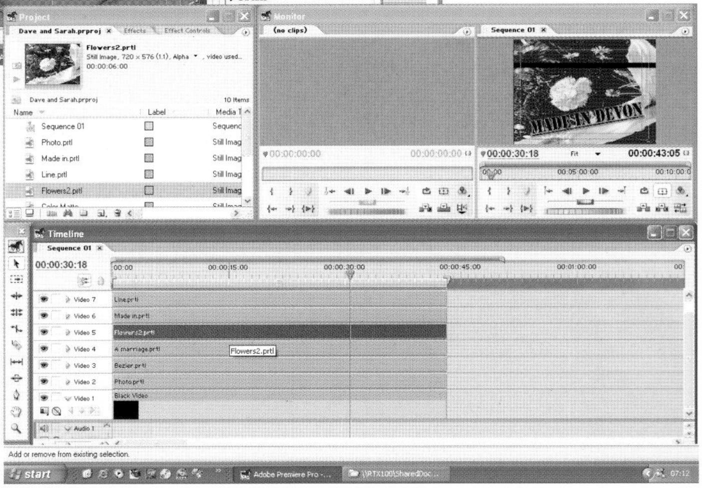

1 *Taking a chance that there might be some hope for the color-corrected wedding template, the first thing to do is to help it along by pulling apart a few of its layers. In* Title Designer, *this is best achieved by copying and pasting any layer that could be used into a new title.*

2 *In* Premiere Pro, *all the stills saved off appear in the* Project Clips *window. Give each of them a video track of their own—including the original final title as a reference—and drag them onto the* Timeline. *Without putting them in the correct track order (with regard to each still's attributes and matte allocation), the order of service will ultimately give you an incorrectly layered image...*

3 *Hopefully, though, you'll have enough logic, preplanning, and experience in fiddling with your template that layer video track allocation will be conducted with military precision. Putting the finished reference title at the end of the clips, creating a new black video clip and putting it in its place on the lowest video track will give you a flat background to whatever you do from here. The next step is to go through the layers, one by one, and work out their relationships—both to the* Timeline *and as transitions between themselves.*

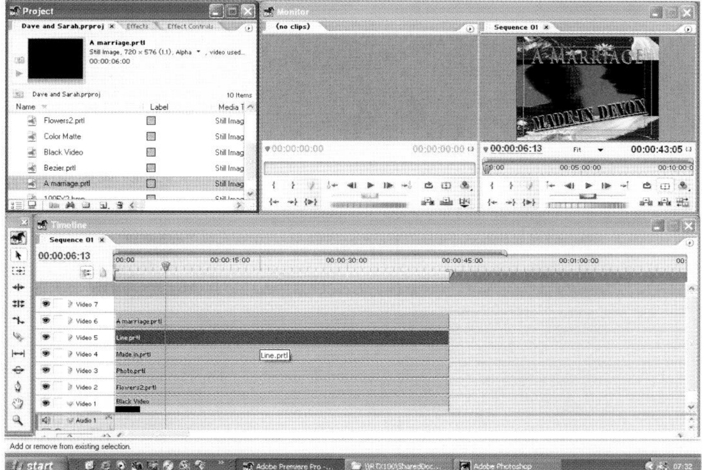

4 *I've put the image of the happy couple up front, but it's still got to find its way out of the black video. To do this, I've chosen a video effect in the* ECW*, as an alternative to a video transition. It's a* Fast Blur*, which works to slowly bring in an image before it snaps into place. A value of 5000 as an initial keyframe, takes the image to the point of absolute invisibility. A second keyframe is given a* Blur *value of 0, indicating absolute visibility. Because the image is stretched horizontally, I'm making sense of it streaking on by selecting the* Horizontal Blur Dimension*. By not selecting* Repeat Edge Pixels*, I'm asking for the blur to treat the edges of the image as semitransparent, easing the transition in.*

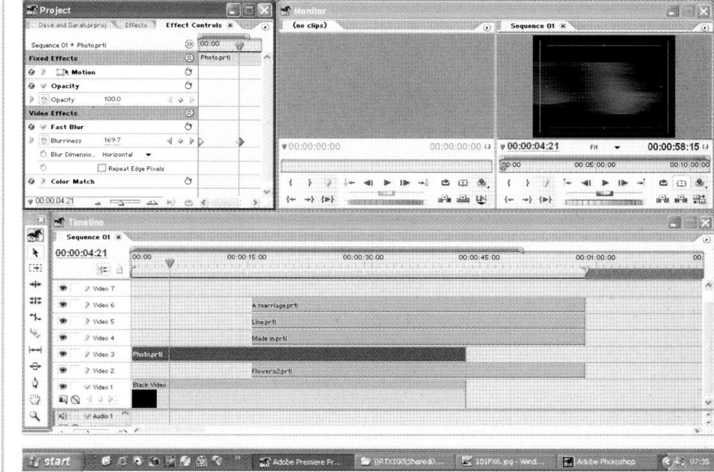

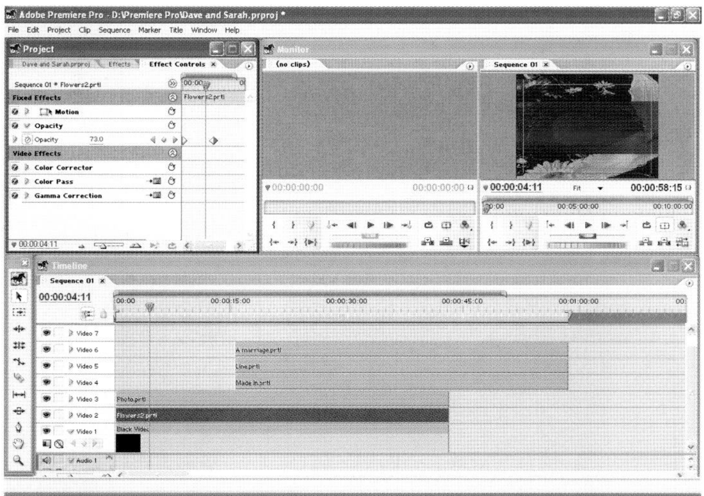

5 *While this is happening, I want the flowers to come in from the black—but staggered slightly later. An* Opacity *change from 0 to 100% brings the flowers into vision...*

6 *...but then dragging a* Stretch > **Stretch Over** *from the* Video Transitions *drop-down will let them work with the "widescreen" happy couple as the opacity change on the flowers runs its course...*

7 Double-clicking on the dragged Timeline stretch transition brings up the Effect Controls in the clip window. The top left-hand "monitor" offers the option of either a horizontal stretch or a vertical stretch. Obviously, only a horizontal is going to work with the very X-axis-based couple...

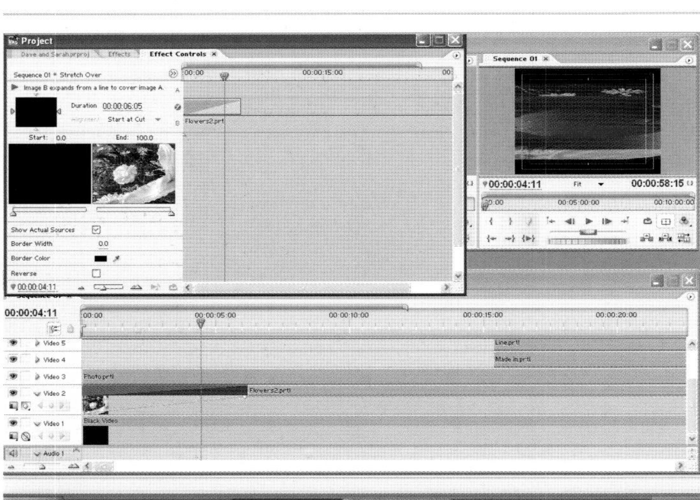

8 Having dragged the length of the transition well over the extent of the 100% flower-opacity mark, I can now scrub the Edit Line in the ECW and find exactly the right running time for the transition to work with the couple stretch and the flower opacity. I want the different layer transitions to give the illusion that the still title is constantly on the move. Therefore the stretch continues to a point after the blur has finished.

9 While the stretch finishes its move, I'm going to bring the subtle black frame-dividing line in. The line is conducive to a simple Slide, perhaps, but let's be much bolder about it: the line is already too shy and needs a bit more encouragement to come to the party. A Swirl slide is the ideal choice to liven up proceedings.

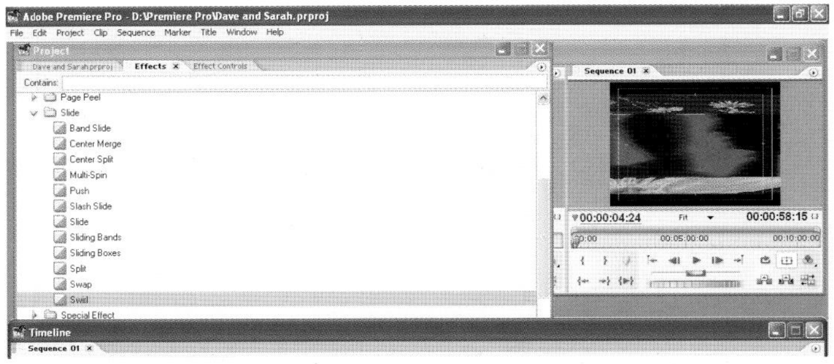

10 Again, stretching the Swirl slide's out-point to continue past the end-point for the stretching flowers, keeps this moving. The other good aspect to the Swirl is that it brings the black band over the red, reinforcing the title's pseudo-Bond effect.

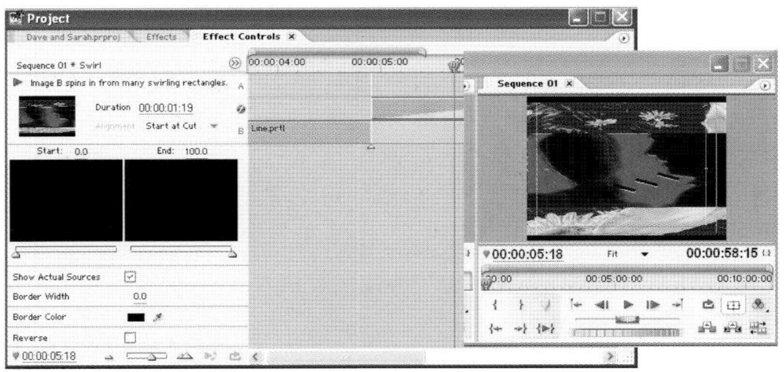

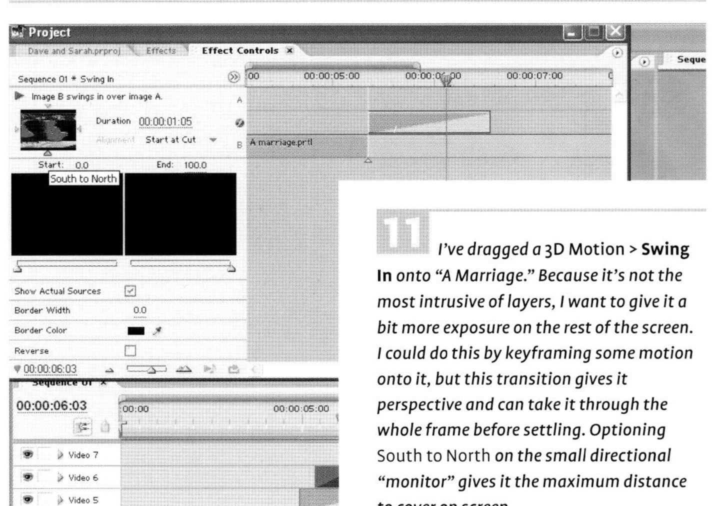

11 I've dragged a 3D Motion > **Swing In** onto "A Marriage." Because it's not the most intrusive of layers, I want to give it a bit more exposure on the rest of the screen. I could do this by keyframing some motion onto it, but this transition gives it perspective and can take it through the whole frame before settling. Optioning South to North on the small directional "monitor" gives it the maximum distance to cover on screen.

12 *I've found a point where the broken black line settles, and positioned the "A Marriage" title on it. Even though this is relevant for a frame, it makes the two movements marry together dynamically.*

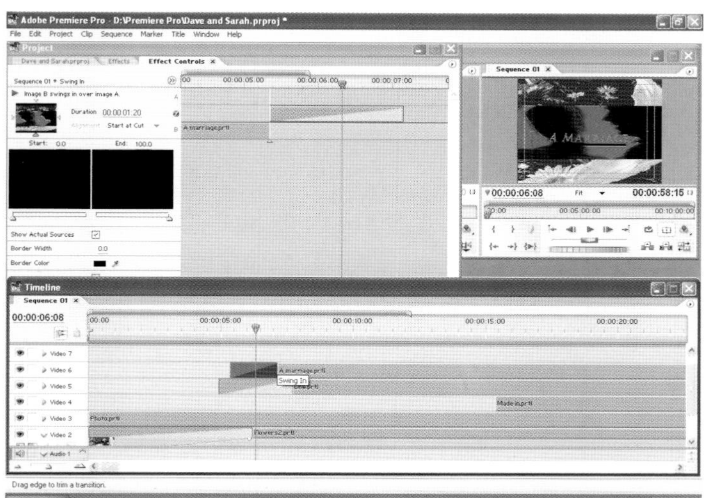

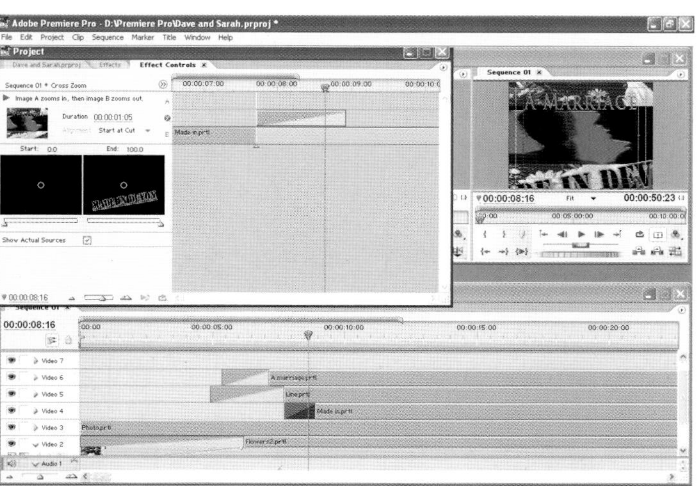

13 *...which just leaves the "Made in Devon" title. Because I've branded it as a rubberstamp, it's exactly that clichéd movement into frame that I want. This can be found as a Zoom >* **Cross Zoom**. *By default, the title comes into frame bottom right. It does the job, but it could look better.*

14 *Moving the start and end frame white circles in the ECW, will change the positioning of the zoom. Because the text is at an angle, I want to work on that same diagonal to bring the title in. Shifting the end positioning of the zoom onto the previewed source locates the perfect angle for the title to come in from the farthest point. As a rubberstamp effect, the transition needs to be reasonably abrupt.*

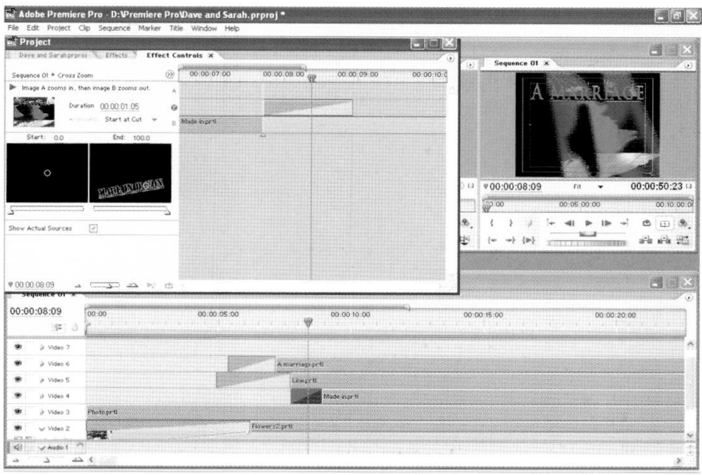

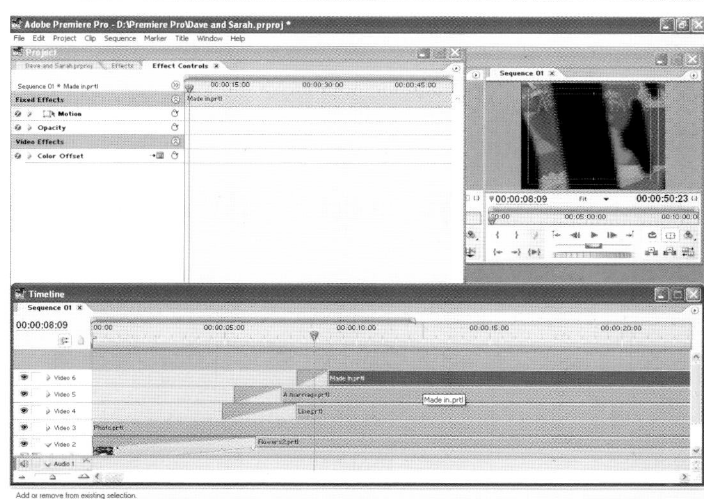

15 *Because the "Made in Devon" title comes in over the rest of the composition, there shouldn't be any point where any of the other layers are over the top of it. This isn't the case as this image shows: the 'A Marriage' on the highest Video Track is superimposing and stealing the show.*

Resolving this is simply a matter of taking the 'Made in Devon' title to the highest available track, and then right-clicking on the original track to delete it.

This title has gone as far as it can, for the moment...

Video effects: creating motion

It's not just transitions that can give a still title the kiss of life. Again, without even hitting the ***Motion*** keyframes, Premiere Pro's video effects can do the same job. Effects are one of those things that can just be thrown on for no reason, or with careful planning, can work with thematic harmony. With stills—glyphs or images without rolls, crawls, or motion control—some effects can create the illusion of movement by being keyframed over time.

The important thing to remember is that to move stills over time, only certain effects work—the keyframable ones. The other thing to remember is that the reason video effects can work so much better with titles than images is that alpha-based titles appear only as your hard-worked title and not as solid black ratio frames with hard edges. In effect, you can sometimes just get away with more with mattes.

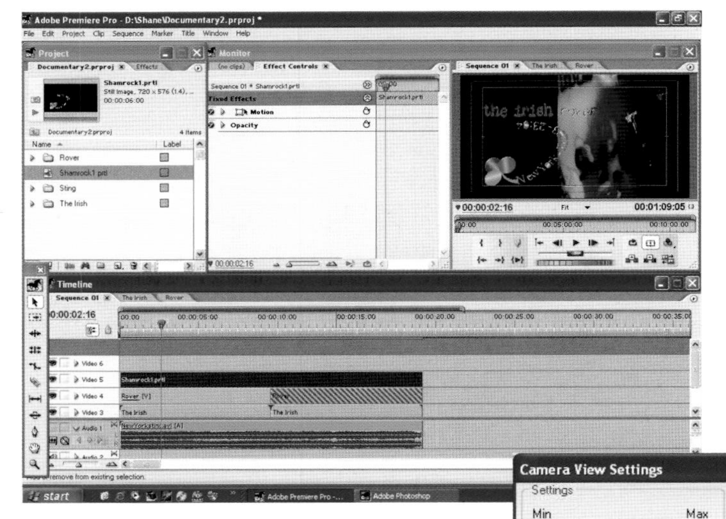

1 *This is the New York version of the documentary sting template. All three layers of the title ("the irish," "rover", and the location stem) are designed to be moving. At present, their only movement is the within-text animation of "the irish rover," and the animated reverse erase/erase transition of "rover" (see page 167 if you want to find out how to get this far).*

2 *To start with "the irish," not only does it need a transition to get it on alongside the "rover," but they both need some distressing motion on screen. The transition first: taking a* Video Effect > Transform > **Camera View** *to the clip allows the entire frame to be manipulated under the guise of it being "reshot" at a different perspective and camera setting. It's a bit of a Band Aid solution, but it's got an all-in-one versatility that's useful. An effect turned into a transition is a reasonable use of creativity.*

Camera View Settings
Settings
Min
Max
Longitude 0
Latitude 0
Roll 0
Focal Length 500
Distance 1
Zoom 1.00
Sample
Fill
Color
Fill Alpha Channel
Reset
OK
Cancel

3 *Starting with the default settings, this is where the image should be placed after having hit the screen. Not knowing exactly the length of the transition to get there, keyframes are placed at the center of the first animated clip with these values before adding any more.*

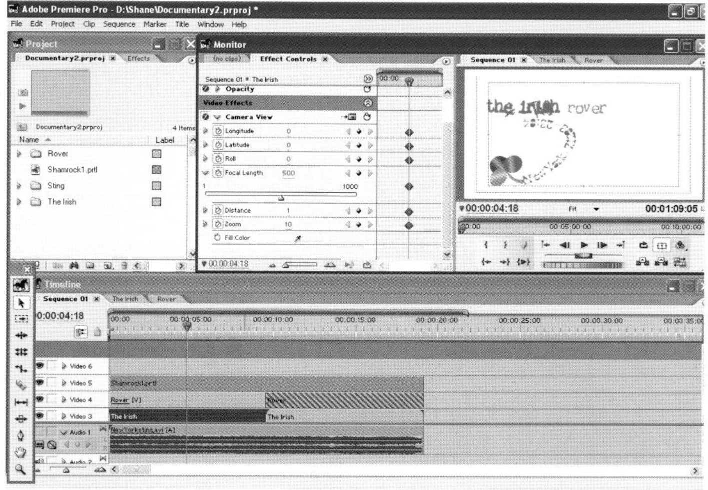

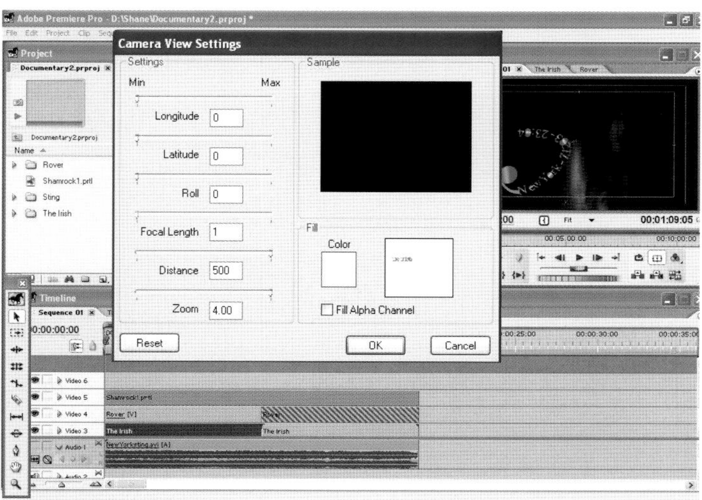

4 *Working with the controls, it's apparent that—like all the X/Y/Z controlling systems—the whole frame is being used. Diminishing or moving the clip in this case would affect a standard solid image (hence the option to* Fill Alpha Channel*). Because the text is already a matte, there is no chance of the edges showing: A Good Thing.*

5 *The settings diminish the text to a nothing onscreen. The default settings mean that the image will get larger and larger until hitting these settings. Because the first clip is half of the overall timing of the title onscreen, this equates to a quarter of the way through the title.*

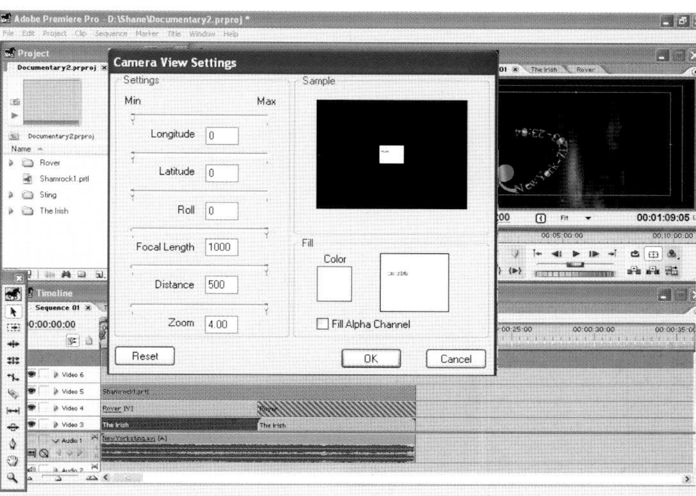

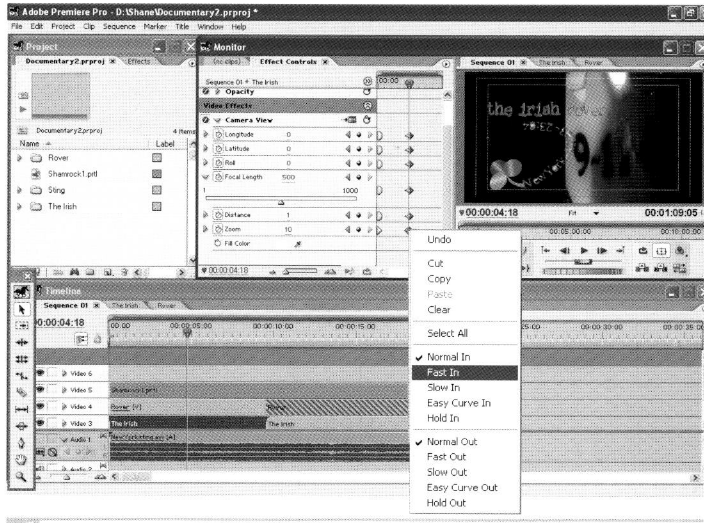

6 *Changing all the default keyframes to* Fast In*, slightly accelerates the speed of the move in.*

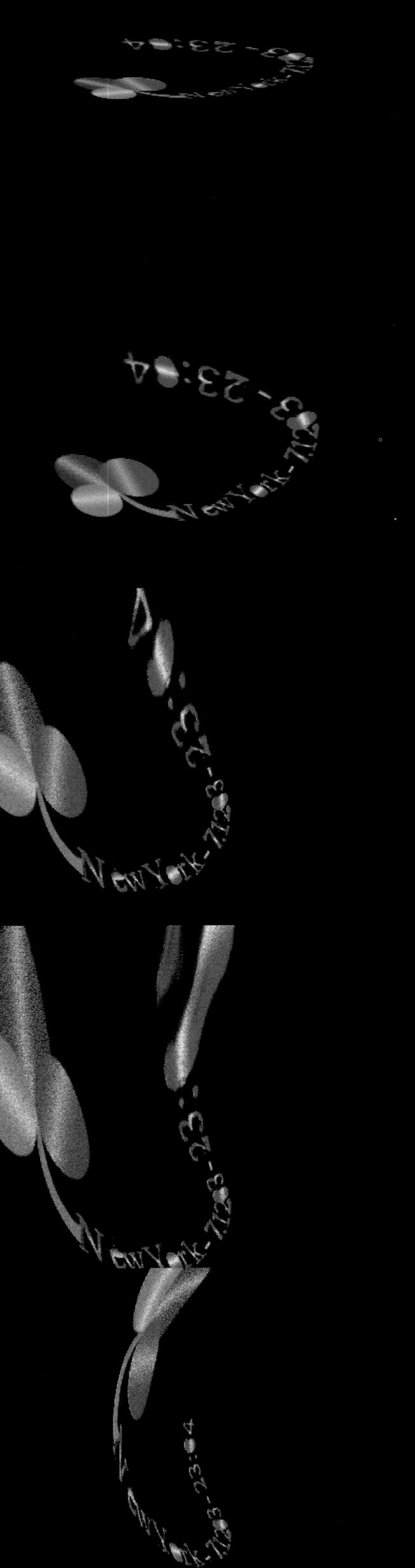

7 Right-clicking on the effect, to Copy and Paste the same values to the second clip, is the next stage. Of course, this means that the second clip starts from nothing again and then zooms in. I want the opposite of this, to create the transition without reversing the already deliberately reversed clip.

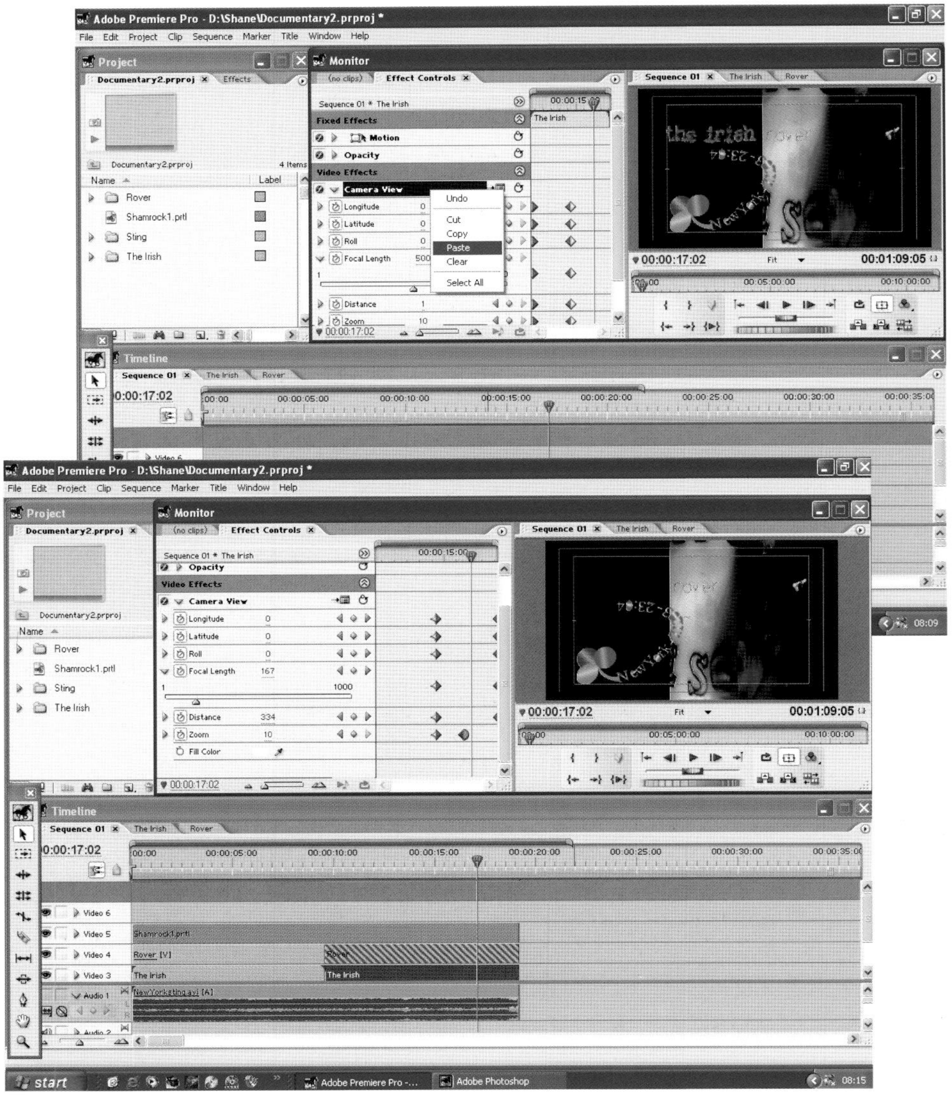

8 And the way to do this is to just drag each of the first (default) keyframes to the end of the clip. The effect is then complete as a move, with the transition occupying the first quarter and last quarter of the entire clip.

9 *Next up: sending the entire three-word title on a merry Irish jig with some video effects trickery. Actually, it's a more jittery effect that I'm looking for to accompany the animation. To do this, it's less tiresome simply to wrap up the whole title as a new and separate sequence.*

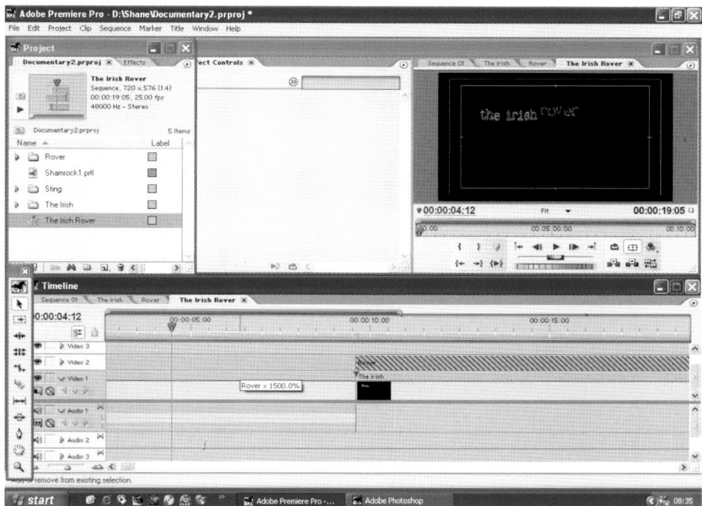

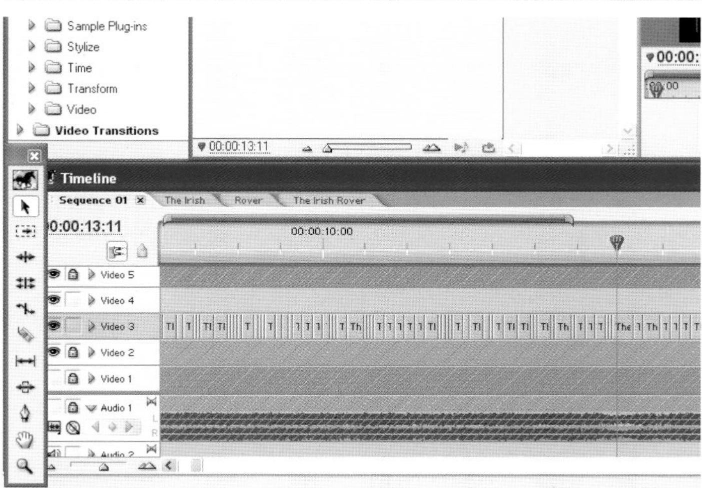

10 *With this in place on the original* Timeline, *it's time to get the razor out. The least painless way of razoring up a clip every one, two or three frames is to zoom into the* Timeline *and work to a right arrow key/CTRL K (razor at* Edit Line*) rhythm. This is done non-uniformly so that each clip is either one, two, three, and sometimes four frames long. The other tracks have been locked to preserve them.*

11 *Selecting a clip at the center of the sequence where both parts of the title are in vision, I've dragged a* Distort > **Corner Pin** *effect to it. The Y values I've put in are such that the title starts at default, shifts slightly downward quickly, and then farther upward less sharply.*

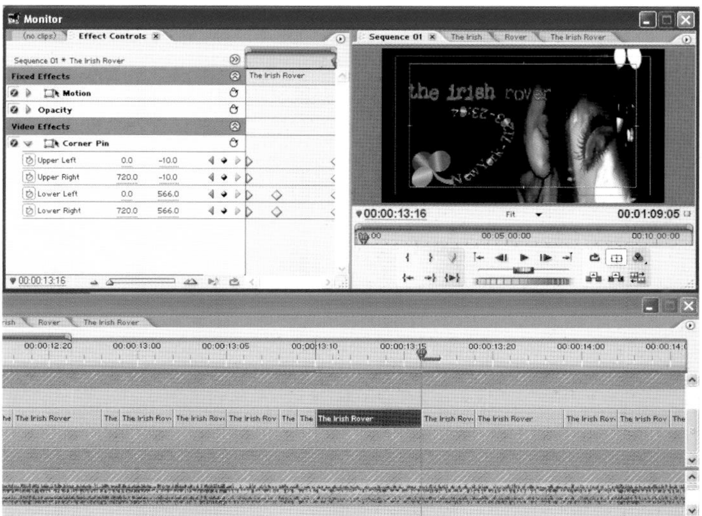

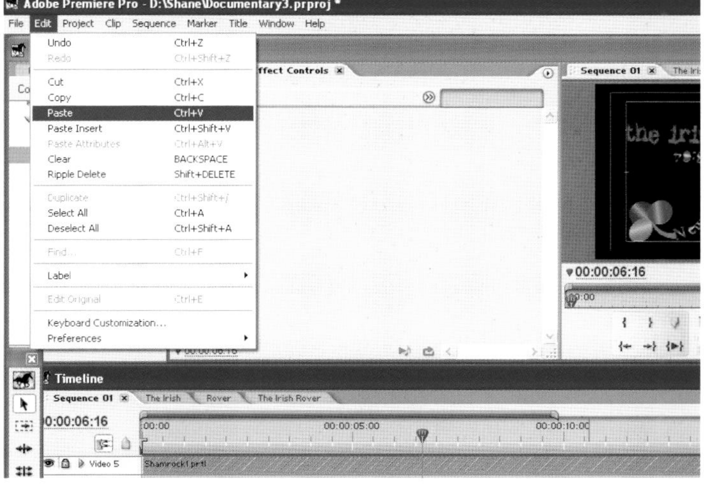

12 *This effect now needs to be applied to all the razored clips to create the frame-jitter effect. Because the end keyframe is not the default value and the next clip's start value is, there's another jitter added by default. To apply it to the whole track, right-click to* Copy *the effect from the selected clip, then* Select All *and* Paste *from the file menu or with shortcuts—again, making sure that any other tracks are locked. Saving this off as a new sequence is a good idea.*

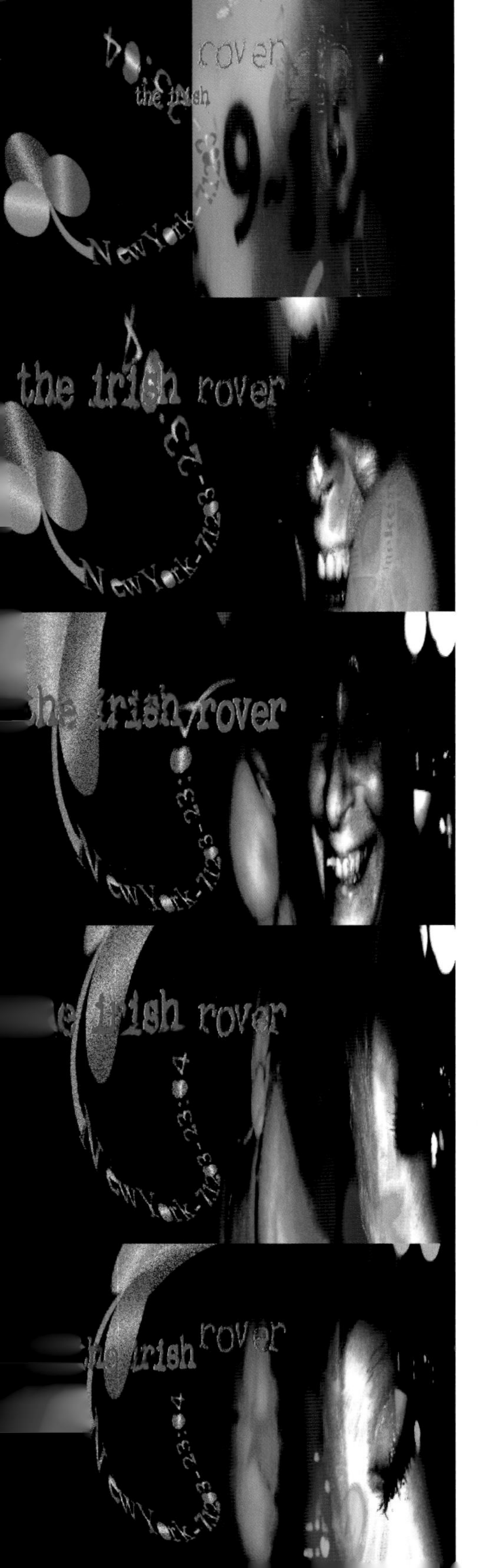

13 Next, the tackling of the shamrock title. Unlocking it and then dragging a Distort > Polar Coordinates effect over will do it some real favors. Polar coordinates re-arrange the pixels from Cartesian (X and Y from 0,0) to Polar (depth and magnitude from the absolute center pixel)—or the other way around. The setup for the effect interprets this as either Rectangular to Polar or Polar to Rectangular. Selecting the former, the curve of the shamrock and stem is allocated depth and the Interpolation value allocates magnitude.

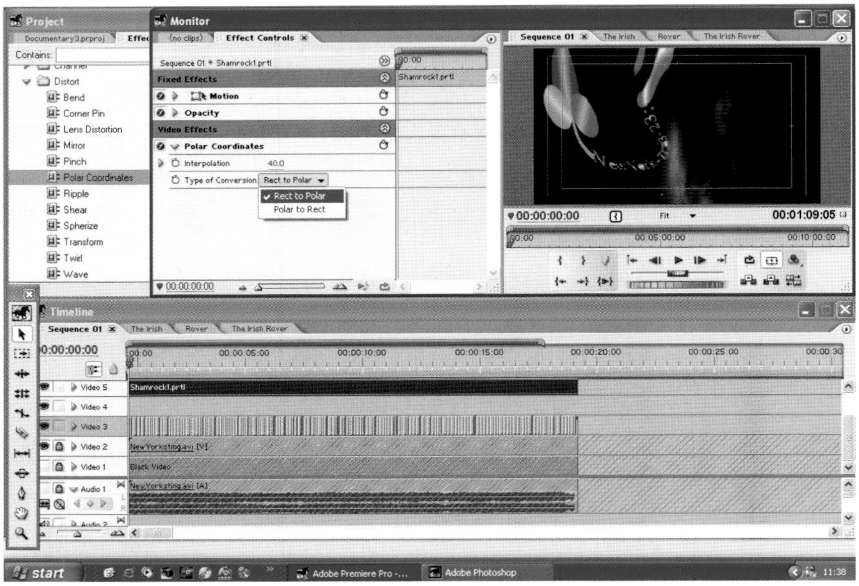

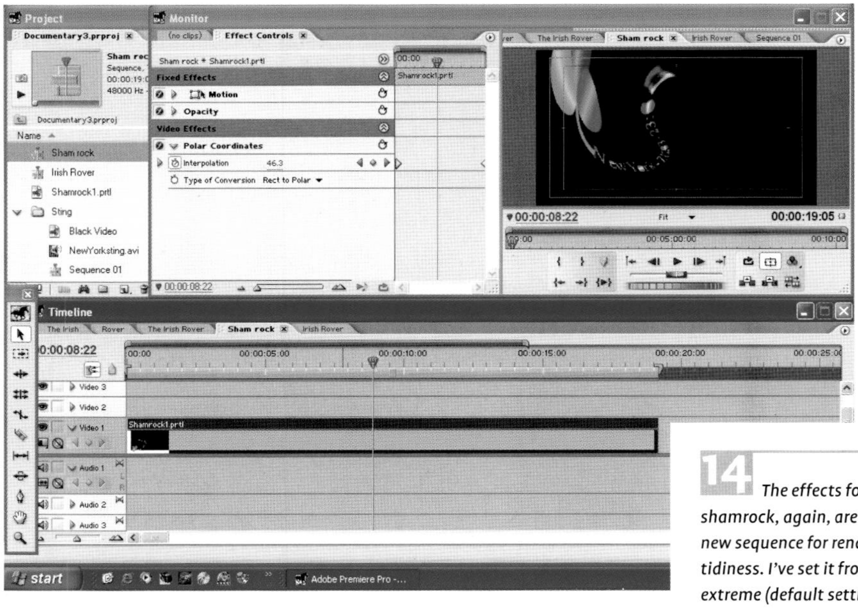

14 The effects for the shamrock, again, are set up as new sequence for render and tidiness. I've set it from one extreme (default settings) to another, which takes it via the middle apex of distance.

15 *What the* Polar Coordinates *effect doesn't do is give the shamrock any transition onto the screen—something that it seems to need with the flow that it now has. Taking a* Basic 3D *effect from the* Perspective *set to the sequence permits manipulation on X, Y, and Z. This means that while the glyph has moving* Polar Coordinates, *it can be made to move around the frame at the same time.*

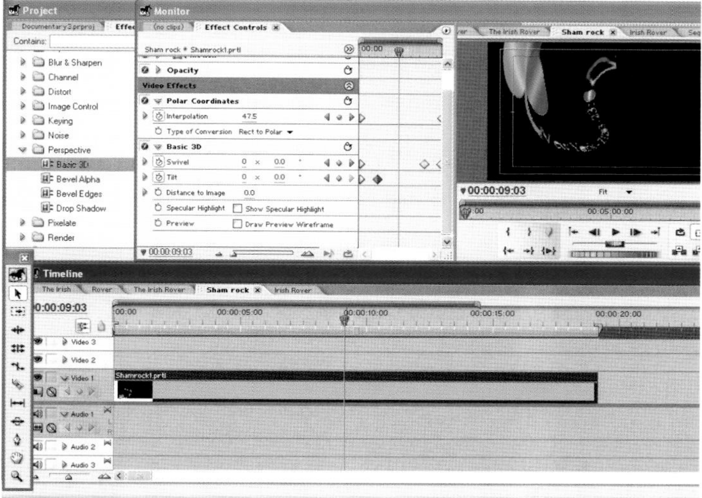

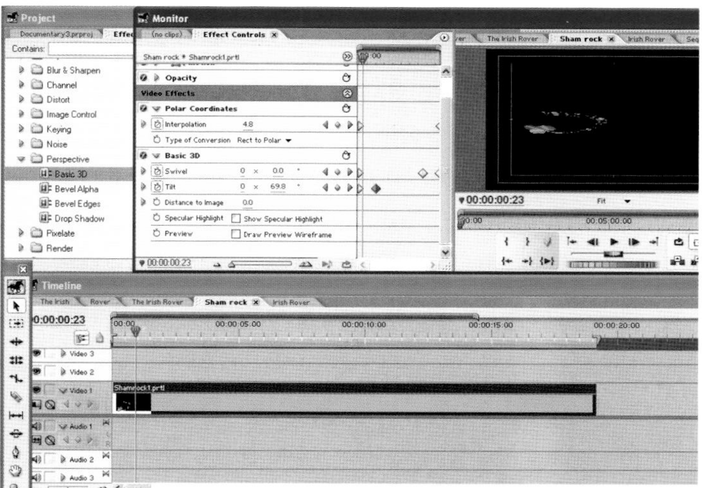

16 *To effect an actual transition out of this, the X and Y co-ordinates for the moving glyph could be inputted so that the start and end keyframes take the image off-screen and move toward the center. Because the effect offers a Z axis, though, I've input values that give the start keyframe 90° on the* Tilt *(horizontal) and 90° keyframe end on the* Swivel *(vertical). An angle of 90° means that the glyph's pixels are given the effect of being perpendicular to the viewer—i.e. as a two-dimension image with no edge thickness, they are effectively invisible.*

17 *With the finished shamrock on the* Timeline, *the one thing left to do is to swap the title tracks to let "the irish" settle and relax on the shamrock bed.*

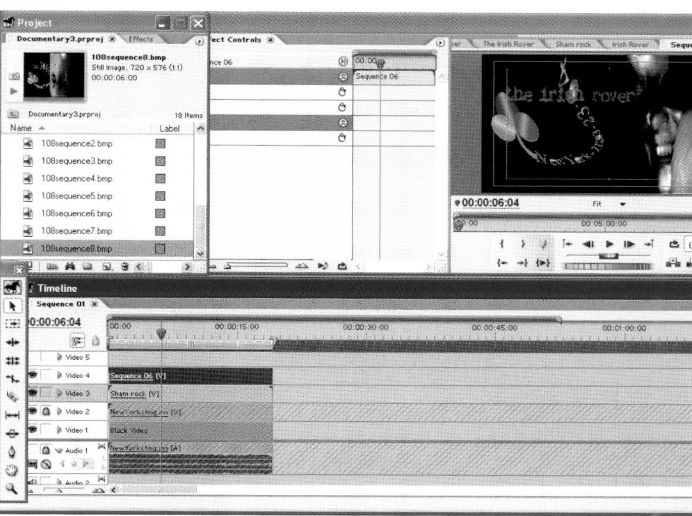

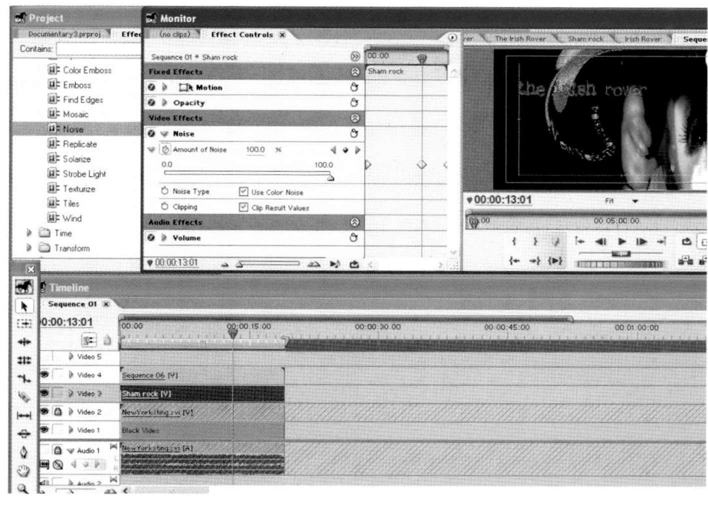

18 *The graphic, though, is still a little too clean for the video—but on the other hand, it can't be too dirty or it'll lose legibility. Taking some* Noise *over onto the clip is going to help, but to up the interest value, and in association with the swell of audio that is going to be applied, the* Noise *is keyframed to grow to the apex of the* Polar Coordinates, *and then die away to the glyph's disappearance from frame.*

Keying layers

A title created in *Title Designer* is blessed with an alpha matte. Once the title is on the *Timeline*, this mask sits between the foreground and the background and offers an 8-bit alpha channel. The translation of this is that there are 256 different levels between white and black—black being read as transparent—which can be applied to each pixel of the image. These values are separate from those of the RGB that forms the video image in Premiere Pro.

When you're working with your alpha channel, then, you're working with those 256 levels and applying them to the image. You're dictating what can be seen between foreground and background. The different keys available are the method (i.e. algorithm) by which the key is applied to the image. These keys are either RGB-based or alpha-based.

1 *The way that this alpha channel is best displayed as a sandwiching mask is through the application of an* Alpha Adjust *from the* Keying *menu. Using the slider, what is termed* Opacity *is really the values between 1 and 256 turned into percentages: 0% is essentially 100% white alpha.*

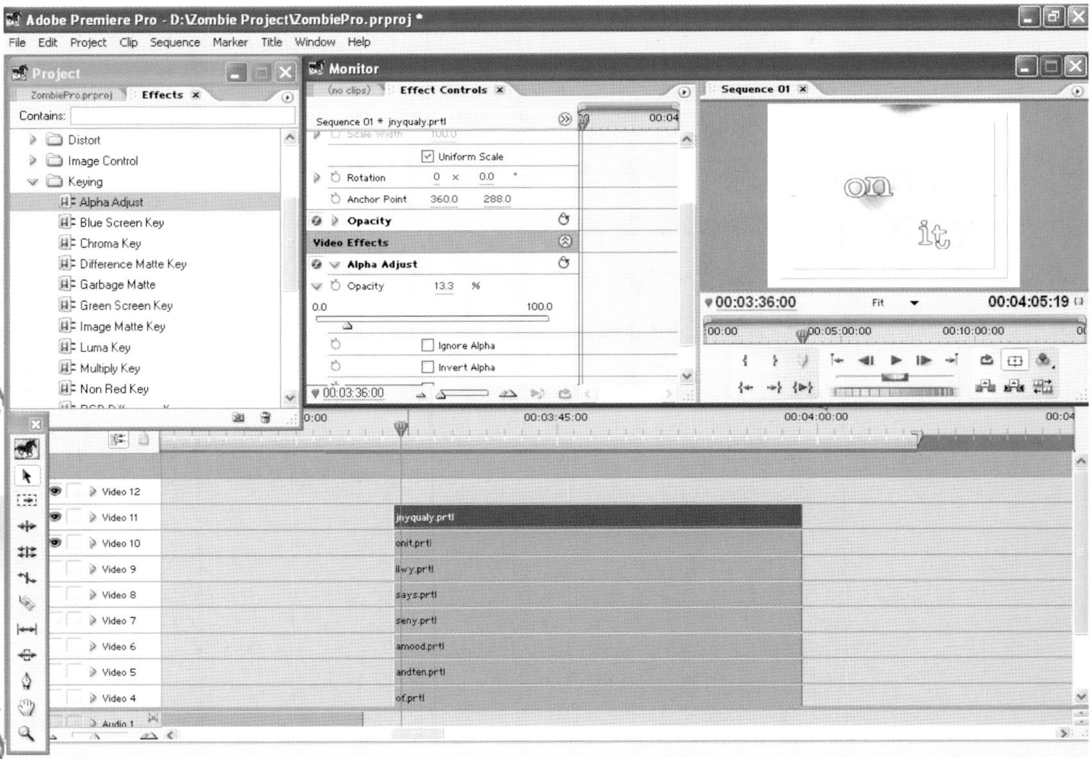

2 *When a particular key is being used, the alpha adjustment is termed* Threshold. *This, again by percentage, is the amount of black alpha channel that is being applied—and conversely to* Alpha Adjust, *the higher the percentage, the less black values in the mask.*

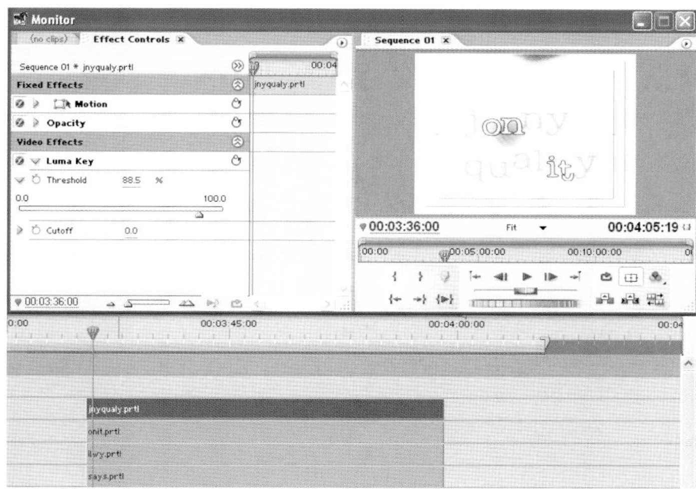

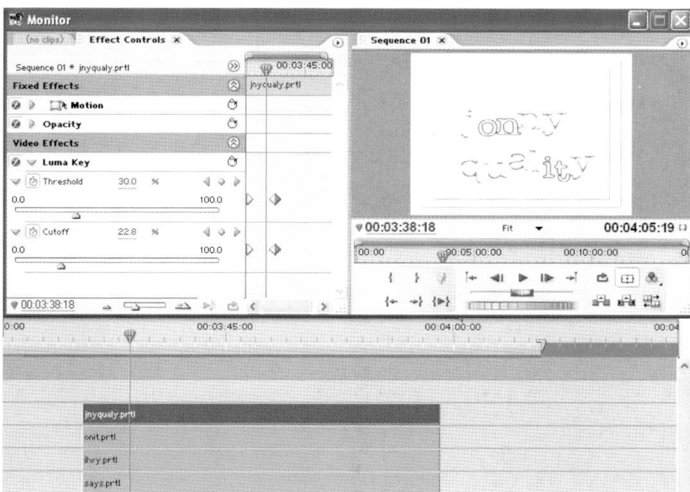

4 *These closing titles are made up of ten layers. Each one of the five complete title screens is formed of two layers each—and all will be required to mix on at different intervals and interact with each other at different times. Because of the predominantly bleached white background that I've put in, I'm using a* Luma Key *to bring on the first layer of the first title. This tears at the* Lit *parts of the title to bring it onscreen in a way that a transition or* Opacity *adjustment couldn't.*

3 *Once a* Threshold *has been set, the* Cutoff *slider operates the amount of opacity set by the threshold. Because both values are keyframable, it enables more interesting (sometimes attractive, sometimes not) transitions of titles—i.e. manifestation and disappearance.*

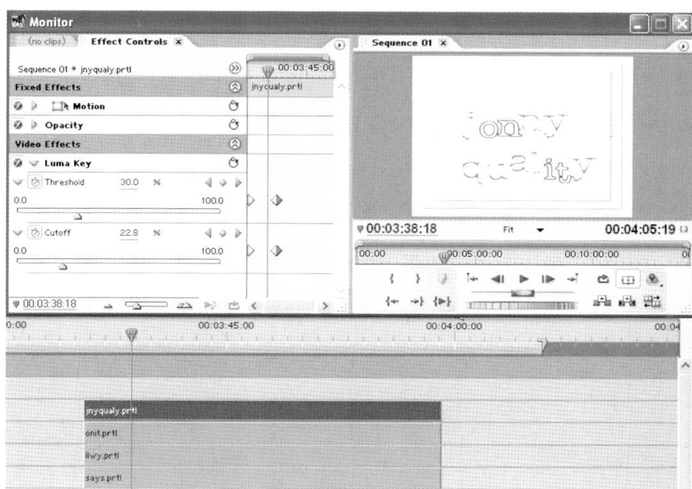

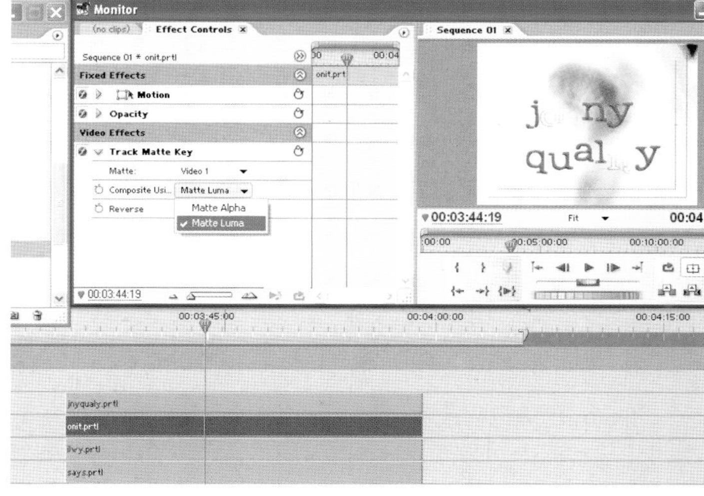

5 *To the second layer of the title, I've added a* Track Matte *to matte to the background track. Because the background image drifts in and out of screen through the bleached white, turning the composite to a* Matte Luma *causes the black stroked white text to drift in and out of vision with the moving image.*

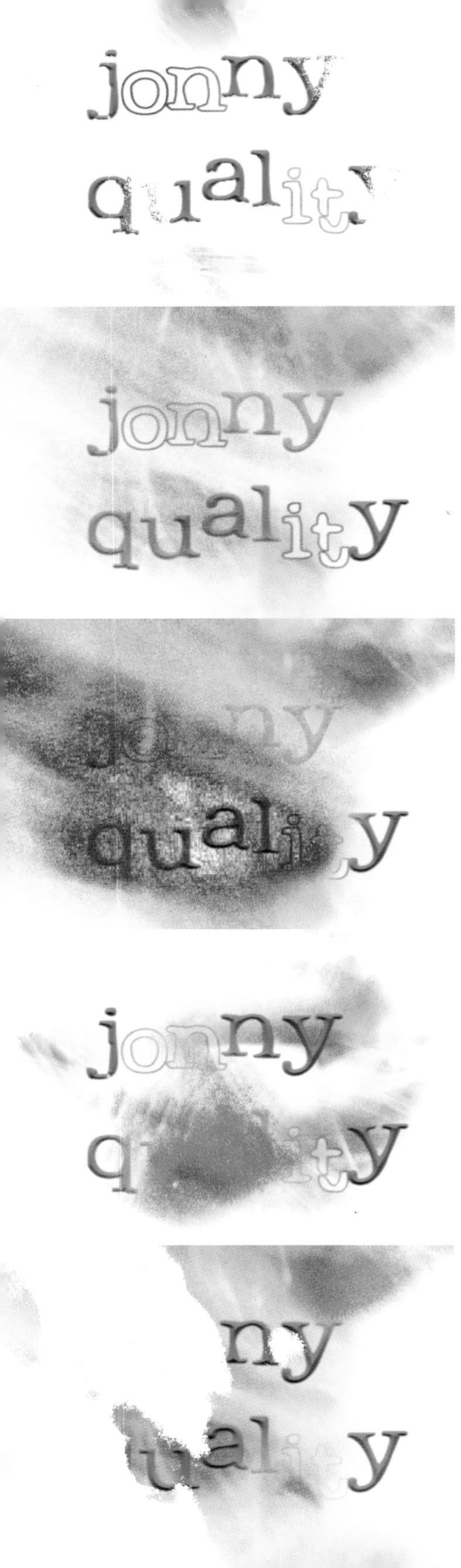

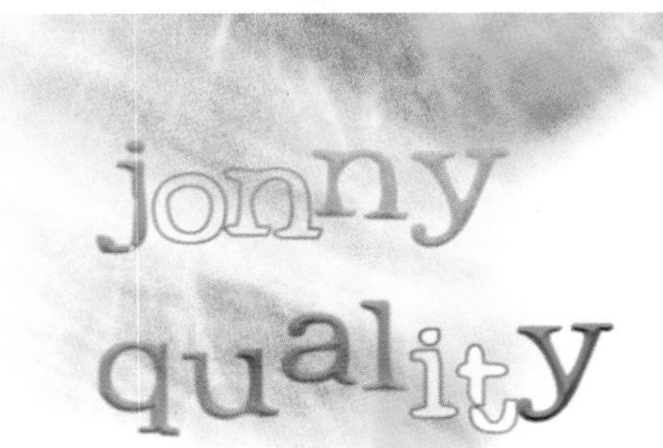

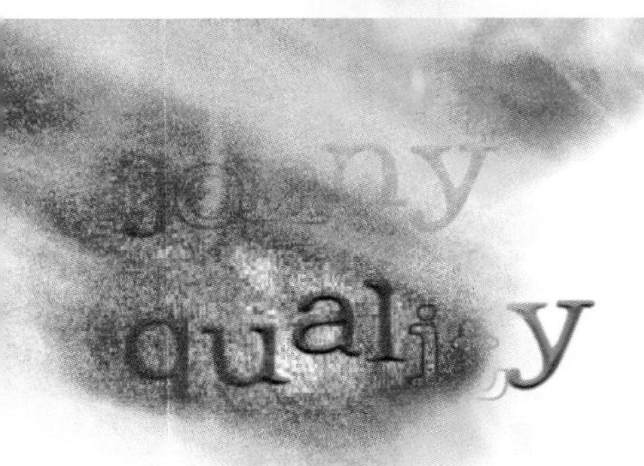

6 *The effect that this will provide once the titles start to move is that I can place the text where their entry and exit onto the screen will be a natural part of the track matte's effect. Even where they are at the moment offers this frame, in which all four letters disappear completely.*

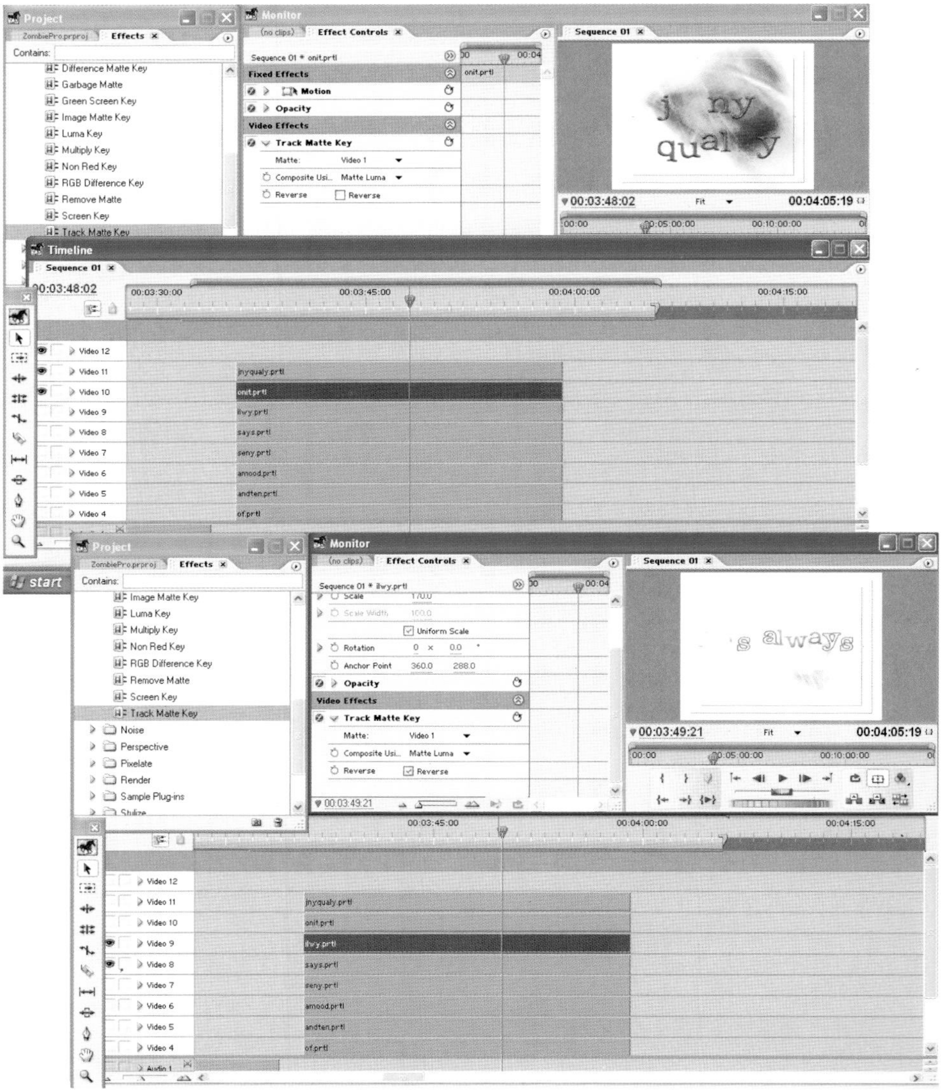

7 *I'm adding the* Track Matte *to every other layer in exactly the same way. For every alternate layer, though, I've checked the* Reverse *box so that any that overlap once transitions and movement are in place, are treated in the opposite fashion by the* Luma*: high* Opacity *becomes low transparency, and vice versa.*

8 *Once this is done, the creative bit happens. There's (by design) a huge amount of bleached white space onscreen. Copying and pasting the background clip above all of the completed titles is obviously going to obscure the entire sequence. This can be fixed with a key. That, however, is only going to create another version of the original background, so what I'll do is turn the background around by right-clicking, choosing* Speed/Duration, *and checking the* Reverse Speed *box to give another layer—roughly along the same lines when it comes to content—but with manifestation at different times.*

There's a certain amount of serendipity to this title. I'm aiming to create relationships between each couple of title screens with movement, and the visibility of the title depends entirely on where the text moves in front of the background, and behind the background in reverse. Movement, then, is paramount to the success of the sequence.

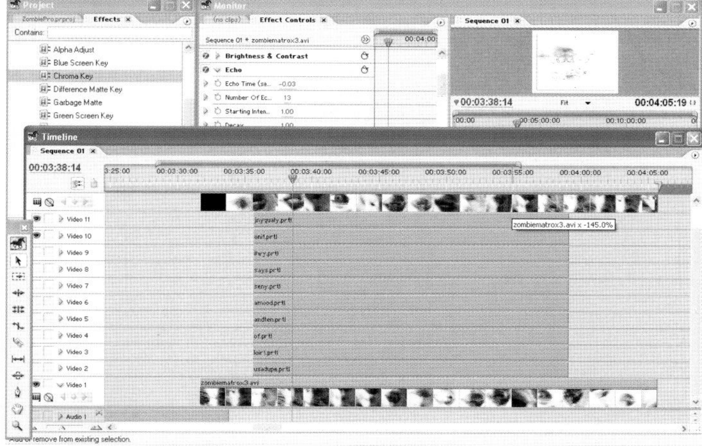

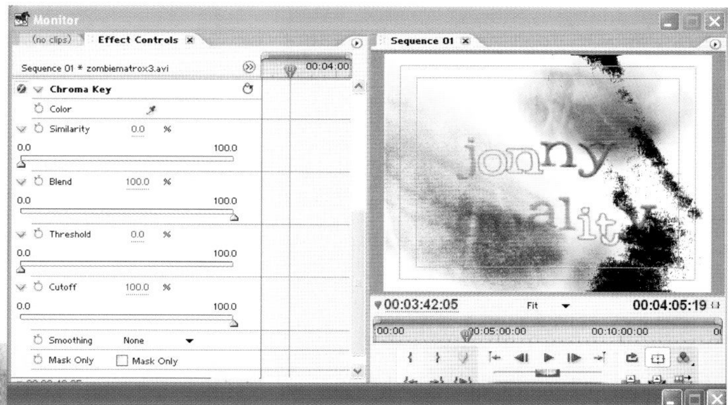

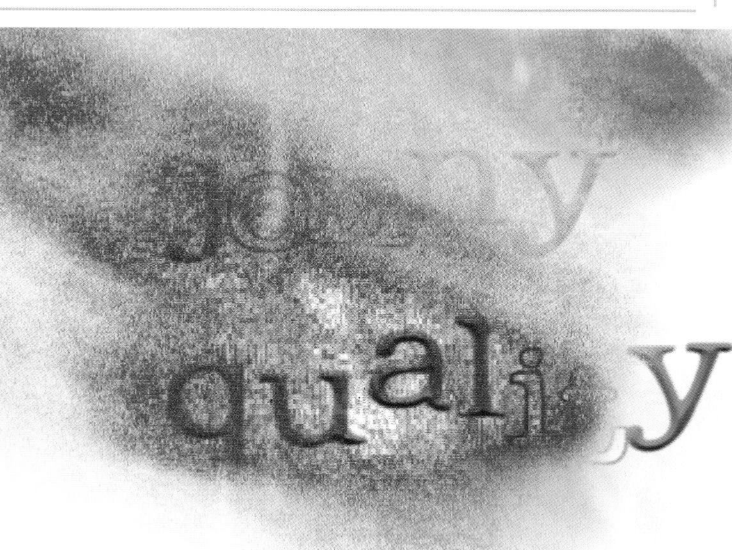

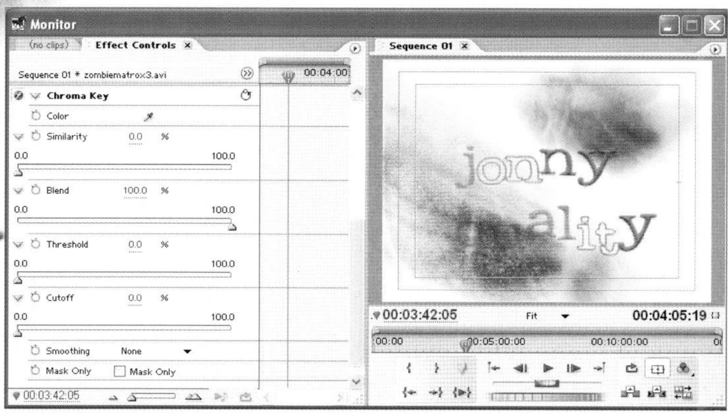

9 *Because of the dominant areas of bleached-out white, I've added a* Chroma Key *to the clip and keyed it white. The new reversed background tears into the text based on a low* Cutoff *percentage, which makes all the difference between the key being read too much (above right) at 100%, or too little (below right). Choosing* No Smoothing *keeps the edges sharp and brittle, creating a more painted look to the transitional text.*

Revising your title

It's easy to lose sight of the bigger picture when you're simply designing in *Title Designer*, but once your work is on the *Timeline* a host of other questions begins: is it working in itself? Is it working with the production? Once on the *Timeline*, a title becomes a different thing altogether.

Revising a title is something that is breakfast, lunch, and dinner for the title designer at their desktop. Double-clicking on *Timeline* titles to get back into *Title Designer* and make fine adjustments is a sign of someone who knows what they're doing, rather than doesn't.

More importantly, taking the short time to Export a contentious Frame, or the entire sequence in the *Timeline* for more complex motion-based titles, is a sure way to identify problem areas in full-frame playback.

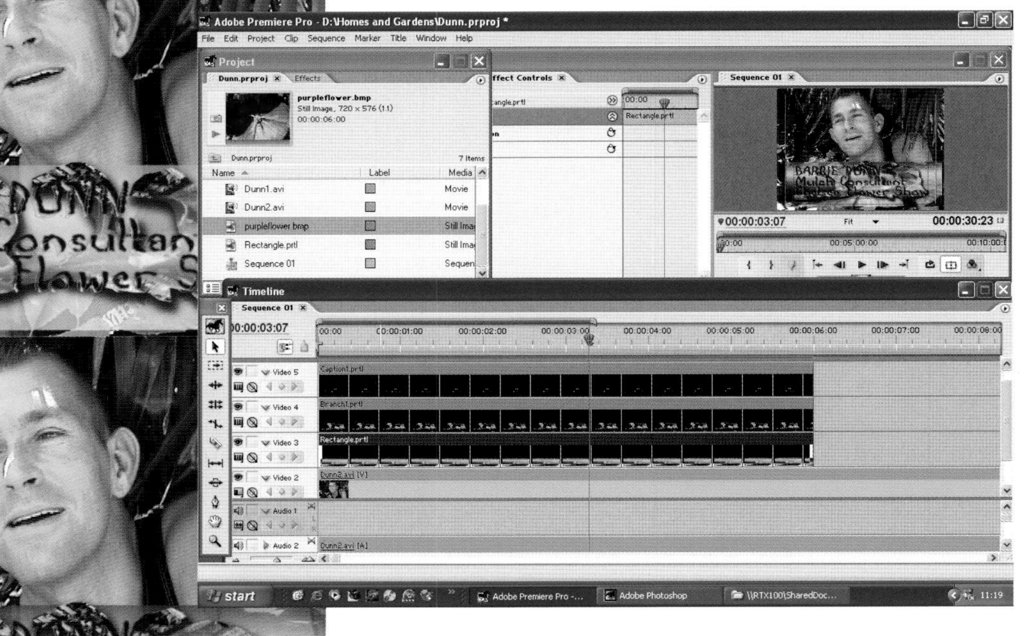

The first and most obvious of the example titles so far that isn't working yet is the gardening promo. Because of the color samples taken from the background in an effort to complement the images, they've actually merged into the background. If captions are supposed to be legible, this is hardly a success story.

1 *Perhaps the secret to revising a title for legibility is not what to add to the title to make it legible, but what to take away. A harsher, more objective source might advise simplifying the font, eliminating the branch, and so on. This is too easy a solution. Working with the ideas that are present is better practice for a professional career.*

2 *Analyzing the three layers involved in this busy caption, it's the branch and the flower-textured rectangle that are too strong for it. Starting with the most dominant part of the title, the rectangle is a large lower-third to accommodate the three-line caption. It's fundamentally instrusive and hides the interviewee. Taking the* Opacity *level down is going to let him reclaim the screen.*

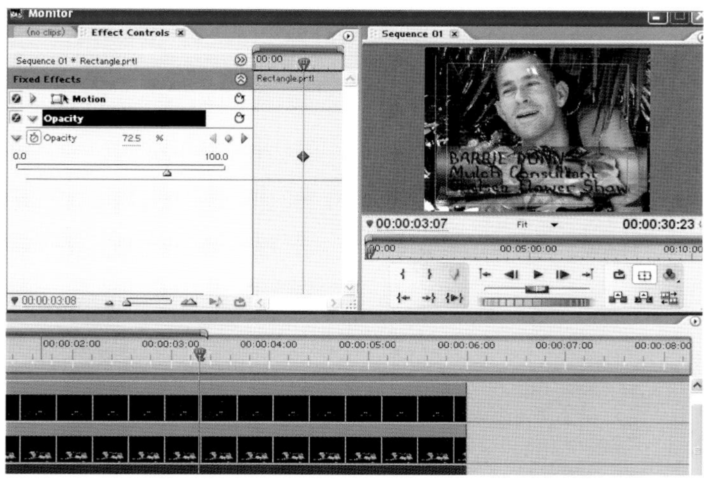

3 *Because of the* Sheen *offset of the rectangle, the reduced* Opacity *has now darkened the area behind the word "Chelsea," and I'm losing it. Taking across the* Levels *effect (*Video Effects > Adjust > **Levels***), I can lighten the entire rectangle by changing the* Black Output Level *for the chroma as a whole (RGB).*

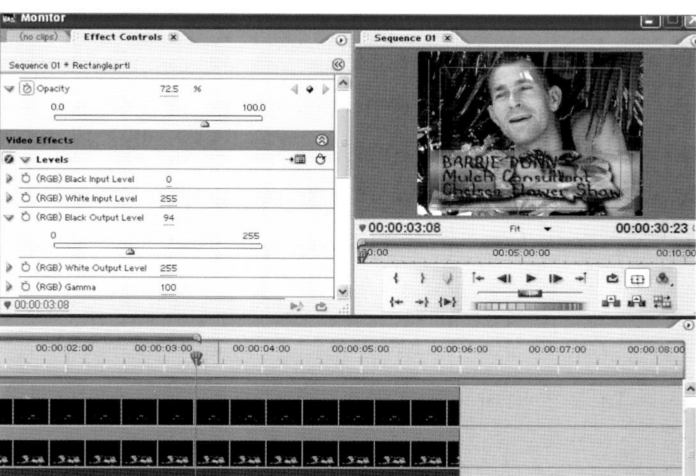

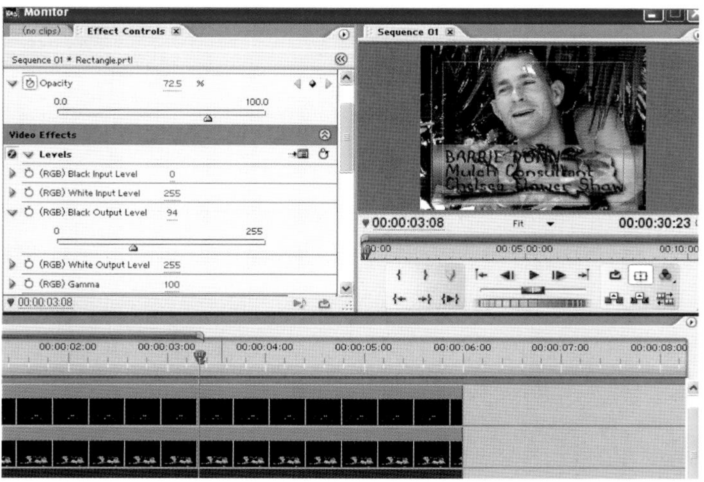

4 *This has effectively washed out the color. Rectifying this is in the same* Levels *options. Because the purple is predominantly a blue hue with a red shade, raising the gamma of the blue channel (B)—i.e. the midtones of the blue—lifts the entire washed-out area. Repearing the process with the red channel(R), to a lesser extent, puts the purple firmly back where it belongs.*

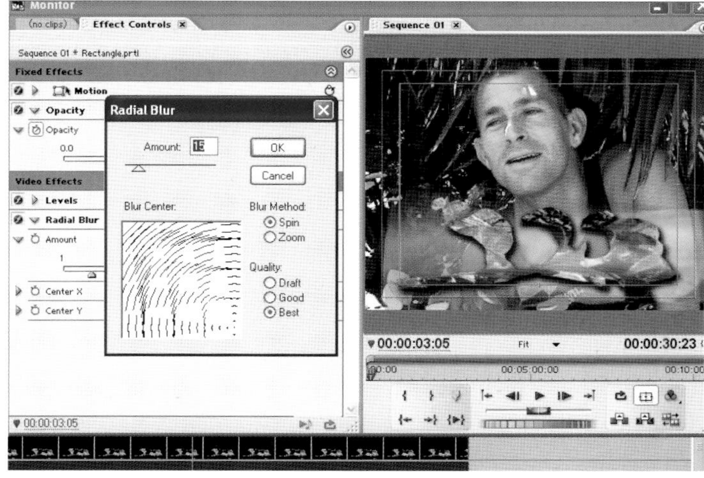

5 *The hard edge to the top line of the strap is maybe just a little too harsh—and a bit uniform. By bringing a* Radial Blur *from the* Video Effects > Blur and Sharpen *menu over onto the clip and then centralizing the focus at the sharper right-hand side of the flower, the harshness is muted and the stronger parts of the flower become the borders to the bezier. With this effect, of course, detail is lost. As a background, it's perfect: significant without being pushy.*

6 *Likewise, the saturation in the branch needs some calming down. The issue with the branch is that the variant shades of green interfere with the text. What I anticipate doing this time is to mute the colors without losing the detail that defines the branch as a branch. The* Convolution Kernel, *found under the* Video Effects > Adjust *menu, should help.*

7 *While the drop-down menu from the effect looks scary, the setup isn't...much. The* Convolution Matrix *contains nine values that each represent the values within each pixel. By default, these have values that represent brightness at the center (2), half brightness north, south, east, and west, and no added brightness on the diagonals. These default values are those of a blur—and using the arrowed drop-down menu to the side shows the effects of other blurs and embosses. The changing values in the grid give some idea of how both the Premiere Pro and Photoshop process blurs and embosses.*

8 *A Light Emboss gives values that serve to pick out brightness values to the top left (minus, shadow) and bottom right pixels (plus, highlight), which gives the image a slightly three-dimensional look.*

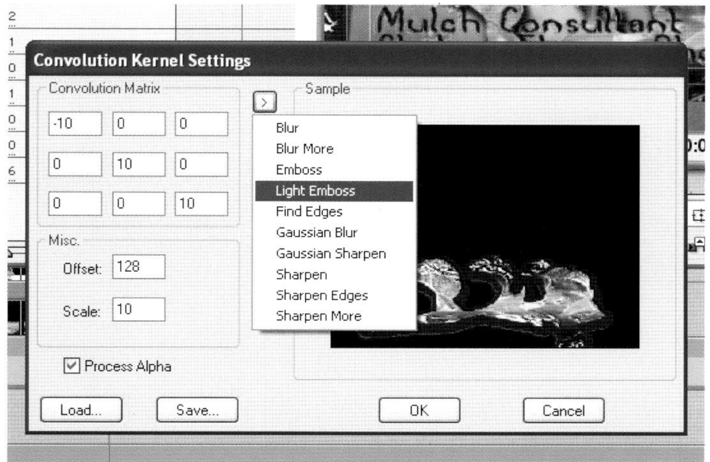

9 *Reversing these values (-10 becomes 10; 10 becomes −10) shifts the forced illumination 180°, and helps the juxtaposition with the surname. Adding another brightness value to the top left (10 becomes 11) in the drop-down menu helps it even more.*

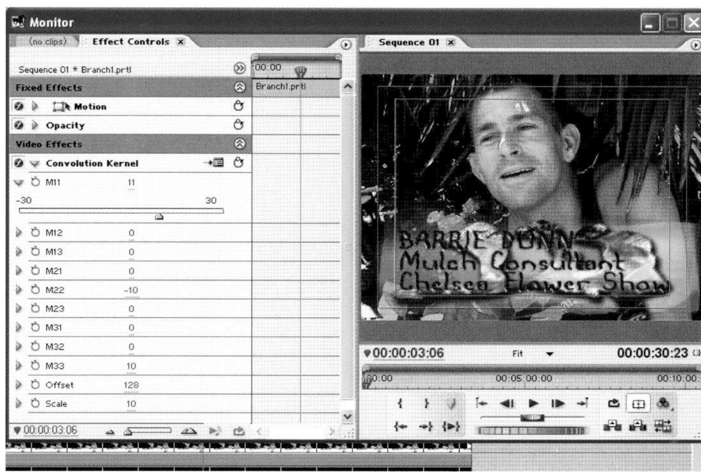

10 *Finally, to clean up the caption a little, I've dragged a Levels effect (Video Effects > Adjust >* **Levels***) onto the text clip. The business of the green midtones here can be mitigated with a decrease of the green gamma output. An effect like Sharpen might seem the right idea, but it actually renders every pixel with brightness and exaggerates difference. Decreasing the gamma lowers the brightness of this unnecessary detail and darkens the mid-greens to appear a lot cleaner against the branch and the flower.*

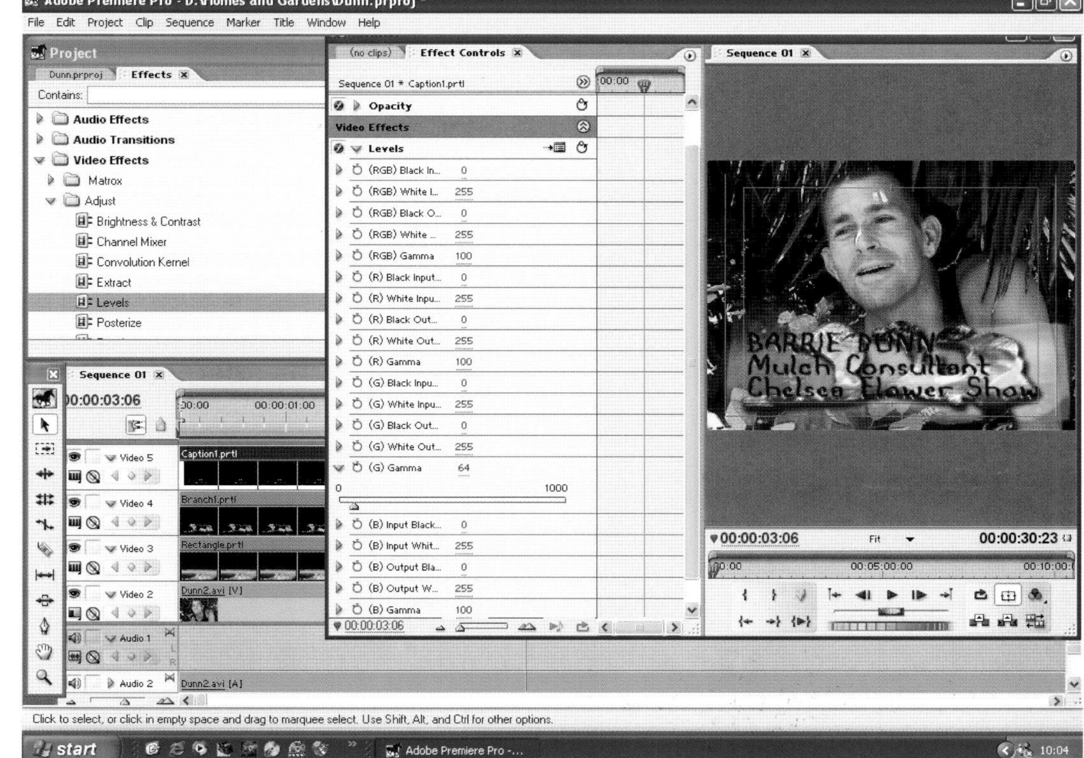

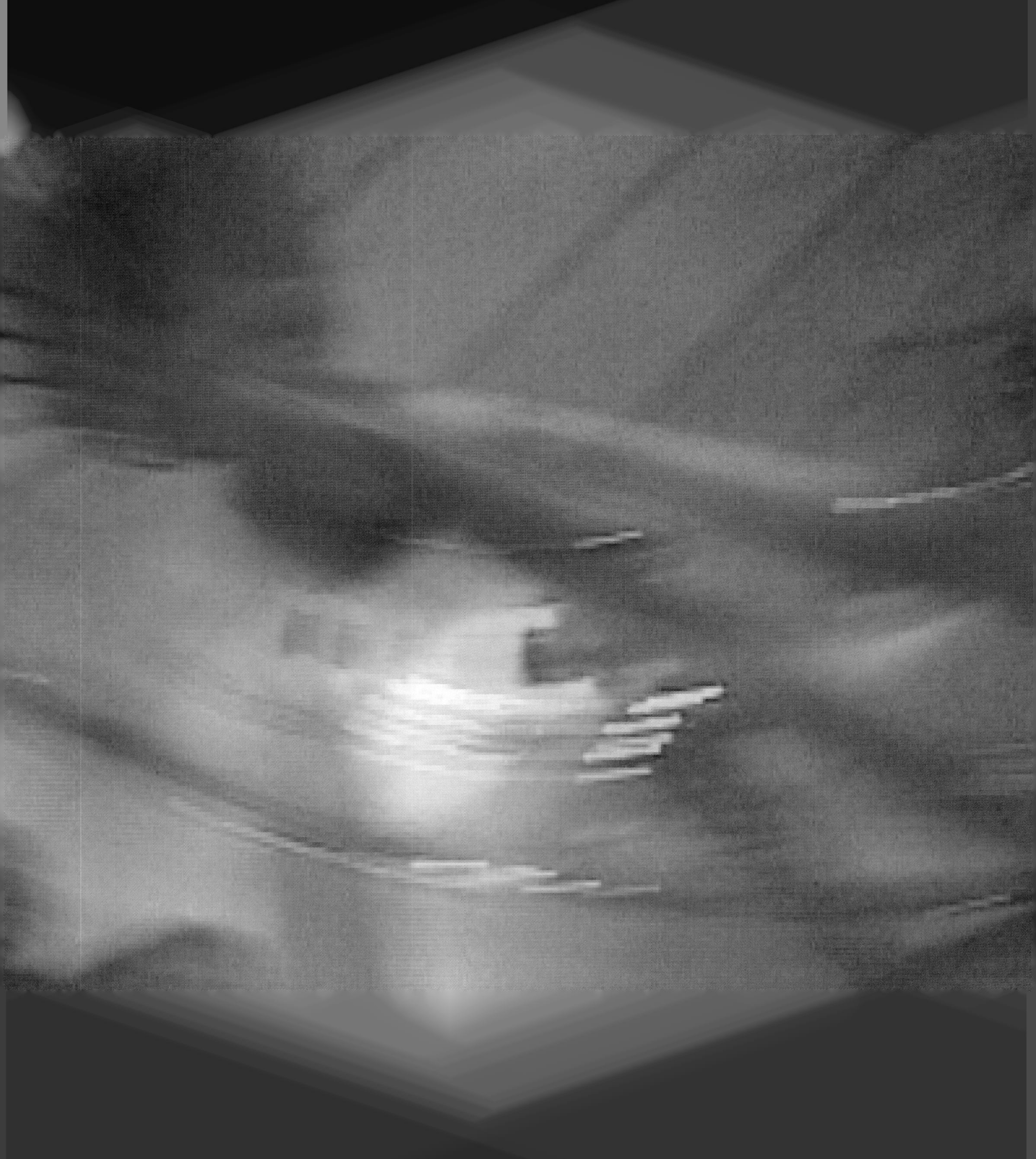

CHAPTER FOUR

titles in motion

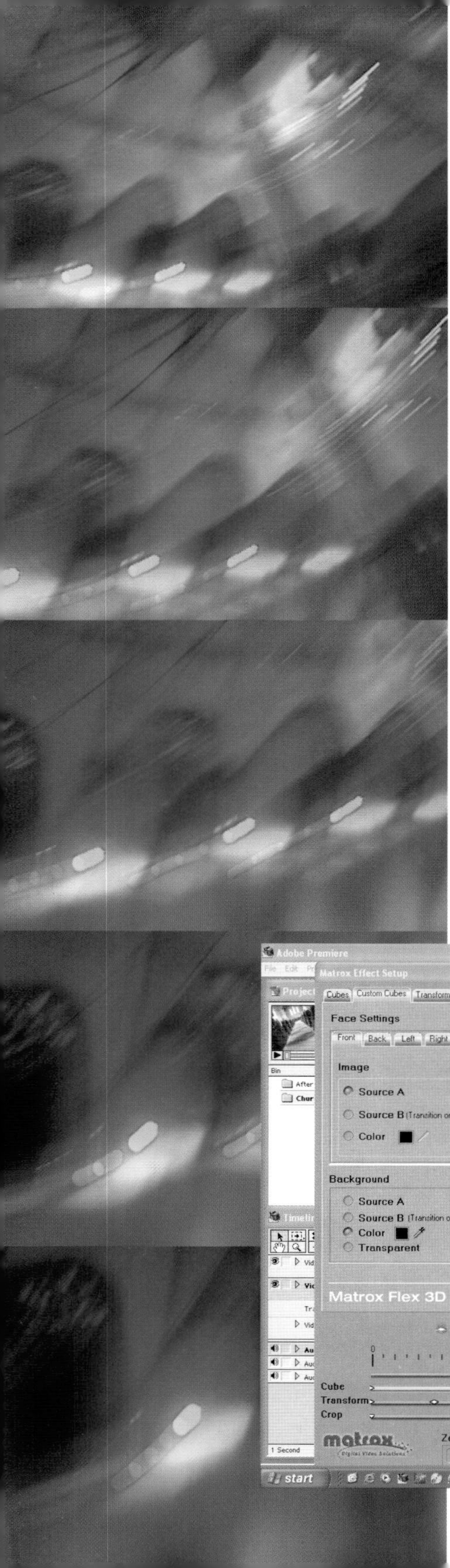

Defining motion

Keyframes in the Effects Control window come into their own when dealing with motion. It's important to define motion with your titles, as they can operate with slightly more versatility than just a simple video clip.

A video clip is not alpha-based. As non-affected/effected digital imagery, it fills the frame at a ratio predetermined in camera. Therefore, any motion applied to the clip will move the entire frame.

Transitions and effects are applied to the events within this frame. Motion, though, is applied not to these events, but to the frame itself. In order to make this relative—i.e. to be able to see the motion—the frame itself has to be relative to something. That something, although looking like nothing, is the composite default (non-true) black video signal.

The default black signal will always be present whenever motion application to the video frame is specified. DVEs set outside a video clip's parameters (say, a simple A to B slide) will use this black on whichever necessary side of the

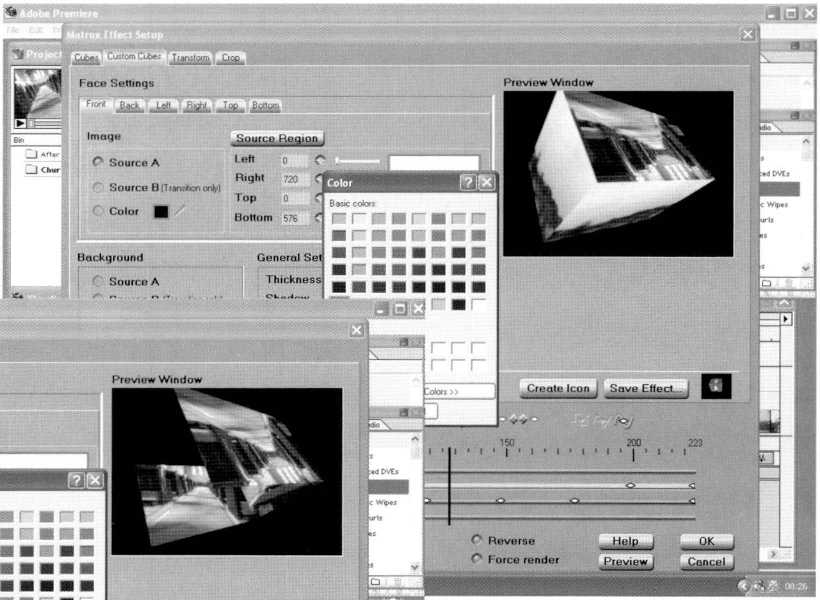

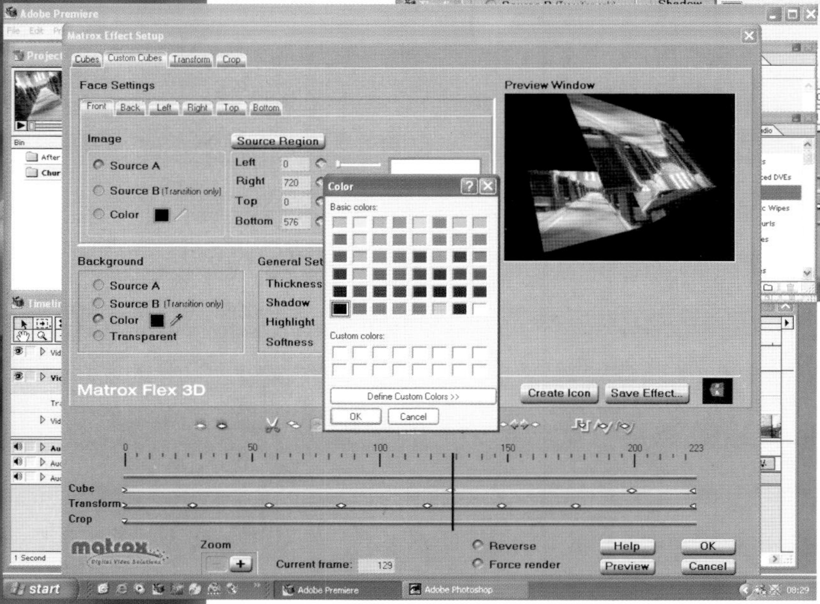

ABOVE: *Premiere Pro, with Matrox's RT.X100 Xtreme real-time editing card,can change the color of this background from black video to any other.*

LEFT: *One frame later and the A source has run out of frames to complete the transition. Xtreme and Premiere Pro use black video to fill in the sides of the cube and complete the transition.*

clip to complete the transition. Motion with titles, though, remains different because the non-affected canvas is not an image, but a black alpha matte. Text won't be legible if it were to fill the frame as a block, unless you've attributed a fill color to the matte canvas. If there is a fill to the matte, the frame operates in the same way as a video clip: the fill is applied to the frame to fill it to the ratio within which you're working (4:3, 16:9). In this case, it has hard edges and, when alone on the *Timeline*, lies on a background of black signal.

Keyframes with motion are a little easier to control because they're more obvious. The eye sees motion quicker than it sees changes in luminance and, relatively, much quicker than it sees changes in chrominance. Motion is also the one thing that gives video the extra dimension that photography is lacking: time.

The *ECW*, as we've seen, is a timeline in itself and this is precisely what makes it easier to understand. Through keyframes in the *ECW* timeline, changes can be made that control the travel of the title for the duration that it's on the project timeline.

Another illusion—this time, space. Travel for the title, whether matted or canvassed, operates in time and space. The analog, real, shootable world, is four-dimensional. Aside from objects in scenery being to either our left or our right, and the perspective that this offers, there's also depth. We know this because we travel through and past objects, and our perspective of them fundamentally changes with three of the five senses: vision, sound and smell. Video can create illusions of two of those. What it can't create is anything more than these. Without straying too far into the realms of Sartre, existentialism and *The Matrix*, we confirm our own and objects' existence in the four dimensions with the sense of touch.

So, time aside, reality exists on X, Y, and Z axes, and this is what digital video captures using light, and the ways in which it falls on objects, textures and surfaces. Titling can emulate this too, and travel is an essential part of the trick.

If you put that same title with fill—i.e. a title with a solid background created with a filled image—over a video clip on your **Timeline**, *any motion applied will move the whole canvas.*

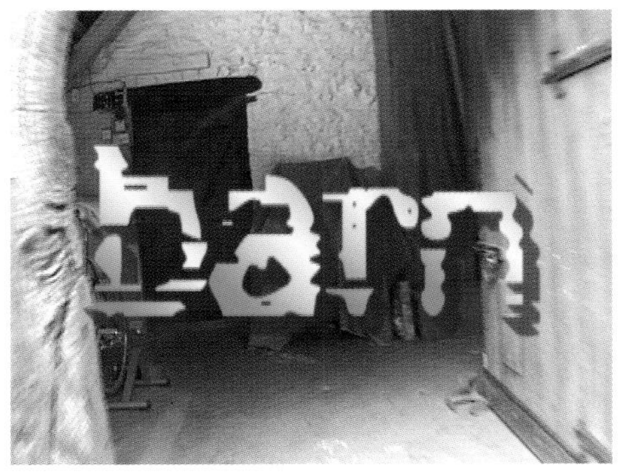

To further the deception of titles in space, motion applied to titling can work with the false reality of the background video motion. This shot moves into the barn, the scale of the title changes from small to large, and the result is that the title becomes part of the background video motion.

There's very little deception involved in left or right, but there is to depth—or rather, as the mind understands it, near and far.

But to the naked eye and the naked video camera, near and far are represented as large and small. Whereas an object can be either large or small, an object getting larger tends to be perceived within the illusion of an analog world, as an object getting nearer. Conversely, an object getting smaller is perceived as an object going farther away rather than simply an object shrinking in size.

By applying this thinking to titling, we can create the illusion of depth, perspective and distance. This is especially true if the title itself is created as a three-dimensional object (i.e. hit by light) using its own X, Y, and Z axes within the XYZ of the frame itself.

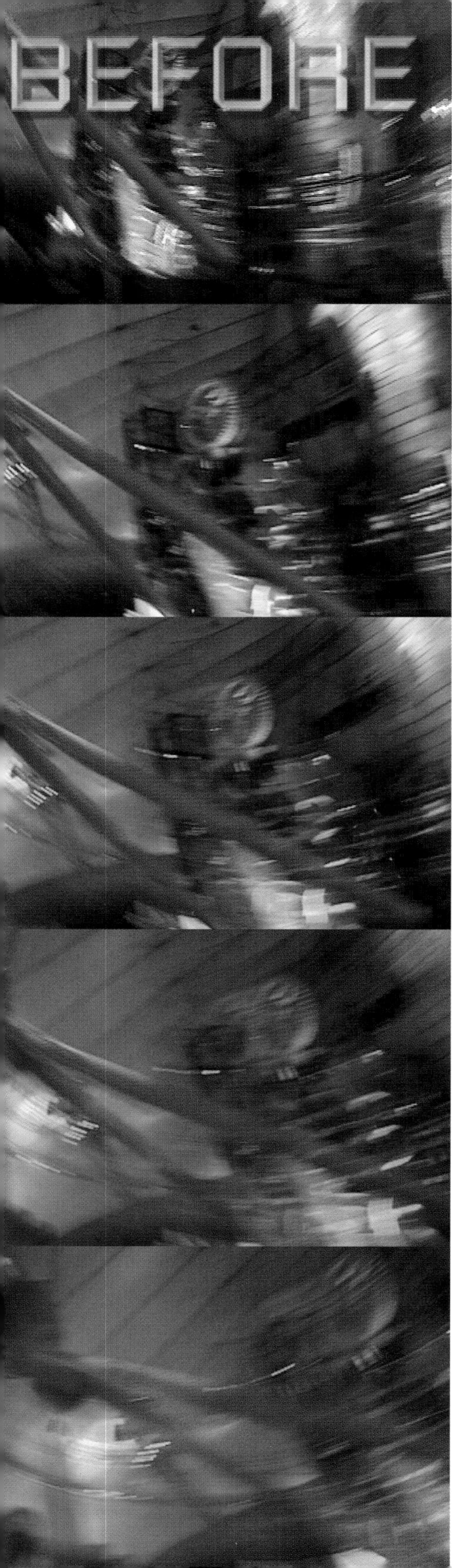

Controlling motion with keyframes

The motion control in Premiere Pro gives you unprecedented versatility, thanks to the ease of keyframing on X, Y and Z axes. If motion in reality is observed as a four-dimensional activity, the best way of translating this in the *ECW* is that *Position* is left/right and up/down, *Scale* is near/far, and your keyframes represent time. With these four basics, creating any type of movement is possible.

The secret to making a title work with—i.e. in the same space—as the background image, is to study the movement of the visuals behind it. In the sequence starting left, continued right, the "before" title is the freeze-frame *Chroma Key* created to move with the pan in the background. The pan is actually a tilt followed by a pan, and moves from bottom right to top left, before a slow zoom to bottom left.

1 *The tilt begins before the 'before' freeze-frame. Therefore any move to make sense of working with the pan should begin here. Before the 'before' is Video Track 3's 'the night before' title. The background counter-clockwise tilt implies an counter-clockwise rotation. Clicking on "the night before" clip with the* Edit Line *at the frame before the start of the tilt, shows the* ECW *edit line at that frame. This is where the keyframe for the start of the rotation should be added. The drop-down menu from the* Motion *option requires the default keyframe set at that point at its default value: 0 (number of rotations) x 0.0° (angle). To set it, just press the* Toggle Animation *clock next to* Rotation.

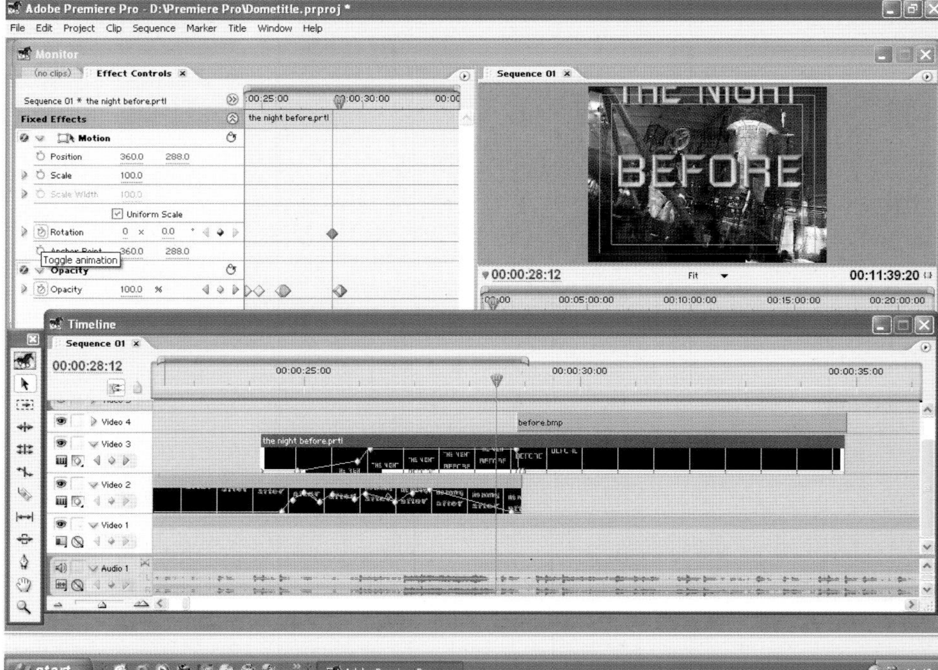

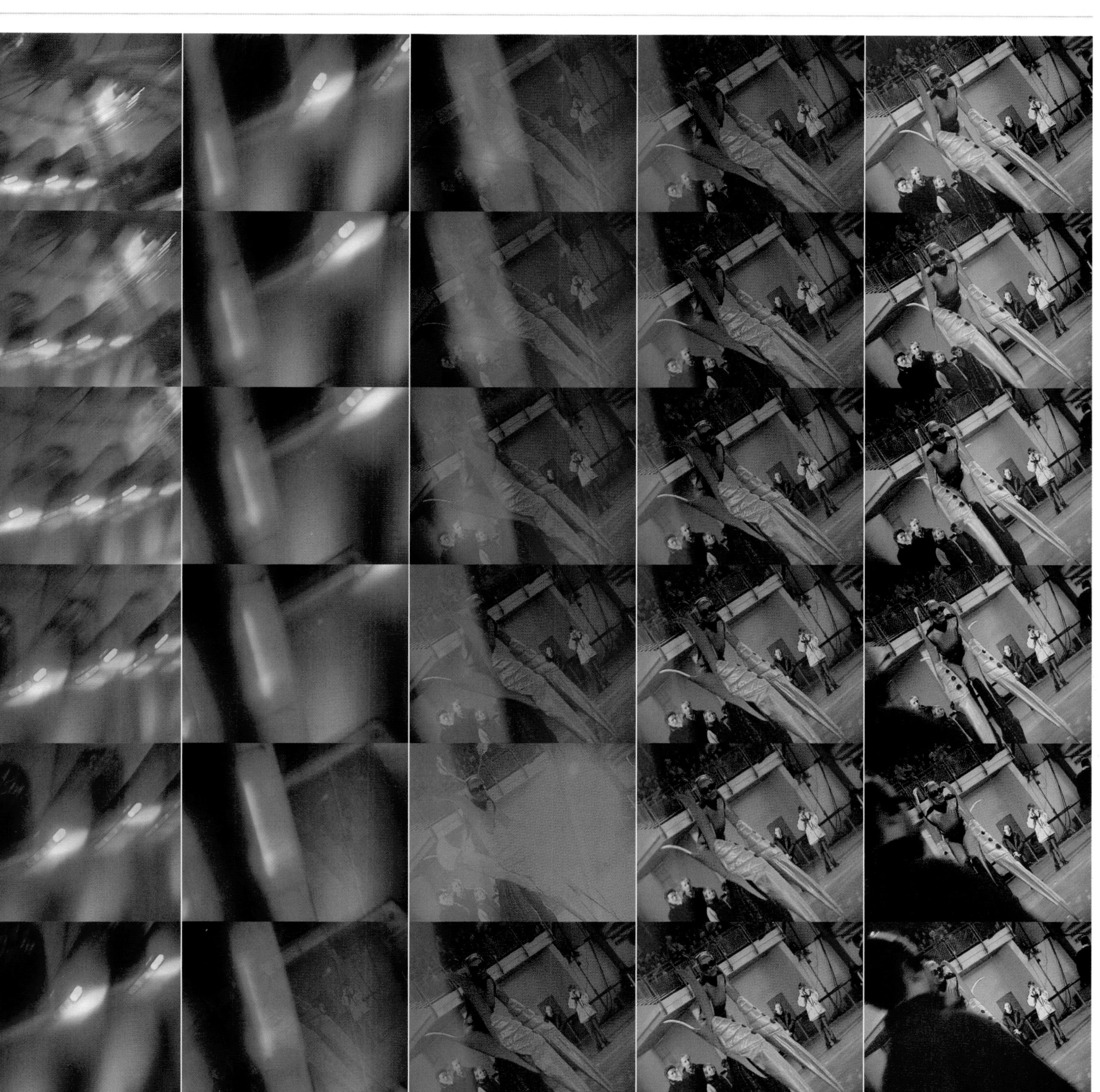

2 *Once this is in place, using the right arrow key advances the visuals frame by frame in search of the next part of the move: the pan. As this image shows, that point of the title is actually covered by the freeze-frame. Continuation to this point on the 0%-Opacity "the night before" title clip won't matter. It's consistent, good practice, and might save any issues with the freeze-frame later...*

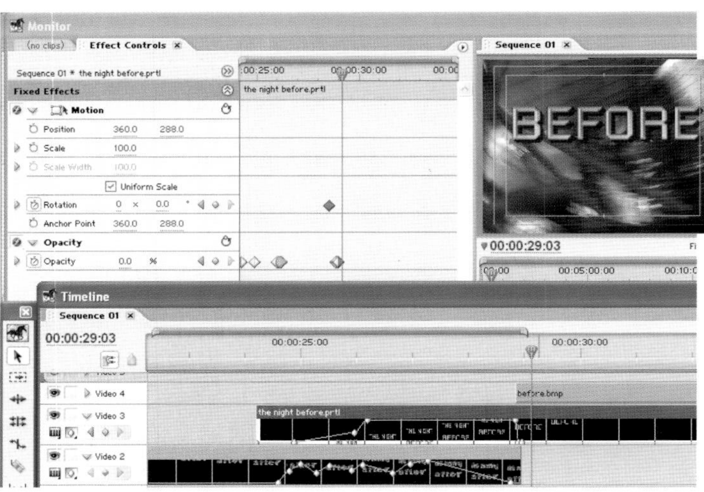

3 *Adding a keyframe at this second "invisible" point gives the outpoint for any move between those points. The outpoint will therefore be the apex of the move—the farthest change from the original 0 x 0.0°.*

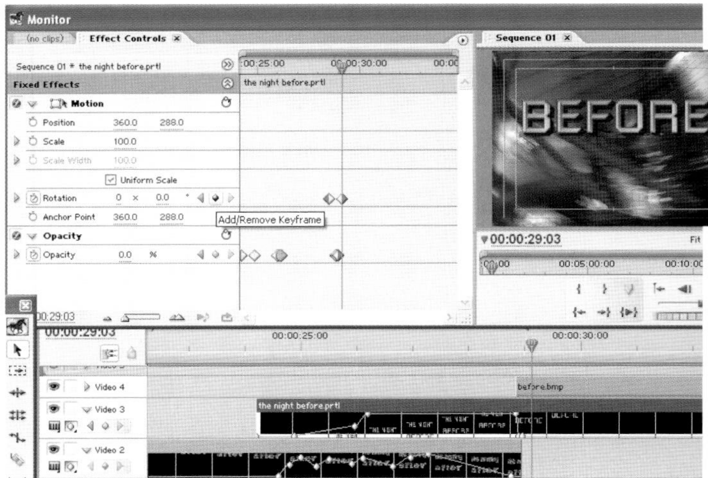

4 *The monitor is reading 'the night before' title clip as invisible, so toggle the* Opacity *effect off, which will allow any changes in* Rotation *at the second keyframe to be viewed, as well as the freeze-frame. Counter-clockwise movement is represented by a minus value in degrees.*

5 *Because the* Rotation *is applied to the whole of the frame and the title isn't centered, it's revolving out of frame. This isn't necessarily a terrible effect in itself, but altering the* Anchor Points *offer a change to the center of the axis of rotation. The values are X and Y co-ordinates and are, by default, set at the center of the screen (which should be 360.0 x 288.0 for PAL, 360 x 240 for NTSC DV, and 360.0 x 243.0 for NTSC Standard Definition).*

6 *The first challenge. Backing up on the roll, the change in* Anchor Point*—moving it lower to keep the "before" onscreen—has exposed the edge of the original alpha frame in the top left. And it's within screen-safe. Alternatively, I could abandon the idea of changing the* Anchor Point*, change the* Anchor Point *to a lesser degree, keyframe the* Anchor Point *not to happen until only the "before" is on-screen, enlarge the font, keyframe the scale, or shift the entire title sequence back a few frames... All of these have different implications either to the design of the movement, the font itself, or the interaction with the background image.*

8 *Everything is in place to lead into the freeze-frame. Clicking on the clip, the same* Rotation *and* Anchor Point *values are added to the respective options. Simply changing the values sets the entire sequence at those values without adding a keyframe icon. This makes for an invisible edit with "the night before" title clip. From here, work on the rest of the "before" can be made to progress it against the background pan.*

7 *The right decision is often dependent on how much unpicking you really want to do—and the wrong decision is often the easy one. In this case, there is sufficient motion to be applied to the title to keyframe the* Anchor Point *without an obvious shift. To do this,* Anchor Point *keyframes are added at the beginning of the clip and at the start of the move to contain the default central value. Once they've reached the* Rotation *start keyframe, five are added—one every two frames—with an incrementally (by two pixels) diminishing value on the Y axis.*

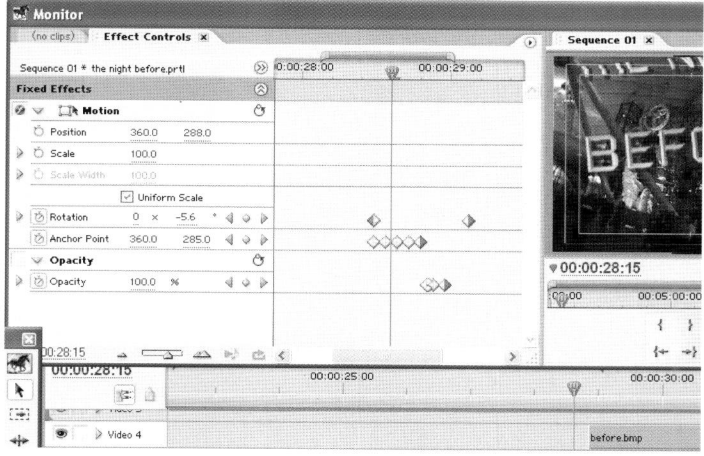

9 *The tilt continues behind the freeze-frame. Leave the* Opacity *effect toggled off the "before" clip, which will let the title's position at the end of the tilt shine through. This now just has to be emulated with the freeze-frame. The "before" clip—as a higher video track—is superimposed on the residue "the night before" title, and this image shows the end of the background tilt.*

10 *The first job is to add the same* Rotation *values as the original clip up until the end of the tilt. The angle of the original clip is our guide to the resultant angle of change to this end point. A keyframe added with the same final rotation angle value fixes the end position.*

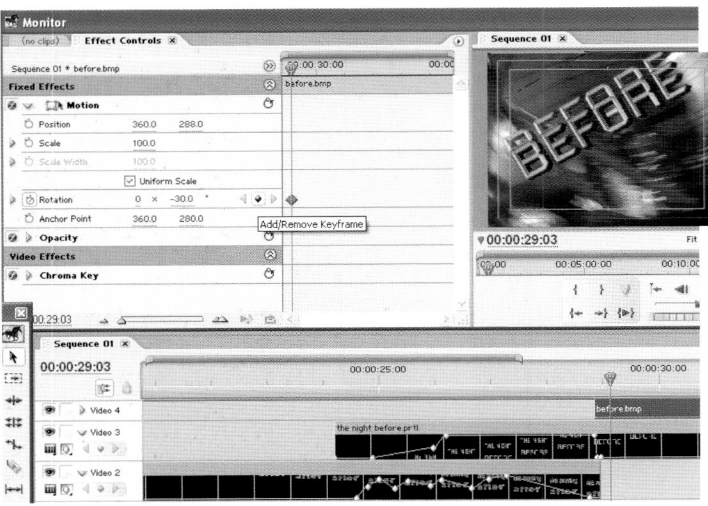

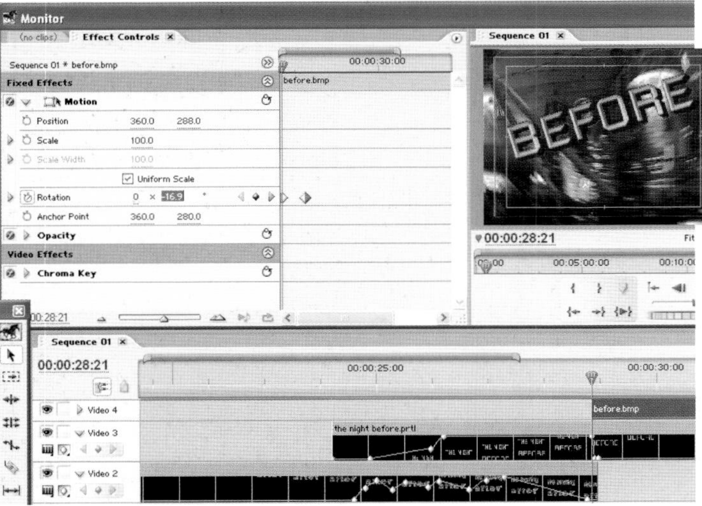

12 *Entering the noted value with a keyframe at the start of the freeze-frame, now gives the "before" title the same speed and angle of* Rotation *that the original title clip introduced.*

11 *Back on the original clip, the first frame of its invisibility gives the angle of* Rotation *at the point that the freeze-frame takes over. Noting this value, the* Opacity *effect can now be toggled back on again.*

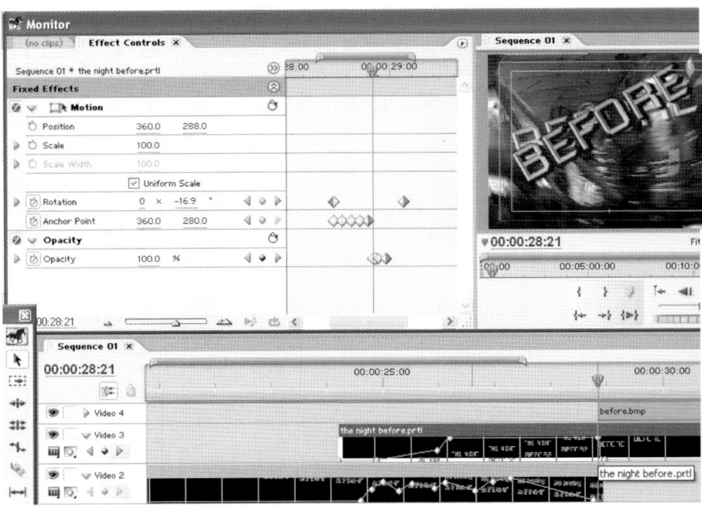

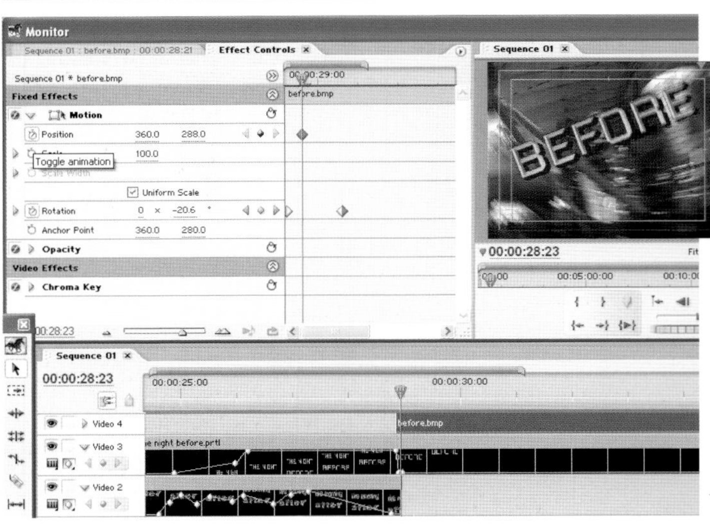

13 *To keep the movement flowing, the pan itself is backed up to start three frames before the end of the tilt. This is where the default value keyframe is added. A pan left to right would just use the X axis of the* Position *values. This pan, though, moves to top left of the frame, and to make the title work with the background would force the title to push off down into the bottom right of frame. Therefore both X and Y values need adjusting.*

14 *Finding the end of the background pan, a keyframe is added to the Position option as the end of the pan for the title. This is where the title should finally end up before the envisaged transition.*

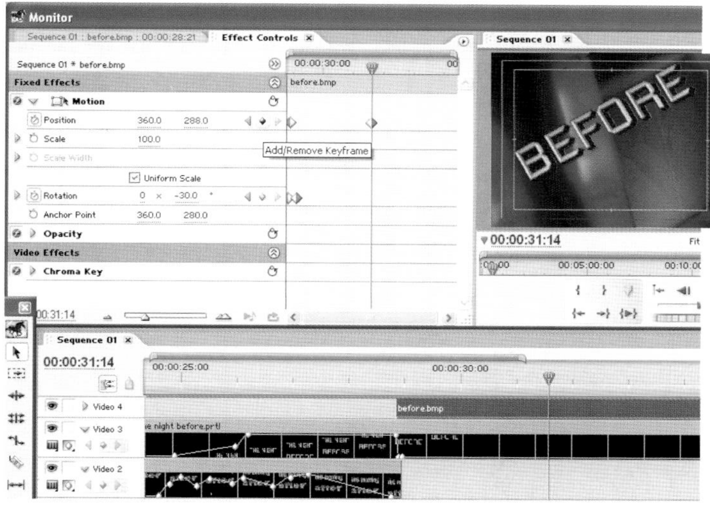

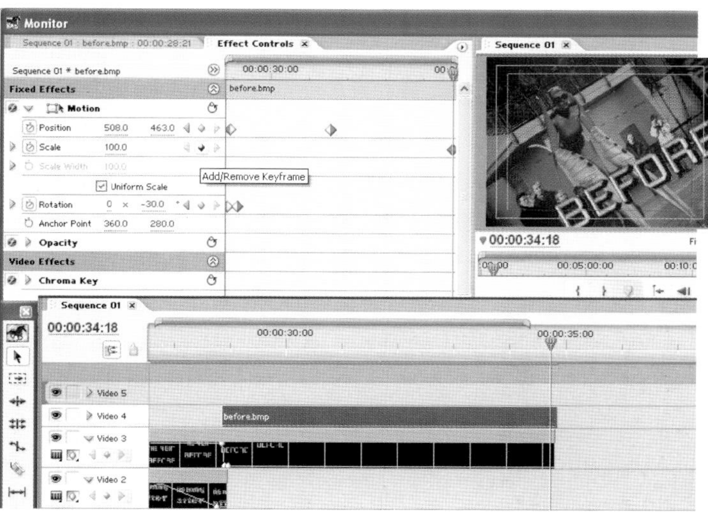

16 *Thinking ahead, the transition of the title to the video should work hand-in-hand with the background mix in the video. To firmly adhere the title to the background action, the zoom should continue while the transition to the video is taking place. So instead of ending the zoom for the title at the end of the zoom for the background (how utterly predictable), the title end keyframe is added at the end of where the transition is conceived to finish.*

15 *Changing the values for the pan end keyframe, the title is positioned for its resting place. Because there's a slight push happening in the background video, I've bled the freeze-frame out of safety and offscreen in order that I can perform a zoom that will bring it back into vision.*

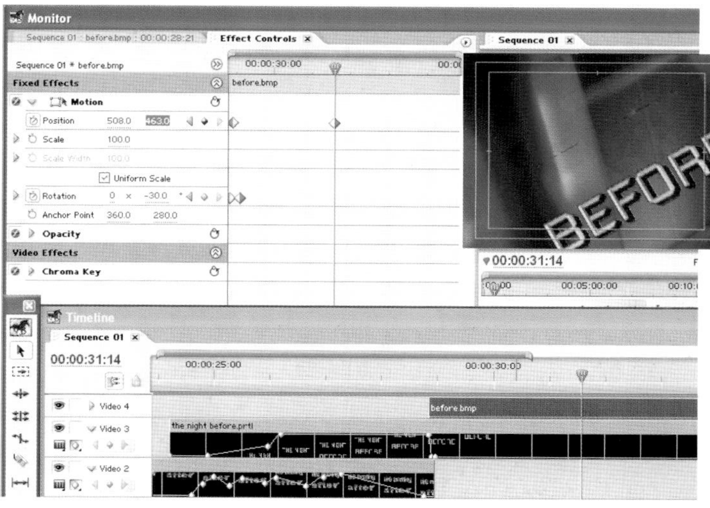

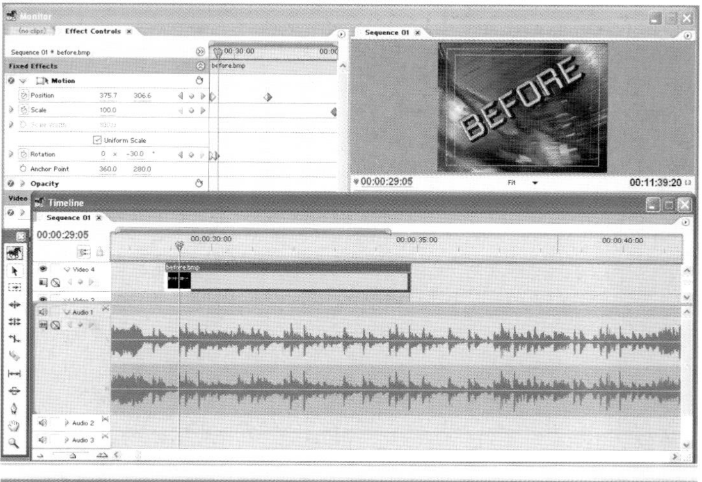

17 *Watching the entire sequence through is always a good way to see what it needs and where. It becomes apparent after doing this that the audio dictates the start of the zoom. The soundtrack is a music track, and the emphasis at the* Edit Line *heralds a synthetic car-braking effect. This screech sounds as though it needs to be accompanied by part of the move, and it makes perfect sense that this should be the start of the zoom—despite the fact that this comes just after the start of the pan.*

18 *Adding the first* Scale *keyframe at this audio point in the* ECW *will make the frame the start of the zoom. Because the zoom is long, though, the entry into it during the pan won't be significantly noticeable with the audio unless the added keyframe is optioned with a* Fast Out. *This automatically turns the end keyframe into a* Slow In.

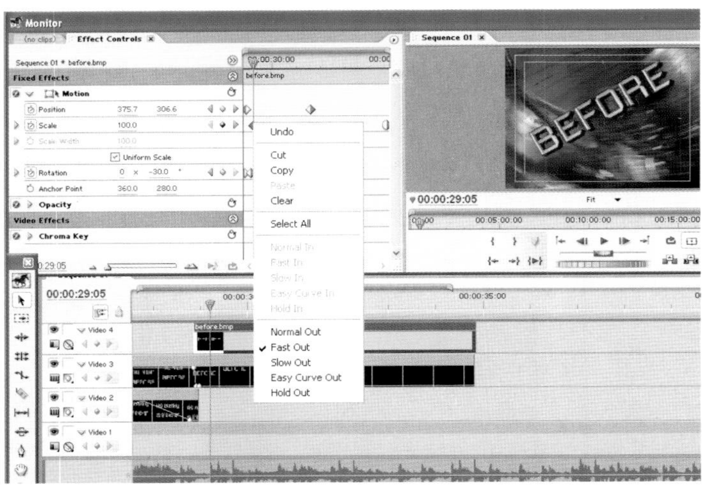

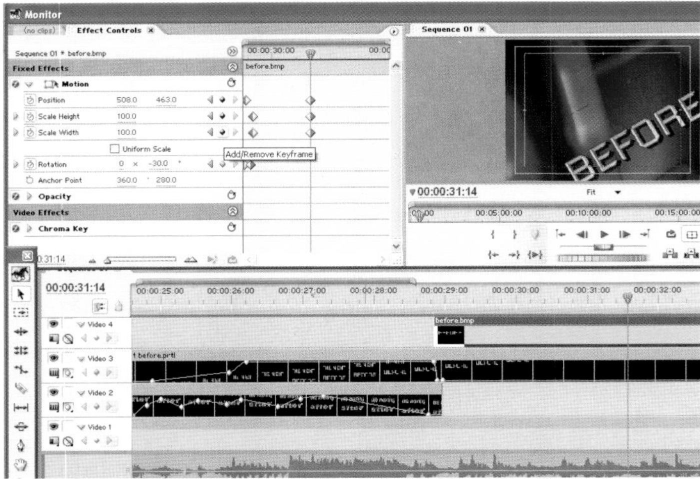

20 *The solution is to uncheck the default* Uniform Scale *box. What you can't do is to change midclip from uniform to non-uniform, which means that the* Scale Height *and the* Scale Width *values need to be input separately. Their increase, in order to emulate the uniform scaled zoom, has to increase with synchronized values. Keyframes are therefore added at the start of the zoom and at the first frame of where the transition will begin.*

19 *This zoom will give an effect that leaves this tight as the start of any transition. It's fine—attractive even—but it doesn't quite use the anamorphic-looking background to the best of its abilities for the transition to it. It also feels as though the zoom should perceive the center of the "O," something very possible with the right positioning—and something that is a bit of a cliché.*

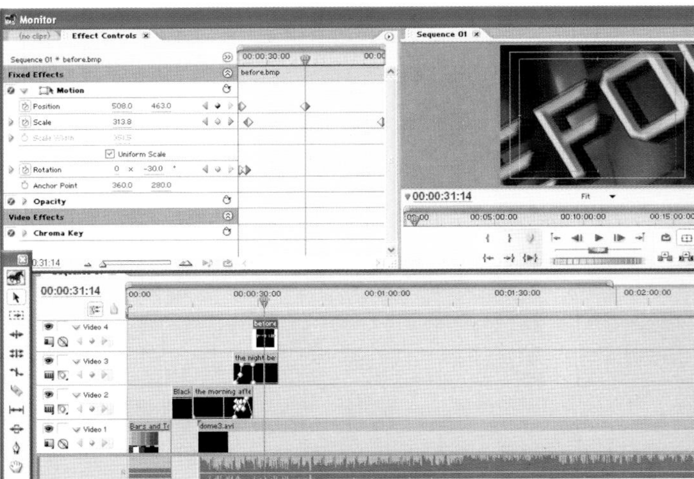

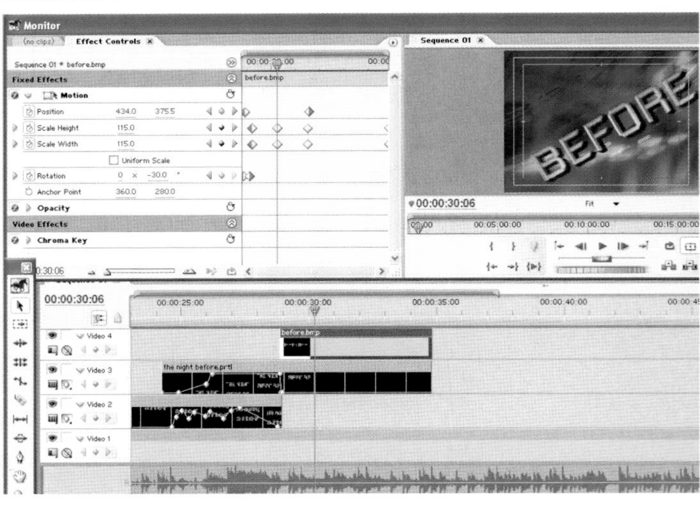

21 *Two more keyframes are added for both* Scale Height *and* Scale Width*—this time for the very end frame of the transition, and for a center anchor between the start of the zoom and the end of the pan. From here, values are added to the keyframes: between the first and the second, a slight uniform increase to introduce the idea of the zoom...*

22 *...between the second and third, a dramatic uniform increase as the zoom itself...*

23 *...between the third and fourth, a rapid decrease in width to compress the title "anamorphically" to the end of the transition.*

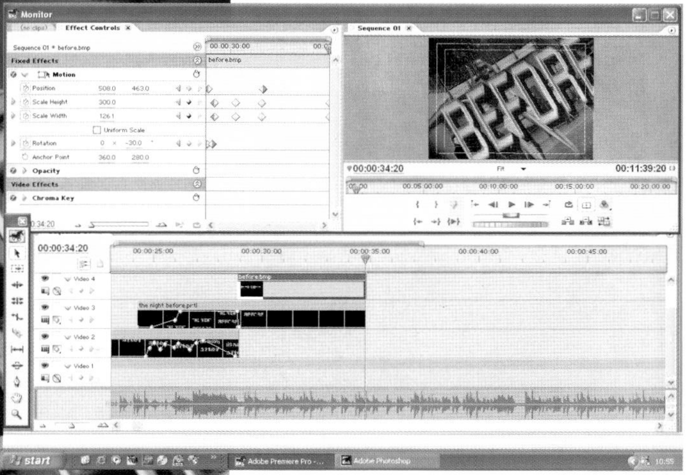

The motion in the sequence is now complete. It's rough around the edges and needs a bit of work. There's always room for tweaking, and Premiere Pro makes it easy to drag keyframes and view your results in realtime. The major issue with this title, though, is that it ought to leave the screen with a little more dignity. The solution? It needs a transition. *See page 122 for details.*

Text and background layers in motion

Adding motion to each layer that you've created can be a very happy marriage. Giving your graphics a more dynamic or kinetic feel can also increase production values no end with little additional effort. While a discreet fade on and fade off will always have their place, a movement can subtly entertain or richly reward the viewer—and the production.

The North Wales Tropical Gardens Company is developing its own house style. This means a nice job for us as there are no harsh boundaries with the clients' branding—aside from a house logo to top and tail the yearly production. That's not to say that I'm out on a creative limb—the caption applied to our familiar interviewee can relate to the captions for the four other interviews that will thread through the video, in design, transition, and motion.

1 *Starting with the original caption, it looks like this—and doesn't do anything. It's also verging on busy illegibility. Captions are there to be brief and to the point, to be read and then get off. I could do this by a simple mix on and off, but frankly the interviews are dry enough. It's time to bend the rules.*

2 *Lower-third captions are strange things. Because they occupy only the space at the bottom of the frame, they don't have much room to maneuver. Specifically, they have more X-axis to work with than Y-axis, which is why any movement they have is usually a crawl. I'm going to pander to this with a crawl for the long thin branch: it makes sense. Selecting Start Off Screen and ending on screen will let this roll from left to right across the bottom of frame.*

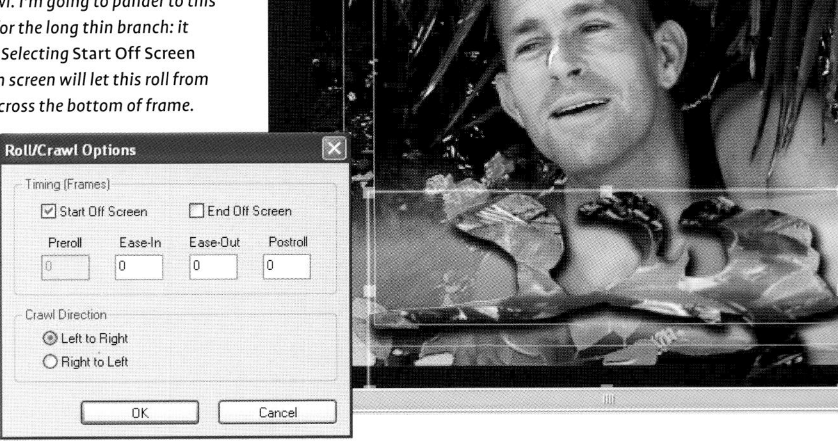

3 *For the flower-textured rectangle, a perpendicular roll will complement the branch overlay crawl—again, choosing* Start Off Screen *and ending on screen, but this time with a* Postroll *value added to slow the motion down. This is because it has less axis (Y) to cover while the branch is moving across the X-axis.*

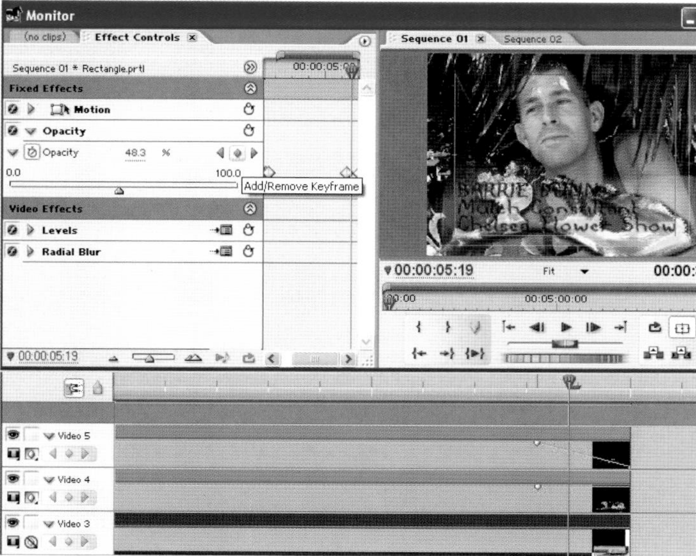

5 *The text itself just needs a simple* Opacity *change to bring it in without any fuss. Fine. The issue now is how to get all the titles offscreen. There are three standard ways of doing this. The first is to simply fade them all off together with the same applied* Opacity *dip.*

4 *In order for the branch to "grow" across the screen as a creeper, I've taken a* Bend *effect from the* Video Effects > **Distort** *menu. In the dialog, slowing the* Rate *down and minimizing the* Width *makes it a little more subtle than the default values.*

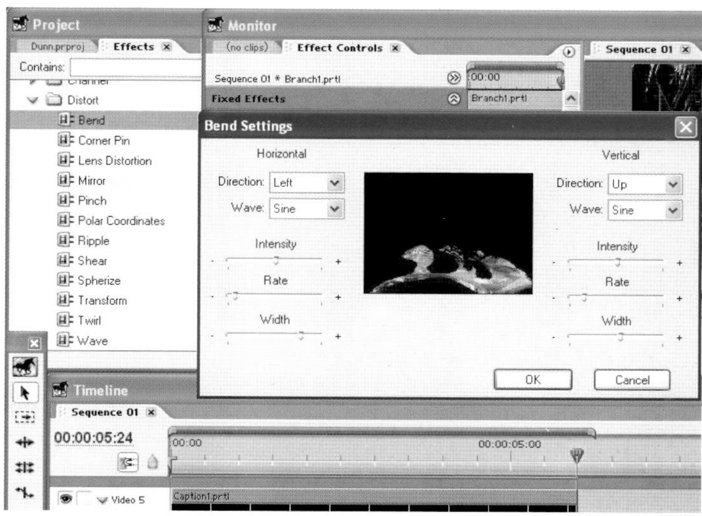

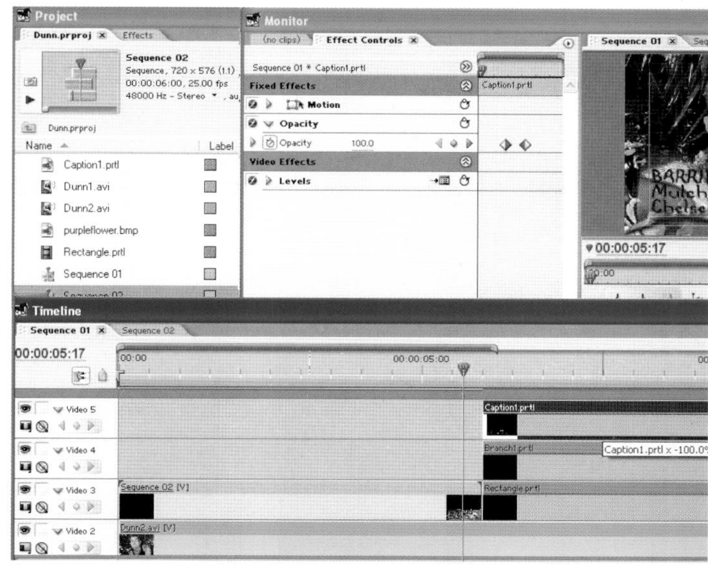

6 *The second way is that each of the images could roll, fade, and crawl back to where they came from. The easiest way of doing this is to save the three caption tracks as a sequence, copy it back onto the* Timeline *abutted next to the original, right-click and apply* Speed/Duration > **Reverse Speed** *to the sequence.*

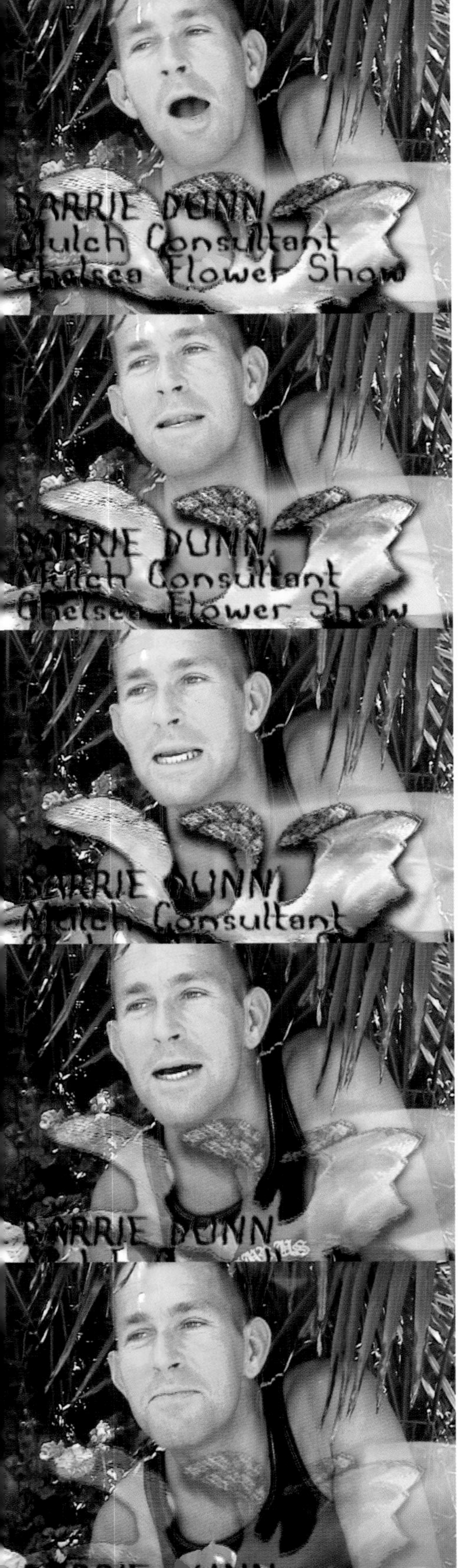

7 *The third way is a different approach. In this case, I think that I could take them off in the same way that they came on, but applied to non-respective tracks. To do this, it's still time-saving (after all the track-tweaking) to save the first title off as a sequence, then insert it back onto the* Timeline *and reverse all of the abutted original clips. From here, the process is to cut and paste any effects, motion, and keyframes from one clip's* ECW *into another.* Bend, Levels, Radial Blur, *and* Opacity *are all applied to each layer.*

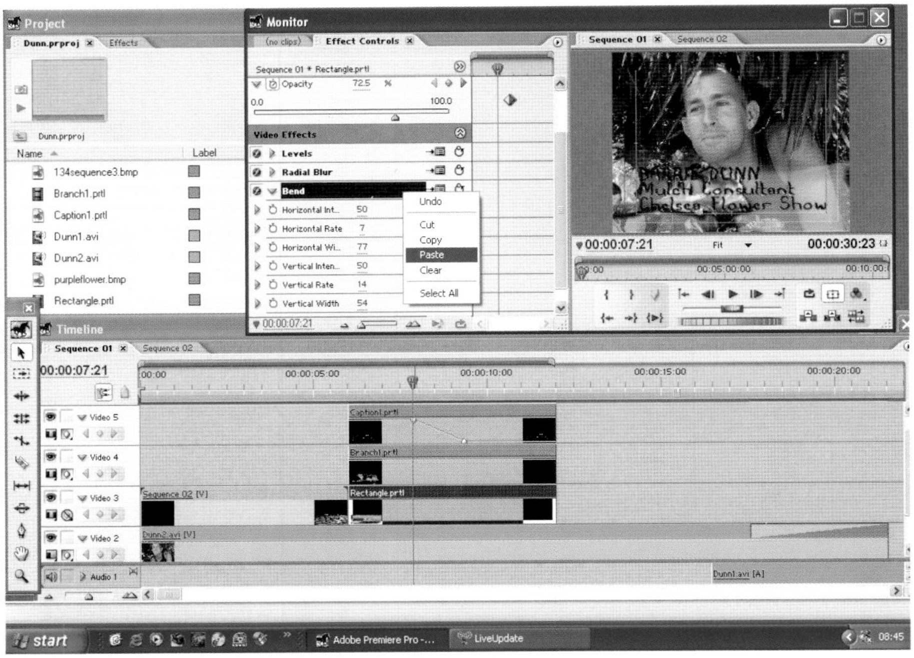

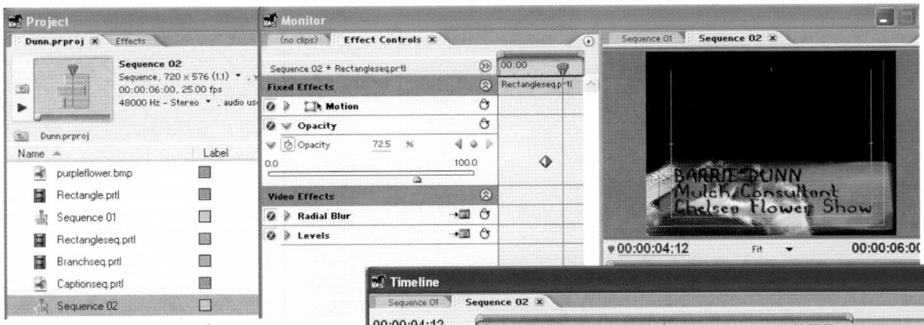

! *A heavily italicized word of warning: make sure that you rename your clips, or pay the price of having all your changes to the newly sequenced clips saved and applied to the clips of the same file name in your original sequence.*

8 *Going back into* Title Designer, *I'm turning the text still to a roll downward. Because the clip is already in reverse, this means applying reverse attributes—i.e.* Start Off Screen.

9 *To take the* Opacity *keyframes from one clip to another (the reverse values for the text to the branch clip), right-click on the* Opacity *effect in the* ECW *to* Select All; *right-click again to* Cut; *click on the new clip and right-click again on the* Opacity *effect in the* ECW, *and* Paste *the effect with all associated keyframes in.*

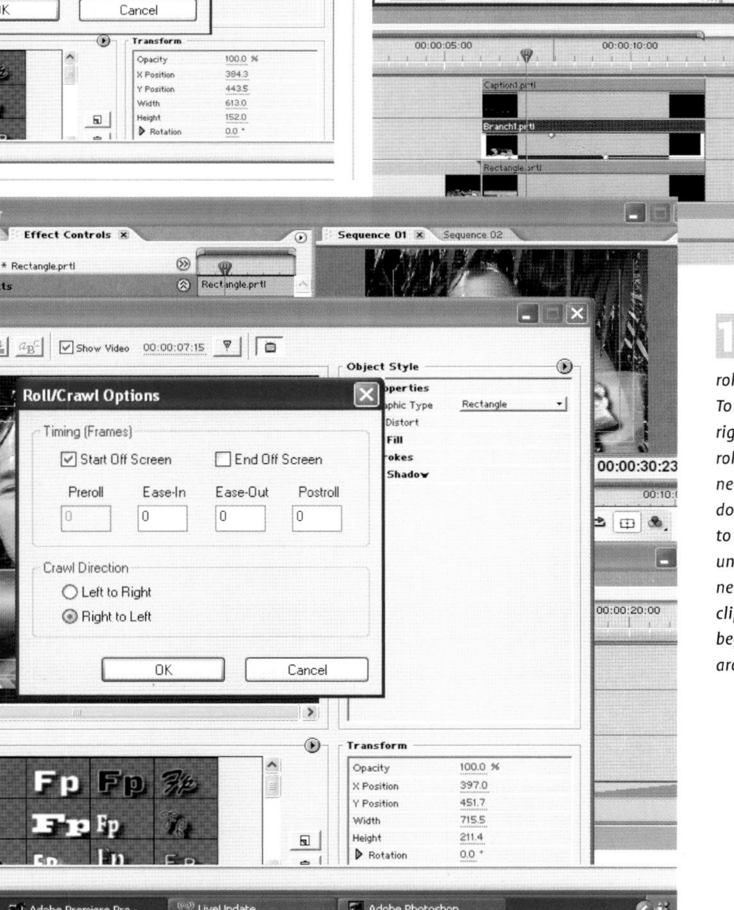

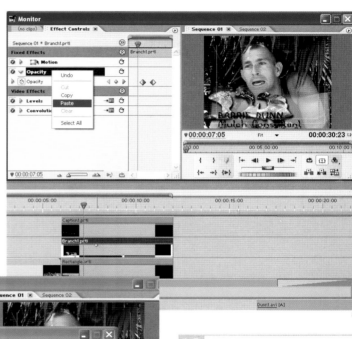

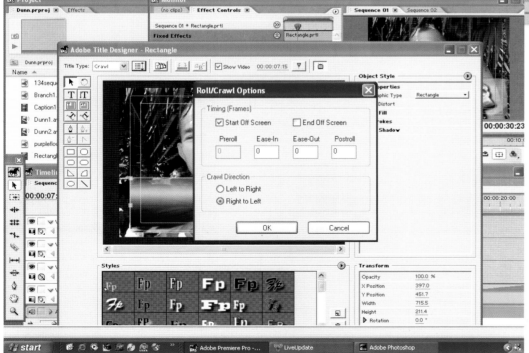

10 *Applying a crawl to the previously rolling rectangle is the final stage for this layer. To complement the branch's original left to right roll, I want the rectangle to continue the roll. Because the clip is in reverse, no changes need to be applied to* Crawl Direction. *What does need to be changed is the* Postroll *value, to stop the rectangle hanging around on screen unnecessarily. Because of the reversed clip, the new value here will be applied to how long the clip remains onscreen without moving at the beginning of the clip. I don't want it hanging around, so therefore a 0 value is applied.*

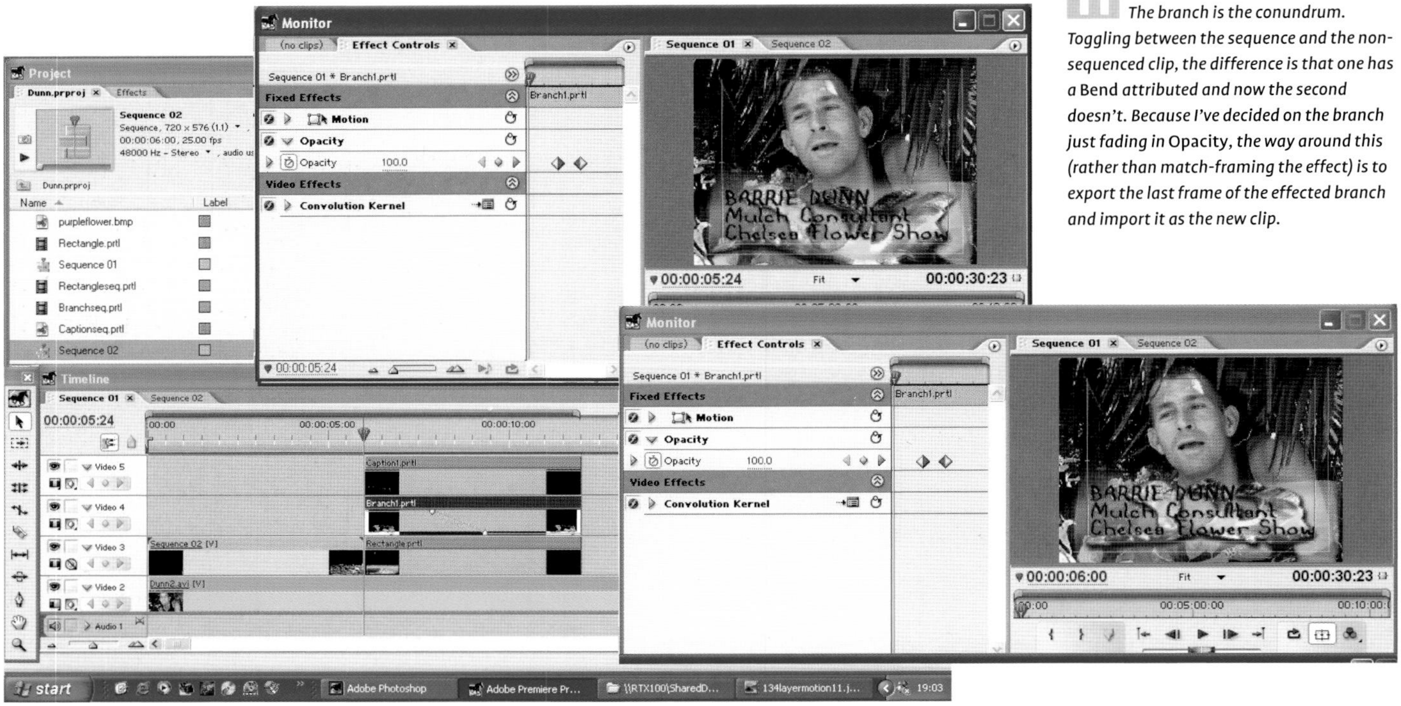

11 *The branch is the conundrum. Toggling between the sequence and the non-sequenced clip, the difference is that one has a* Bend *attributed and now the second doesn't. Because I've decided on the branch just fading in* Opacity*, the way around this (rather than match-framing the effect) is to export the last frame of the effected branch and import it as the new clip.*

12 *We need to go back into the original sequence, as it is the only place now that the layer exists as a solo matte. Making sure that it's rendered first and that the other tracks are toggled out of vision, the frame can be exported before attending to the new sequence on the* Timeline*.*

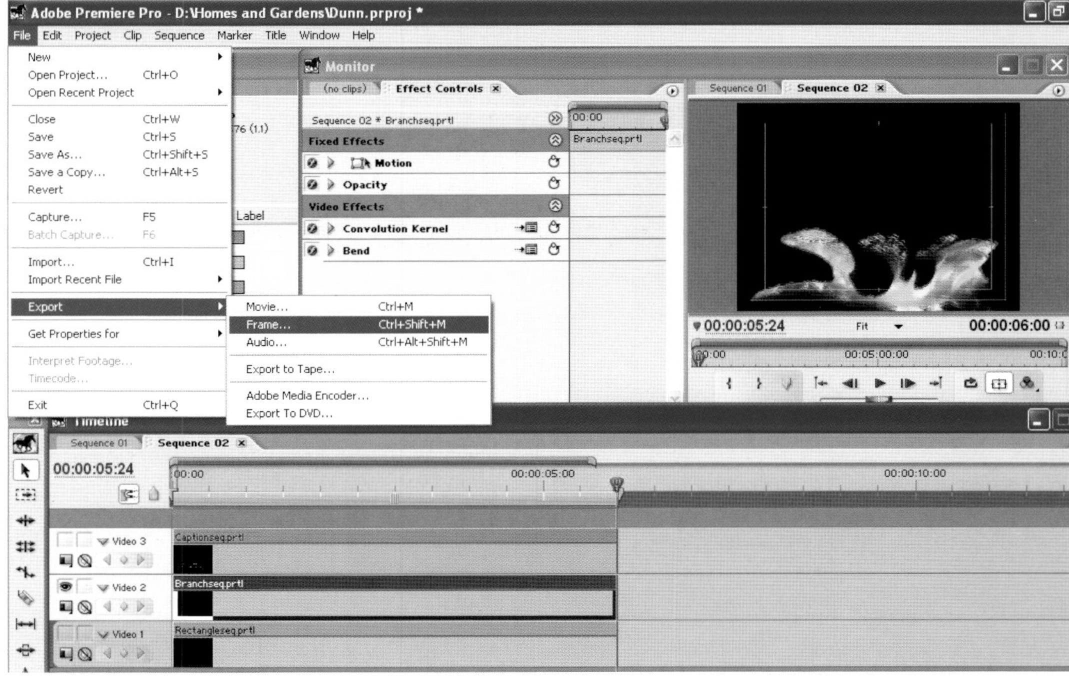

13 *Once put in place of the unbent branch on the* Timeline, *the* Opacity *values for the former clip need cutting and pasting onto the new still frame. As a still frame, though, the black matte is read as a black and not a matte.*

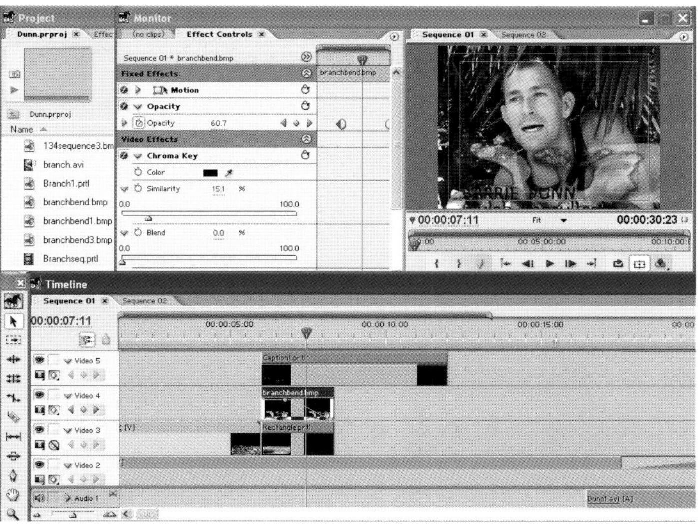

15 *Rendering up and analyzing the entire sequence, we can see that the dissolve effect on the caption is too labored, so the clips have been shortened to suit.*

14 *Dragging a* Chroma Key (Video Effects > **Keying**)*, sampling the black, and using* Blend *and* Smoothing *values enables the black to be read as a matte again and the interviewee to come through the composite.*

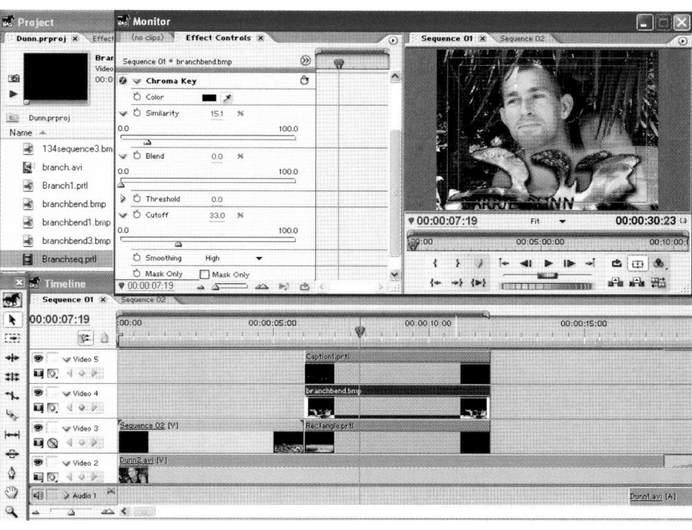

16 *The final stage for this caption is to sequence the caption's movement out of frame and then sequence the entire title to keep it neat and render-free on the* Timeline. *For the rest of the captions in the video, we can copy and paste the effects and motion from the tracks here and use them within each individual sequence.*

Keying and motion

Keying with titles in motion tends to be a slightly more dangerous thing. Having a lot of different frames on show increases your chances that a key will be on show too. Tearing, bleeding, and matte lines are common adversaries to a good key and can ruin a good title.

Because titles are there to be read, they're scrutinized more than a badly shot image that's accompanied by dialogue. And because titles tend to be graphics, they can often create havoc when keyed onto a background, especially when they're bold, brash and colorful, or in a different file format—or, in particular, moving.

Choosing the right key is essential—as is planning the key that you're going to use when you're designing the titles. Remember that the battle is not lost from the start: to your advantage is the fact that Premiere Pro's keying now offers so many high-quality options and tweaks that there's really little excuse for a bad key. As well as fine-tuning, keying can be keyframed, making your alterations as specific as to a still or even to each individual frame.

There are two ways of keying in Premiere Pro. One is for the transparency to be understood as color. The other is for transparency to be read as grayscale. There aren't just two keys, though. Premiere Pro has enough to ensure that you can choose at least one that works efficiently.

1 *A good example of a key required is within the up-and-coming Dome Title. As we'll see, the title has had a trail applied of 30 subsequent titles with a distance of 0.05 seconds between them. The Starting Intensity of the first trailed frame from the original title is keyframed to diminish from 100% to 29% of the original's chrominance and luminance over the course of the motion. Each subsequent title that forms the trail is degenerating in image from the last one at a 7% rate—i.e. each title loses 7% of chrominance and luminance from the title before it.*

2 *In order to demonstrate the particulars of keying motion, it's important to bear in mind that the outcome of the key needs to reveal our whole trail against a background that is of similar hue (in this case, blue) to the title itself. While the close framing on the trail has lightened the image, I've put the chrominance back into the sequence with changes to the RGB output levels (White and Blue Gamma).*

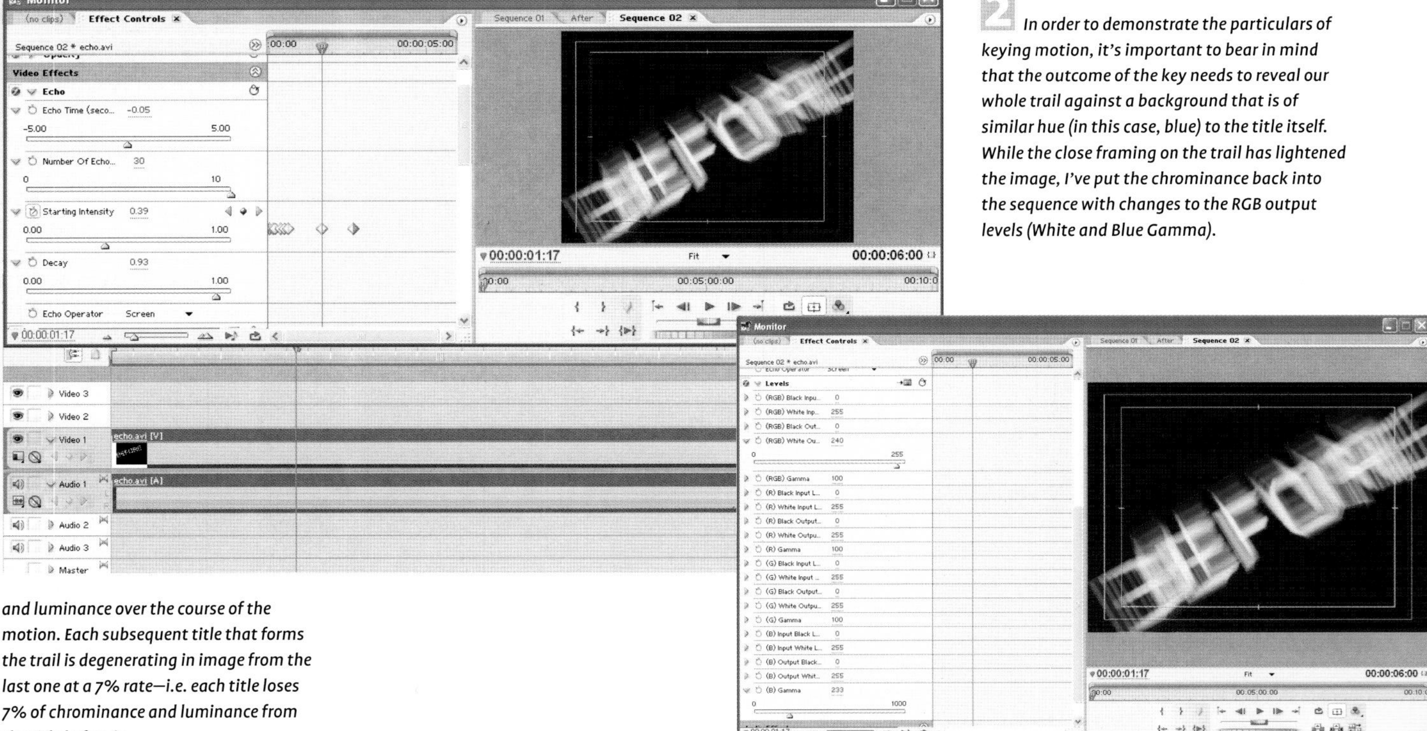

3 Without being too obvious, I'm applying a Blue Screen Key to the blue-hued title on the blue-hued background. At a Threshold of 50% and 0% Cutoff, the background is let through whatever is blue within the title. Because the trail is a degeneration of the original chrominance, there is less blue in it. Because there is increasingly less blue, the trail remains progressively faithful, but the less degenerated and the more original the title, the more background comes through to renders it illegible. Using a Blue Screen Key is entirely the wrong thing if you want anyone to read a blue-hued title, unless it is just designed as background detail.

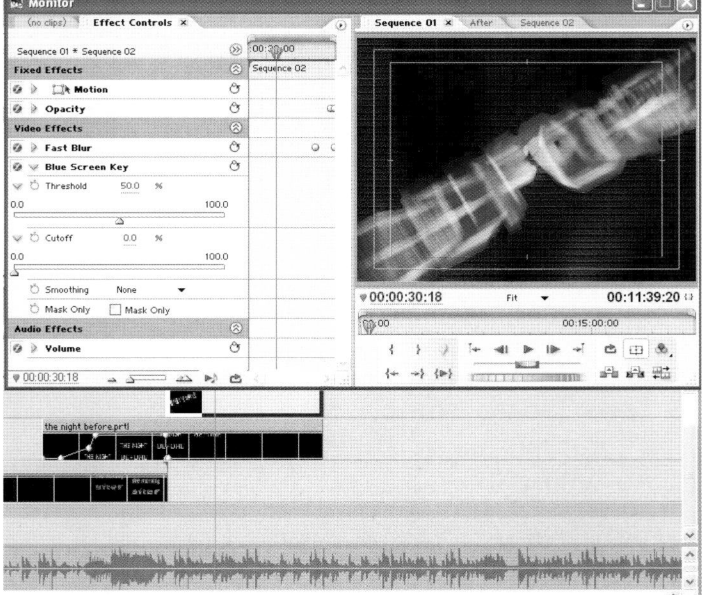

4 A Green Screen Key acts in exactly the same way, searching for any sign of green. With a Threshold value, there are obviously a few elements within the text fill that bring the background through.

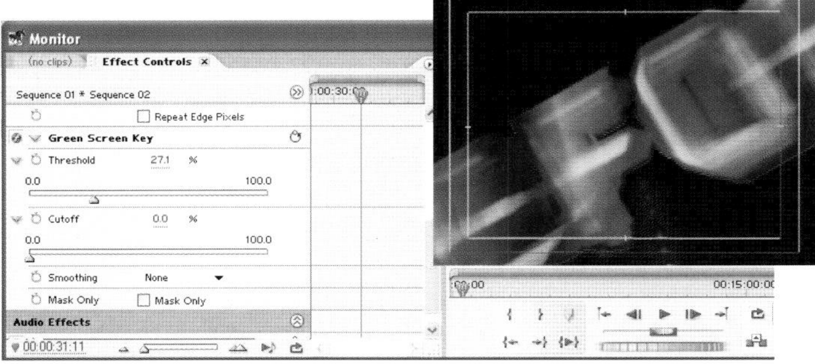

5 An alternative to the blue and green keys is the Non Red Key. This can be used in conjunction with other keys, as it is very good at softening backgrounds and edges. Despite its inability to key the background, here, it certainly would be useful if I wanted to keep the trail fluid. Unfortunately, in the process, it also softens the hard bevel of the moving text.

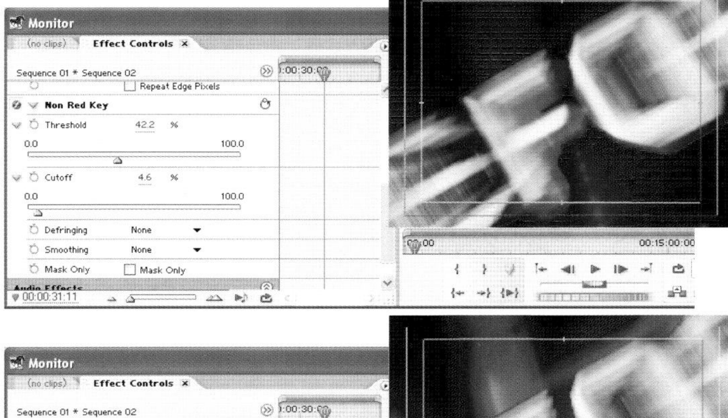

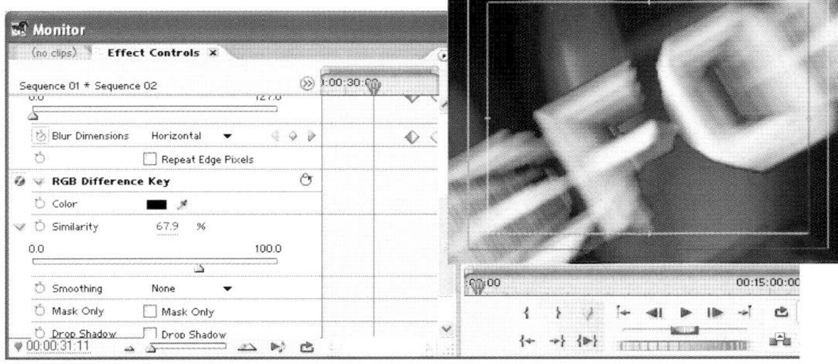

6 My next choice might be the RGB Difference Key. Not specific to any particular color, it allows for the Color Picker or a sample to be taken in order to key it. It's perfect for broadspread flat colors—and in this respect, good for graphics such as this. All in all, it is a definite contender...

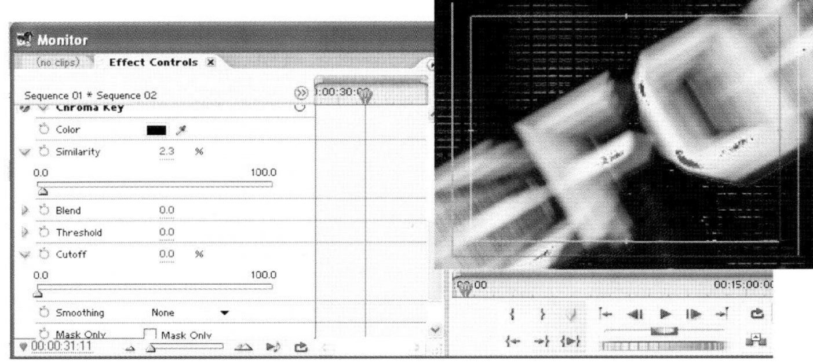

7 Premiere Pro's Chroma Key is the apex of its chrominance keying capacity. On this clip, though, it doesn't want to be read at all. If the alpha matte background is interpreted as black, inputting a black value in the Color box creates real problems with the text itself, which contains black between every close-knit trail frame.

8 *Finding the point of transparency to let the background through with the* Similarity *of color, and adjusting the* Threshold *and* Cutoff *to best possible delineation with the key, is still too much for a degenerating trail. A* Chroma Key *is very versatile and giving in* Premiere Pro*—indeed it's the best all-rounder, indicating that the most efficient way to undertake this particular key is with one that deals with luminance.*

9 *So bring on the* Luma Key*. Because the echo is duplicating the values of the pixels at a higher rate than it is degenerating (hence the trail), it's adding luminance when each echo is combined with another. The brightness of the pixels is therefore the most prominent feature of the text in motion. The* Luma Key *serves to recognize this and keys it to a degree that it doesn't require the additional* RGB Difference Key *that I had as backup.*

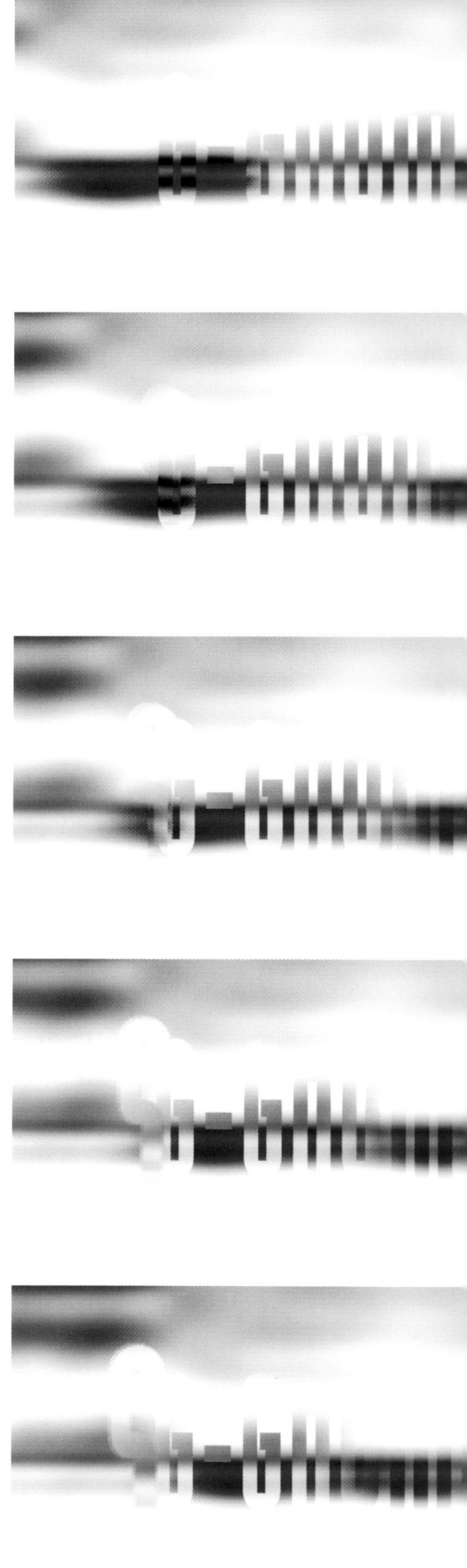

Keying and motion: 2

The second work-through we're going to look at is this one. It's a green screen scene, that we'll actually look at producing later on in the book (*see page 152*). As we'll see later, the question is the question mark. At the moment, there are three fundamental layers in the title…

1 *The background with a* Crawl *from left to right…*

2 *The main title with a* Track Matte *background keyed to crawl right to left…*

3 *…and a question mark "hidden" within the initial "G" of the main title, with a* Green Screen Key *with the same reversed background crawl keyed through.*

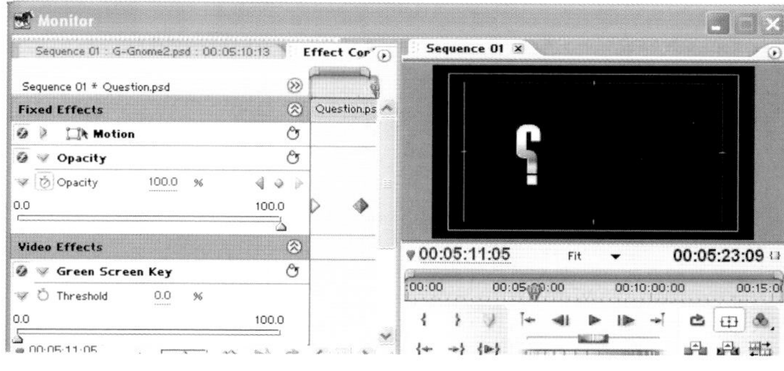

4 *Together, they're almost magical…*

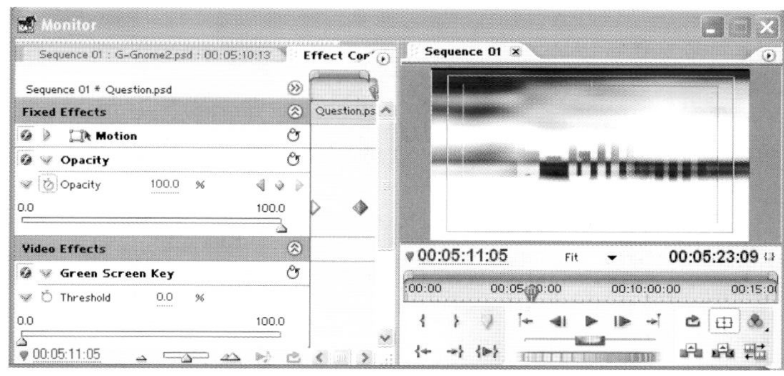

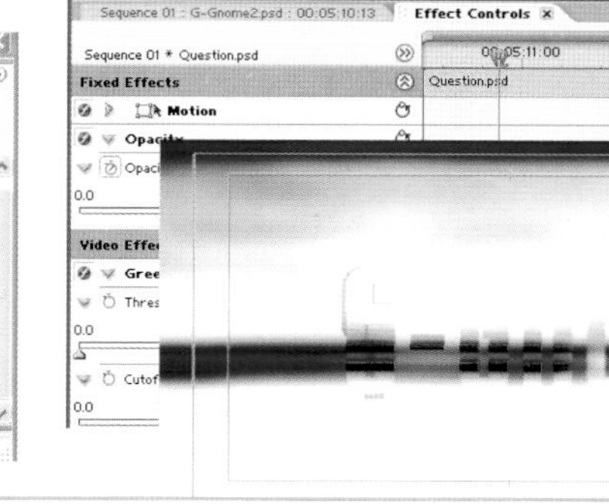

5 *…almost. Under scrutiny, it's quite obvious that the* Opacity *change, which I applied to the question mark in order that it emerged seamlessly from the "G" has had no effect whatsoever. None. In fact, under scrutiny, all the* Opacity *change does is to change the "hidden" question mark from a very noticeable poor key, to the desired key.*

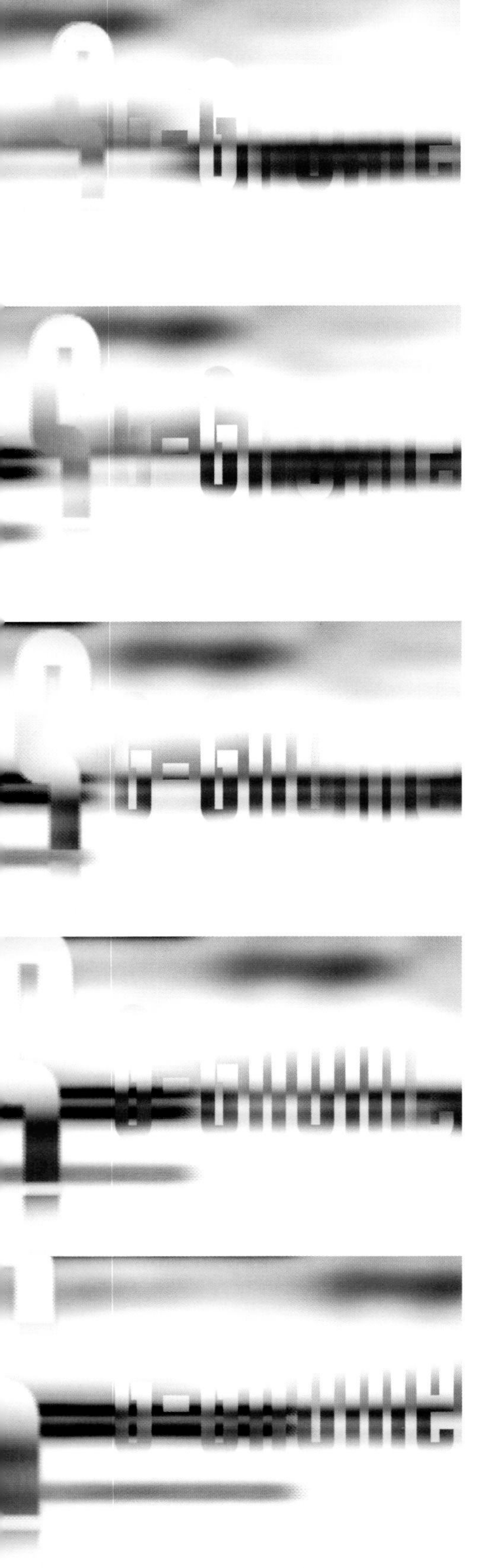

6 *There are two important layers: the question mark and the background. To make them work together, the* Opacity *change from the question mark needs duplicating exactly to the background. This is the essence of making any keying transition work: all associated layers have to work together, or risk too much or too little of one or the other.*

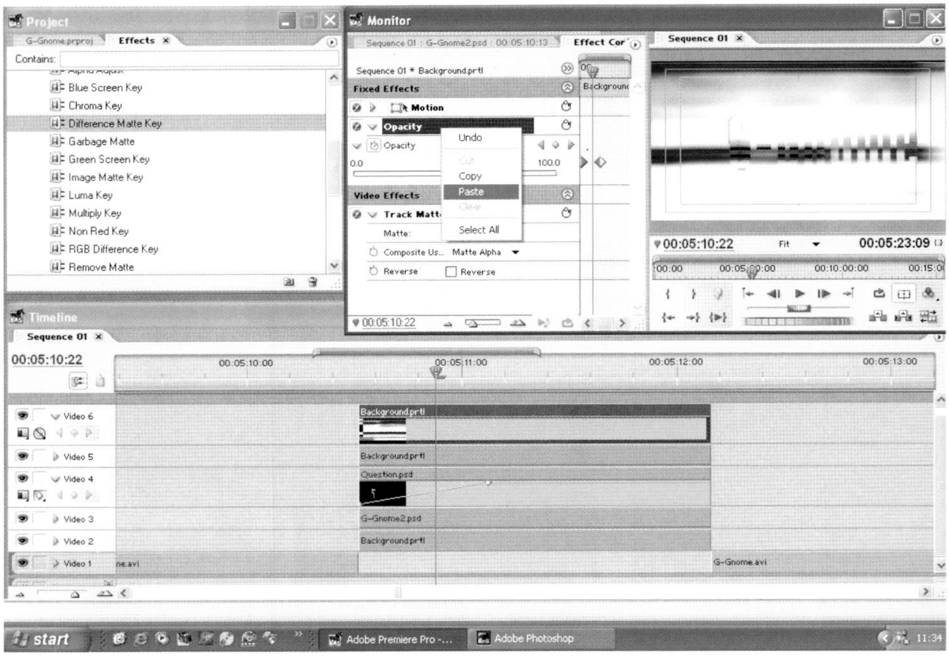

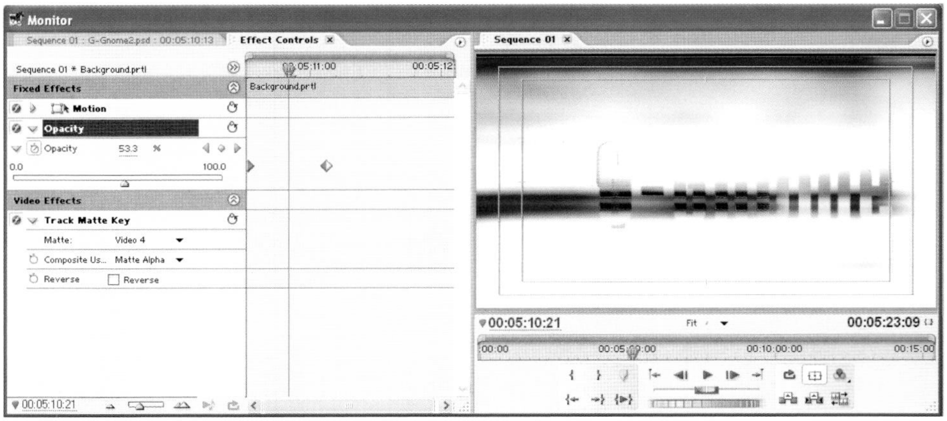

7 *The issues with keys are that they are incredibly sensitive to change. Using both of these layers at half* Opacity *still deforms the "G" beyond all recognition.*

8 *Taking the second full Opacity keyframe back down to zero, highlights what I require up until the point of movement.*

9 *Therefore, both values are changed to create a very steep change—from 0 to 100 in three frames. Even that causes an issue in the middle frame, though—and that one frame can make a jarring difference on the eye.*

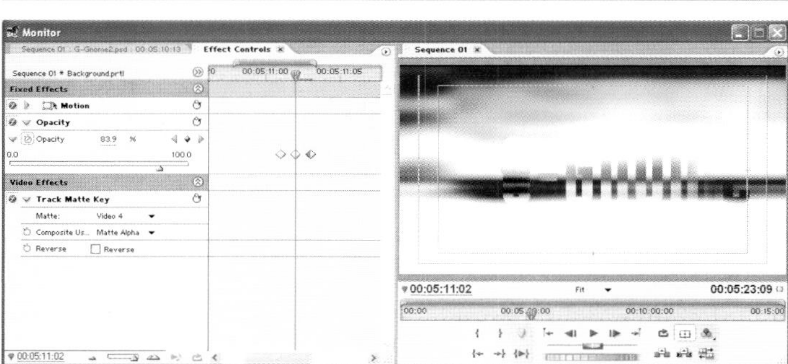

10 *This is fixed with a higher Opacity inclination on the background, which makes it a smoother ride to the apex.*

11 *The final objective, though, is that the question mark moves out of the "G" glyph, like a clone. This needs to take place at that precise change in Opacity. Dropping down the Motion menu at the first keyframe, I've keyframed as the default position. For the second one, I've made my move out of the "G" to the left on the X axis and added a slightly higher Scale value. For the third, I've cleared the "G" and continued with the Scale increase, before keyframing final values at the end of the clip to take the glyph out of screen safety.*

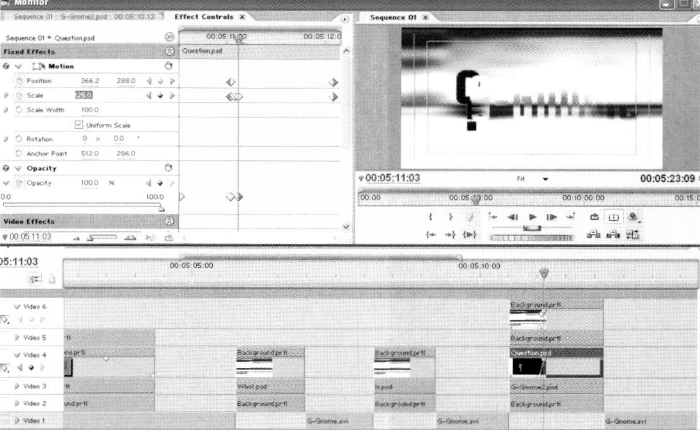

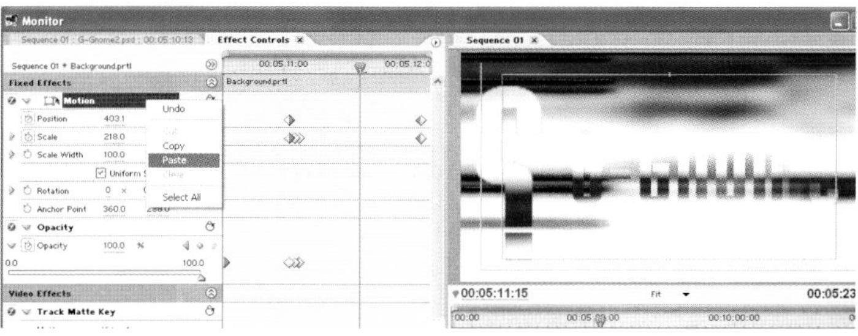

12 *Copying and pasting these Motion values over to the background clip completes the effect. What I'm not so keen on, though, is the rather obvious keyline around the question mark.*

13 *Taking an RGB Difference Key over from the Keying Effects menu enables this to be softened. Sampling one of the lightest blue hues and checking the Mask Only box also gives us a Drop Shadow that works well with the three-dimensional increase in scale of the glyph. The result works exactly as I want it to.*

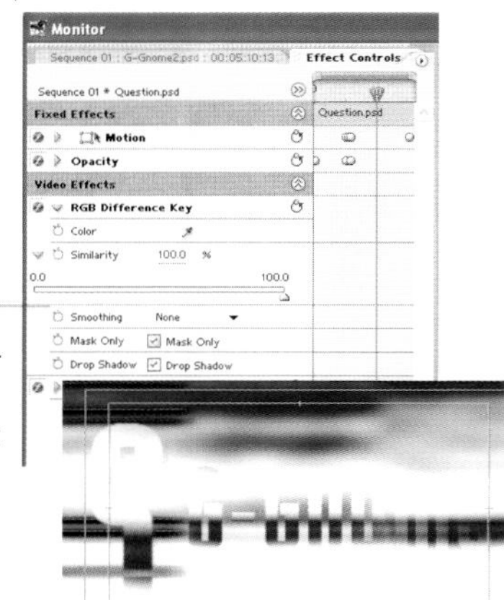

Motion in space

Motion is an integral part of titling. Rolls and crawls are standard practice for title designers, but their common exploitation often prevents viewers from actually reading the titles themselves.

Designers, though, are on a constant mission to be noticed—which is why some title sequences scream "Look-at-me." While you have to be pretty cunning to find an effect that has never been used before, the permutations of different movement over time in a 400,000 pixel playground should make it a huge arena for creativity. Fashions change in video and titling, but the current evolving trends are towards the dynamic interaction between titles and individual glyphs—rather than merely dolling glyphs up in text effects. You could say it's "the new black (matte)." Natural transitions are in, and video effects are out.

1 *To progress the "Jonny Quality" title, the entire beast is made up of one big* Timeline *block: a reversed speed* Chroma Key *overlay of the background, the background itself and five pairs of title layers track matted to the background. Each layer, by default, occupies the same area of the screen and the same space in the* Timeline. *Because of the* Chroma Key *overlay and the* Luma Track Matte *background, each layer (depending on the lenght of the titling) is therefore visible and invisible in precisely the same areas of the screen. All of this will be changed with motion within the space.*

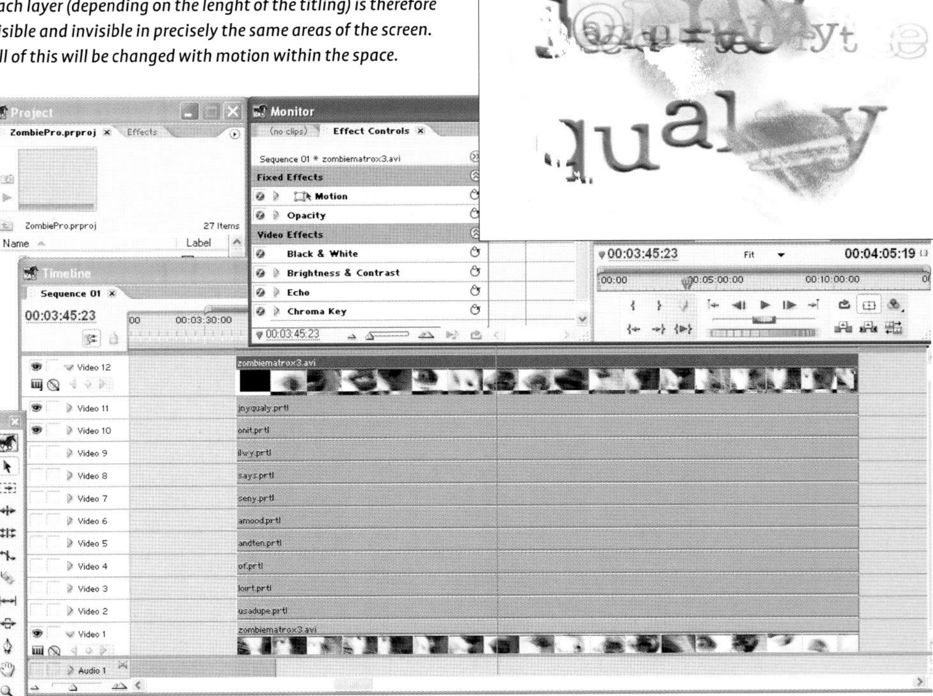

2 Because of the complication of the Timeline, the best bet is to get a reduced amount of sequences—or better, some AVIs—out of the whole thing to simplify the Timeline, in order that each pairing can have its moment with the overlay and background. Working through them chronologically is the only way to continue. The reason that all the layers remain there is that it makes for easy toggling between different views of tracks to see what lies ahead. The cost of this is render time.

The first pair's green text already has a transition in place of its own: a Luma Key that brings it in from the white. Coupled with this, the Chroma Key and Luma Track Matte seem to have ideas of their own about where to come into frame.

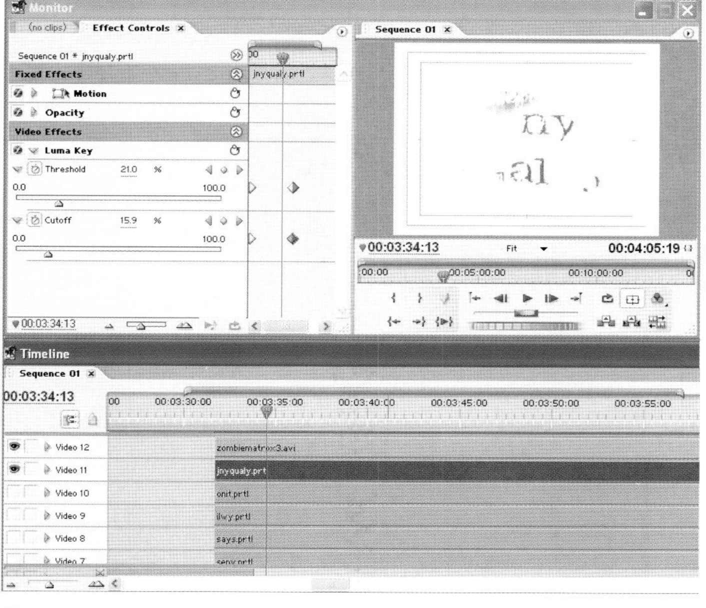

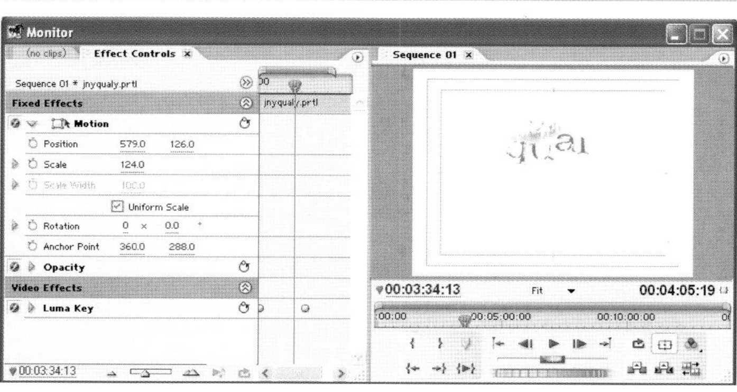

4 At exactly the same point on the Timeline, simply changing the Scale and Position in the ECW affects how much of the title shows through, with the Luma Key transition, Chroma Key, and Luma Track Matte all interacting with each other.

3 A word about the background. In order to understand the following process, the background itself must be understood. Shot on DV using a slow shutter and high exposure in bright light, the clip in Premiere Pro with an Echo, slow-mo, and a high contrast is dreamlike with frame-by-frame shifting hot (white) and cold (image) spots. What this means in terms of use as background and overlay is that no part of it is particularly identifiable. This kind of background is useful with a complex title like this—especially when the text changes the usage of the background. Repetition is unlikely to be noticed, and therefore any time-consuming adherence to using strictly different parts of both AVIs will produce results that aren't really worth the effort.

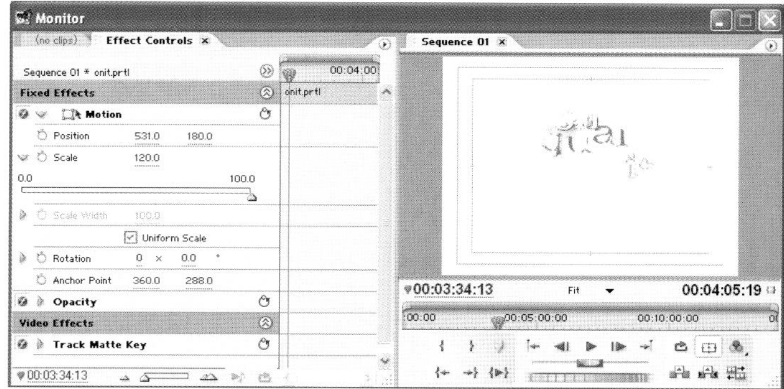

5 Toggling the second part of the title into view—and knowing that, at some time during the motion applied, they both have to be in vision to be legible—we can see precisely the sort of complication that makes good housekeeping and focus so important for titles.

6 *This, though, is the title at another part of the* Timeline*—and this demonstrates the reason why...*

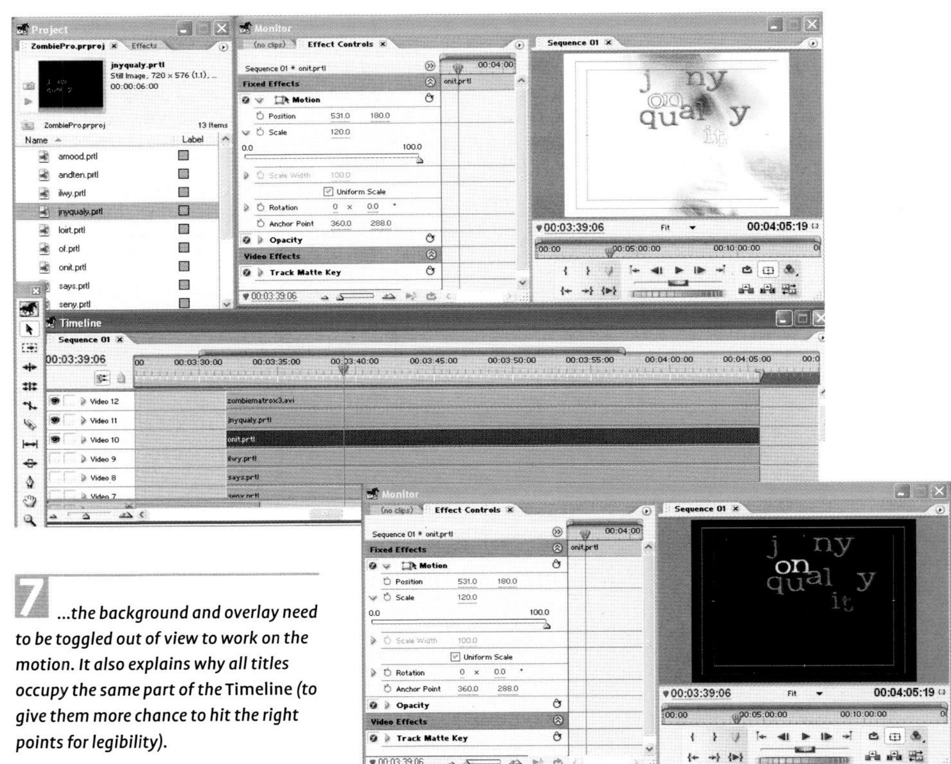

7 *...the background and overlay need to be toggled out of view to work on the motion. It also explains why all titles occupy the same part of the* Timeline *(to give them more chance to hit the right points for legibility).*

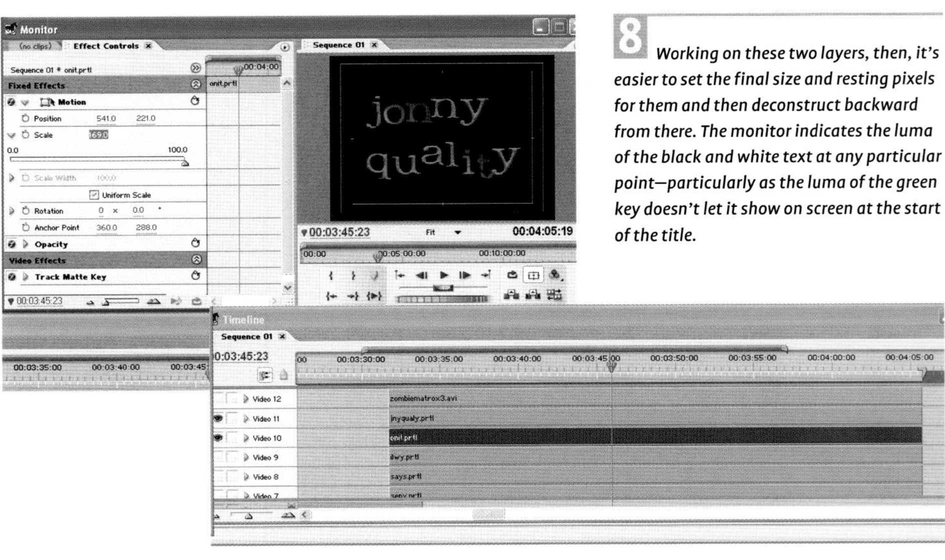

8 *Working on these two layers, then, it's easier to set the final size and resting pixels for them and then deconstruct backward from there. The monitor indicates the luma of the black and white text at any particular point—particularly as the luma of the green key doesn't let it show on screen at the start of the title.*

9 *Working backward, there isn't such a luma transition for the monochrome text: it starts hard onscreen. The* In *position, then, forces a creative work-around (in case the* Chroma Key *isn't overlaying the text) to take the text off screen. This, I've done, with a massive* Scale *increase.*

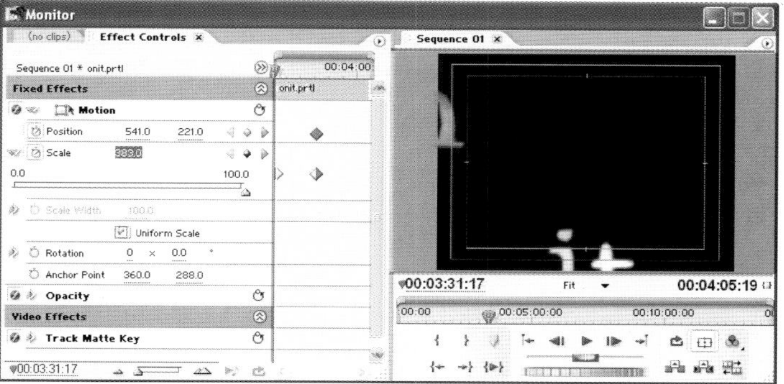

10 *Rendering up with background and overlay in vision, I've exported the clip as an AVI...*

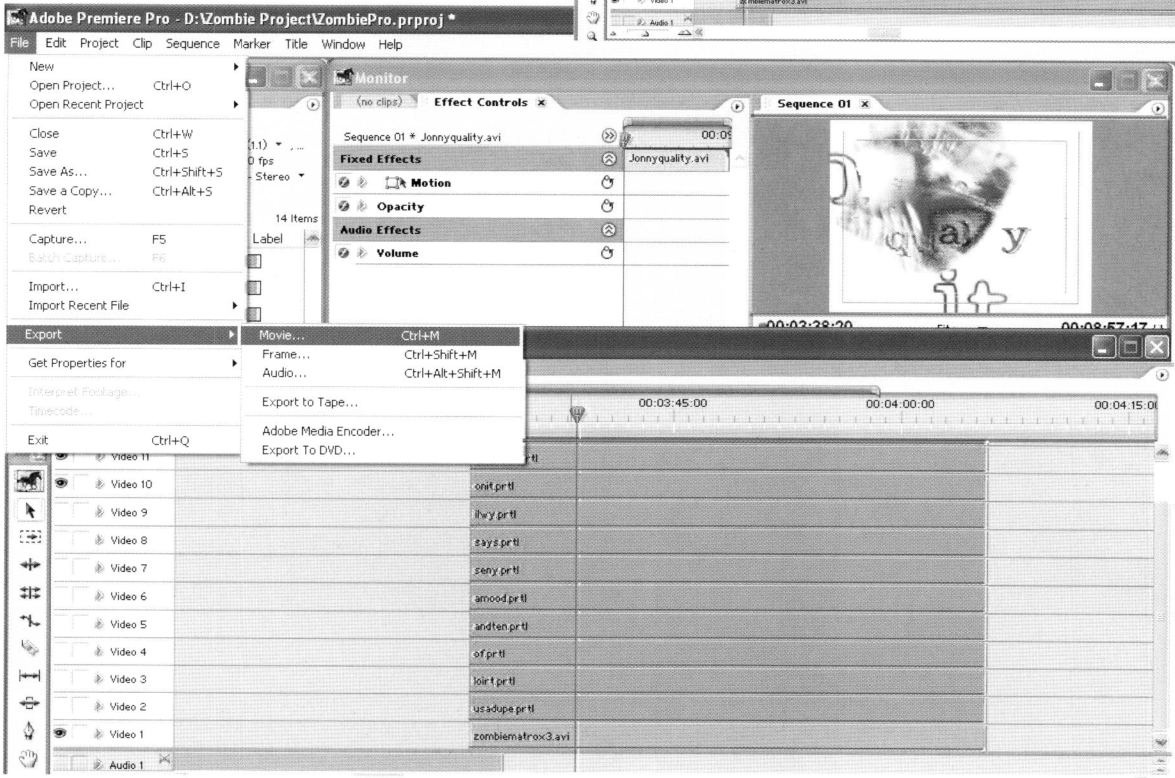

11 *...which means that I can then clear the two layers and work on the next two. The trick to avoid giving yourself a hard time not seeing the bits that you want to see, is to check for screen safety, see how the whole sequence is working, and keep toggling vision on each track, with your* Edit Line *in the same place.*

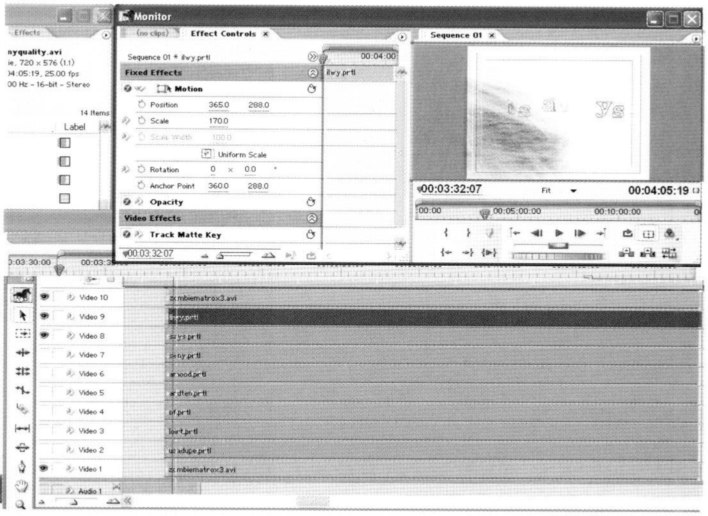

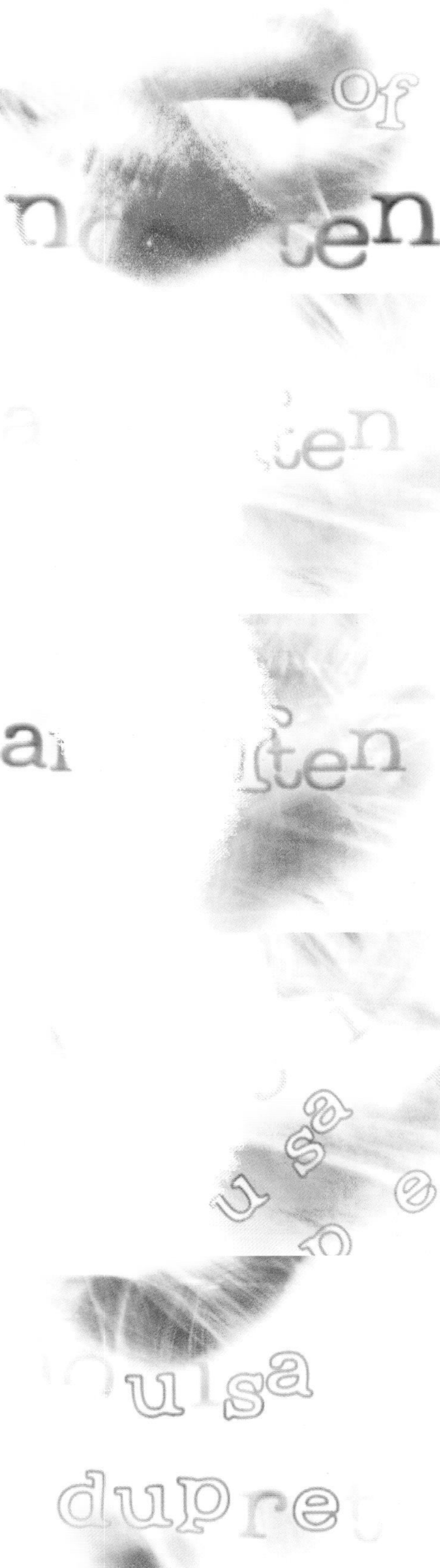

12 *I've no luma transitions that bring any of the text on anymore, so all text will be coming in from different angles. These second two layers are coming in—one from the top and one from left of screen—and they will both* Scale *up and settle in their correct legible position. Both in-points are slightly delayed to get a different background and overlay to the first title. The monochrome text is even given slightly more scaling once it gets to its final position. This just keeps things moving beyond the requirements of the title.*

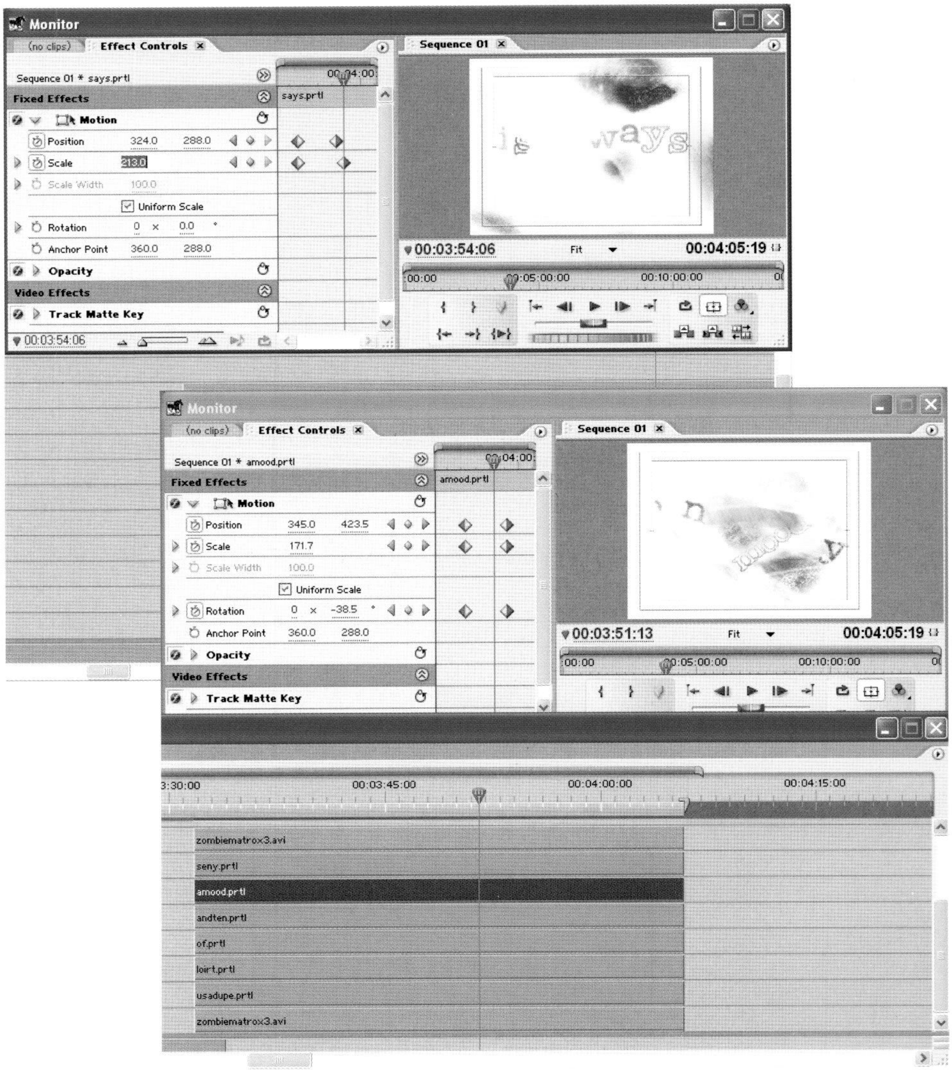

13 *Again, exporting the clip with all four layers, and then eliminating the used text layers from the* Timeline*, enables work on the next two. This begins and ends slightly farther down the overlay and background clips. For the transition, I'm starting out of frame with two upscaling, rotating layers that move into their correct position at the end of the move.*

14 *Render, export, clear tracks, start again: this track's transition is much easier to see without the overlay toggled on, which means that much of the transitional motion is likely to be hidden. I've therefore extended it over time to ensure that some of it is seen. If there's a speed issue, this can be adjusted when the clip exists as an AVI. This time, I'm back using the X and Y axes, taking the titles to the bottom and to the right of screen. The green clip will be descaled as it travels, the monochrome text will upscale.*

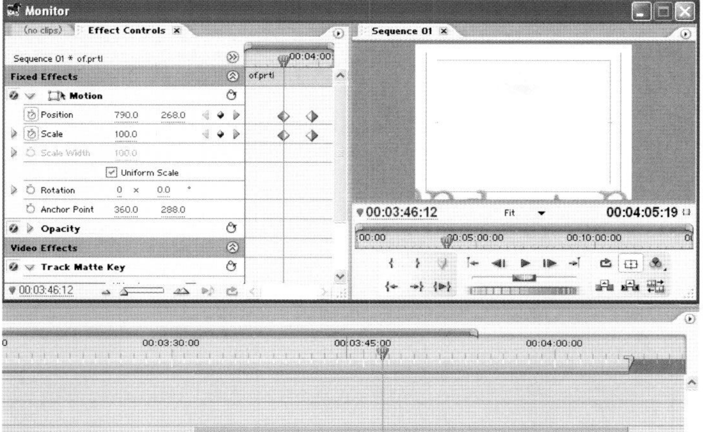

15 *For the last clip, I've used another Rotation to get both layers out of frame at the start, but altered the Anchor Point on each—one on the X axis and one on the Y.*

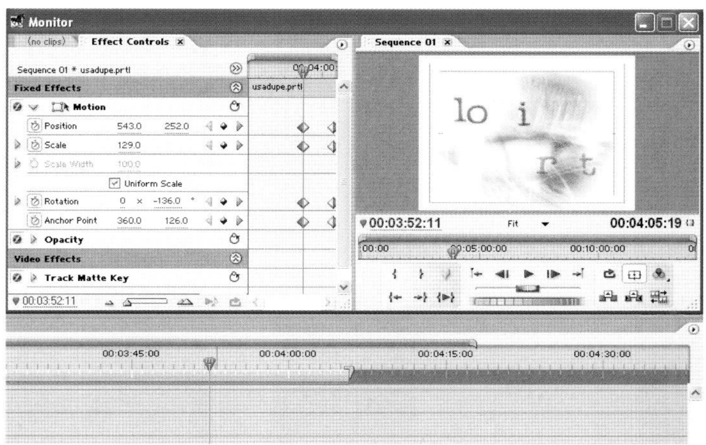

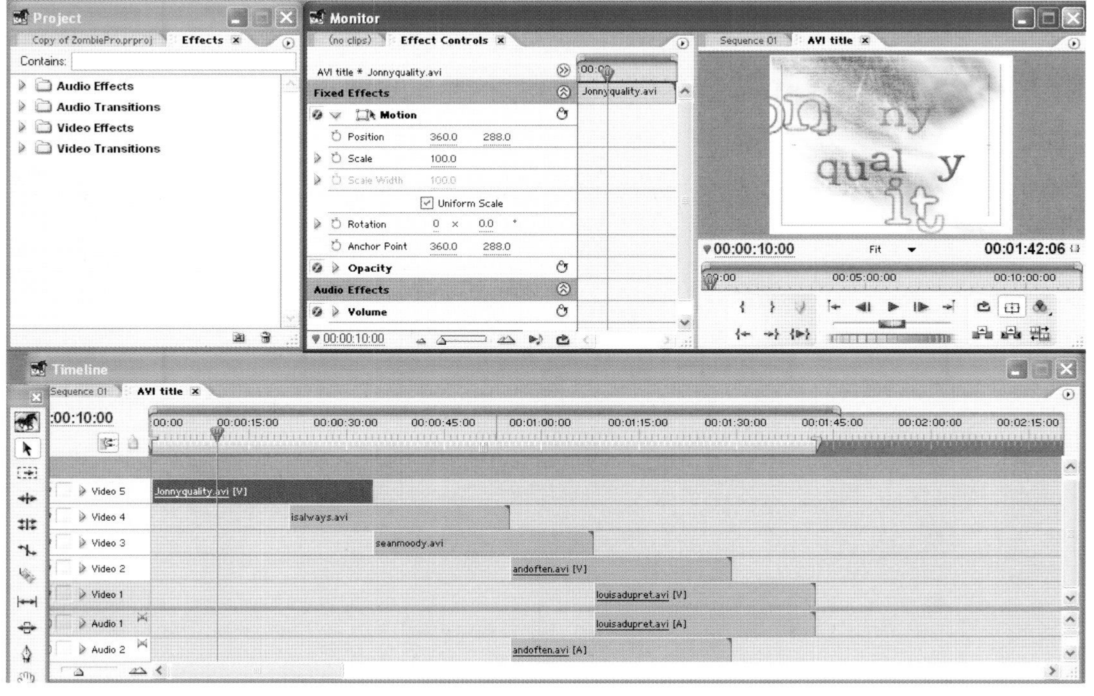

16 *This done, the next stage is to create a new sequence, using all of the new AVIs. I've stepped them roughly, giving them all their own video tracks once more. The speeds of the moves, transitions, and flow are all entirely wrong at the moment. This, though, cannot be done without the aid of the soundtrack...*

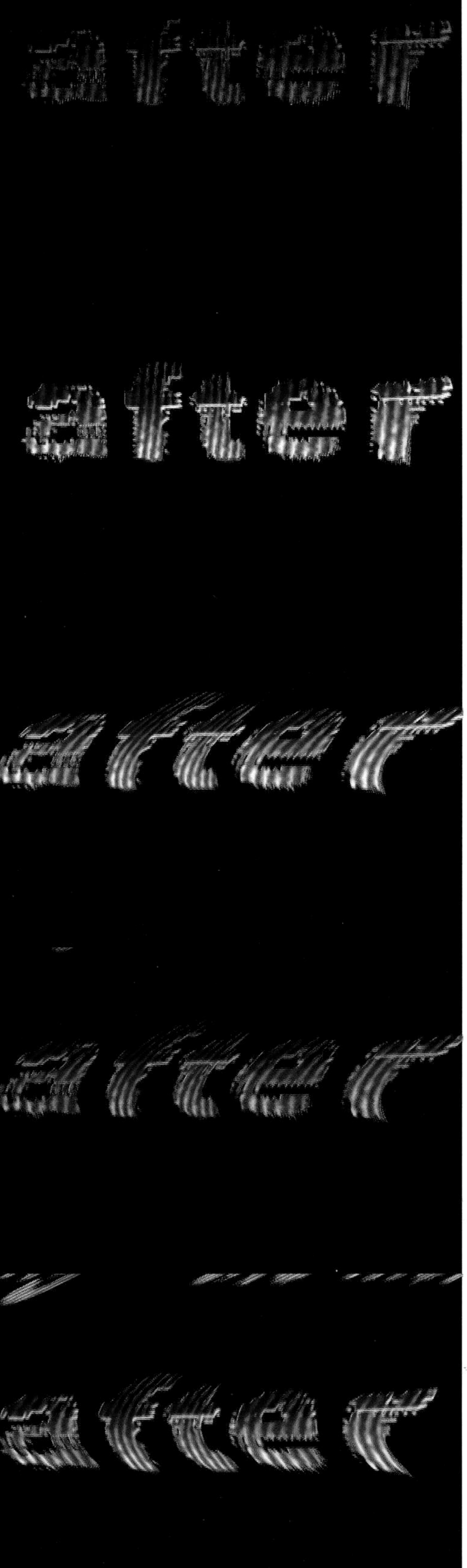

Video effects in motion

When everything's moving and functional, there's always something else to do: add a video effect, for example. But it's vital that you choose your effect and your moment wisely, to avoid being flashy or gratuitous.

We've seen how to use an effect as a transition and to create motion. If you've already got motion, there are certain effects that can add to the movement, to give your title even more impact.

The Dome title has been sitting on the sidelines waiting for its moment of glory. This is it.

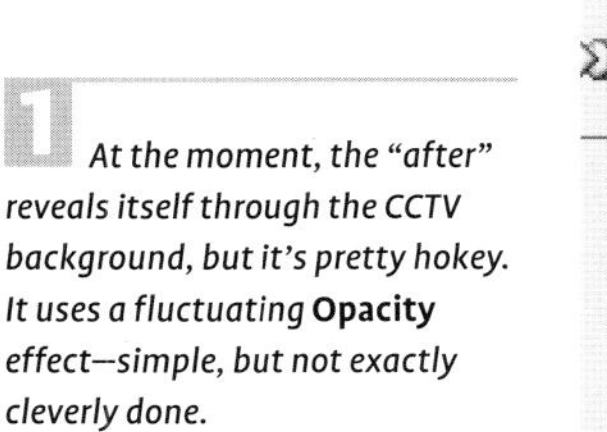

1 *At the moment, the "after" reveals itself through the CCTV background, but it's pretty hokey. It uses a fluctuating* **Opacity** *effect—simple, but not exactly cleverly done.*

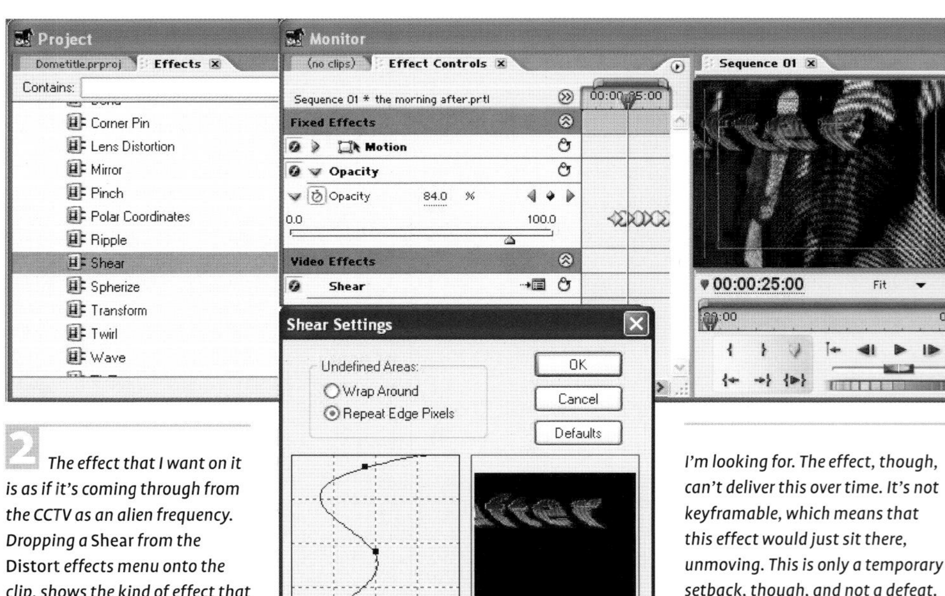

2 *The effect that I want on it is as if it's coming through from the CCTV as an alien frequency. Dropping a* Shear *from the* Distort *effects menu onto the clip, shows the kind of effect that I'm looking for. The effect, though, can't deliver this over time. It's not keyframable, which means that this effect would just sit there, unmoving. This is only a temporary setback, though, and not a defeat.*

3 There's always a way. The problem with razoring up the clip as is, is that it's in reverse—and this only leads to more problems with Premiere Pro's rather odd behavior. Creating a new sequence solely for the clip, and then exporting the clip as an AVI, is a good start.

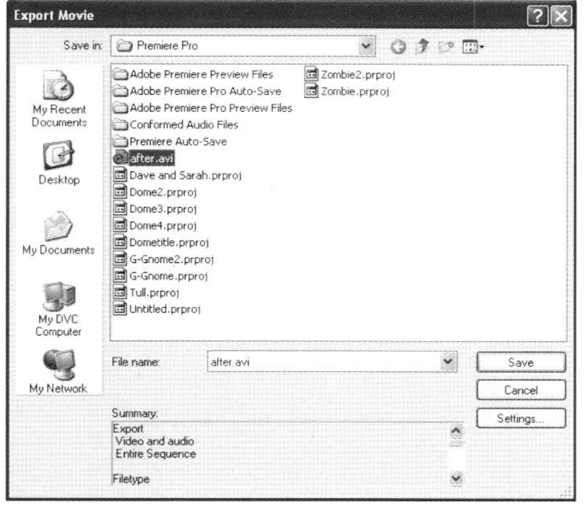

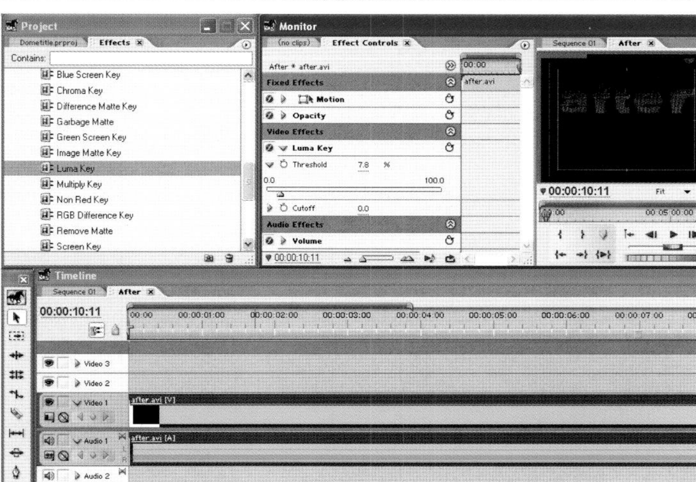

4 Clearing the prtl clip from the sequence and importing the AVI leaves the clip open for razoring. Before getting carried away, it's important to remember what exactly an AVI does to the clip. As an AVI, the title is no longer based on an alpha matte. Instead, the black alpha is now black video. Before razoring, it would make sense to drop a Luma Key straight onto the AVI and change this. However, because this sequence relies on the matte working well, it makes more sense to add it to the entire sequence when it's back on the original Timeline, enabling some immediate and incremental adjustment.

5 So, without the Luma Key, I've hacked away at the Timeline with a razor at various random points where the Opacity is letting the title through.

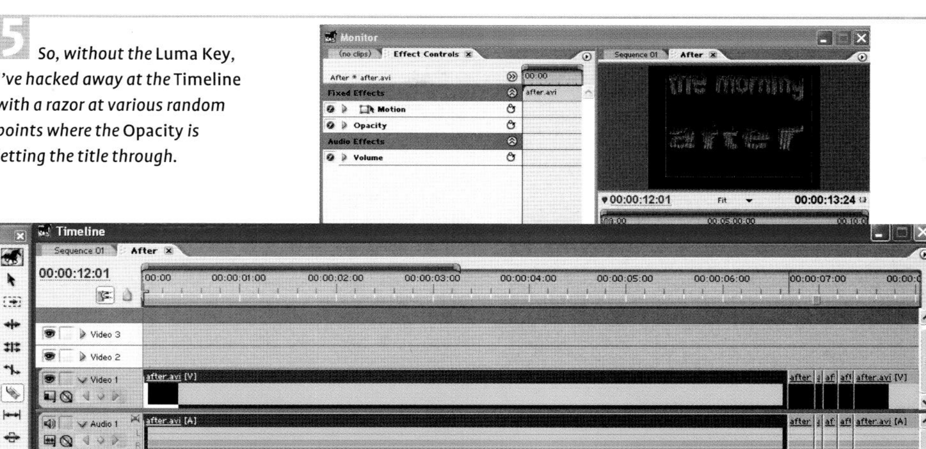

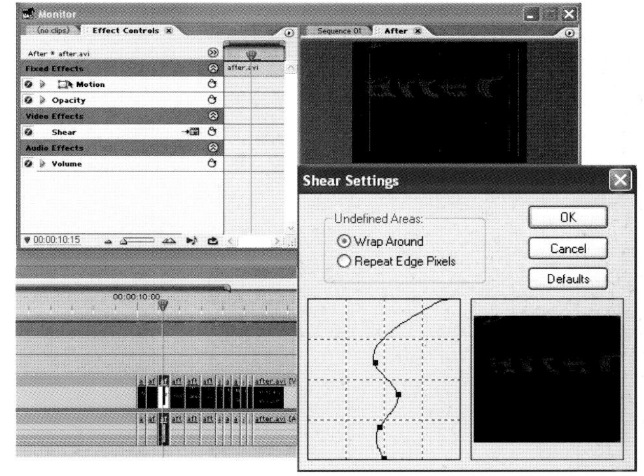

6 For every other one of these small clips, I've dragged a Shear from the Distort menu and tweaked it to suit in the settings dialog. It's perfect for the roll of the title as the settings screen represents the whole of the output screen, not just the title. The rolling title will therefore wave in these fixed directions as they move down the screen over the effects applied.

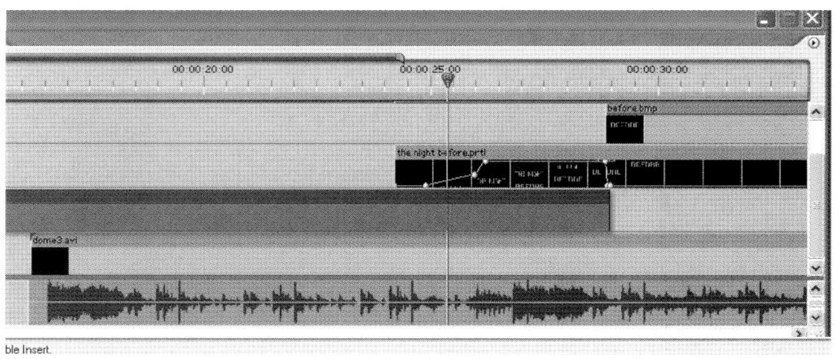

7 Rendering and saving this up, I've dragged the sequence onto the original Timeline to replace the cleared prtl file.

8 *The next thing is the application of the* Luma Key. *Dragging it onto the new sequence, I've found a point where all layers are onscreen to scrutinize the* Threshold *and* Cutoff *points required on the slider scales. Because the title itself has elements of black in it, it becomes an exact science...*

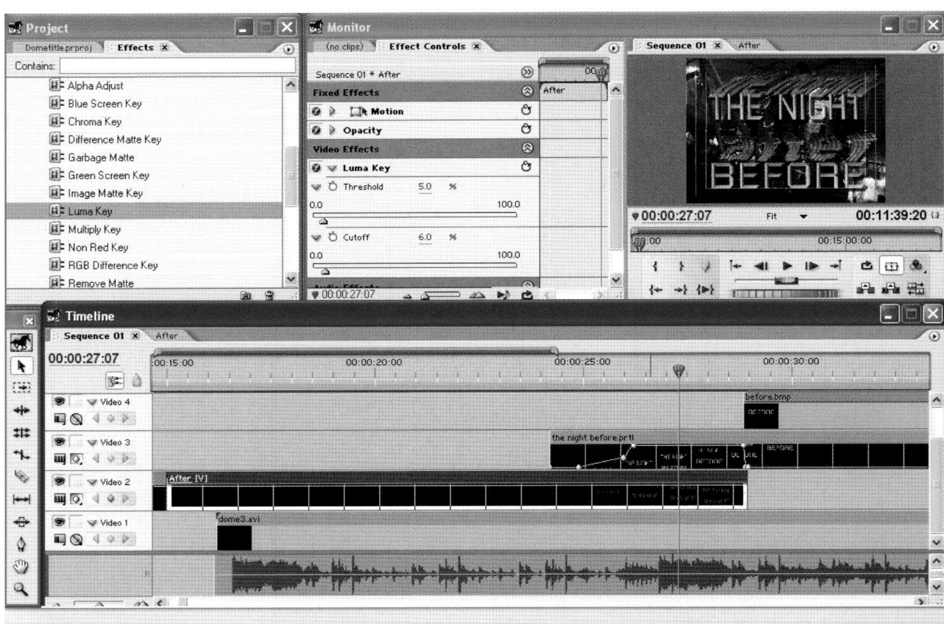

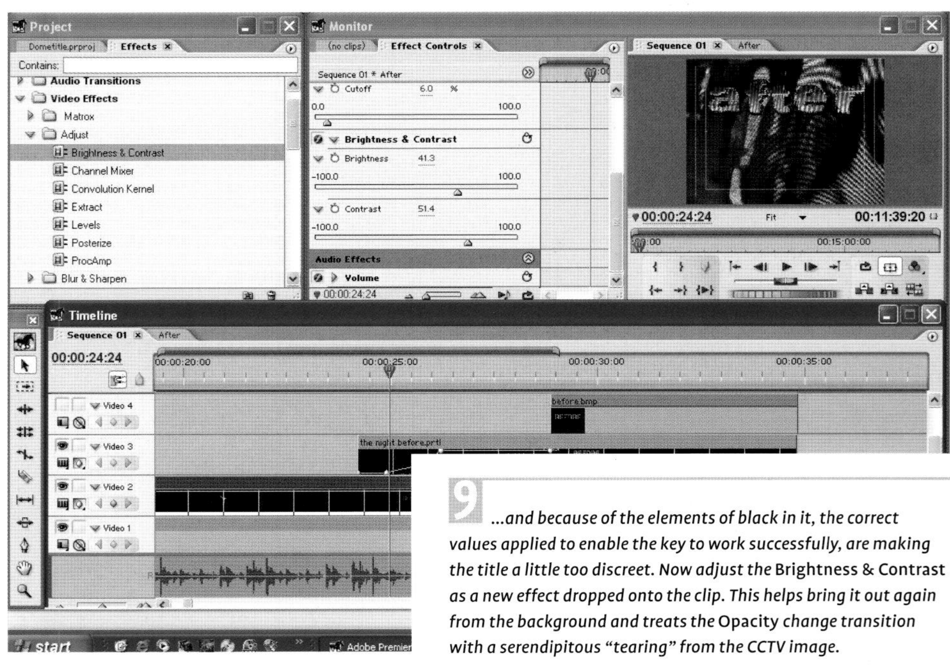

9 *...and because of the elements of black in it, the correct values applied to enable the key to work successfully, are making the title a little too discreet. Now adjust the* Brightness & Contrast *as a new effect dropped onto the clip. This helps bring it out again from the background and treats the* Opacity *change transition with a serendipitous "tearing" from the CCTV image.*

10 *In all this activity we've almost forgotten about the rolling "the night before" caption. Here, we're bringing together the two different styles of title, each of which alludes to a very different mood. It follows, then, that their respective motion should be different. It's time to give the second title the attention it deserves. Dragging an* Edge Feather *from the* Transform *menu works well with the title matte. Tingeing the edges of the frame with a slight* Opacity *change keeps the title looking good as it enters, rolls down, and then leaves the frame.*

11 *We'll also use a* Lens Flare *from the* Render *drop-down, which will give it that extra lift as if the title is entering the limelight, and create a larger contrast between the feathering. The* Zoom Lens *setting retains more saturation of the blue fill than the* Prime *options and adds a slight flare reflection.*

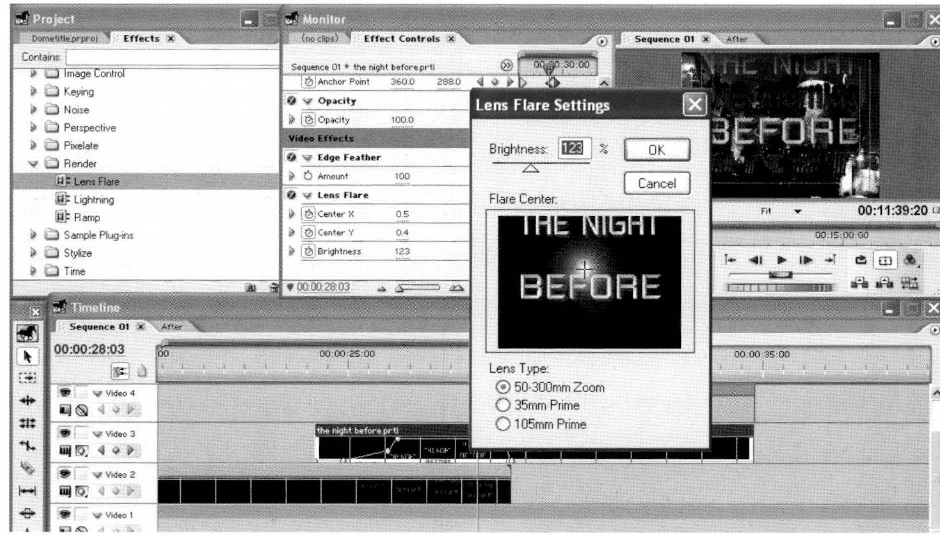

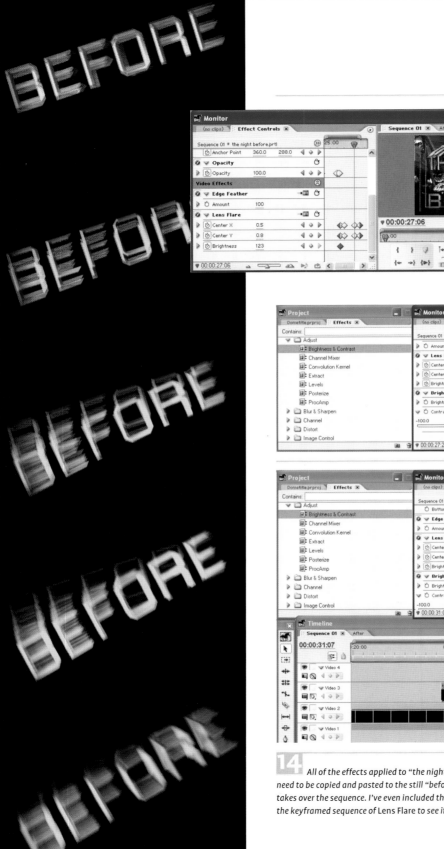

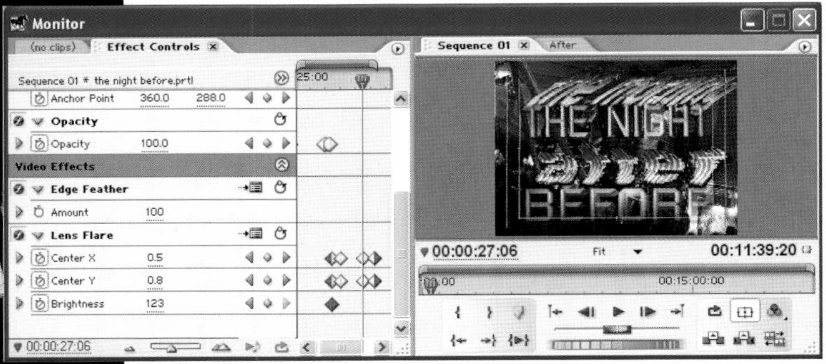

12 *The* Lens Flare *is keyframable, and because of the roll, I've put in different X/Y co-ordinates to move the* Lens Flare *across the screen, covering certain letters at certain times during the roll. It highlights them and makes them a little more special.*

13 *In doing so, though, it has the knock-on effect (especially in the areas of the feather) of washing out some of the fill saturation. Again, dragging a* Brightness & Contrast *adjustment to the clip, strengthens the luminance once more.*

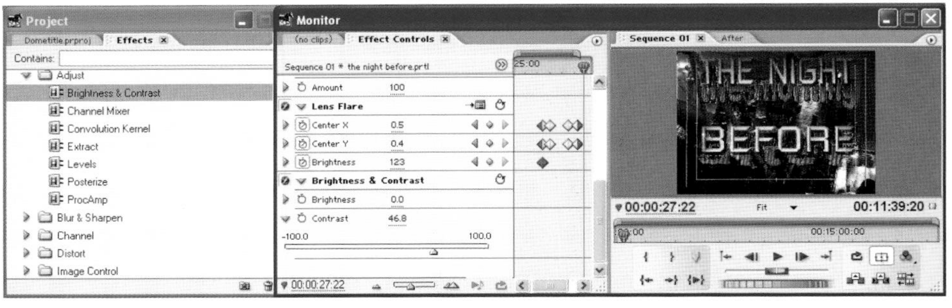

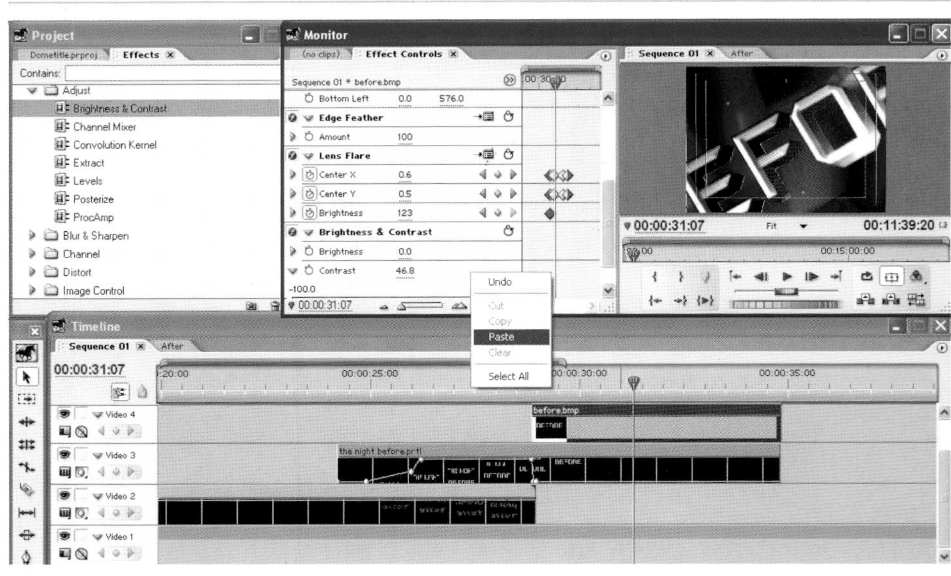

14 *All of the effects applied to "the night before" need to be copied and pasted to the still "before," which takes over the sequence. I've even included the whole of the keyframed sequence of* Lens Flare *to see if it works...*

20 *The* Echo Operator *is the method in which the echo is interpreted. An* Add *option combines the pixel chrominance and luminance channels, which can lead to a completely overloaded image...*

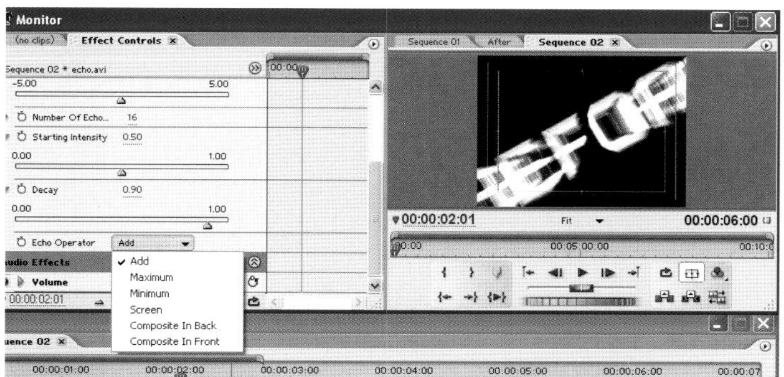

21 *The* Maximum *option combines the image, using the maximum values possible from all frames together and thereby producing a tolerance limit...*

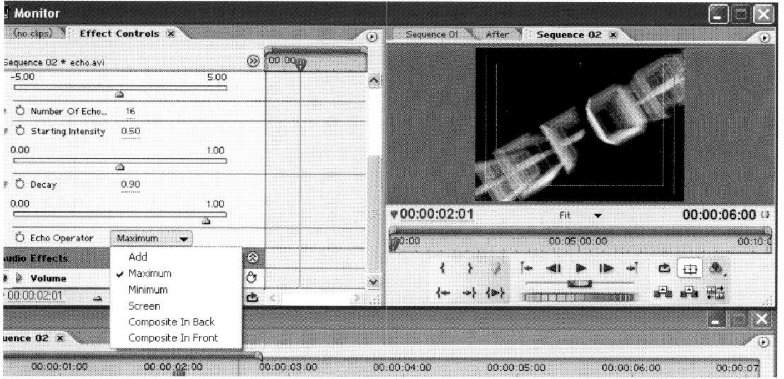

22 *...while* Minimum *does exactly the same but with the minimum values, thereby producing a dark echo.*

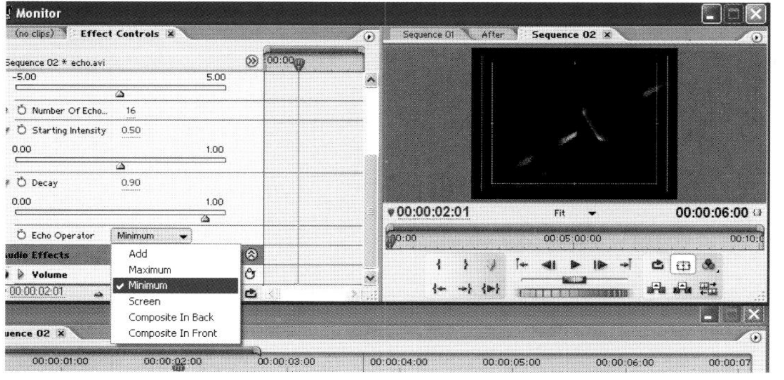

23 Screen, *like* Add, *also combines the pixel intensity, but distributes the pixel values between fields, balancing the brightness.*

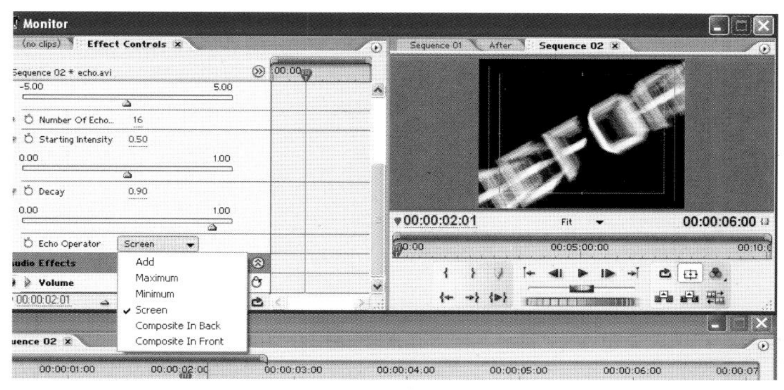

24 Composite in Back *uses the alpha channel to compose the echoes from the back to the front...*

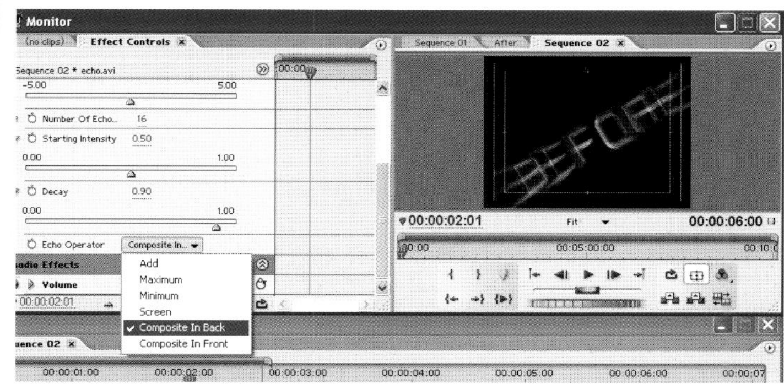

25 *...and* Composite in Front *does exactly the opposite...*

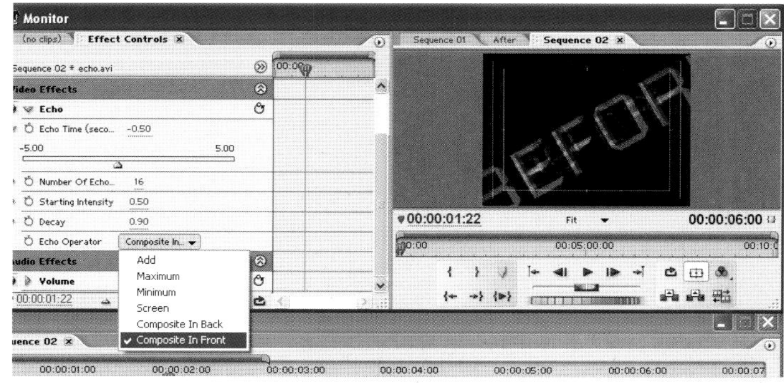

26 *Suddenly the choice of effect—and the choice of options—hots up. There can be only one winner, though, and that is always the one which works when keyed. In this situation, where close-knit trail frames are at once lightening the image, washing out the color, and blurring the original, the combination of* Echo *and key is vital. The closest I can get to success with the effect that I want is by using* Screen *as my composite option, but I've keyframed the* Starting Intensity *values to ensure that I keep the brightness of the pixels in check.*

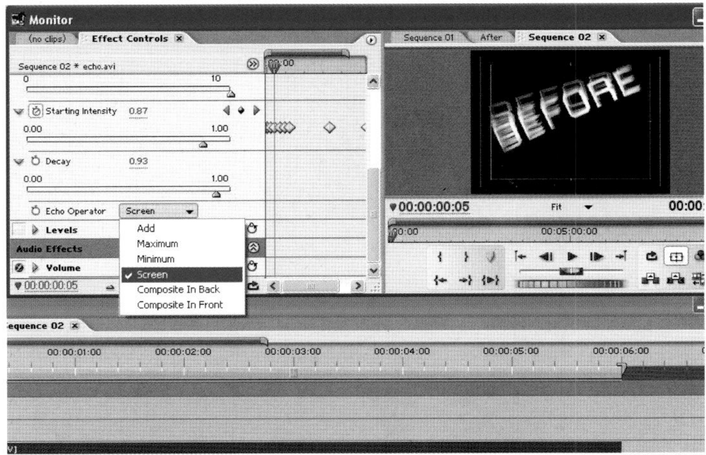

27 *That said, there's far too much white in the title—we want to dazzle, but not to blind—and the difference between the original moving title and the superimposed moving still will be too great unless some of the blue is put back in. Dragging a* Levels *adjustment onto the clip allows for a decrease in the overall chrominance (RGB)* White Output, *as well as the blue midtones* (Blue Gamma) *to temper this.*

28 *Dropping it in place on the original* Timeline, *a* Luma Key *does the job in getting it to be seen* (see page 122-127), *and adjusting the* Threshold *makes it far less painful on the eye.*

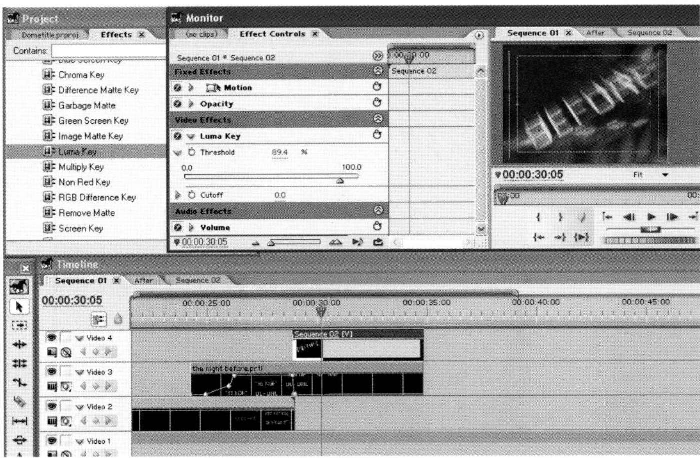

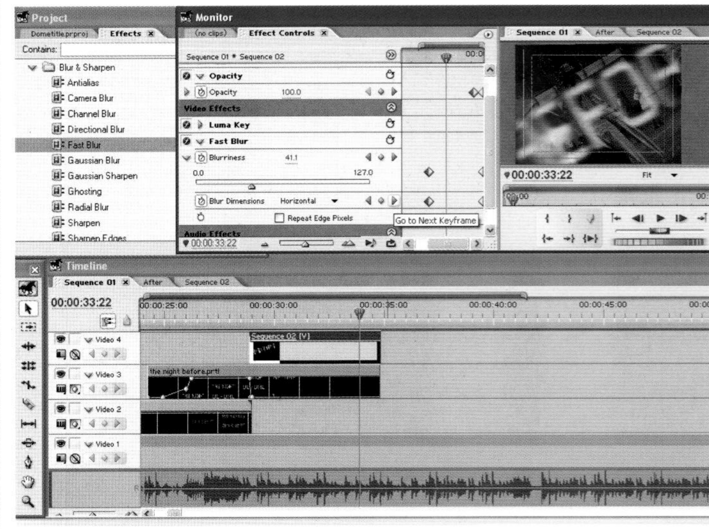

29 *All that remains now is the exit of the "before" title. Once due for a simple mix, it now looks as if it needs something purely based on the horizontal axis to work. With* Effects *at the ready, adding a* Fast Blur *on the* Horizontal *axis to take the title to the extremity of blur (i.e. invisible effect), works dynamically as a transition. Keyframing a final* Opacity *drop to rid the final frames of any blur residue seals the work. Truly a night to remember: and our title draws out the themes of the video.*

THE NIGHT
BEFORE
THE NIGHT
BEFORE

the irish rover

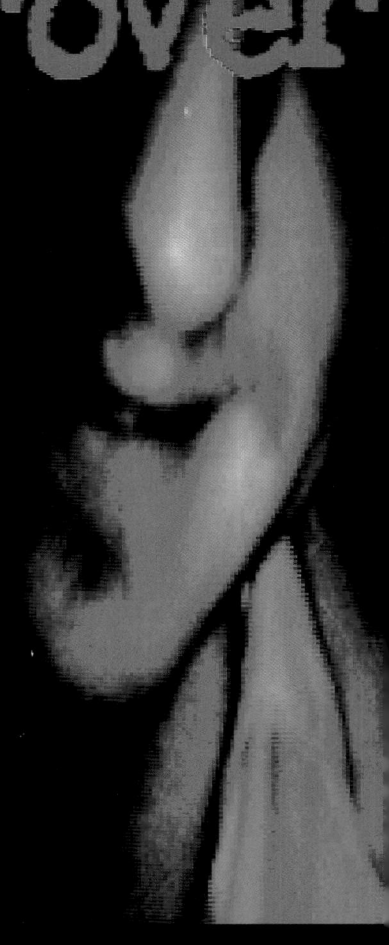

5

CHAPTER FIVE

using Photoshop with titling

Photoshop and Premiere Pro

Premiere Pro is now fully compatible with another Adobe package: the image-editing giant Photoshop. Using Photoshop alongside Premiere gives you all the versatility of a dedicated image-editor and graphics and text creator—but there are some basic concepts to take on board first...

Like Premiere Pro, Adobe's Photoshop (the industry-defining image-editing suite) is at heart a pixel-based program. More accurately, it is a bitmap-based application, designed to work with photographic material. However, like Adobe's graphics and drawing package, Illustrator, Photoshop incorporates a number of vector-based drawing and text tools, which work alongside the pixel-based tools that enable us literally to paint with light.

When we say these tools are vector-based, this means that they use mathematical algorithms to define shapes and lines based on calculations of magnitude (size) and direction (X/Y). Such graphics can be scaled to any size with no loss of resolution. Non vector-based applications, on the other hand – such as Premiere – rely on pixel information to form an image. Pixels, short for "picture elements," are the smallest elements into which such a digital image can be broken: dots of chrominance and luminance that form images derived from those ones and zeroes (ons and offs) in which all digital information is stored.

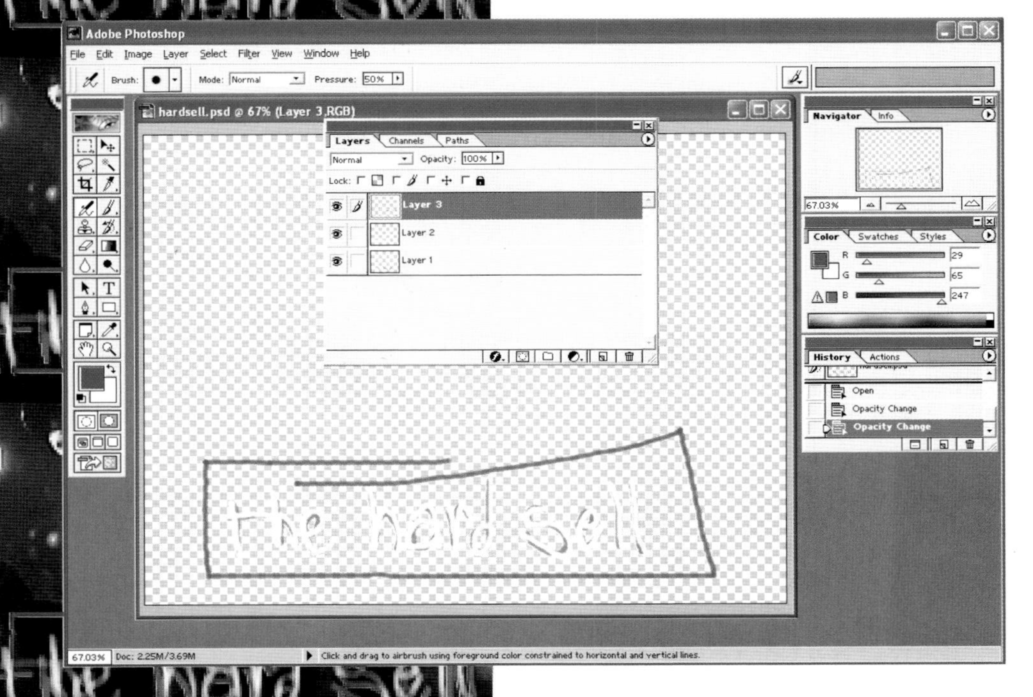

Graphics and image-editing applications are historically tailored for the still image, not the moving one – although most can now deal with animations (rapid sequences of still images). The moving image has always used non-square pixels of 4:3 ratio, while graphics and image-editing applications (and computer monitors) use square pixels that are less prone to artifacts.

It used to be, therefore, that in order to take a still image into a moving, pixel-based environment, the image would first have to be resized, deinterlaced, color-corrected, and alpha-adjusted. Premiere Pro can now deal with all of these in *Title Designer* or on the *Timeline* itself. In short, it is now delighted to talk to everything that Photoshop can throw at it.

Things get slightly more complicated with vector-based images, including text glyphs. These demand an additional process called rasterization, which turns the vector intructions into a more conventional pixel bitmap format (.jpg, .bmp, etc) that Premiere can understand. This translation, though, is not always a perfect one, and antialiasing is often needed to mitigate any irregularities.

Today, Premiere Pro has a much deeper understanding of Photoshop, and this can be seen as soon as an image is imported. Not only are Photoshop's native .psd files now recognized,

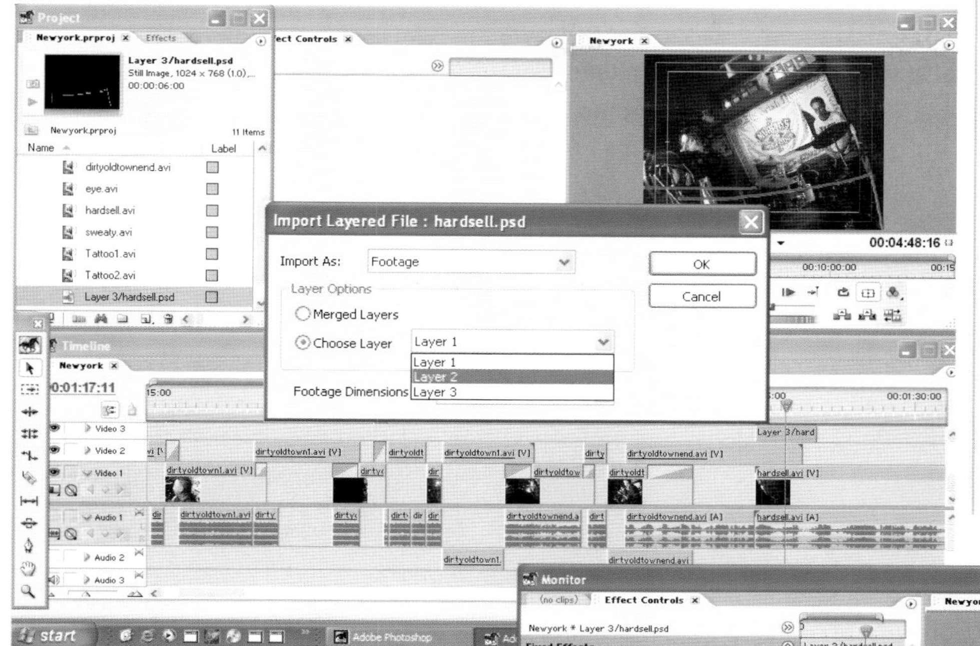

but a dialog box will ask if you want to import all the original layers, or a "flattened" version of the image (one with the layers merged so that they are no longer separately editable). Once in Premiere Pro, .psd files remain .psd files, and any transparency in the file becomes an alpha matte.

In addition, a .psd file can be quite happily imported as a logo into *Title Designer* and worked with from there – again with any transparency appearing as an alpha matte (see right). This is echoed on the *Timeline* – .psds are removable and resizable, and are open to color and opacity change as happily as any moving clip when dragged home (below right).

You can also modify them with video effects and transitions, making Photoshop one of your most flexible friends when creating titles. Used creatively with moving images, you'll surprise yourself with what you can do with Photoshop (and the cheaper Photoshop Elements) and Premiere very quickly. Now there really are no limits.

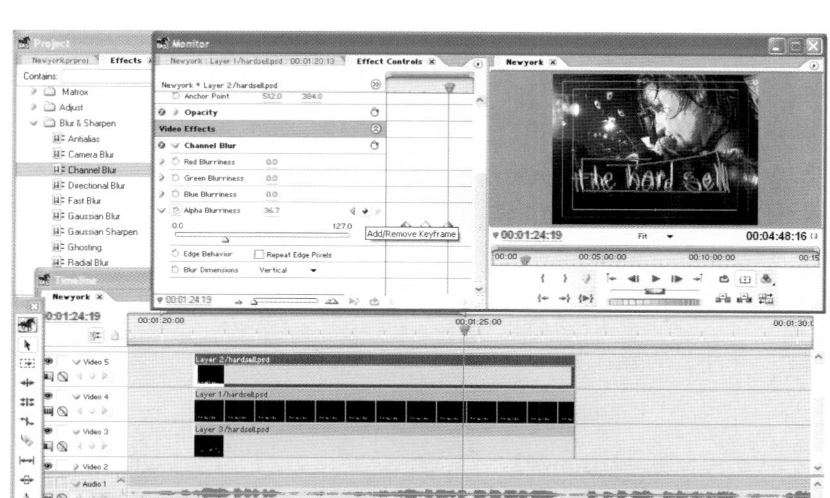

Creating backgrounds

Photoshop gives you the freedom to do a lot more with background images for your titles. Even though Premiere Pro's *Title Designer* allows for the import of images or logos, you can get precisely the image that you want with a bit of pretitling creativity in Photoshop.

Once you've opened Photoshop, it's good practice to get your image size and resolution right from the start. You will get a prompt when you create a new file, (*File* > ***New***) or you can take a look on an existing project by selecting *Image* > ***Image Size***.

If you start to change sizes once you've taken the image into Premiere, your image can be in danger of showing its pixels to the world. In practice, it helps if you know the size of your video in pixels, and use that as the image size with the resolution set to at least 72ppi. Otherwise, you should at least make sure that the aspect ratio of your image matches the aspect ratio of your production. If you're operating at 4:3, there should be 4 horizontal pixels for every 3 vertical pixels in your Photoshop project. Having a low resolution, increases the chance of pixelation, but having too high a resolution makes your files large and cumbersome. But if you want to retain detail, then remember: you can always make the image lower resolution, but you can't make it higher without losing detail.

Make sure that you're working in RGB color space, as none of your other options translate to video. If you're operating Photoshop 7, you'll find a number of presets available that will make your options a lot easier, as long as you know the format of your Premiere production.

Other *Image Size* options are crucial to your success. Your pixels and resolution will be set, but uncheck the *Constrain Proportions* box and check your *Resample Image* option as *Bicubic*.

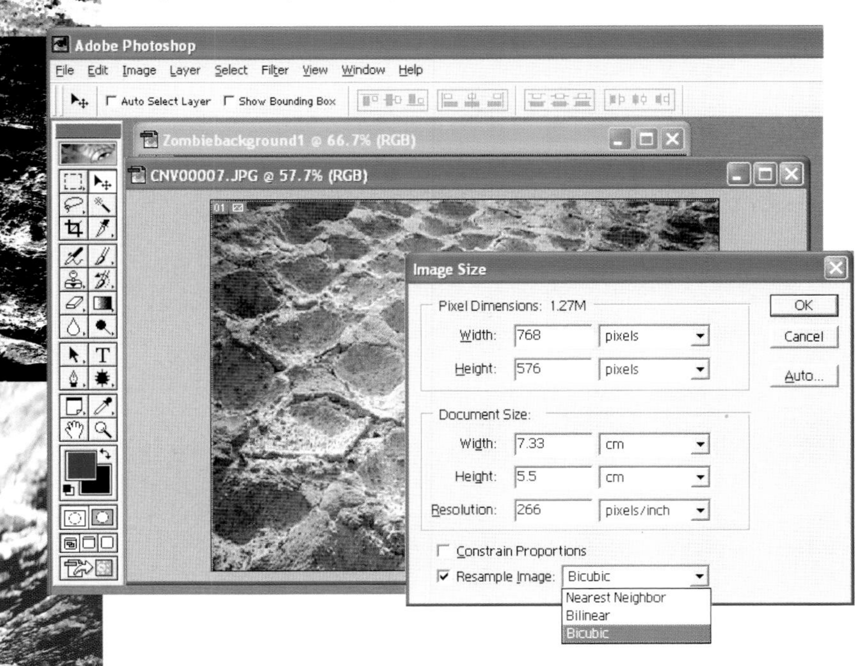

Of course, your image size (and subsequent resolution) is entirely dependent on what you plan to do with it. If the background is going to be used for a DV Effect such as a zoom, your image size and resolution should be enlarged to accommodate the image at maximum scrutiny.

Now that you've created your blank image to the correct size or imported your image, Photoshop will let you modify it as you wish. Remember that you can create a work of art that makes your eventual title illegible or unwatchable...or you can create a background that works with your text, complementing it without intrusion.

If you do create something that becomes too busy, then there is always the *Opacity* option in *Title Designer* to at least temper the background. The danger of this, though, tends to be that the image becomes so obscure that you have wasted your time creating it. Conversely, you risk supplying an image that the viewer would rather look at than the text.

Your success at creating background images in Photoshop is obviously dependent on your creativity and ability with the software, but even if you're just starting out, there's substance in "less is more" theories when it comes to title backgrounds.

The background is the base to your titling and, as such, it does not necessarily require mattes and masks to be applied. If you're compositing layers, then this is something that is often more versatile when taken as separate layers into *Title Designer* as a time-based tool.

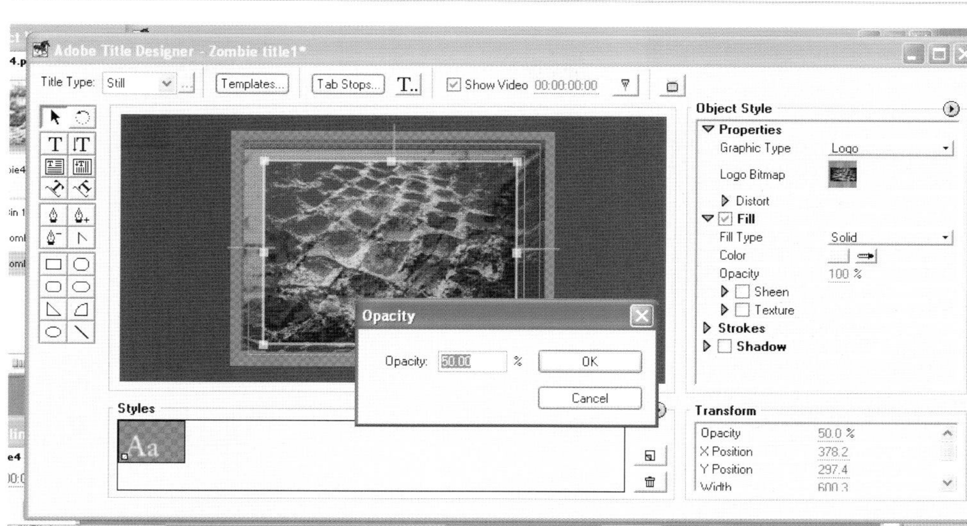

Imported images within Photoshop act as a single-layer file and operate slightly differently. These might be stock images, or still images that you have scanned into the application. Instead of manipulating the image size to produce nonsquare pixels, it's easier to change the ratio once the file is in *Title Designer*. Here, percentage calculations for non-square pixels simply require an input of 89.886%—call it 90%—applied to the height of the image. Once an image or logo has been imported into Premiere, right-click on it to transform the scale to a non-uniform vertical value of 90%.

Images, such as photographs, are easy to work with, as they rely on how pleasing they are to the eye when undergoing transformation. Sometimes, complex calculations—no matter how precise—are no substitute for simple esthetics. *Title Designer* will show this realtime transformation using the same process as Photoshop.

Importing logos in *Title Designer* also lets your image be seen in its aspect ratio beneath your title, enabling you precisely to fit your background to fill it. Right-clicking on the background also offers you the options you need if you're importing various layers. *Transform* > ***Opacity*** and *Arrange* > ***Send to Back*** (et al) can create the compositing you need with the added bonus of testing the text to see if the background becomes too busy or intrusive.

If you do take your layers separately onto the *Timeline*, motion effects and scaling can be applied to each of them with keyframing. A background in motion behind your text can add both dynamism and sophistication, raising your production values.

Backgrounds in practice

Creating backgrounds from source can throw up challenges specific to graphics onscreen. Resolution is always an issue, particularly when many graphics are created for the Internet (one of the primary marketing outlets) where they are only intended to be used at a small size and a low resolution. Taking those images and trying to produce something that will look good when viewed at full-size on a CRT screen can be a suprisingly tricky process.

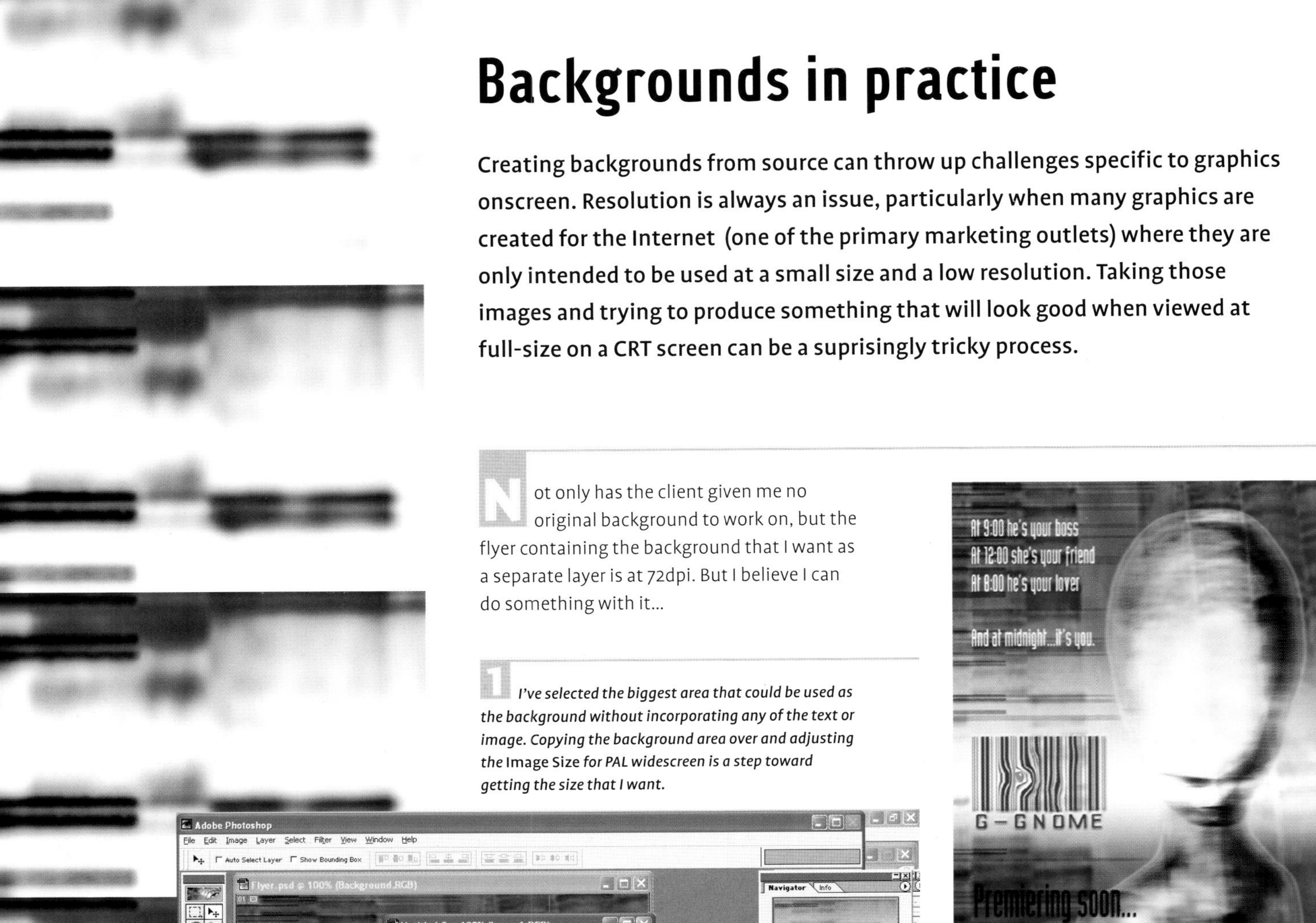

Not only has the client given me no original background to work on, but the flyer containing the background that I want as a separate layer is at 72dpi. But I believe I can do something with it...

1 *I've selected the biggest area that could be used as the background without incorporating any of the text or image. Copying the background area over and adjusting the* Image Size *for PAL widescreen is a step toward getting the size that I want.*

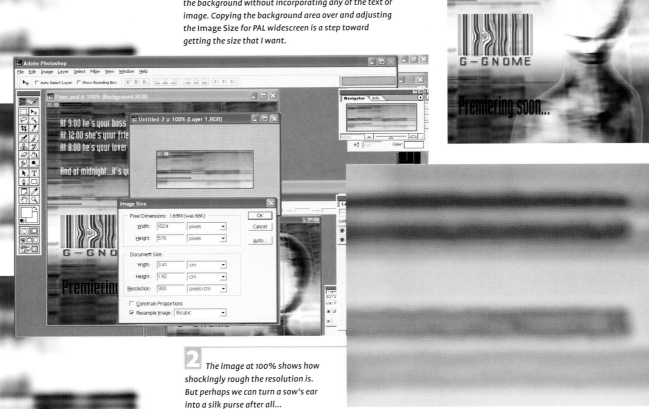

2 *The image at 100% shows how shockingly rough the resolution is. But perhaps we can turn a sow's ear into a silk purse after all...*

3 *Having reasonable carte blanche over the manipulation of the imagery, while still using the references, I've sharpened the image and adjusted the brightness and contrast. Any excitement about what effects are becoming visible onscreen is easily tempered with the knowledge that any additional filter won't add to the quality of the image.*

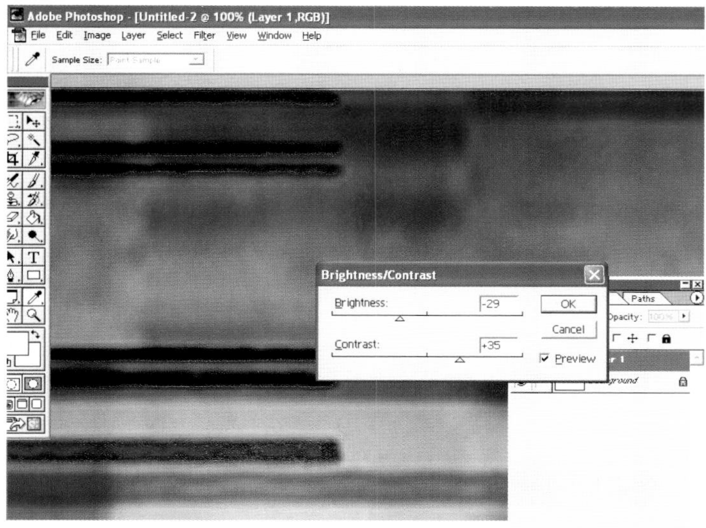

4 *The image itself is a composite of chromosomes and their digital representation, thematically appropriate to the video itself (which is about cloning). A blow-up highlights the detail to make it more obvious as a quickly viewed title background. Using a diffuse glow not only blurs the blocky pixels, but bleaches the lighter accents to distinguish the chromosomes.*

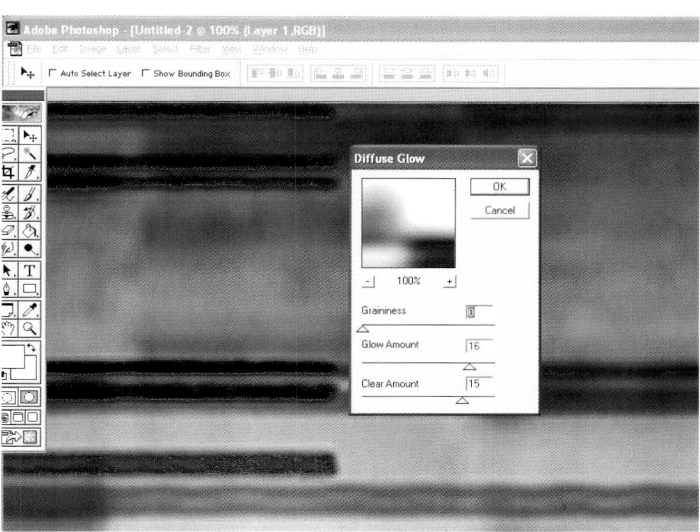

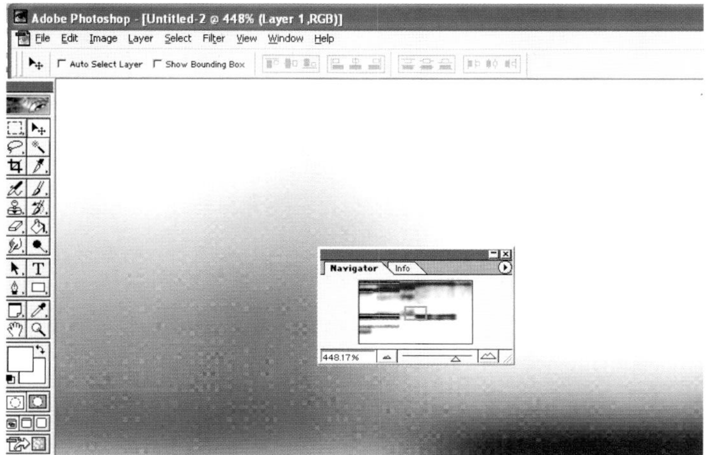

5 *Magnifying your image will give you an idea of just how much scrutiny it will bear, and at what size your final product will begin to show its true colors. Part of video production is always keeping in mind where your product is going to be shown—and this consideration is never clearer than in this kind of situation.*

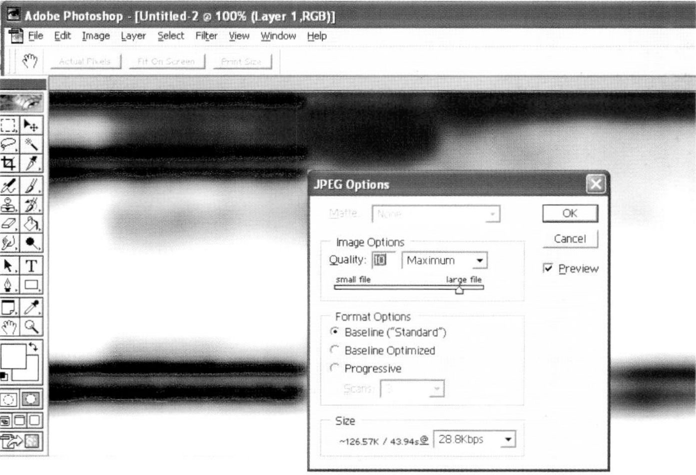

6 *Make sure that you save the background off at maximum resolution, or you'll waste your work. The point is always to make the inherently ugly less noticable and offensive. Although bumping up the contrast, lowering the brightness and adding filters might seem to draw attention to the image's resolution, it also offers a lot more for the text to hang onto, and more room to maneuver in the edit itself.*

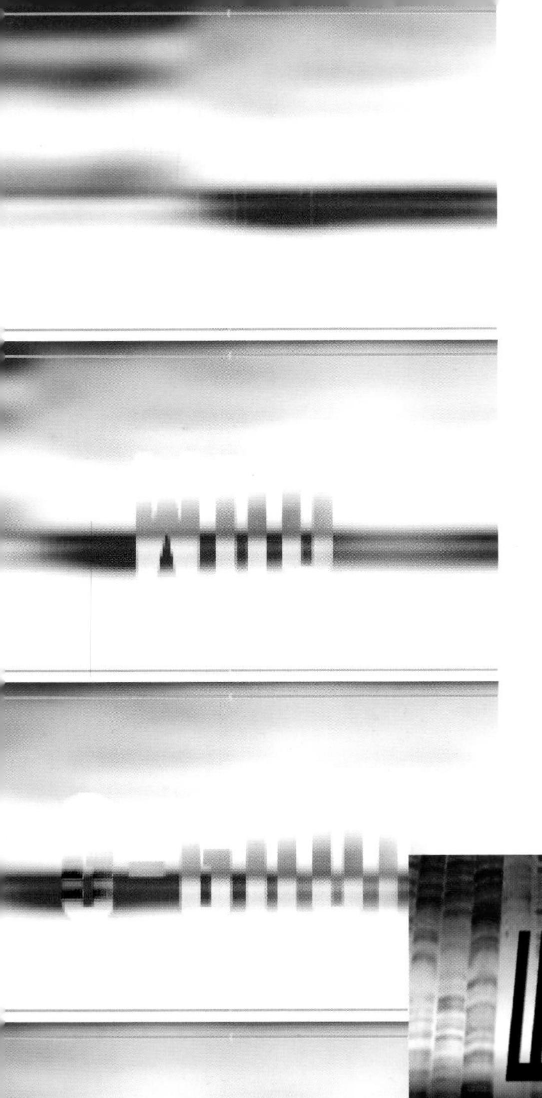

Creating, importing, and manipulating text

By design, Photoshop offers you far more options for textual creativity than *Title Designer* can. Pro's *Timeline* will deal with placement, motion, and effects, and *Title Designer* with the fine-tuning of your title, but Photoshop lets you create exactly what you want as flawless source material.

The teaser video for the G-Gnome project has three Photoshop stills thrown in toward the end of it. The only way that they've been modified, is by a small push-in (a scale increase), but basically they're flat, dull, and don't add any drama or visual urgency between each one. They look like this:

The background is to come, using the techniques described, but the text is another matter. Given that these three words form the marketing push (a twist on the video's main subject, which is cloning), and that the font was included in the material that was sent, it's probably best to reconstruct everything.

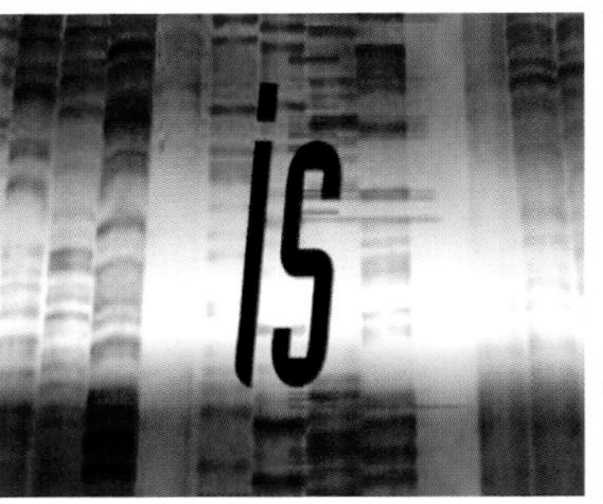

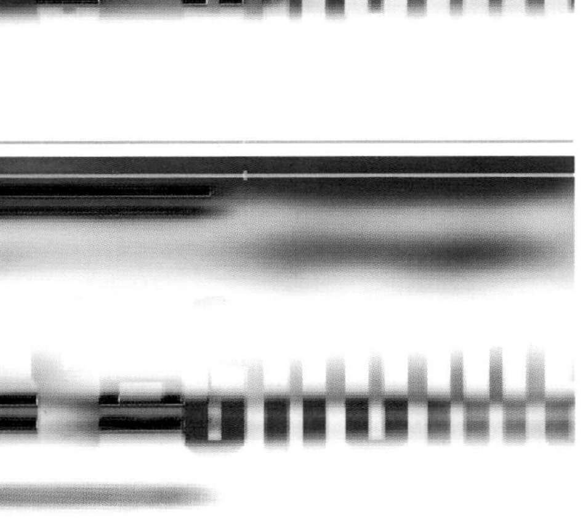

1 *Just. Three. Words. It should be easy enough. The video is in 16:9-ish. It's Super 16 film on video and the ratios will be roughly 1024x572, to be fine-tuned in* Title Designer *once they're on the* Timeline. *Creating this with a transparent background will allow for the introduction of another layer—the background—and anything else I need to add to apply the dynamism that the words need.*

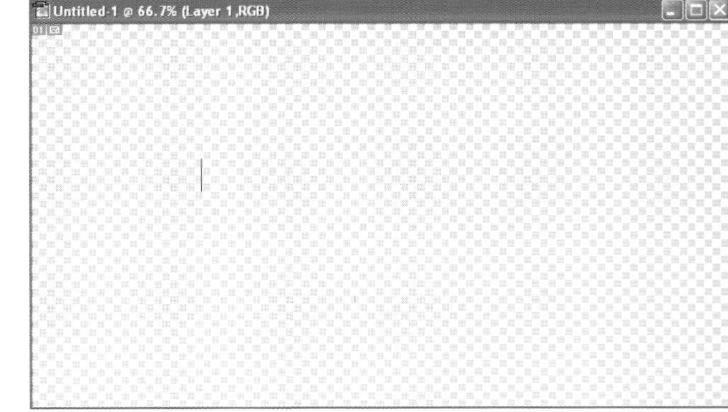

2 *The good thing about these words is that each title is just one word. This allows for embellishment, given that each is easily processed within the amount of time on screen. It takes a 250-point Assiduous font to get the first title up to somewhere near the right size to command the screen. What I do have to think about, though, is that if each word (as part of a sentence) is going to be created similarly, does that mean that the font has to be the same size for each? And if so, I should perhaps start with the longest word to see if it fits on screen at 250 points. Conversely, the solution might be to look at the smallest word, "is," and see if it needs more than 250 points to look right—which might throw up new resolution issues. And at what part of the process do I hand over to the* ECW *and* Title Designer *to control the size and scale of the words?*

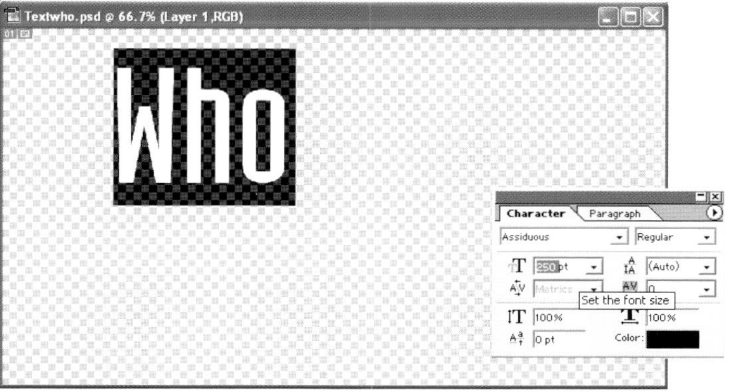

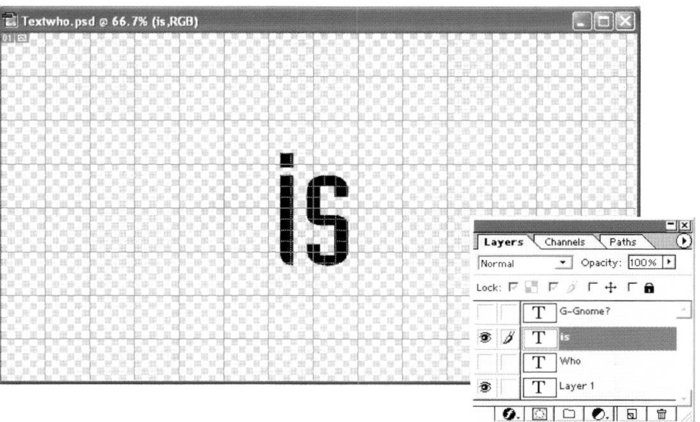

4 View > Show > **Grid** *will assist from the start in getting the position of each visible layer right. I like the original version's central placement, and it gives me enough room around the word to play with when the text is back home on the* Timeline.

3 *Well, I'd love to have the answers, but actually the best way is to create all of the images as separate layers within the same frame and work them individually together. Your best friend here in avoiding confusion between layers will be the* Layer Visibility *toggle.*

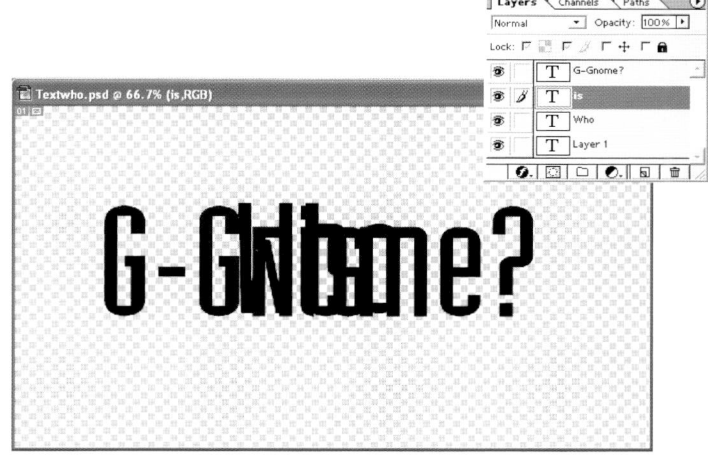

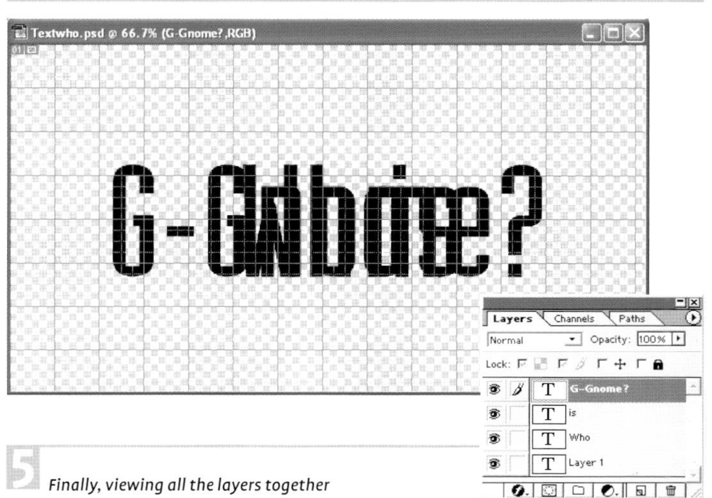

5 *Finally, viewing all the layers together enables a little adjustment of position—particularly bearing in mind any use of capitals, and in this case the full-sized, bookending question mark. In fact, the more I look at the question mark and its similarity to the shape of the first capital "G," and the more I think about the theme of cloning, the more I'm inclined to do something creative with it.*

6 Cutting the "?" and putting it on a separate layer, I've still left the "G-Gnome" in the same position, anticipating that the question mark will eventually end up at the end of the word. Checking it against the "G" for size and shape, though, is enough to make me change my mind. If the question mark was reversed, there's no reason that I couldn't make it appear to the left of the initial "G"...

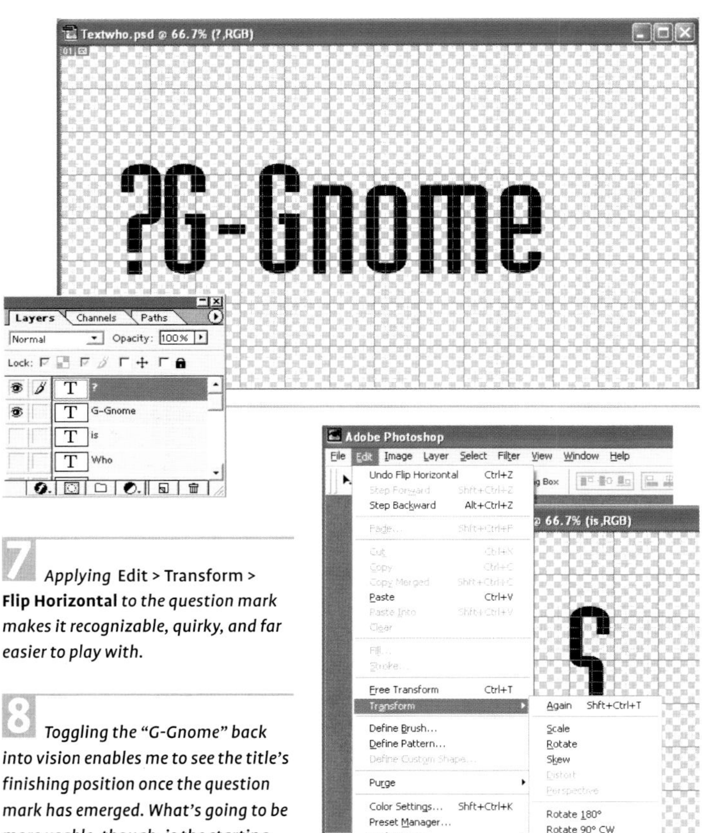

7 Applying Edit > Transform > **Flip Horizontal** to the question mark makes it recognizable, quirky, and far easier to play with.

8 Toggling the "G-Gnome" back into vision enables me to see the title's finishing position once the question mark has emerged. What's going to be more usable, though, is the starting position for the "?"...

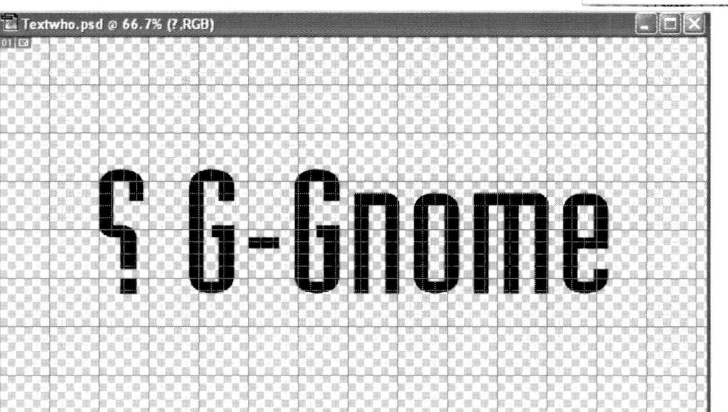

9 ...and this is it. Using the arrow keys to fine-position the question mark, all the text is now layered and in position. Still doesn't do anything, though.

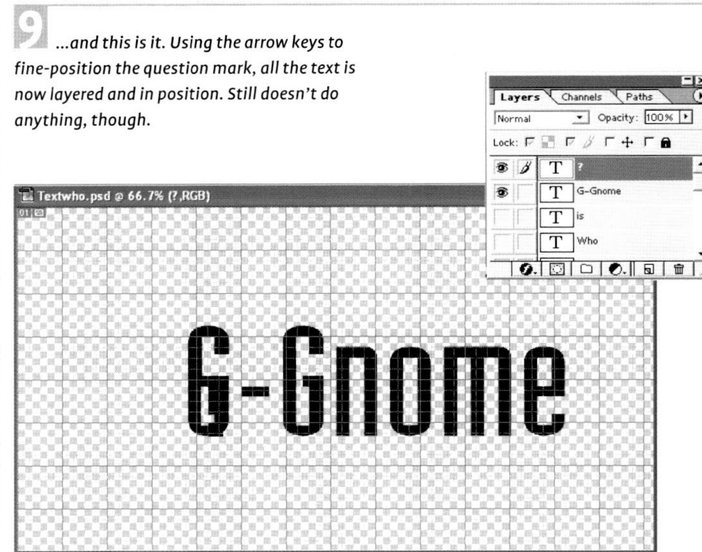

10 Because the words are so simple and stark, I can not only get away with a texture, but make it work hard for me. To make it impressive, though, requires a bit more surface area than I've got. If your font doesn't have a bold version, like Assiduous, Photoshop is only too eager to please with a Faux Bold in the character menu. Applying this will increase the area all around the characters, which means that you don't have to reposition them.

? G-Gnome

11 *Instead of just taking the text into* Title Designer *and applying a texture, I want to use the background for the text. This is going to require some kind of key, so all the layers need a green fill. Selecting the* Color *in the* Character *menu, I've picked a suitably horrific hue for all of the layers. It may not be necessary for the question mark, but it's best to avoid any problems at source.*

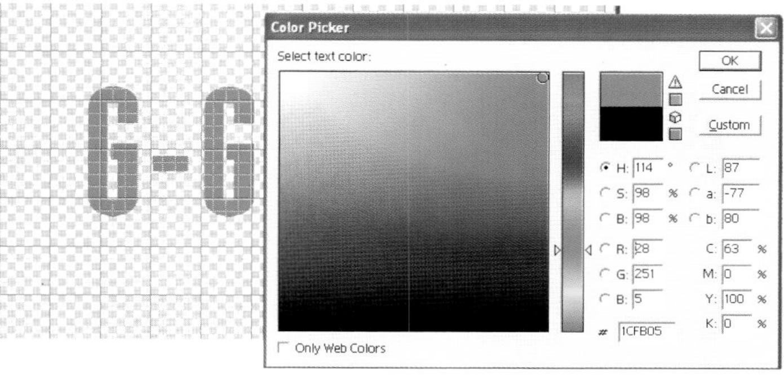

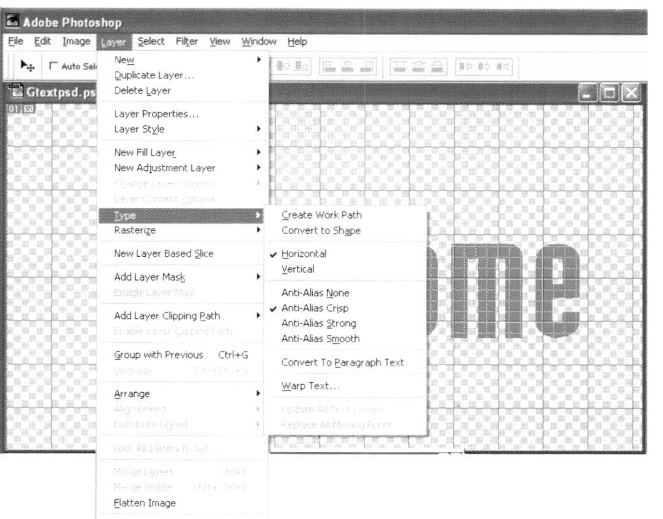

12 *Finally, a* Crisp Anti-Alias *is applied to each layer to define it. This is especially appropriate for any keying that has to be done.*

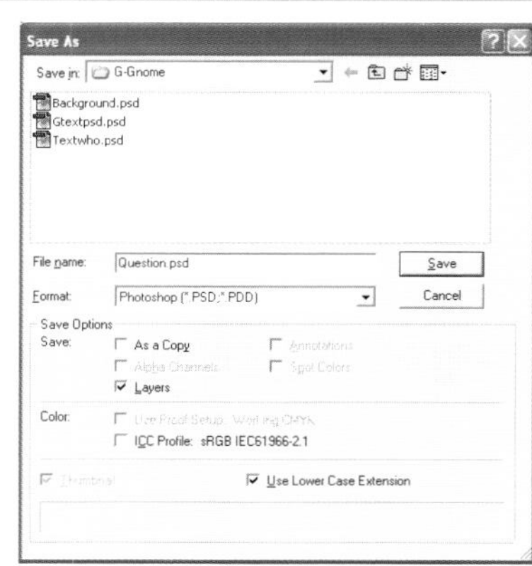

13 *When saving, make sure that if you've been working (like this) with a transparency, that you don't save as a JPEG. All this will do is turn the transparency to flat white.* Title Designer *loves .psd files and will interpret them as they were designed.*

14 *I've razored away at the original boring insert titles, and cleared them out of the* Timeline*. Copying and pasting the background title over the three residual gaps is the next step.*

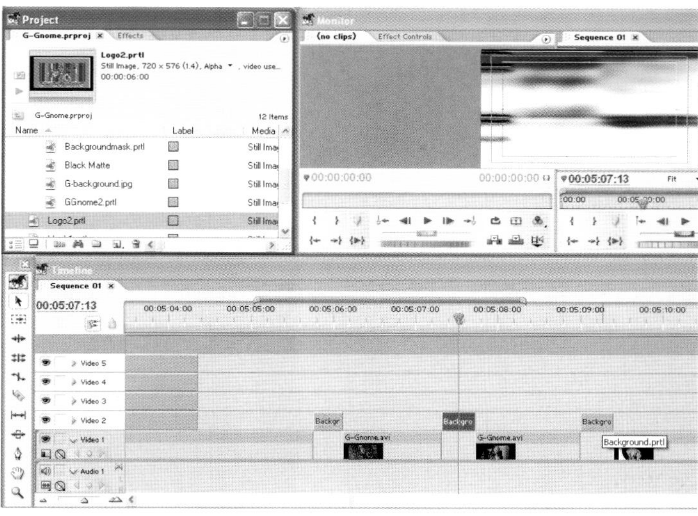

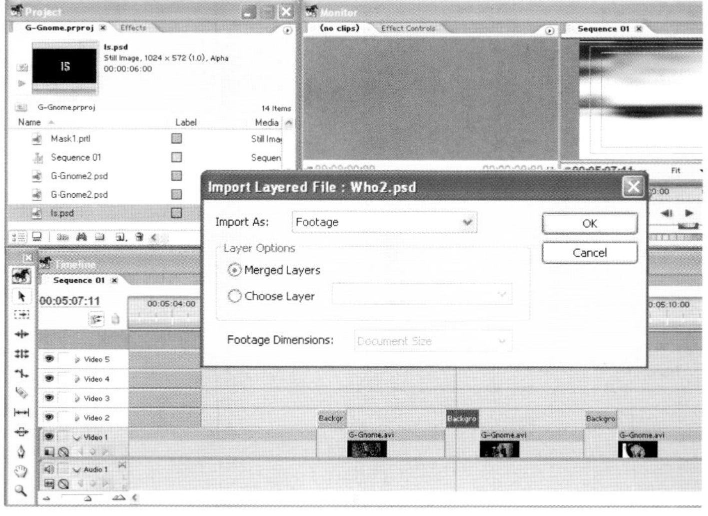

15 *When Importing each Photoshop file, make sure that you're importing them as* Merged Layers *in the dialog box that pops up. This will ensure that your transparency stays true.*

16 *Dragging each clip over the backgrounds lets the background replace the transparency. The background is moving left to right; what I want to do is to greenscreen the text for a background moving right to left.*

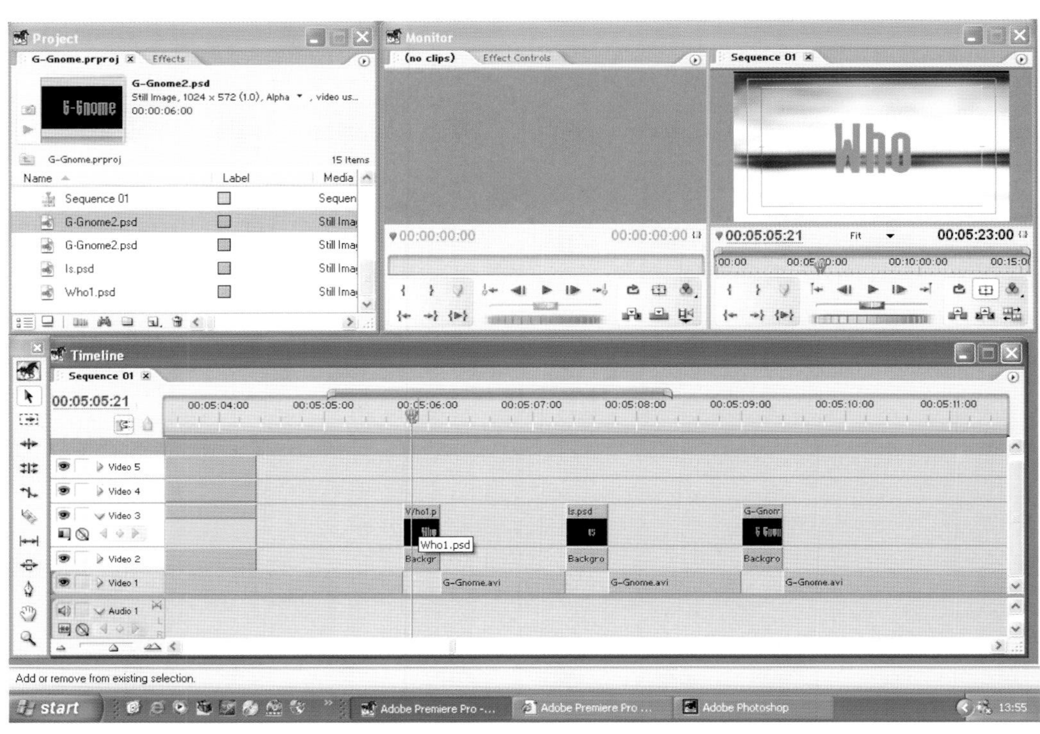

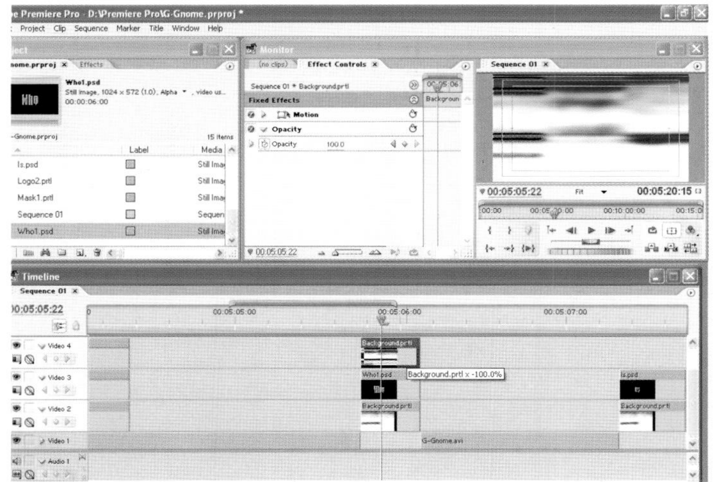

17 *Right-click, Copy, and Paste gives me a duplicate of the background. Right-clicking the duplicate, selecting* Speed/Duration, *and checking the* Reverse Speed *box gives me the texture for the greenscreen. Putting it on a video track over the text gives me the text sandwich that I'll need, but the effect that I don't.*

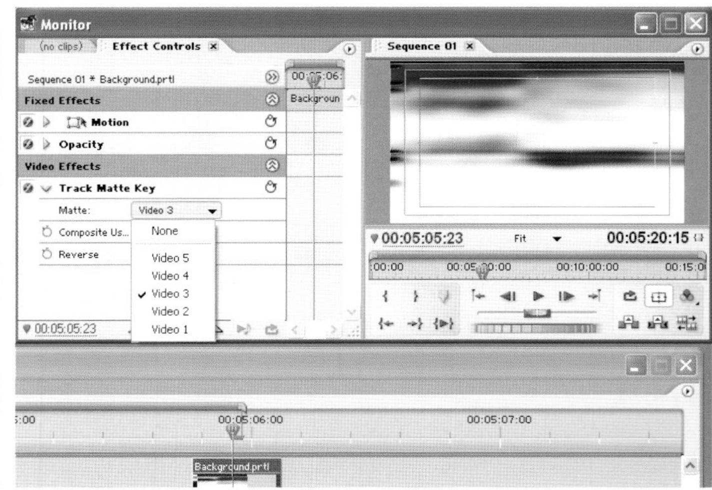

18 *Time to get started. The reverse background on Track 4 is to be applied to the greenscreen. Dragging a* Track Matte *to the clip and allocating an alpha matte to the text (Track 3) will do this.*

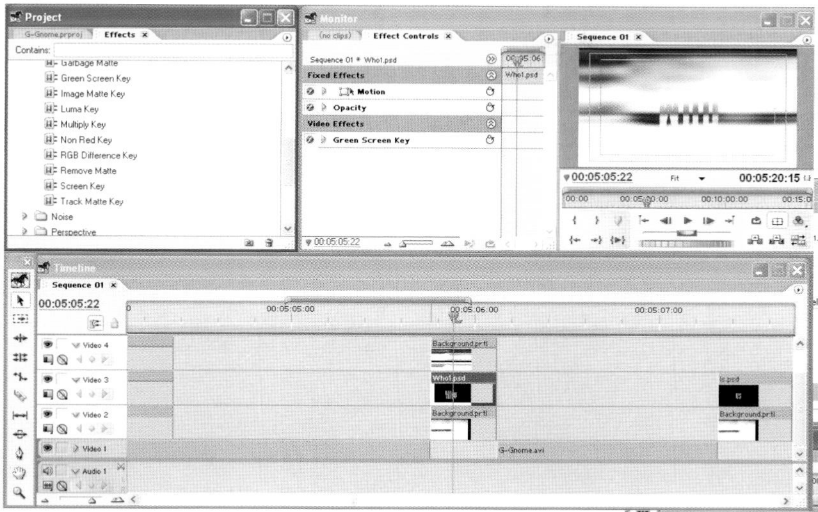

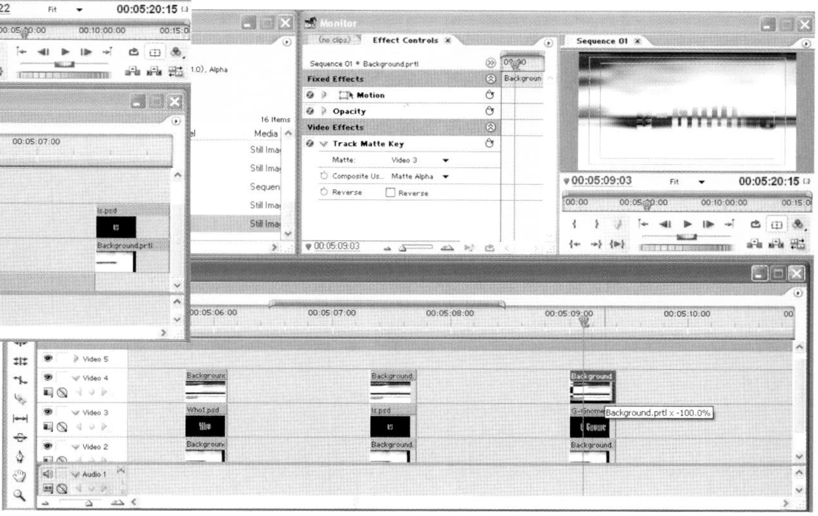

20 *Right-clicking, copying, and pasting brings me to a point where all three words' textures are complete and uniform. All that's left now is the question of the question mark.*

19 *It's time for the text to get rid of its green sheen and take on its new colors. The application of a* Green Screen Key *makes the text reveal the track above, leaving the previously invisible original background track to fill in the transparency around it.*

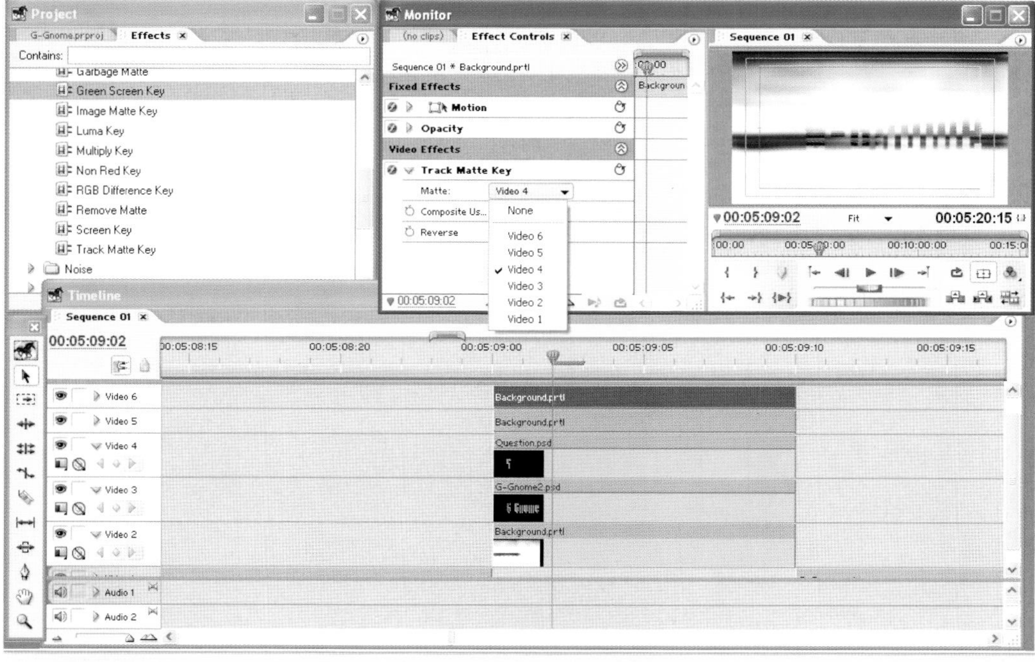

21 *Moving the text texture up a track, then dragging the "?" into the text sandwich and adding a* Green Screen Key *to it is a good start. Copying yet another reversed text texture onto another track above is the next step to getting the question mark noticed. To make it visible, though, requires a change of* Track Matte *on the new layer to relate to the question mark track.*

Using mattes and keys for imported files

We've discussed how Premiere Pro translates logos as solid objects. This may provide a good, strong image, but it also makes it hard to apply a key to the logo. This is because the image doesn't have the default alpha key that video clips have applied to them.

For the G-Gnome teaser, there are now two files to composite: the logo and the background. They're not designed to be keyed, but given that the logo is on a plain white background, there is a way that this can be done. If you have a background that isn't uniform, and you want to pick out a logo, the best way to do this in Photoshop is to create a new path layer with the *Pen* tool around the logo itself and take it over onto a plain background.

1 *These are the two images in place on the* Timeline. *Both have been bitmaps imported as logos into* Title Designer *to become prtl files. The logo, as superimposed, is on a track higher than the background.*

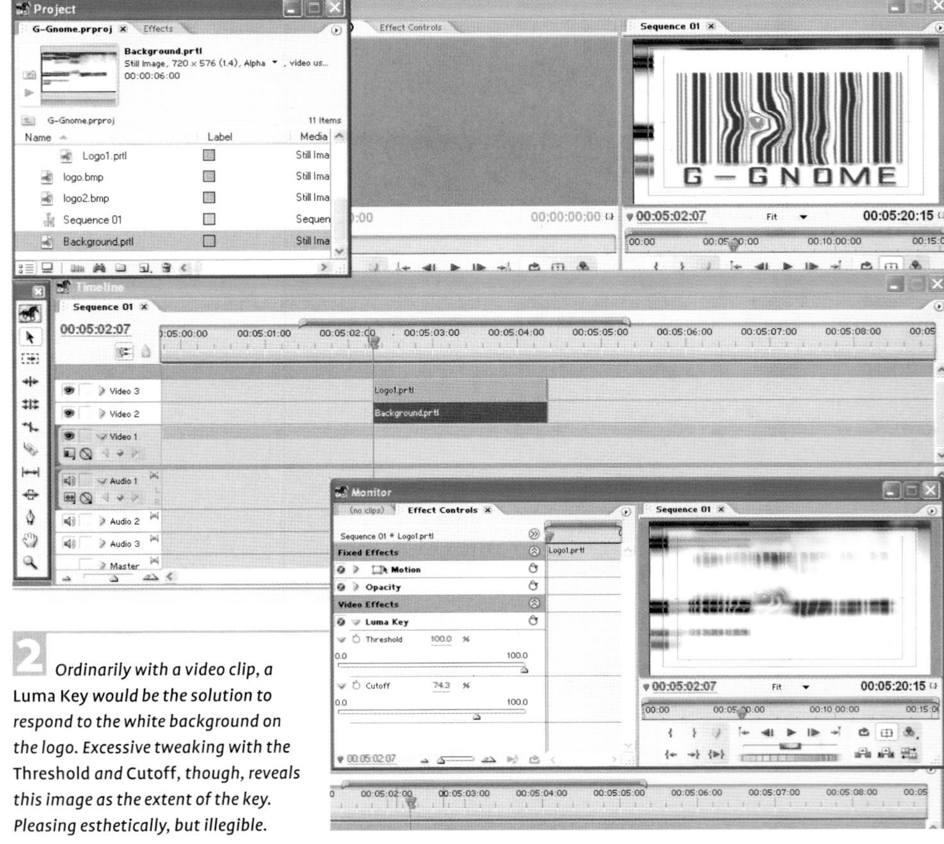

2 *Ordinarily with a video clip, a* Luma Key *would be the solution to respond to the white background on the logo. Excessive tweaking with the* Threshold *and* Cutoff*, though, reveals this image as the extent of the key. Pleasing esthetically, but illegible.*

3 Going back to the original source is the one way to redeem the situation. If the problem is the file, the problem has to be fixed in the file. Opening the bitmap in Photoshop will let me doctor it to be more Premiere Pro-friendly.

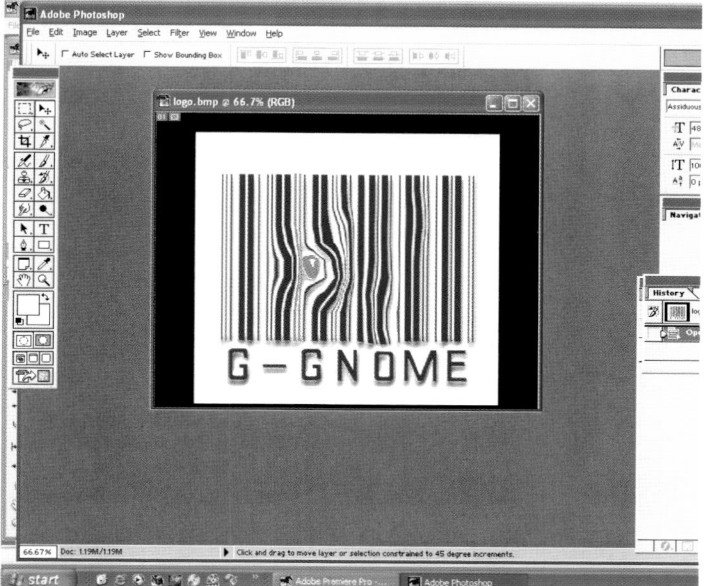

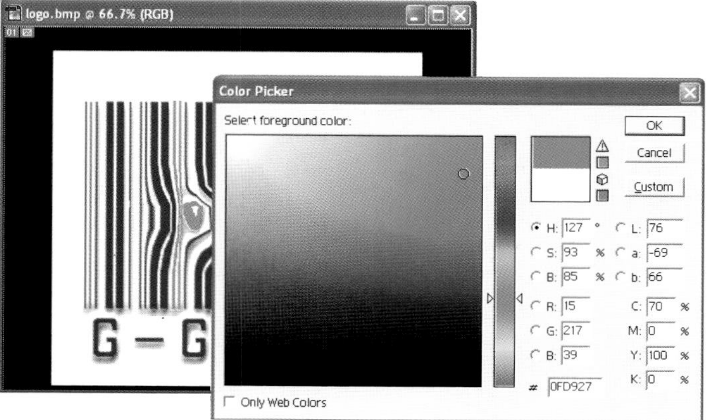

4 And it really is as basic as replacing the white with green. A Green Screen Key in Premiere Pro is a strong key and will absolutely read anything green as a zero value. Because there is no green in the graphic, it becomes an easy task.

5 The Paintbucket tool is hardly the most subtle way of replacing the white, but it's a good place to start. What it also does is reveal the problem areas for fill—but if the job's to be done, it's got to be done properly...

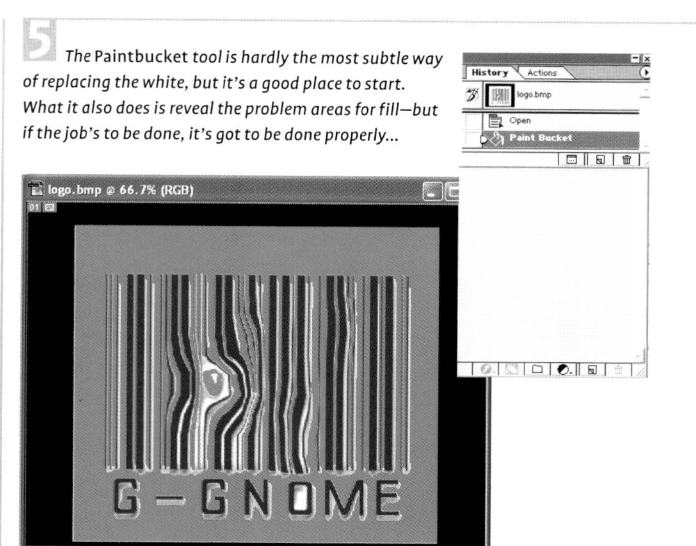

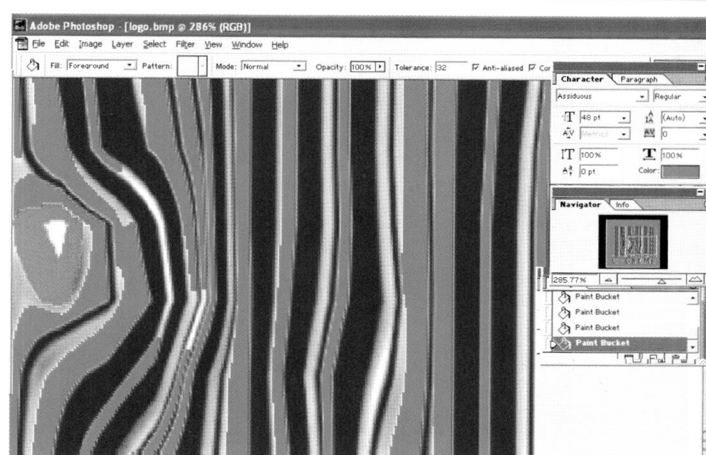

6 Use all the tricks in your Photoshop book. Fill, spray, paint, and keep magnifying to make sure that you're covering all areas. All the white has got to go...

7 When you're done, save it as a recognizable version of your logo in the appropriate Premiere Pro project folder, then shut down Photoshop and import it into your project.

8 *Back in Premiere Pro, you might as well ditch the original logo prtl file (right-click then* Clear*) and start again. Open up a new title and import the new image into* Title Designer *(right-click then select* Insert Logo*).*

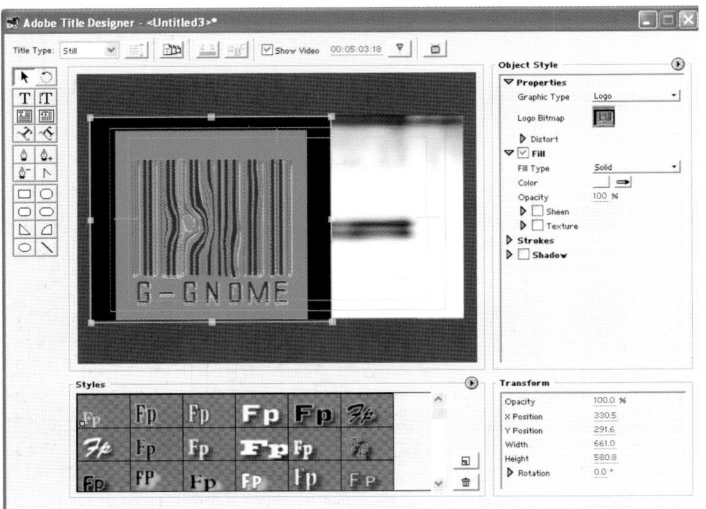

9 *Size it up, using your drag cursor to cover the screen-safety and beyond, and save the project as a new title.*

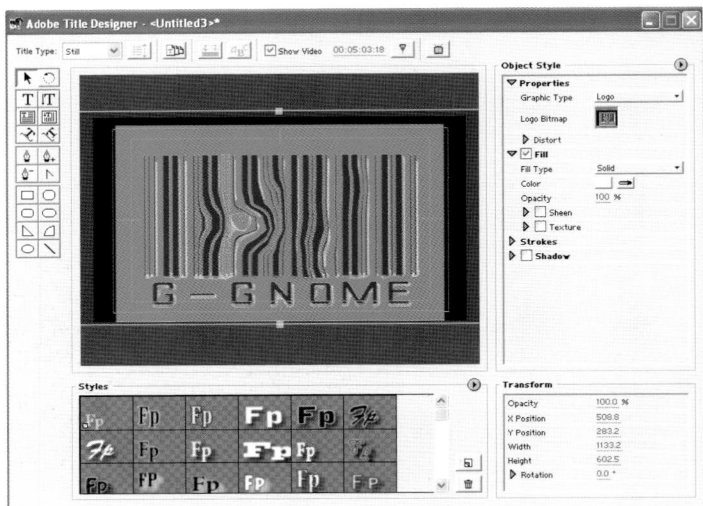

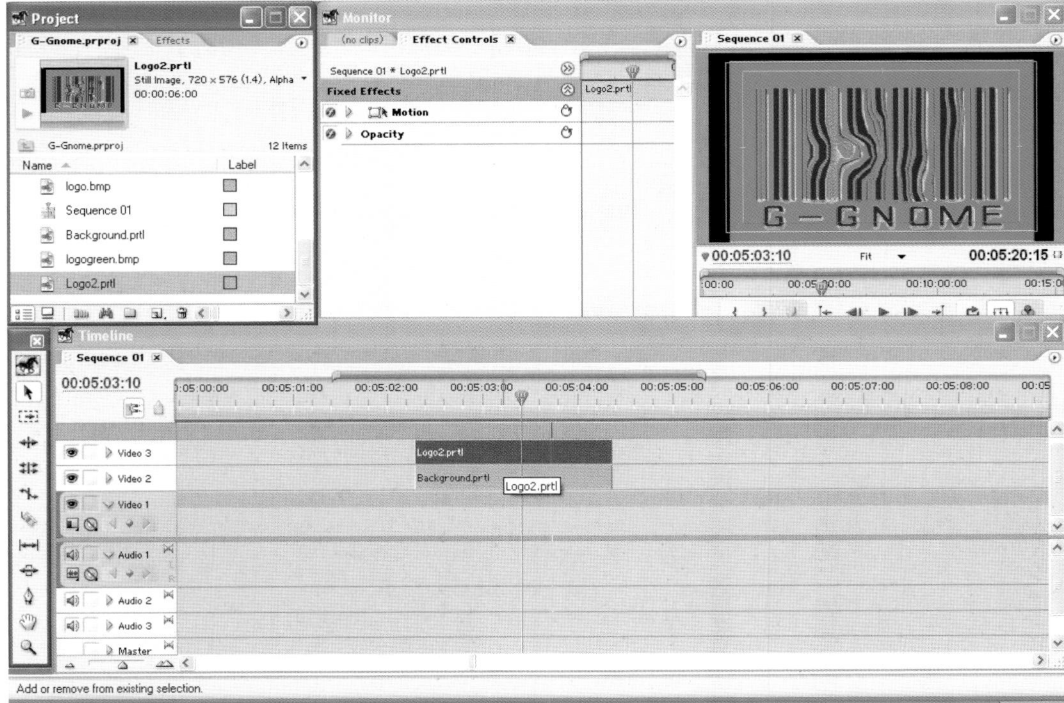

10 *In the Premiere Pro* Timeline*, drag the new logo into the place where the original, unusable graphics file was and witness the beauty of green.*

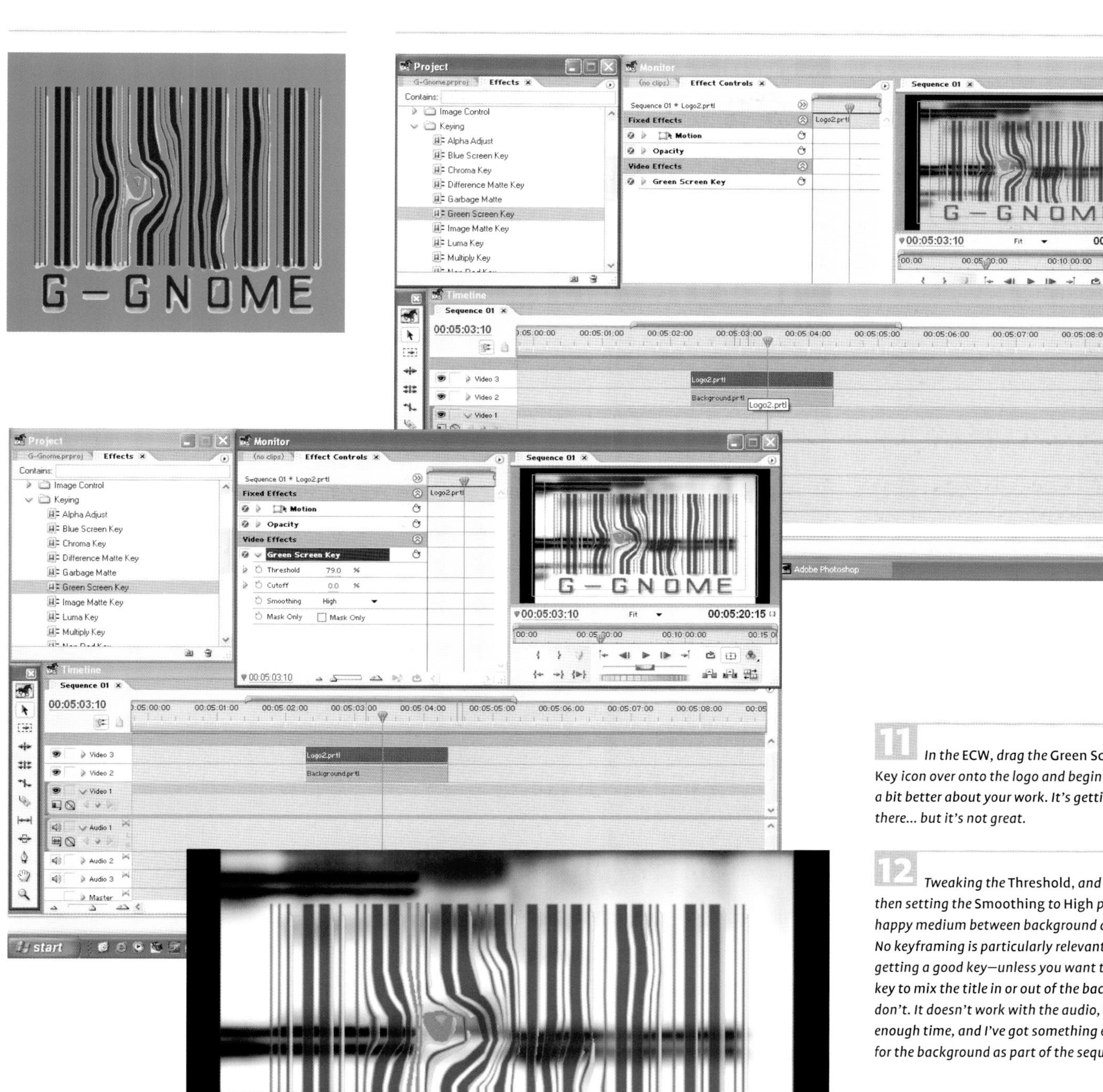

11 *In the ECW, drag the* Green Screen Key *icon over onto the logo and begin to feel a bit better about your work. It's getting there... but it's not great.*

12 *Tweaking the* Threshold, *and* Cutoff, *then setting the* Smoothing *to* High *provides a happy medium between background and logo. No keyframing is particularly relevant to simply getting a good key—unless you want to use the key to mix the title in or out of the background. I don't. It doesn't work with the audio, there isn't enough time, and I've got something else in mind for the background as part of the sequence.*

Framing Photoshop files

Although you might have spent time keeping your Photoshop graphic at the right size, there are times when this either doesn't happen, you've got better ideas for it, or the rest of the video that you're working with isn't in an obvious ratio.

The latter is true of the "G-Gnome" layers—coupled with the fact that they were straws grasped from the hands of print marketing.

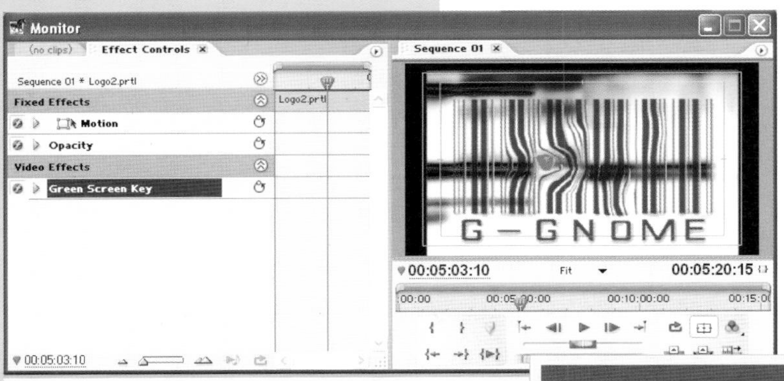

The key is in place, the two layers are in the right place. However, there is a problem as this image just hard cuts in, sits there, and then hard cuts out. This is a harsh video graphic sitting toward the end of a trailer shot on Super 16 film. It looks out of place, and the fact that it's the only thing in it not moving, doesn't make it sit in well at all. Let's be honest, it stands proud and screams "I'M A VIDEO GRAPHIC." It's time to make it sit down and shut up.

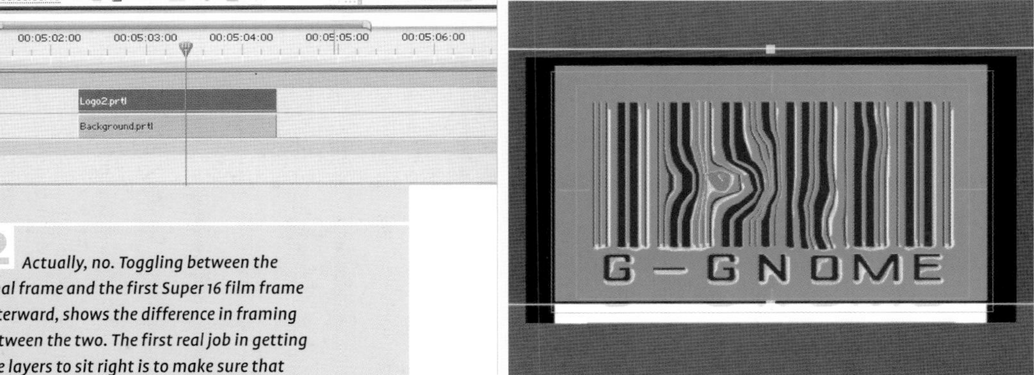

1 *The first thing to do with it is to resize the logo. It's dropping out of screen-safe at the bottom. Going back into* Title Designer, *it's simply a question of dragging the baseline to match the space between the top of the logo and the screen-safe margin....or is it?*

2 *Actually, no. Toggling between the final frame and the first Super 16 film frame afterward, shows the difference in framing between the two. The first real job in getting the layers to sit right is to make sure that they're masked off to the same degree.*

3 *There are four specific ways to do this. For each of them, you'll need to extend both of the title layers over the video on the* Timeline *and then lower the* Opacity *of each to enable the viewing of all three layers together.*

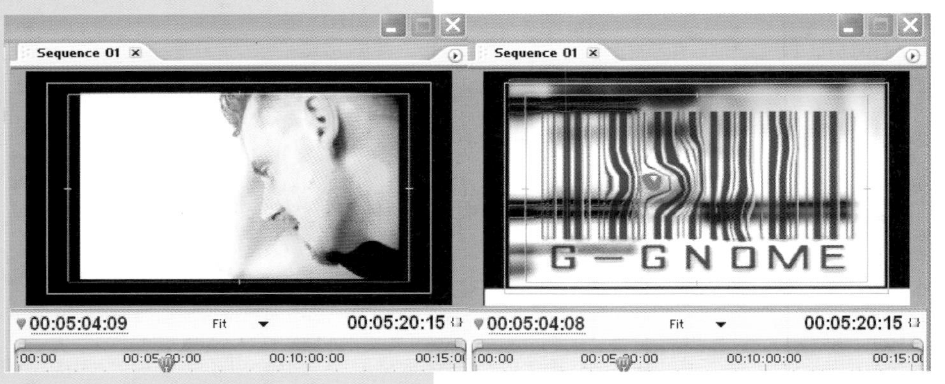

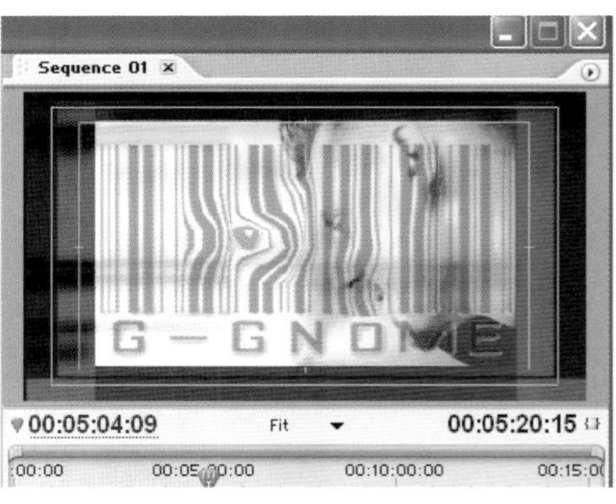

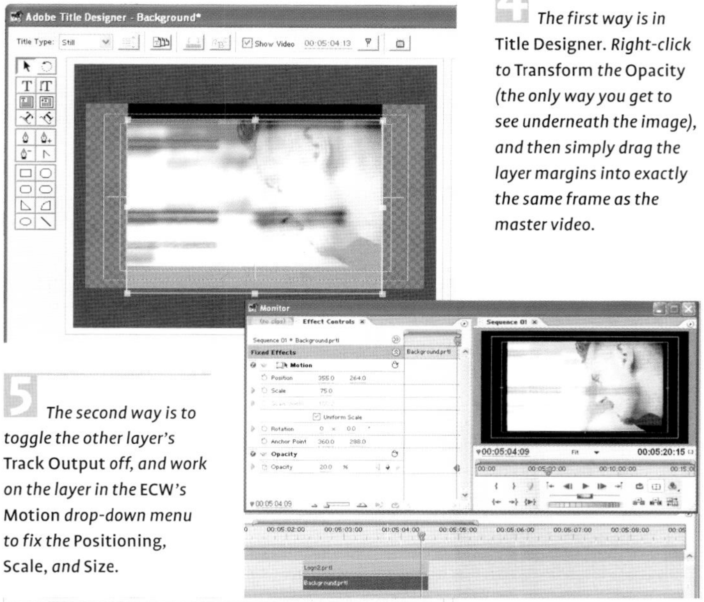

4 *The first way is in* Title Designer. *Right-click to* Transform *the* Opacity *(the only way you get to see underneath the image), and then simply drag the layer margins into exactly the same frame as the master video.*

5 *The second way is to toggle the other layer's* Track Output *off, and work on the layer in the* ECW*'s* Motion *drop-down menu to fix the* Positioning, Scale, *and* Size.

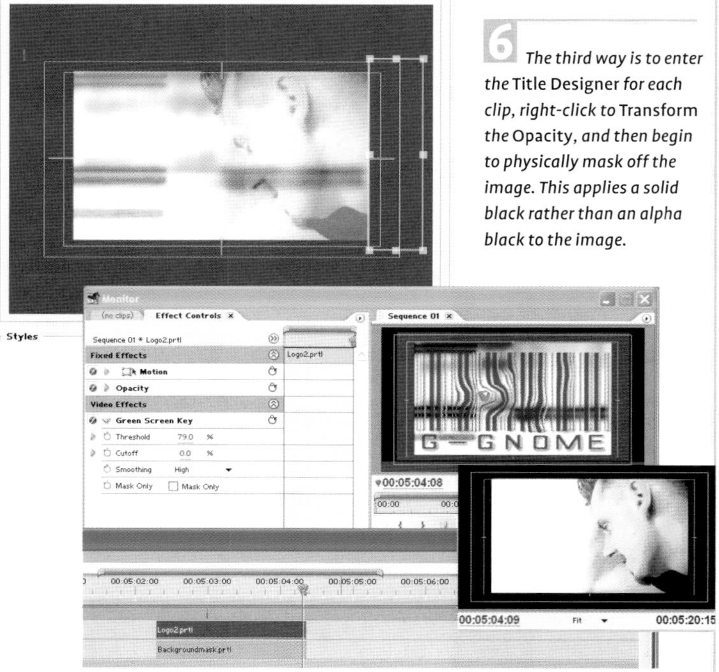

6 *The third way is to enter the* Title Designer *for each clip, right-click to* Transform *the* Opacity, *and then begin to physically mask off the image. This applies a solid black rather than an alpha black to the image.*

7 *Not forgetting to* Transform *the* Opacity *in* Title Designer, *return to* Premiere Pro, *drag the layers back to their original, then position and toggle the* Track Output *of both back on again. This should give you the results that you want, with a seamless framing between the new images and the old video.*

While this looks fine—and it is if that's all you want to do with your layers—it's not enough for me. It's a pill for a still, but hardly a potion for motion. Remember, you've applied the solid black to the layer itself, which means that any manipulation to that layer is going to affect the black as well. It's also going to be tedious to apply the same masking to each of the other Photoshop images that need to be inserted here. There has to be another way. And there is.

8 *Create another* Video Track *above your layers, if you haven't got one: you're going to need it. Extending the layers over the* Super 16 *video, the* Opacity *in the* ECW *for each of the title clips is dragged down to 50%, and a new title opened.*

9 *From here, just create your own masking device as a separate object using the rectangular marquee tool.*

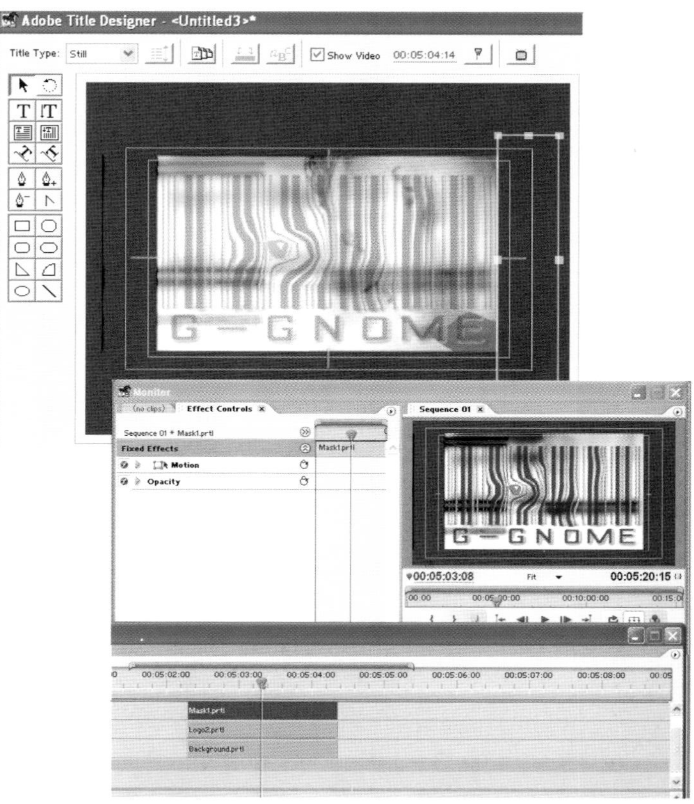

10 *Save it to your project and then get the* Opacity *and length of clips back to where they were on the* Timeline. *Drag the new title mask to the new video track above the other layers and find yourself with the effect you want and a mask to use for any other Photoshop layer in the same project. Better still, it will stay in place when any of the other layers are moved or manipulated—because, boy, does this graphic need to do something...*

Compositing and animating files within Premiere Pro

Still frames don't have to be dull frames. They can be effected and affected. In other words, they don't have to sit there and bore the audience until they finally leave the screen.

Instead, they can be one of the most effective weapons that you can have in titling. If a better title is one that has a simple idea, and which is legible, then graphics created specifically for the task can be dynamite.

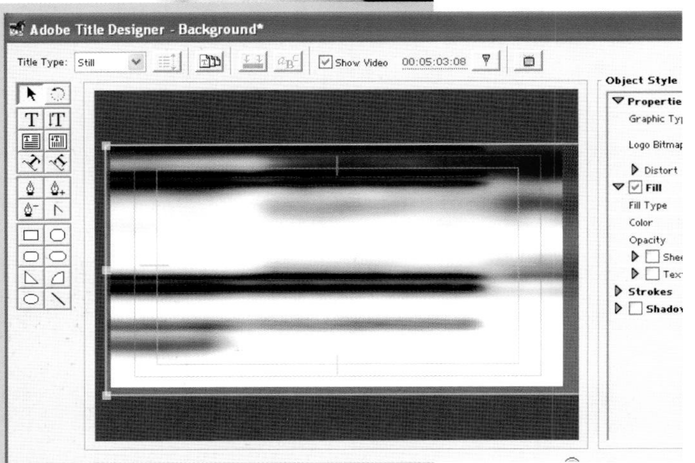

1 *Going back to my original oversized background before the black frames were applied, I'm going to make use of the fact that the frame is too big. This is another important factor when creating Photoshop images: if you want it to move, you need excess baggage to move with. There's still not quite enough image to play with, though, so at the slight expense of resolution, I find myself back in Title Designer again, stretching the image.*

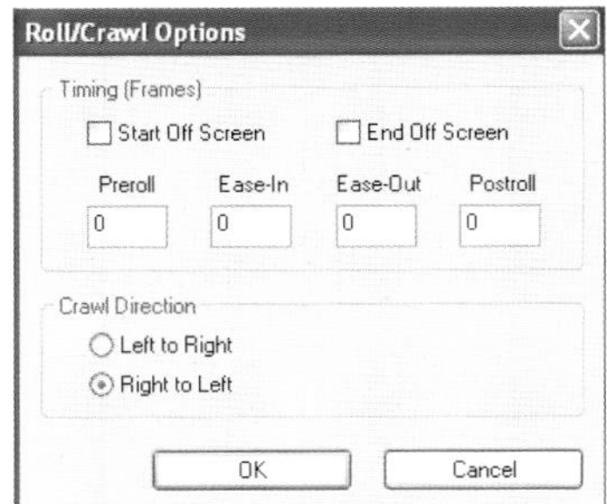

2 *What's in my favor is that the background image lives its secret life on the Y-axis, so any noticeable resolution change will at least flow with the image and motion. Just like any text, adding a crawl to the image will save me positioning by keyframe in the ECW. A crawl is a perfect companion to the stretch and the chromosome image itself.*

3 *The logo needs to be doing something else at the same time—something slight, given the short amount of time on screen. The theme of the video is cloning, and it seems to make sense that the logo should duplicate itself. Taking this literally, right-clicking to Copy the logo will give me some versatility to do this.*

4 *I've pasted it in at the end of the video (by default it pastes to Video Track 1), then dragged it back into view. Right-clicking and renaming it will help distinguish between the original logo and the copy.*

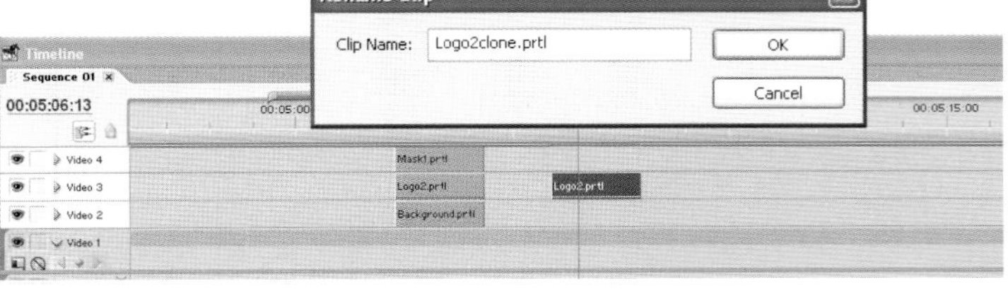

5 *What it really needs, though, is its own video track. Create one for it, but if you do have a black mask like this one here, ensure you shift it up a track to override the new layer.*

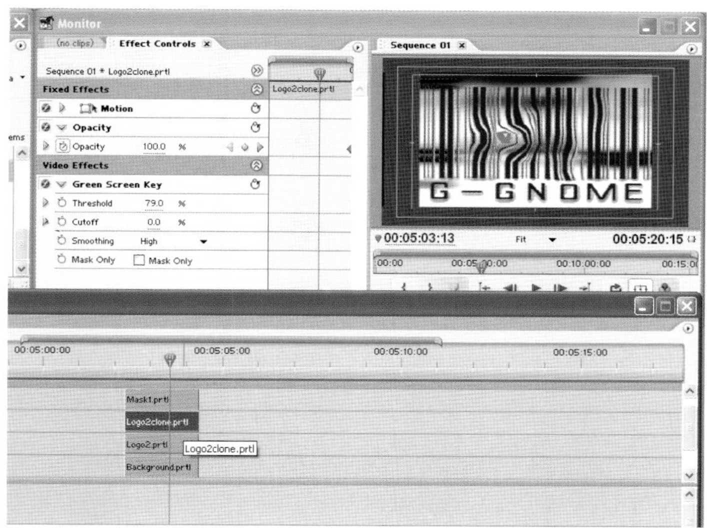

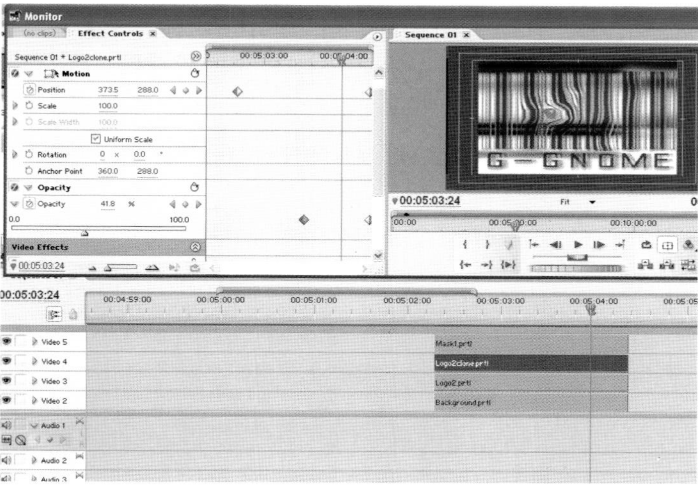

7 *It looks unsubtle and busy, so I've set the* Opacity *to fade out to 0% from about halfway through the clone move.*

6 *In the ECW, I've set the copy's* Motion > **Position** *at it's default center for about half a second. After that, I've set the final keyframe of the graphic at a slight X* Position *shift to create the "cloning."*

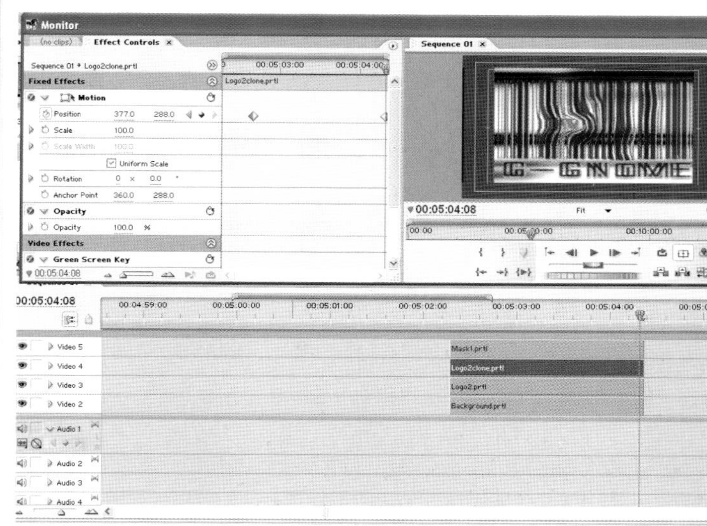

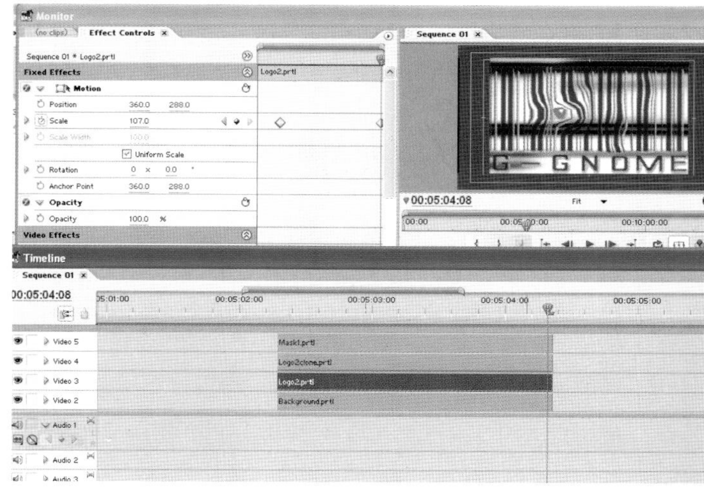

8 *Keeping the* ECW *edit line in place, I've returned to the original logo and—at the start of the clone's motion—put an initial keyframe where I want to begin a* Uniform Scale *increase. It goes to the end of the title clip, and edges the logo text close to bleeding off the edge of the screen. This works so well that I decide to duplicate the effect on text in the rest of the teaser.*

9 Back to the "Who is G-Gnome?" title. Because of the move—and because I've already razored away at the video production itself—I've extended the time for all of the graphics to make room for changes to the text. They will always require just that bit more time...

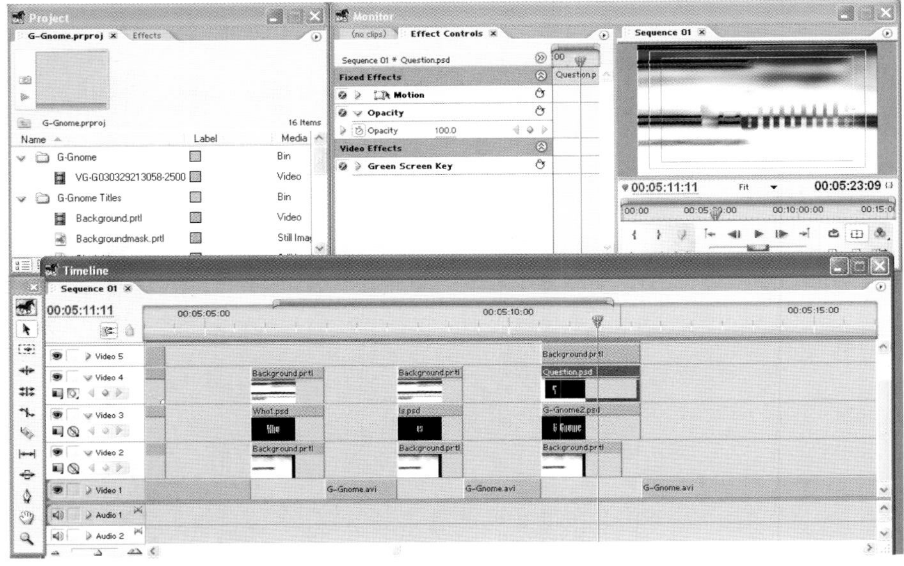

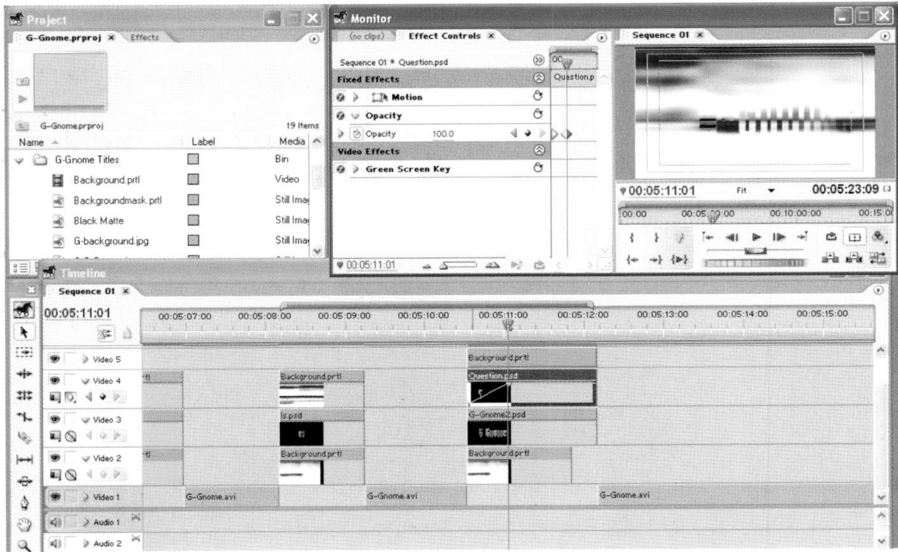

10 To start with the question mark, all I've got currently in composite is a slightly misshapen "G." If the question mark is going to emerge subtly from this initial letter, it's going to have to start with a zero Opacity and then quickly get to 100% as it separates from the "G." From the start—even at 0% Opacity—the '?' needs to start moving away from the "G." Of course, if you remember back as far as page 125, you already know what we have to do next. If not, all you have to do is turn back and remind yourself.

Compositing and animating files within Premiere Pro: 2

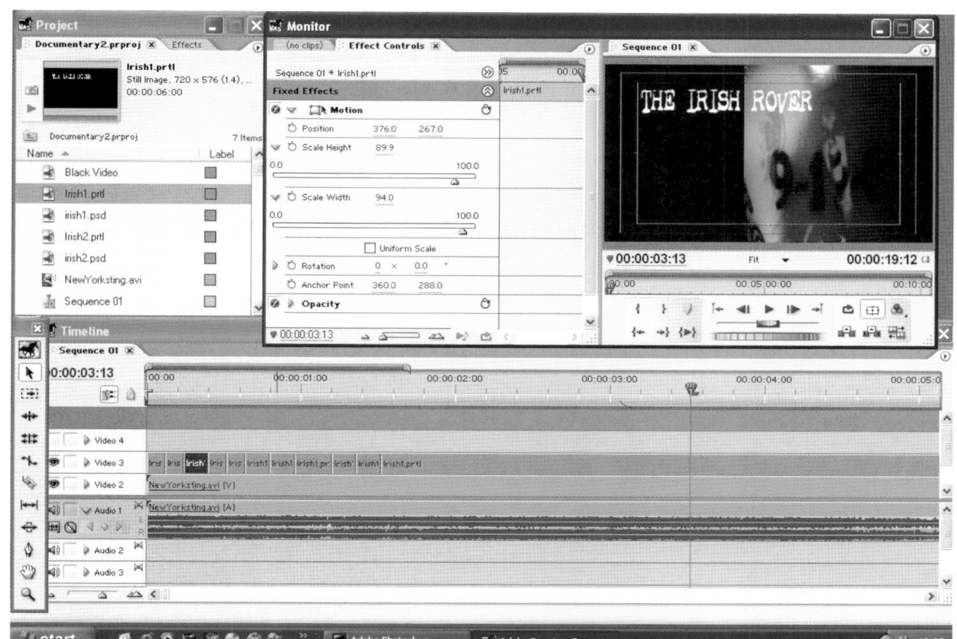

Creating the feel of animation contributes to the video in a very particular way. Creating flickbook movement between still frames draws attention to the distance between images. We're now at a time in film and video history where the viewer understands that animation used to be the only way of achieving certain effects, and knows that there are no such boundaries of possibility any more. Budgetary constraints are almost as historical, and seldom offer an explanation for animation.

Nowadays, it's an effect more than anything else, purely because a viewer will always know that smoothness could have been attained, but animation was chosen. That effect can be of the retro, the comedic, the quirky, or the distressed.

Keyframing motion in Premiere Pro is a surefire way of animating titles to the point of perfection. If you don't want perfection, though—if you want the feel of "true" animation (actual distance between fields using video)—there are three fundamental ways of achieving it.

1 *The first is in Premiere Pro itself. By razoring up the title on the Timeline, different motion values can be attributed to each part of the title with hard cuts between them. It's as painful as animation tends to be, but the effect can be worth your while—especially if coupled with an effect.*

2 *This overexaggerated Ripple effect (sequence left) has been added to the same razored-motion title by copying and pasting the effect to each clip and altering the values between them. The difference in values, coupled with the jump-cuts, gives it a heavily animated quality.*

3 *A slightly less tedious way is to keyframe motion or an effect from the start of a title clip to the end of it. Rendering this and exporting it as an AVI to be introduced again in another sequence...*

4 *...allows for the clips to be razored as short sharp clips and either re-abutted...*

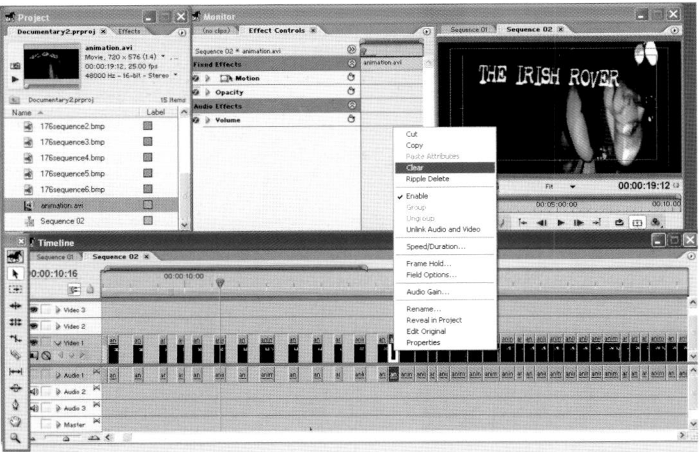

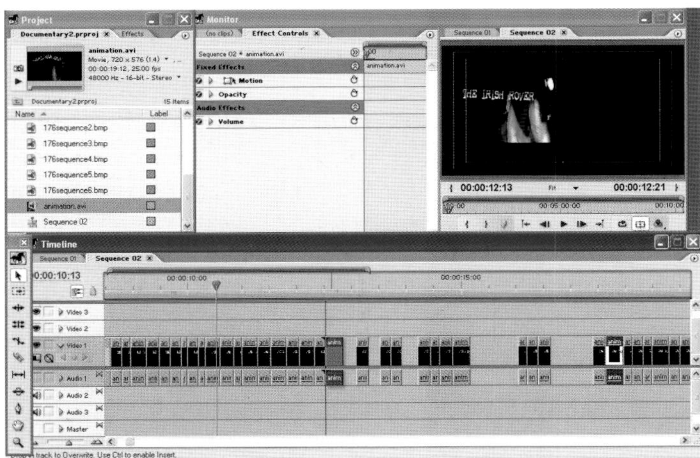

5 *...or for the clips to be arbitrarily dragged around between themselves to give the jittery title effect of, say, something like the titles in* Se7en.

The point of all this is to say that any still image can be copied and moved within the frame, using the ECW motion controls or a 2/3D DVE until an animation is created. The third way of doing this is to use Photoshop and Premiere Pro in tandem. The object in this example is to achieve something different—and a lot more effective.

6 *I've created two matte files in Photoshop to act independently in Premiere Pro, dividing the title into two and saving them both off. The font has been chosen to work with a punky, distressed look, and the color to work as juxtaposition against the green night-vision video.*

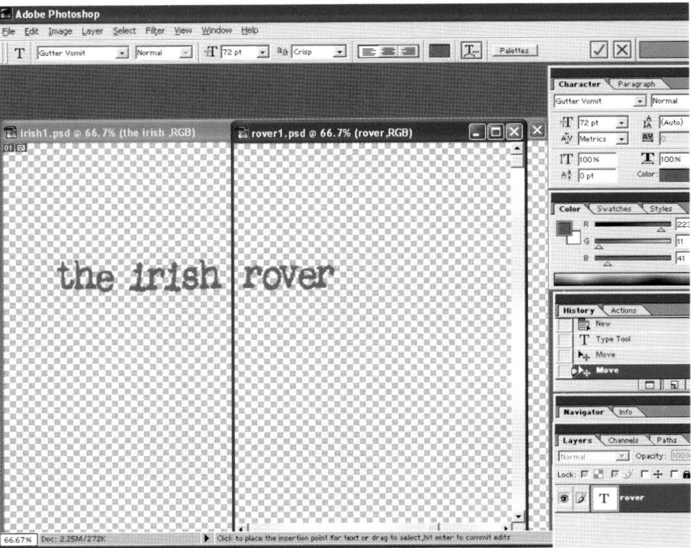

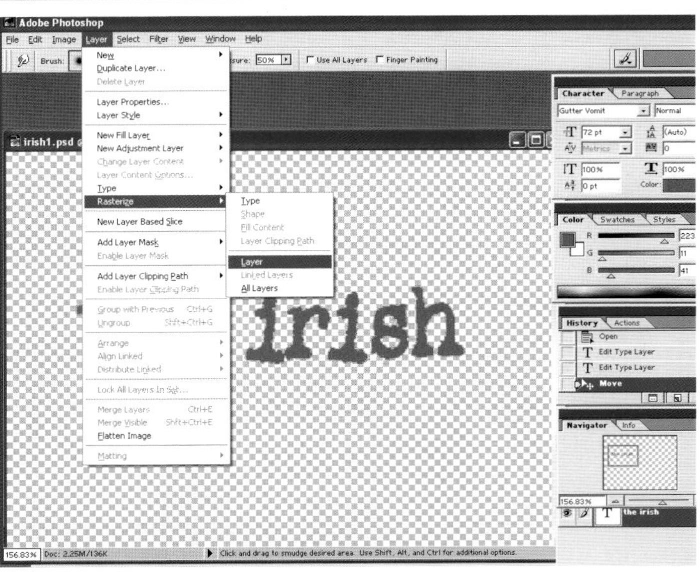

7 *Before each layer can be worked on, they have to be rasterized. This ensures that all edits to the new "normal" layer (rather than text layer) can be made.*

8 *Selecting the* Smudge Tool, *then checking the* Finger Painting *box and a suitable brush size with the magnified text, gives the text the ideal 'distressed' look to go wit a punky animation style.*

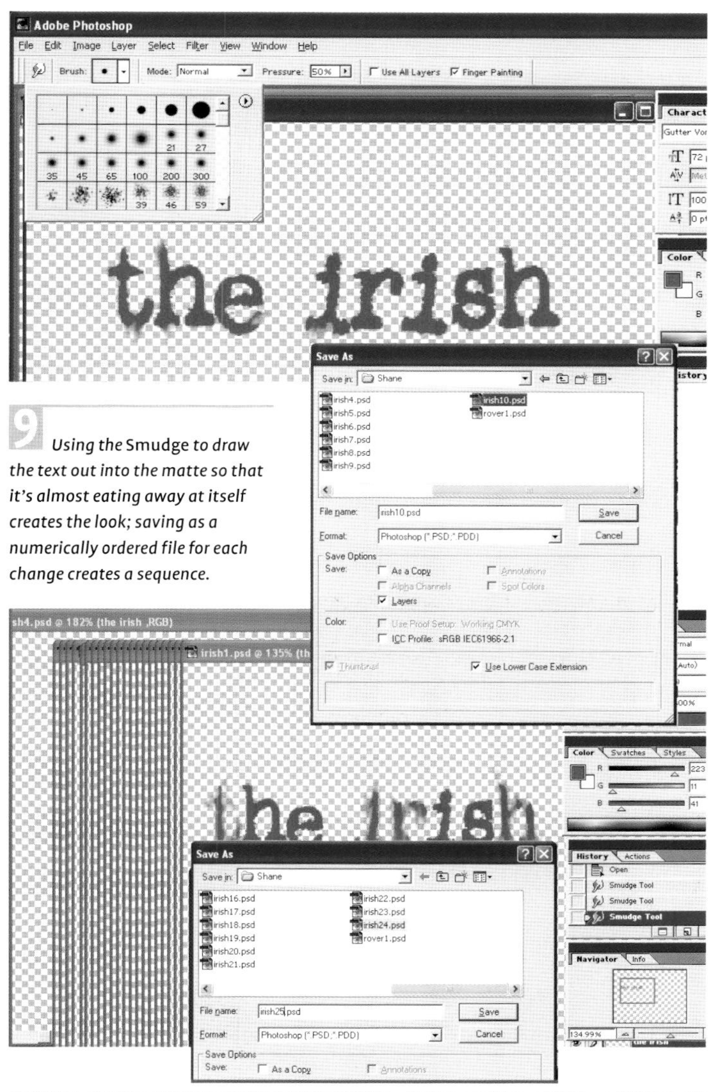

9 *Using the* Smudge *to draw the text out into the matte so that it's almost eating away at itself creates the look; saving as a numerically ordered file for each change creates a sequence.*

10 *Each time I make changes, I'm making them to the original .psd file. Therefore as progress is made, the process becomes simply a matter of* Open Recent File, *"Irish1"; magnify; smudge;* Save As *"Irish22.psd";* Open Recent File, *"Irish1"... ad infinitum—or at least until I've completed a round and convenient 25 frames. Note an additional, thematic trick: I've occasionally paid particular attention to leaving "he is" as an untouched part of the two-word title.*

11 *Turning to the separate "Rover" part of the whole title, I'm adopting a slightly different method. Instead of a* Smudge *tool, I'm going to use the* Eraser *to gradually eat into the word. At overstated magnification with a small airbrush, it's possible to make the slightest of changes over the course of the 25 frames.*

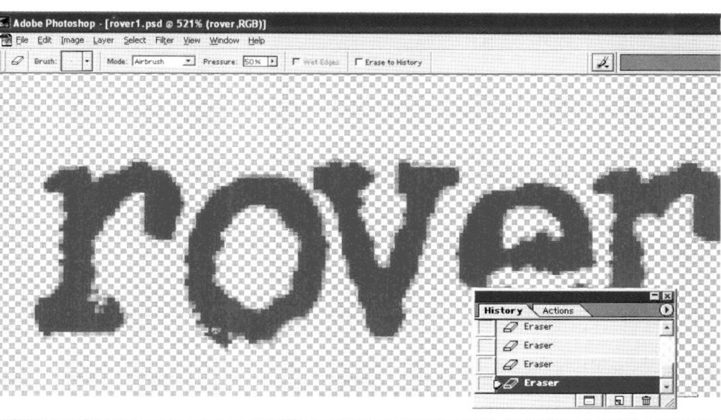

12 *The process is exactly the same, but without reverting back to the original text. This time, each change is made progressively, and I save numerically and sequentially in reverse...*

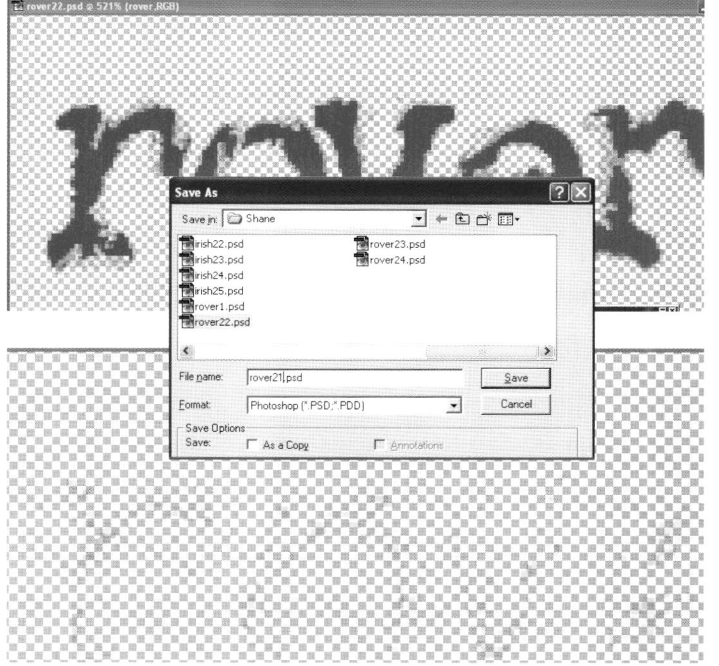

13 *...until there's nothing left of the title at all.*

14 *Importing all the files as footage into the Premiere Pro project, it's tidier to create bins for each title away from the video footage...*

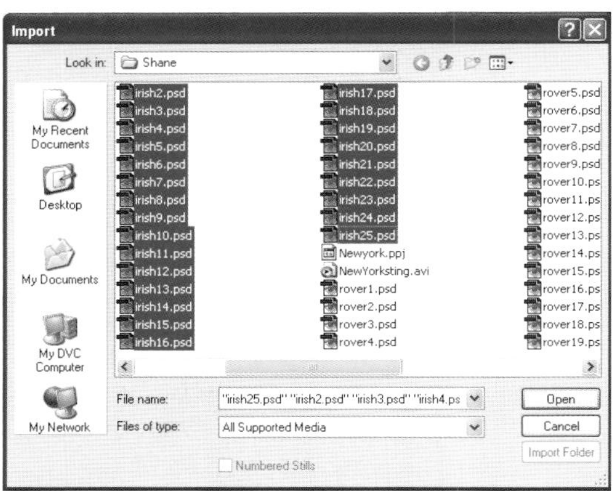

15 *...and once there's some kind of order, it's time to introduce the madness.*

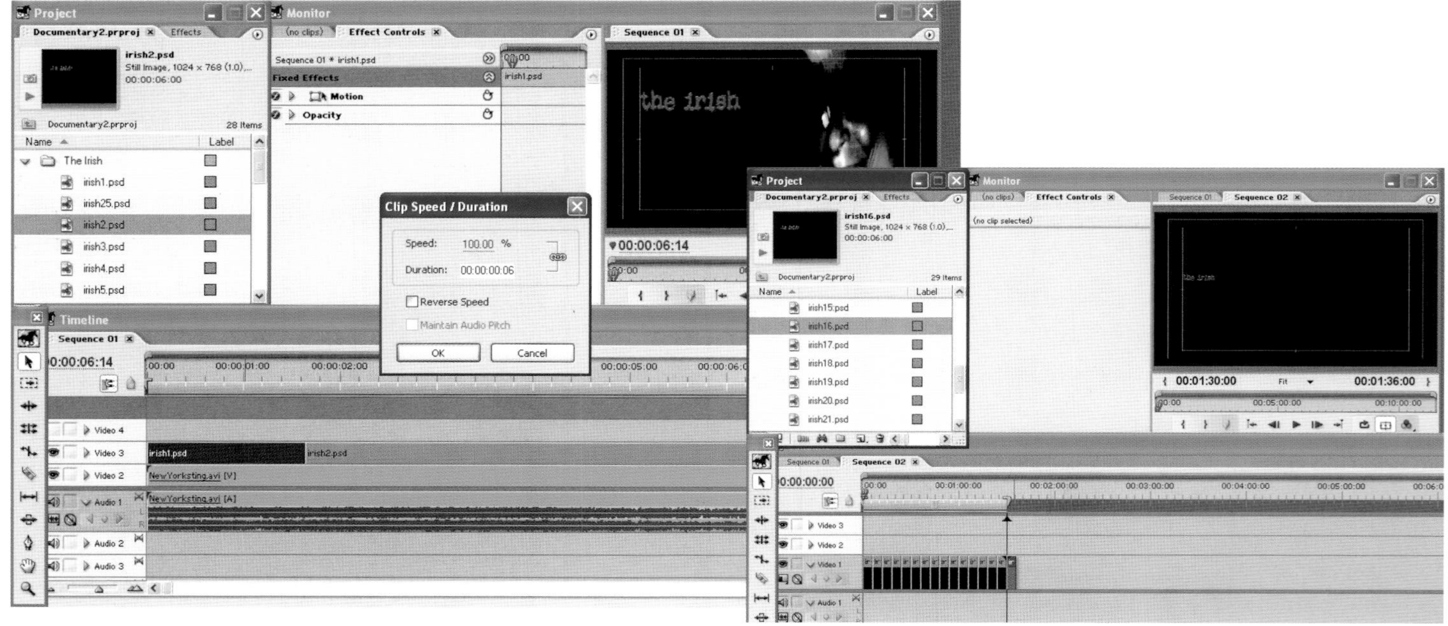

16 *Of course, the point of animation is that you notice it as animation—but not so much that it becomes a slide show. Dragging each clip onto the* Timeline *and right-clicking to* Speed/Duration *lets the value be input for each still. Video is a seamless parade of images at 25/30 fps, so I'm reckoning on noticing animation at roughly half of that. Therefore, inputting a duration of six frames for each still should be conspicuous enough without overdoing it. But wait a minute...only six frames, not 12? Why? Well, there's one more trick up my sleeve yet...*

17 *You want animation without any more tedium. Six frames per second defaults the* Speed *value to 2500%. This is because each psd file dragged to the* Timeline *has a default duration of six seconds. Zooming out of the* Timeline*, then, it's quicker to simply drag all of the clips in order into a new sequence and then speed up the whole of that sequence at 2500%.*

18 *Because this is so entirely easy, it's worth thinking ahead at this point. If the animation is likely to go on for a few seconds—and the animation is conspicuous—then it will be conspicuous too that the animation is repeated sequentially every four seconds. To break up this repeated cycle, it's no real sweat once all of the stills have been dragged in, to randomly keep dragging them in until reaching the amount of time required to avoid repetition.*

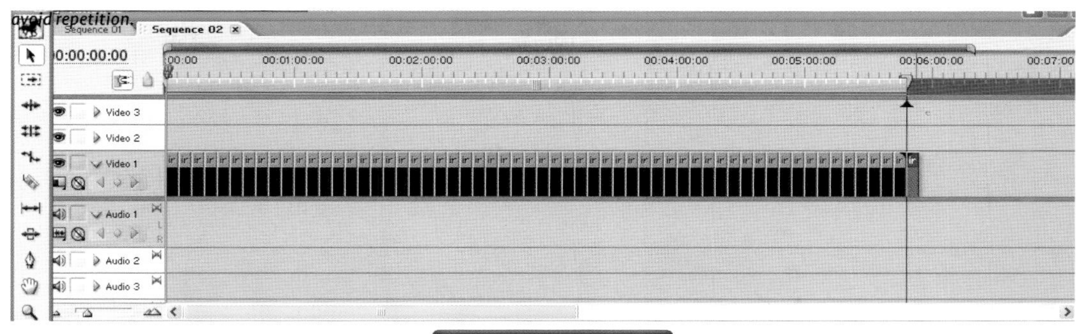

19 *Dragging the new sequence on the* Timeline *and right-clicking to alter the* Speed *to 5000% gives only, of course, enough for half this sequence.*

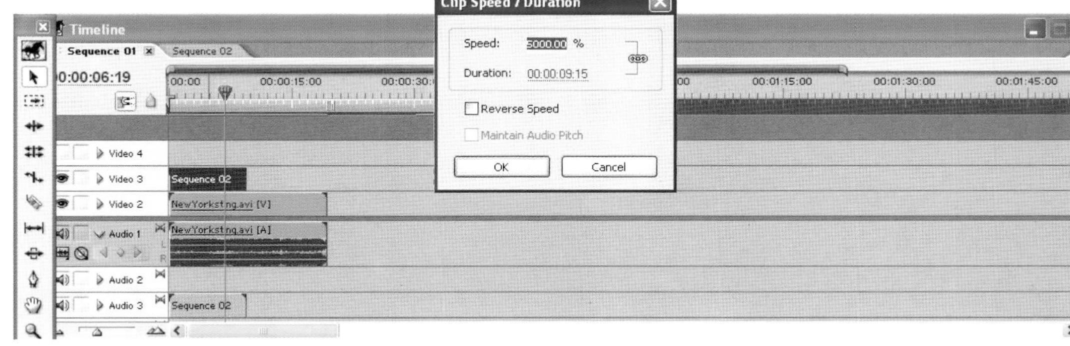

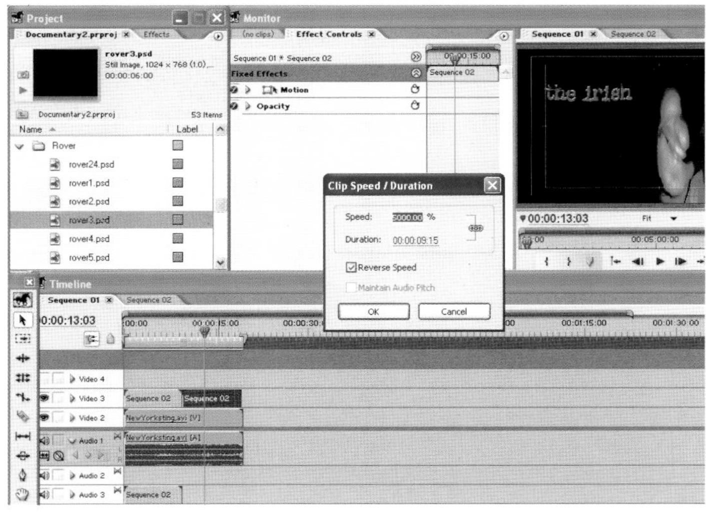

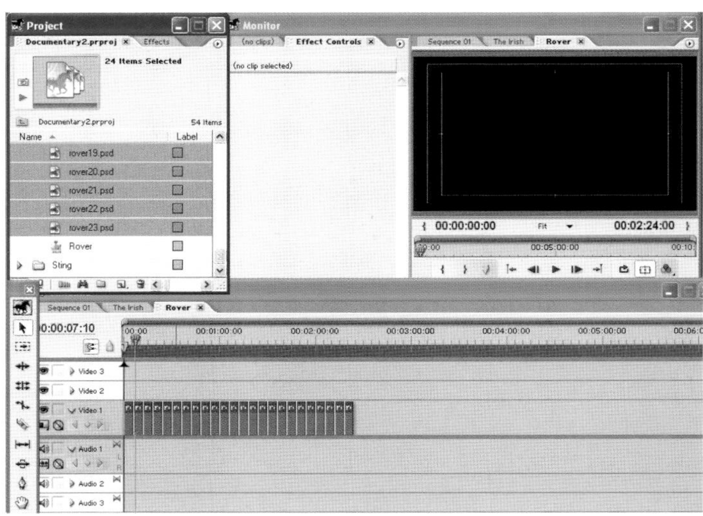

20 *To achieve full randomness at half the boredom rate, copy, paste, and abut a duplicate of the sequence—and then right-click and select* Speed/Duration > **Reverse Speed** *to make the most of your sequence.*

21 *Next up, the second part of the title. Again, creating another sequence to drop it into is going to help. Because this is numerically sequential rather than random and because the file numbers were allocated in reverse to the respective erased files, highlighting all of the Rover psd's and then dragging them onto the* Timeline*, will do most of the work.*

22 *Dragging the new sequence back onto the original* Timeline *shows its default length—5 seconds x 25 stills = 150 seconds.*

23 *Setting a new speed of 1500% brings it to the halfway mark of the sequence on the* Timeline*...*

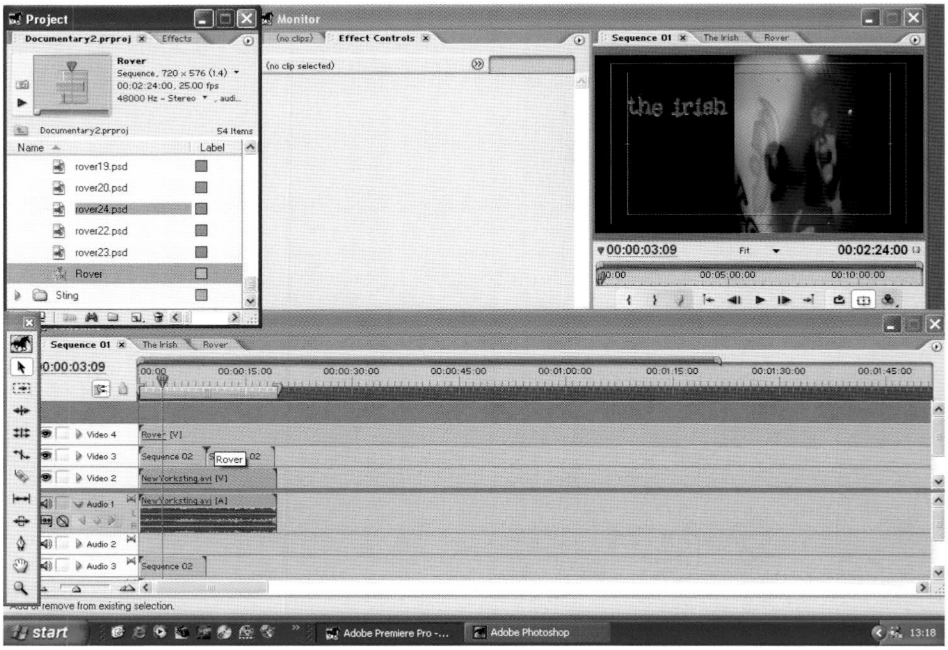

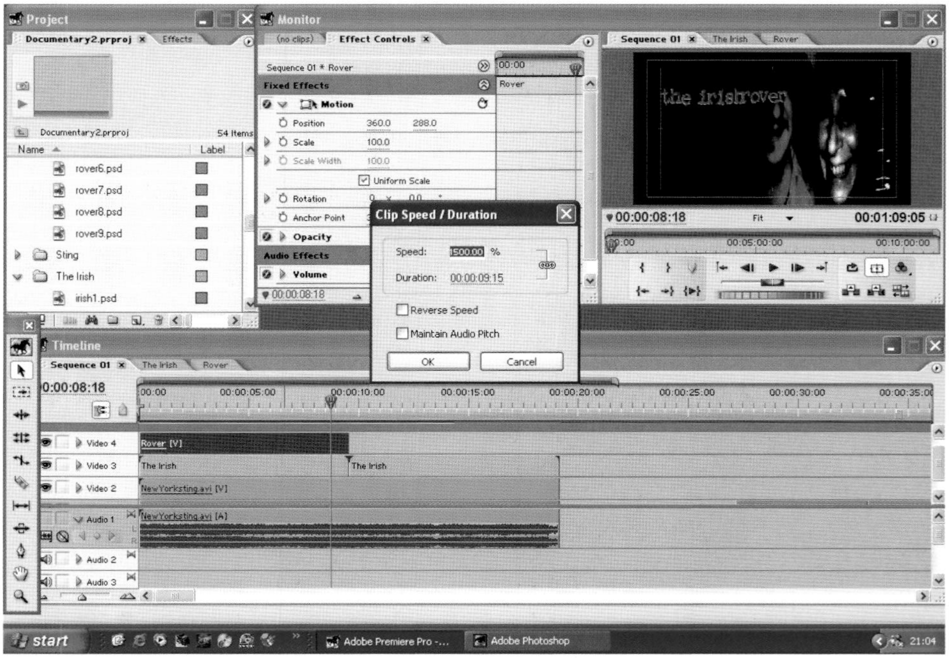

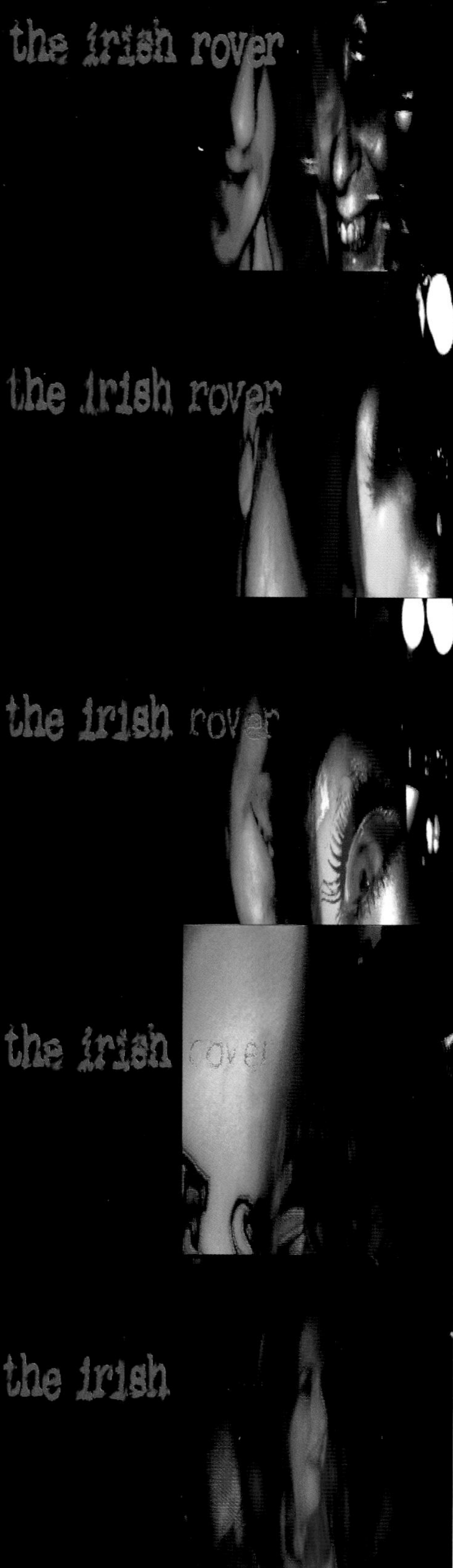

24 *...and again, copying, pasting, and right-clicking to select* Speed/Duration *then* Reverse Speed, *adds a clip to be dragged and abutted to be the transition back to the fully erasered start of the title.*

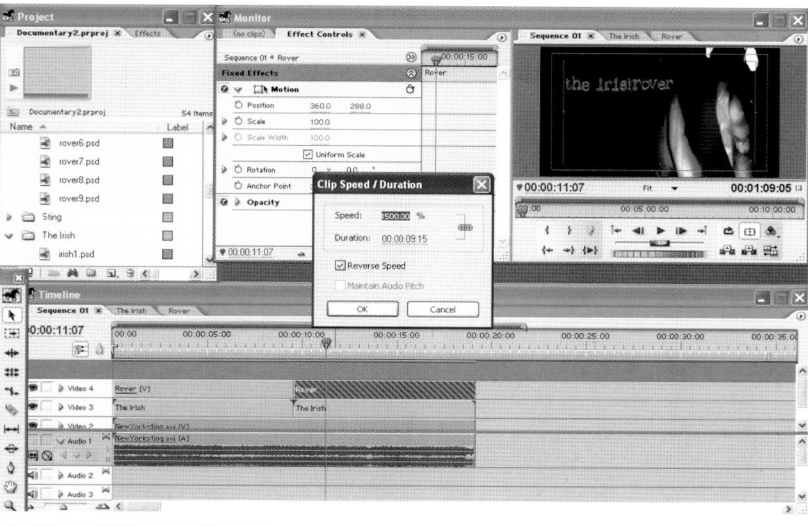

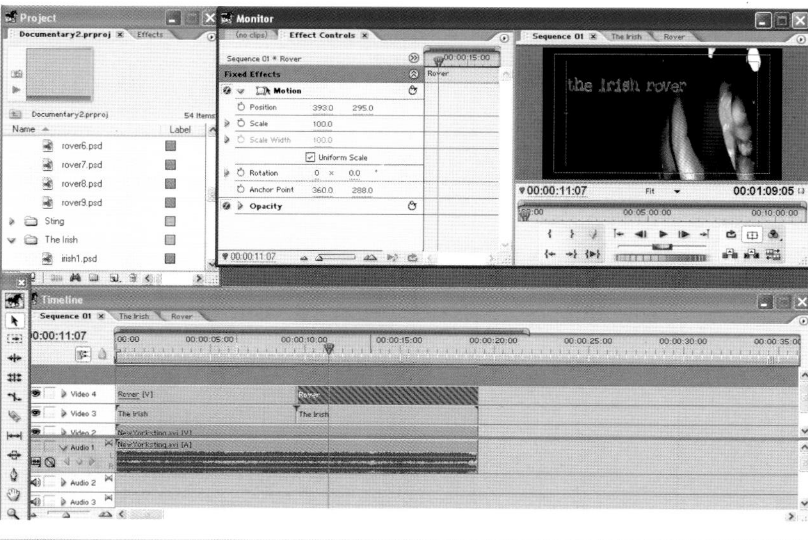

25 *The animation is complete bar one thing: the rough-and-ready placement of titles has ensured that there isn't enough gap between the two layers—and the last two words. To align the text, the X and Y are adjusted using the* Position *control in the* ECW's Motion *dialog for both the forward and reverse clip.*

It's missing a lot. The forward/reverse clip acts as a transition that the first layer still needs to bring it on and off at the same rate. If you turn back to page 90, you can remind yourself how we achieve this using video effects.

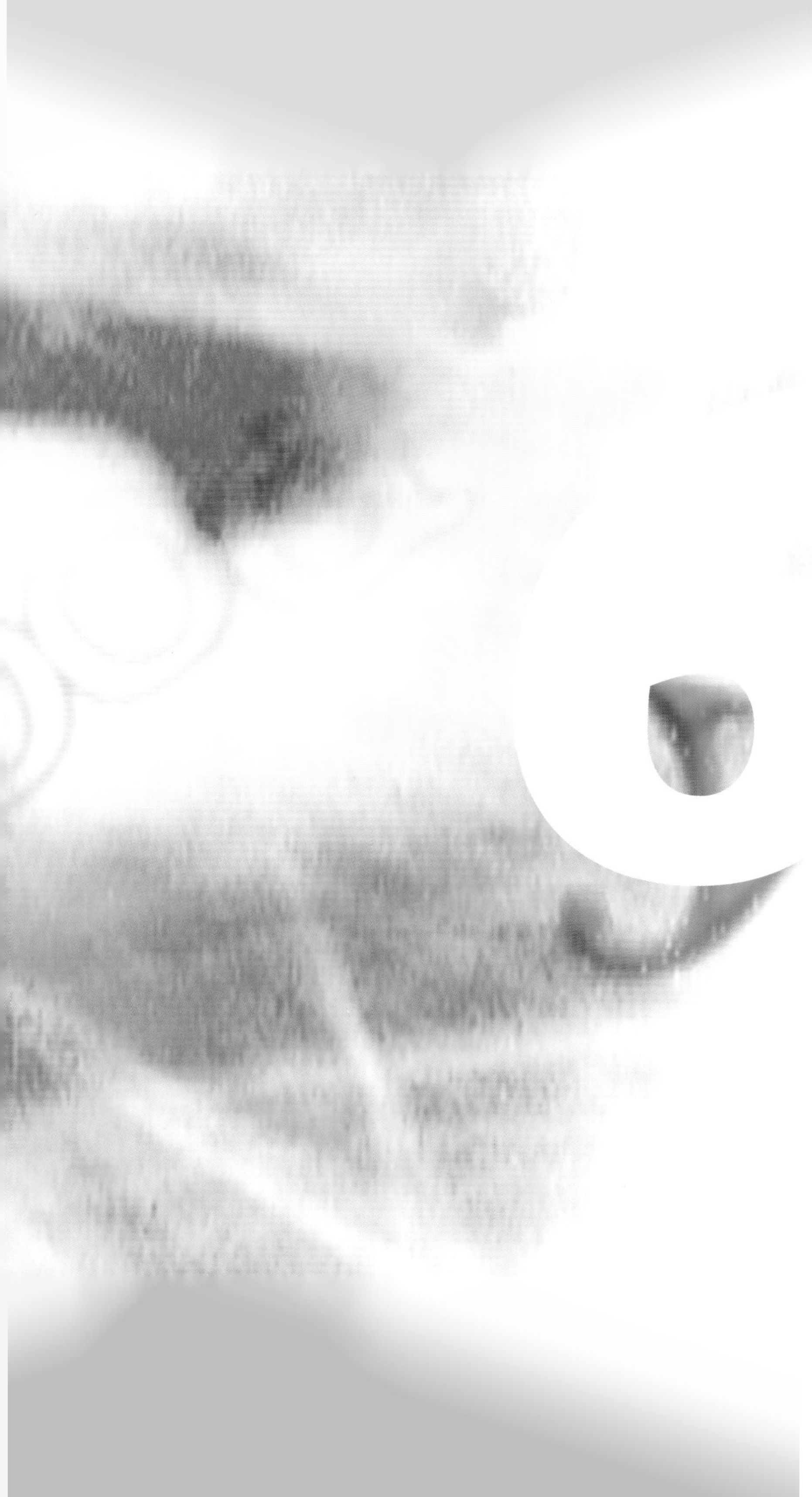

CHAPTER SIX

the full effect

Final checks

We've learned some of the creative techniques for backing your titles out of the garage, giving them a lick of paint and a polish, and taking them for a spin. But all of the elements of a good title, including your images, harmonious audio, composition, and screen safety need a final admiring glance.

If you've got this far, it probably seems like a long journey. There've been many twists and turns on the road , but finally I hope you've got something to be proud of. Nothing's ever *quite* right, though, so it's time for the final check-through.Run through the title sequence in its place with the production. Is it too long? Too distracting? Are all the vital elements in place? Is all the information there? Most of all, does it do what you set out to do?

There are always ways of fixing a title sequence. If you're generally happy with it, the best idea is to put the entire *Timeline* into a new sequence and apply adjustments to that. If it is too long or too short, can you get away with a simple speed change? If it's too busy, will muted colors tone it down?

The simple fact is that the combination of a perfectionist title designer and the awful reality that nothing's ever perfect can be pretty lethal. There are infinite ways that titles can be improved, just as there are as many ways that titles can be changed. You just need to decide whether the changes are worthwhile.

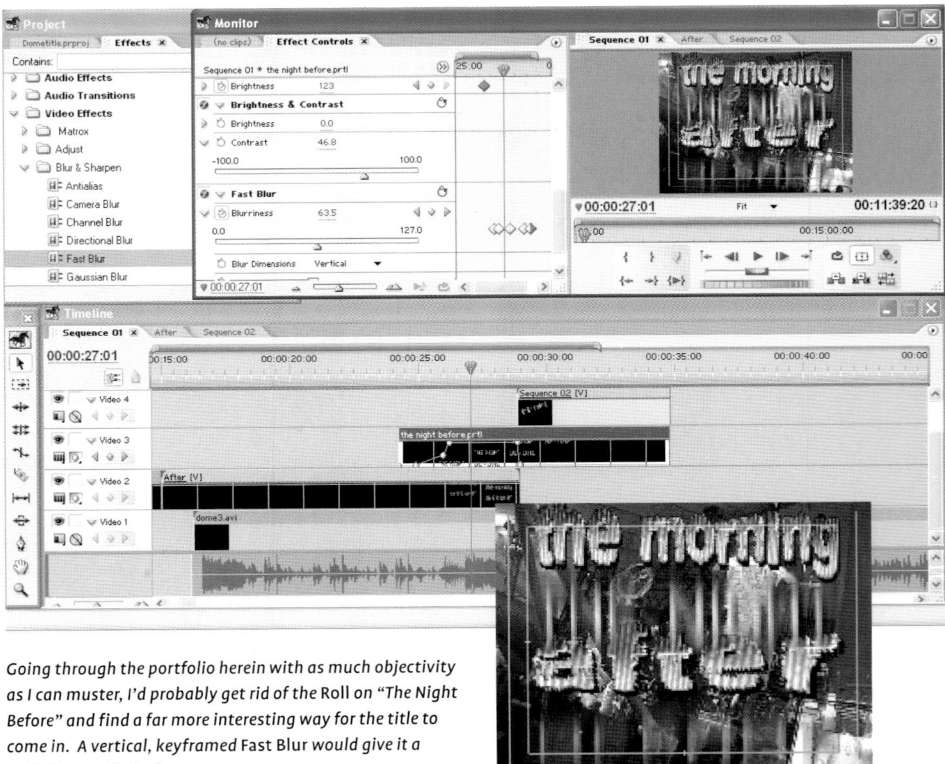

Going through the portfolio herein with as much objectivity as I can muster, I'd probably get rid of the Roll *on "The Night Before" and find a far more interesting way for the title to come in. A vertical, keyframed* Fast Blur *would give it a suitably sparkly look.*

The poor married couple: I've turned them into James Bond and Pussy Galore—which may be an improvement. It's still too static, despite the still moves. Exporting it as an AVI, the entire frame needs livening up in time to a suitably upbeat soundtrack. A video effect should sort this one out.

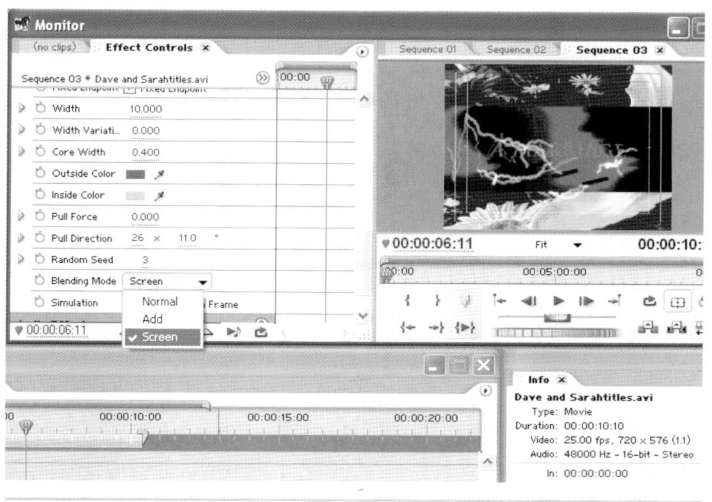

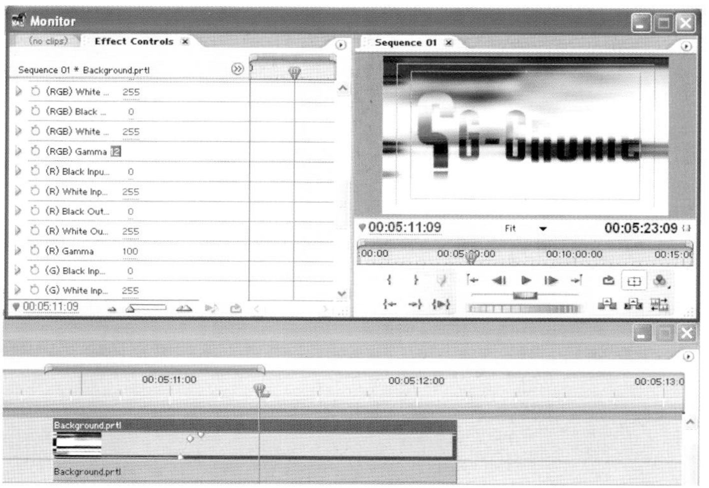

The issue with the "G-Gnome" title is that it's slightly too short to process what it's saying. I could fight for more space and permission to loop the soundtrack. Instead, I've found a better way: lowering the RGB Gamma *in the* Adjust > **Levels** *drop-down, and inputting a high* Color Offset *(in* Effects > Image Control*) to the backgrounds keyed to the text and question mark, bringing them both out from the resident and unchanged background.*

This gardening caption is really far too busy. If I ever wanted it to be distracting, I've got it in spades. Added to this is the fact that there are other interviews that will follow suit, and it's too much. The caption and flower background are toggled into vision in one sequence, exported as a frame, Chroma Keyed*, and mixed on and off. The branch animation matte is knocked back in opacity behind it.*

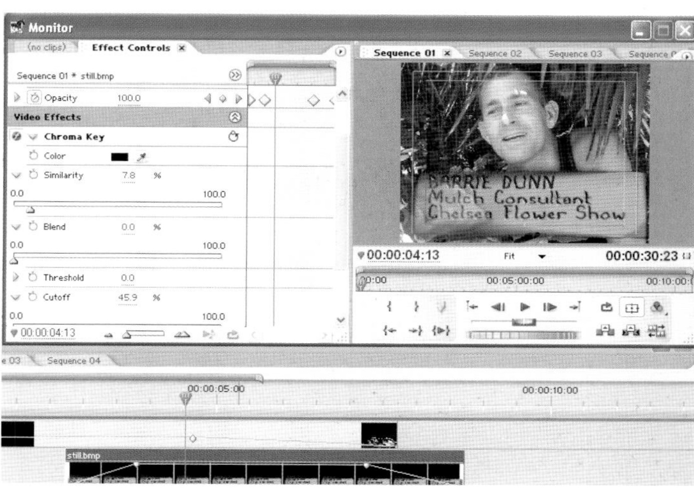

This title I'm happy with visually. In fact, if anything, it's the audio that needs cleaning up...

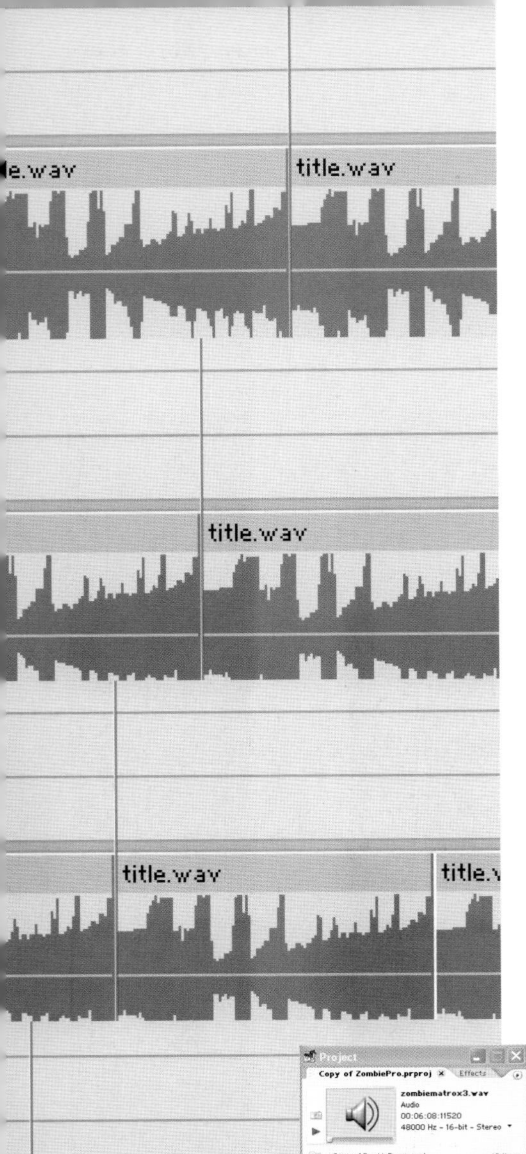

Choosing your audio and fixing it to fit

Audio is the crucial element of any title sequence's success. Audio takes a viewer through the titles—at the very least making reading fun. At most, it can direct the viewer to the text itself, predicting how long they've got to read them, how they're going to come in, where they're going to be placed on screen. When sound and text work together, the effect can be more entertaining than the production.

Audio isn't music: audio is audio. Audio is dialogue, sound effects, voice-over—even silence. And yes, audio can be music, or a layered combination of any sound.

Captions don't tend to have sound effects—sometimes they do, if the programme is amusing, zany, or intended for children. All the same, it's not a great example. Opening titles absolutely love sound—and fall over themselves for music. End titles likewise, but if it's cinema, the majority of the audience isn't listening to it.

The example here is an end title sequence. There's absolutely no reason why this pop promo actually has titles, aside from the fact that it's a demo and the names may register with potential managers as they get up out of their creaking leather swivel chairs and turn the monitor off. The end titles cut is as loose as you like with no audio. The only audio that I actually have of the band is the track itself, which of course has already been played—and the natural audio from the promo's source clips.

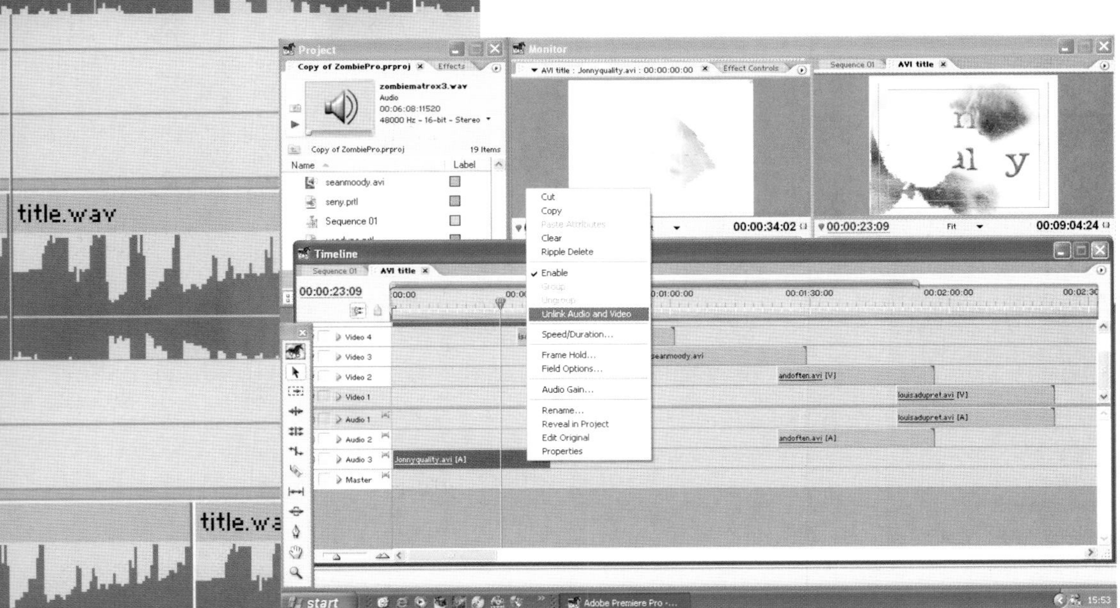

1 *Because of the background and overlay clips, Premiere Pro has been kind enough to keep them for me as linked audio clips. As grateful as I am, they've got to go and leave the audio clean. Making sure that they're unlinked, I'm clearing them away...*

2 *What I do have to hand is the audio track for the promo. Recognizing that these are end titles and the opening bars haven't been heard by the viewer for at least four minutes, I'm going to take these and razor the rest of the music away. With the residue opening bars, I've right-clicked to change the Speed/Duration to 40% of its original speed, then checked* Reverse Speed *and the* Maintain Audio Pitch *box.*

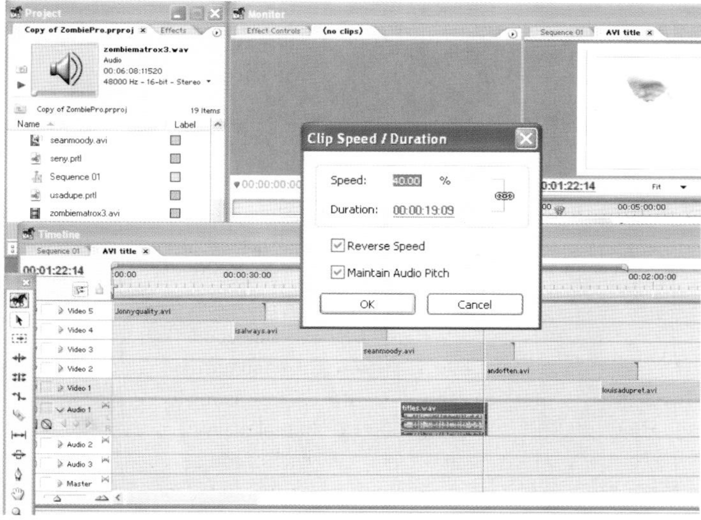

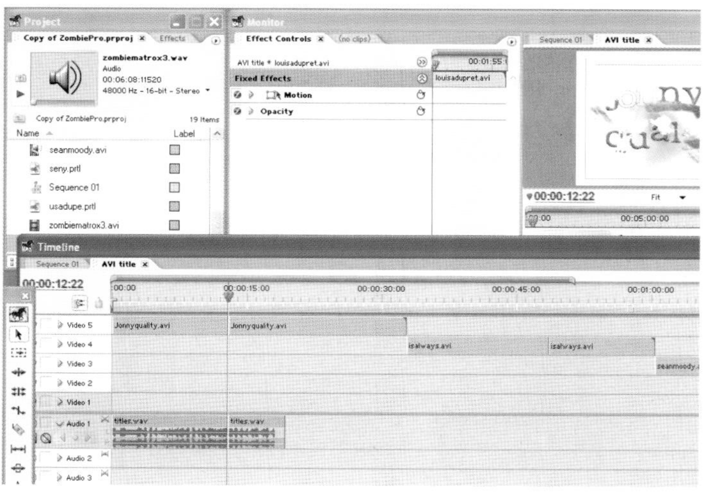

4 *The editing process continues from* *page 133**. Each clip has a transition and a legible timeframe onscreen. Each AVI's transition needs a speed check to make both the transition quick and the text flicker-book legible. Both the transition and the resting point of each clip therefore need razoring to apply different values.*

3 *It's short and not so sweet—but ultimately interesting. Don't let anyone tell you otherwise: length does matter. And knowing exactly how long this audio sample is at 40% is a good enough method of starting to compose the pictures. With video and audio, neither the chicken nor the egg comes first—they both work in tandem. Using the audio clip as a reference (it can be repeated as many times as necessary), and knowing that each title needs to be legible for three seconds plus the transition that gets it onscreen, provides acceptable rough values to begin editing with.*

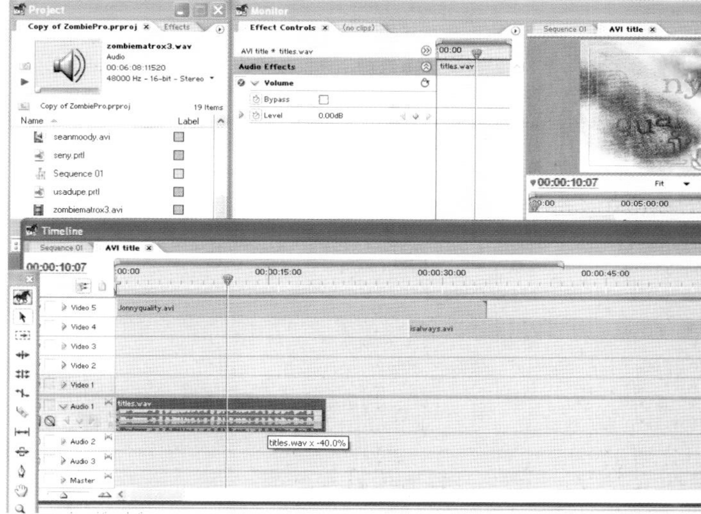

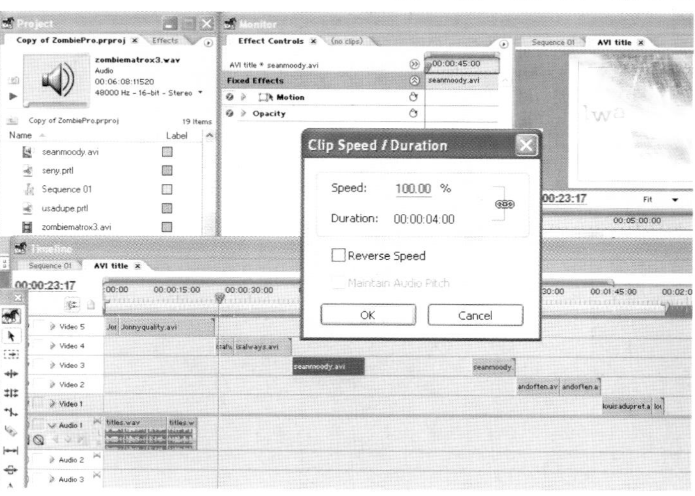

5 *The speed of the transition is easy because it doesn't rely on legibility—just an indication of legibility. Therefore altering these values to be four seconds (three seconds plus a one-second mix to the next title) is easy to input as timecode values. The exception is the start clip, which runs for only three seconds.*

6 *The question of timing for the final positioned text of each of the five titles then has only two criteria: they have to contain enough of the ever-fluctuating clip to be legible, and they have to have one second clear from the outset for the transition into the following motion of the next clip. Speeding up each clip certainly provides enough digestible information to the eye to piece together a legible title, so I'm going to give them the same amount of time as a starting point: four seconds (aside from the end clip with three seconds).*

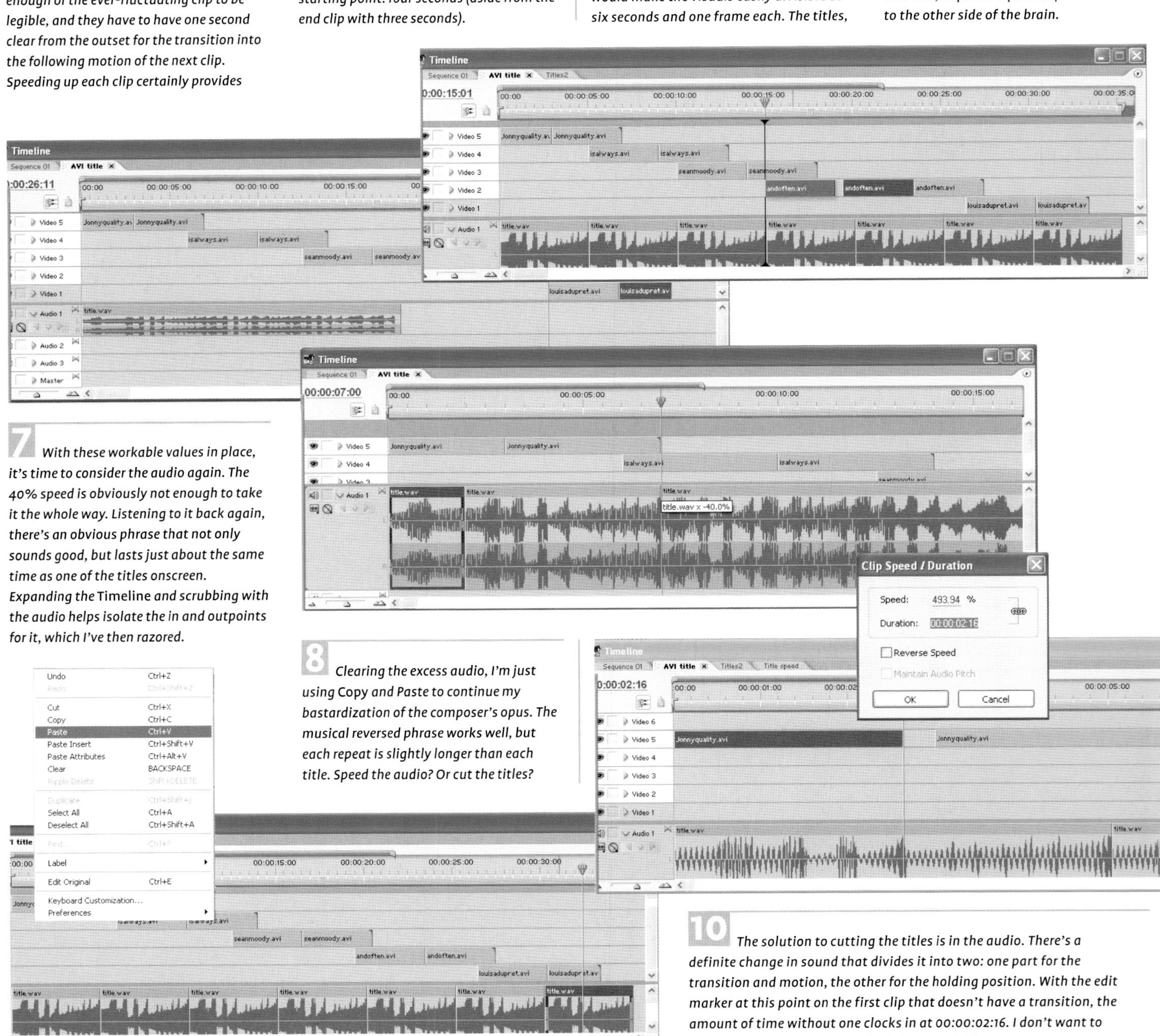

7 *With these workable values in place, it's time to consider the audio again. The 40% speed is obviously not enough to take it the whole way. Listening to it back again, there's an obvious phrase that not only sounds good, but lasts just about the same time as one of the titles onscreen. Expanding the* Timeline *and scrubbing with the audio helps isolate the in and outpoints for it, which I've then razored.*

8 *Clearing the excess audio, I'm just using* Copy *and* Paste *to continue my bastardization of the composer's opus. The musical reversed phrase works well, but each repeat is slightly longer than each title. Speed the audio? Or cut the titles?*

9 *They both win—or lose. Removing the last audio phrase, the audio comes in at 00:00:30:05. Without any transition, this would make the visuals easily divisible at six seconds and one frame each. The titles, though, are too pregnant, too look-at-me. Five seconds is more than adequate for each, easilt divisible—and with a transition involved, requires a quick trip to the other side of the brain.*

10 *The solution to cutting the titles is in the audio. There's a definite change in sound that divides it into two: one part for the transition and motion, the other for the holding position. With the edit marker at this point on the first clip that doesn't have a transition, the amount of time without one clocks in at 00:00:02:16. I don't want to cut the clip—I just want to make it faster so it fits.*

11 *The second part of the conundrum applies to the second part of the clip. For flickerbook legibility, it needs speed and not cutting. The five allocated seconds minus the 02:16 comes in at 02:09 (PAL). Fine, but I still need an additional allocation for the duration of the transition to the next title...*

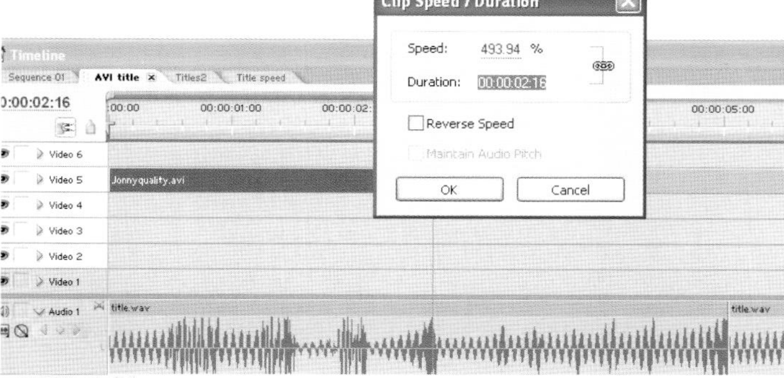

12 *Determining a transition time of 12 frames, I've added it to the second part of the clip for a running time of 02:21.*

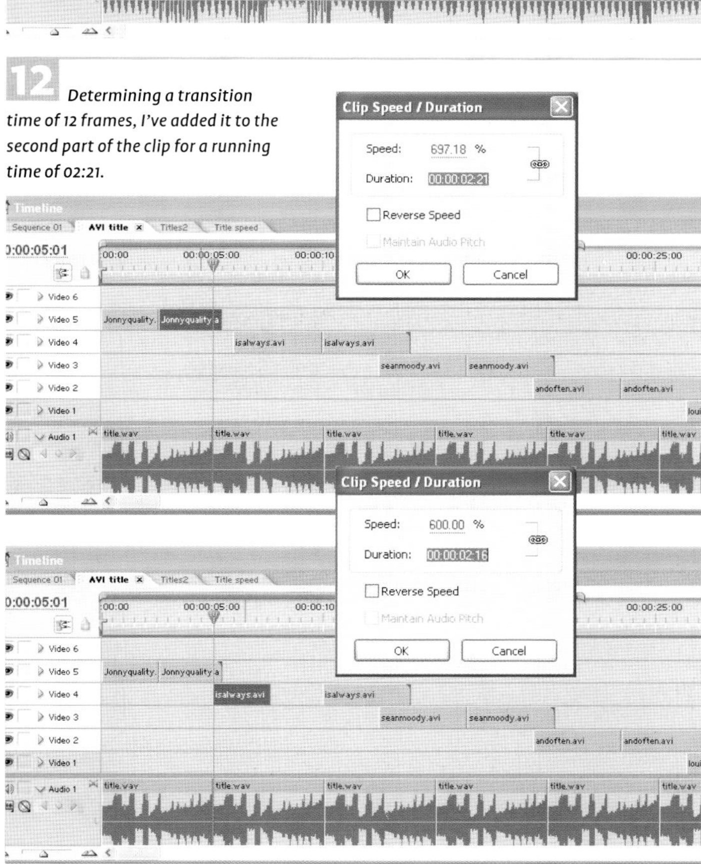

13 *Dragging the next motion clip to the five second mark and altering the speed to 02:16 creates the start of a chain reaction all the way down the* Timeline.

14 *The holding position of the final title doesn't need the transitional extra 12 frames and therefore clocks in at the original 02:09 duration to keep it neat with the audio cut. Take the last clip of audio off and the* Timeline*'s looking a little better.*

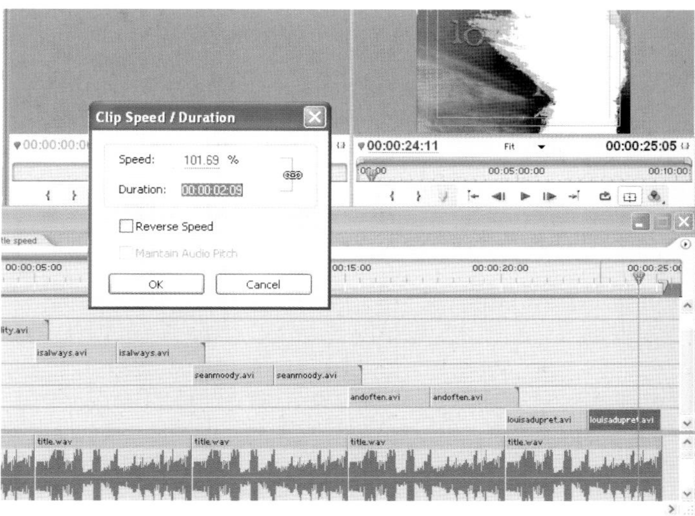

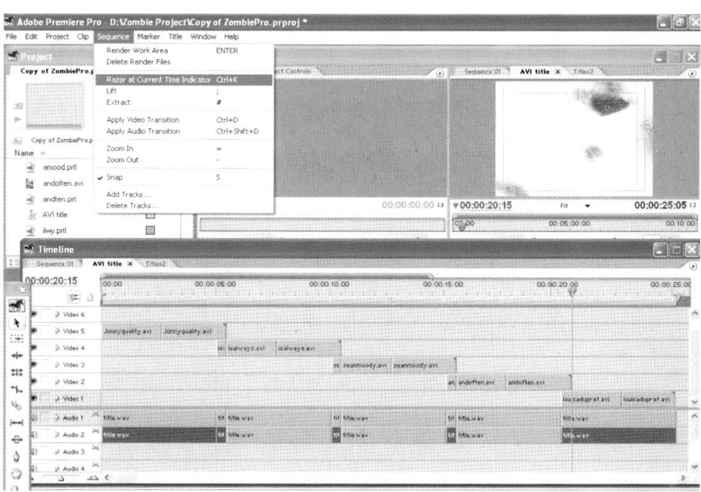

15 *It might seem obvious that the audio dictates the choice of transition—and ordinarily I'd probably try and find a snip of audio from a source tape to corrupt into a sound effect. Instead, though, I'm going to work with the audio that already exists. Now I know the positioning of the transition, I've duplicated the entire audio onto a track below and have begun razoring it at the future transition's outpoint.*

16 *The inpoint is already there as the start of the new audio phrase, and I've taken a stereo* PitchShifter *audio effect over onto the first of the duplicated clips. I'd probably keyframe this for absolute control, but for the sake of 12 frames, Applying the* A third higher *option adds the slight whirlwind sound that inspires a transition.*

17 *Finally, adding a* Channel Volume *filter, then keyframing for a quick left to right pan, completes the actual effects for a dynamic transition.*

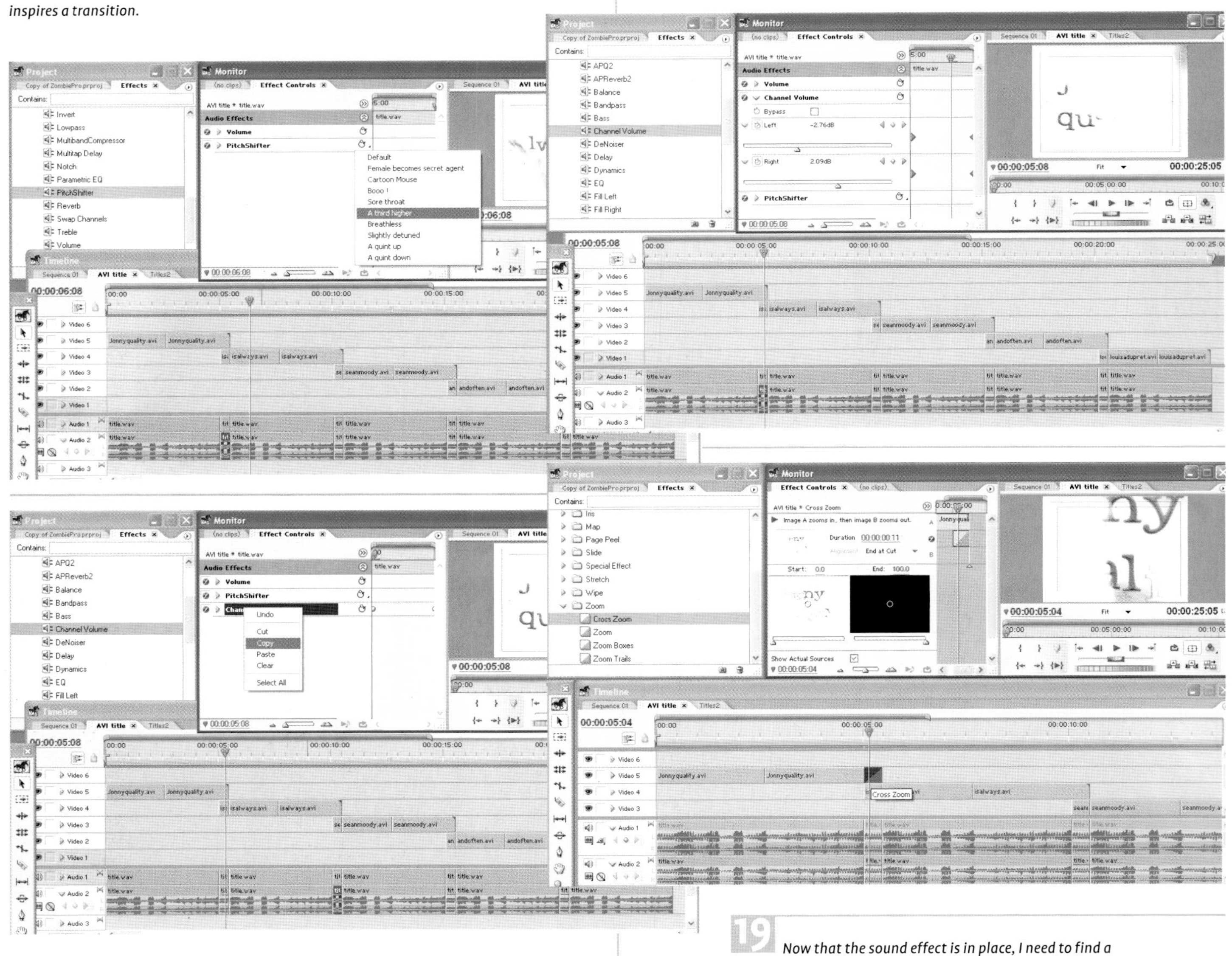

18 *Copying and pasting the audio effects to all of the duplicate audio track's razored clips ensures the rhythm. The duplicate audio keeps the original track running—and the audio transition effect popping in—without the need for any audio transition.*

19 *Now that the sound effect is in place, I need to find a transition to complement it. There's the whirlwind side of things, and the pan to consider. The whirlwind could be a* Spin *or* Tumble Away *quite happily, were it not for the fact that the transition is just 12 frames long. Whatever happens has got to be short, sharp, and instantly comprehensible. A* Cross Zoom *gives us motion and instant recognition of what has just taken place.*

20 *What it also offers is the ability to interpret the pan. Clicking the start move's directional cursor to the right of the screen, shifts the whole title off to the left for the first part of the pan effect.*

21 *Repeating this* Cross Zoom *on the second clip with reverse values (directional cursor to the left of the screen), brings the second title in from the right and completes the audio pan effect made visual.*

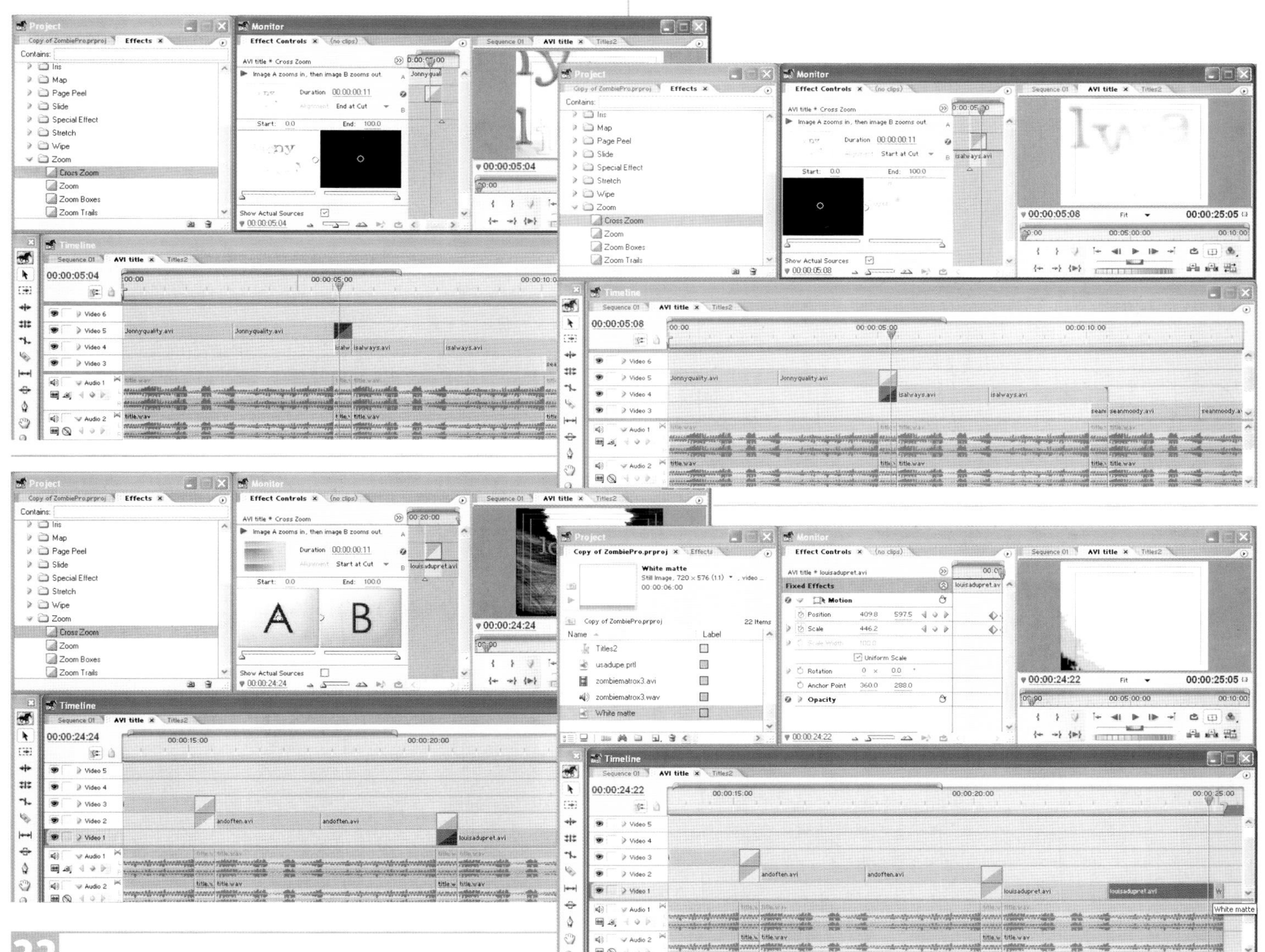

22 *I've applied exactly the same effect for each of the audio transitions and the title is almost complete bar an entrance and an exit. The sequence starts abruptly, the audio starts abruptly; the sequence finishes abruptly, the audio finishes abruptly. So far, so perfect. The beginning starts from a pure white screen, which, coming off the back of the video itself, works well enough. The end, though, has—again, with some serendipity—a screen rip a couple of frames in.*

23 *The frame shows the apex of the rip. To reinforce it, I'm keyframing a* Scale *and* Position *change to move into the white area as if the screen has ripped apart. Untidiness beyond this point is then razored off and replaced with a white matte (*File > New > **Color Matte***).*

24 *To match this "ripping," I've taken a* APReverb2 *over from the* Audio Effects *menu and extended the clip slightly long enough to let the* Church *default take effect.*

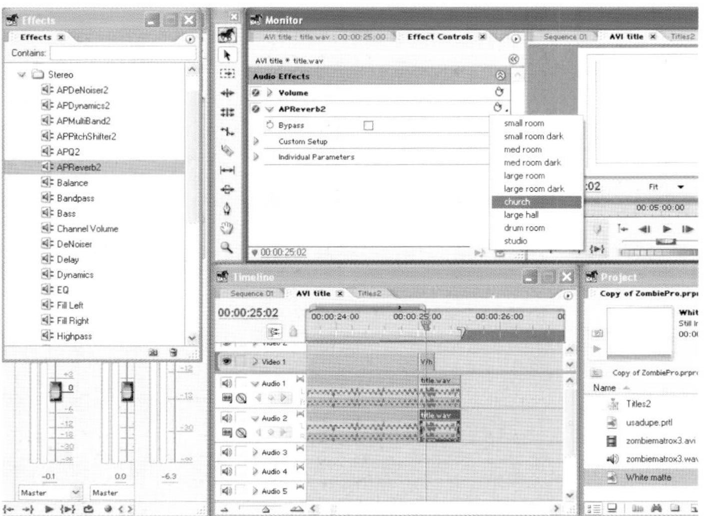

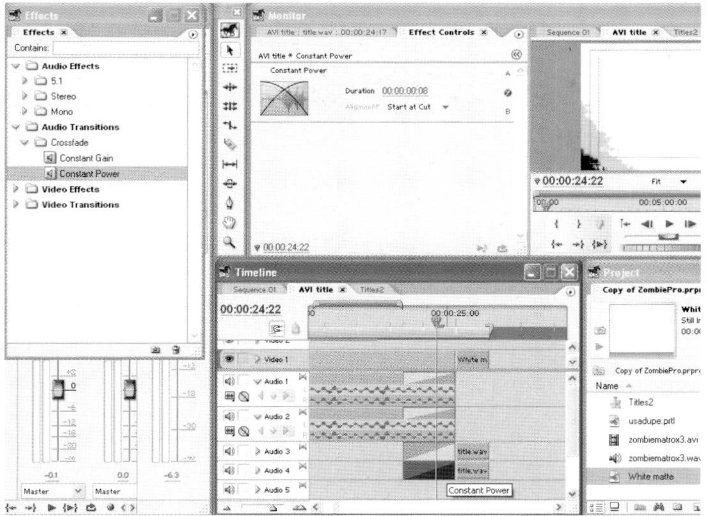

26 *Finally, locating the position of the rip, I've taken both razored tracks and placed them both on audio tracks beneath to coincide with the visuals. Dragging over a* Constant Power Crossfade *from the* Audio Transition *drop-down onto the two original clips and onto the two new ones, seals their part in becoming an invisible part of the soundtrack.*

25 *The harshness of the sound is created by unchecking and taking off the* Audio Pitch *that I'd maintained throughout.*

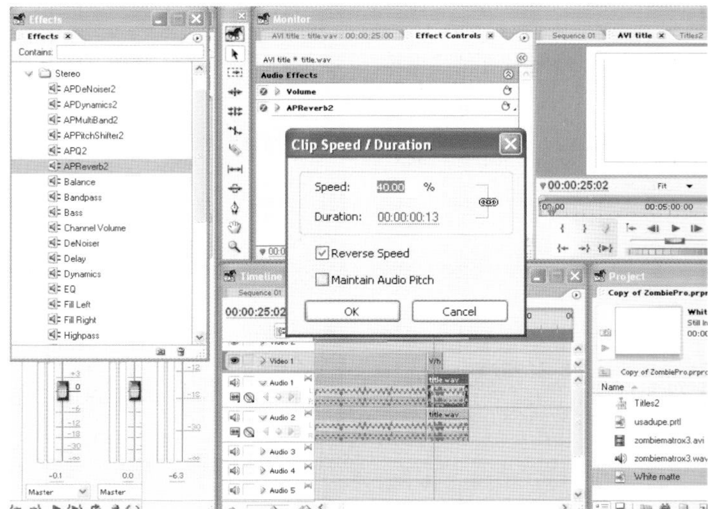

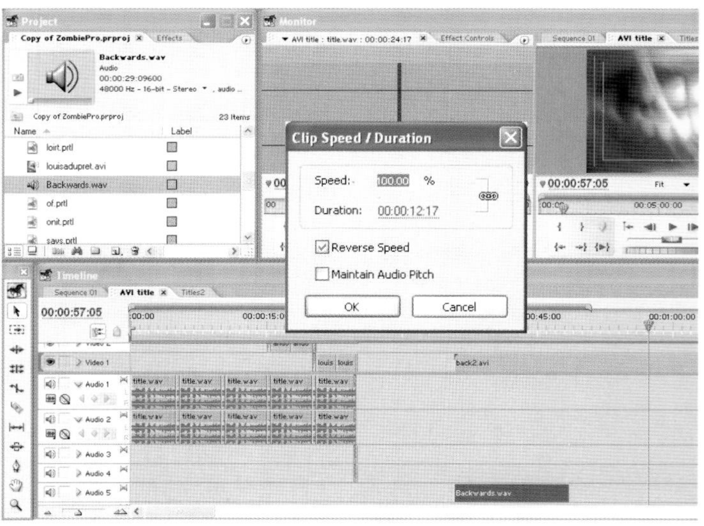

27 *Of course, finesse can be infinite. There is one last audio track, though, that I've had in mind since cutting the video. The singer was required to learn to mime her chorus backward in order that this part of the video could be reversed in the promo to create an awkwardness to her now forward movement and the environment around her. While shooting, the singer had very cleverly learned her lines backward and sung them as appropriate. Taking the audio of this to the* Timeline*, I'm reversing it for a WAV of the singer singing very strangely forward.*

28 *It's just a pay-off, a nod and a wink to the singer's efforts, and it certainly doesn't need to fit the current audio slot perfectly. As a pay-off, though, it needs to stop at precisely the rip point and therefore fits onto one of the razored rip tracks without needing its own. I'm not interested in distorting any of the strange singing and neither will I be altering the speed to fit. This dictates the in-point, and the voice coming into the audio sits quite happily in the sequence.*

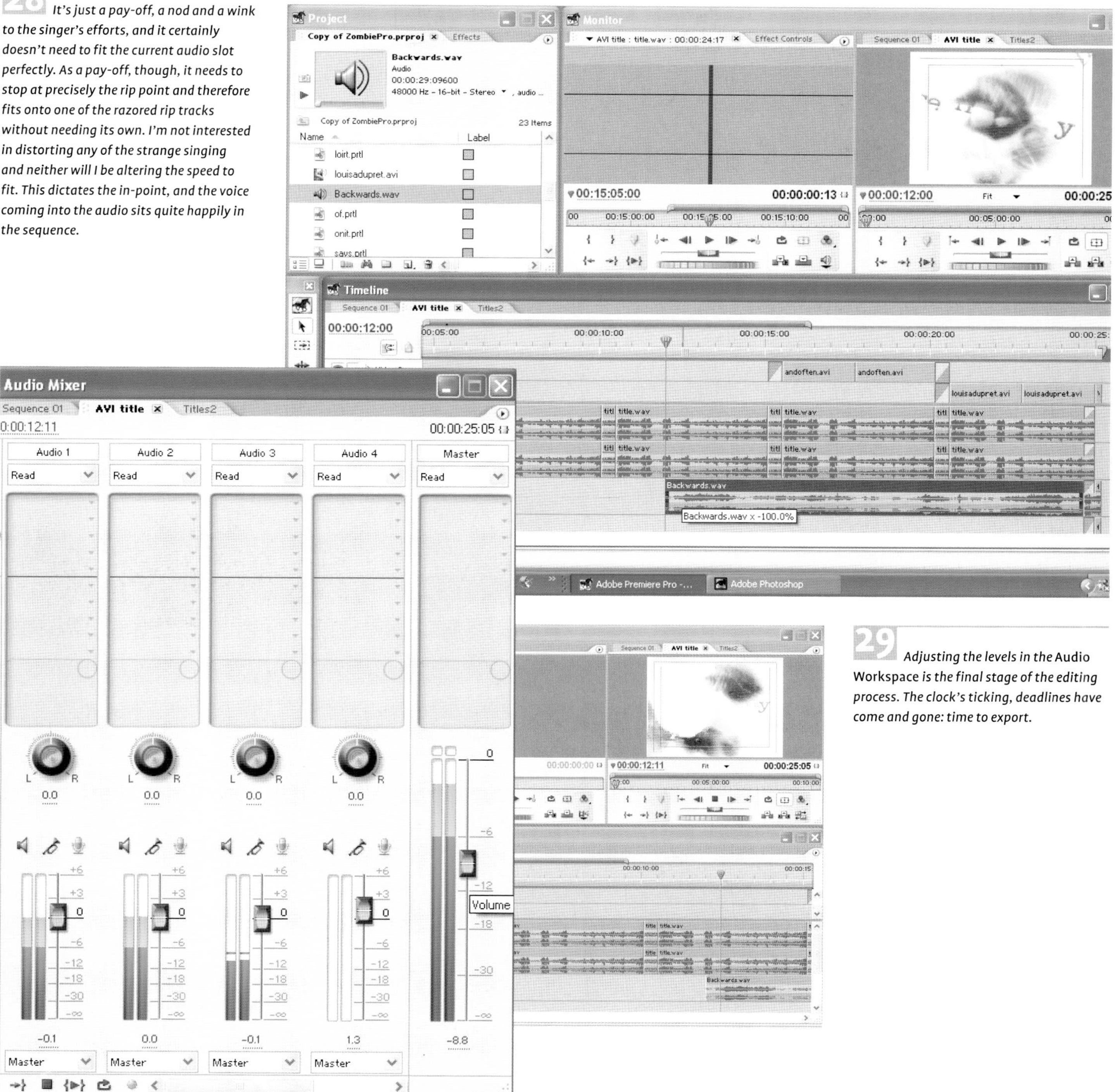

29 *Adjusting the levels in the* Audio Workspace *is the final stage of the editing process. The clock's ticking, deadlines have come and gone: time to export.*

Exporting, printing, and analysis

Just as the ideal is for you to be working with a production as a separate and complete AVI on the *Timeline*, so in return, you should be providing a separate and complete title sequence in a compatible file format.

Exporting a title sequence can be just as valuable as an end product as it is providing a reference to see what, if anything, requires changing. In the real world, beyond that of Premiere Pro and a computer monitor, things can look very different. In this respect, an exported file can be as much of a continuing process as may be the final stage. This is particularly relevant when it comes to issues of pixelation, colors, or screen-safety—and all of these for broadcast requirements. Exporting doesn't have to be a hit-or-miss affair, though.

Graphics and glyphs are incredibly sensitive to being encoded. Everything that you've ever done to them—effects and filters—ruins their original purity. And even their purity was never going to live up to what you once saw on a computer monitor. Sometimes, in fact, the cleaner the graphics and glyphs are, the more they're inclined to show us what they're made of (the digital equivalent of slugs and snails and puppy dogs' tails).

The less compression, the better. Once saved, a file will tell you exactly how large it is, an indication of how much compression has been applied for the file format. Compression is the way that pixels

Work with your scopes. If you're not using external monitoring devices, use Premiere Pro's to go through your title and see if there might be any problem areas when you do export.

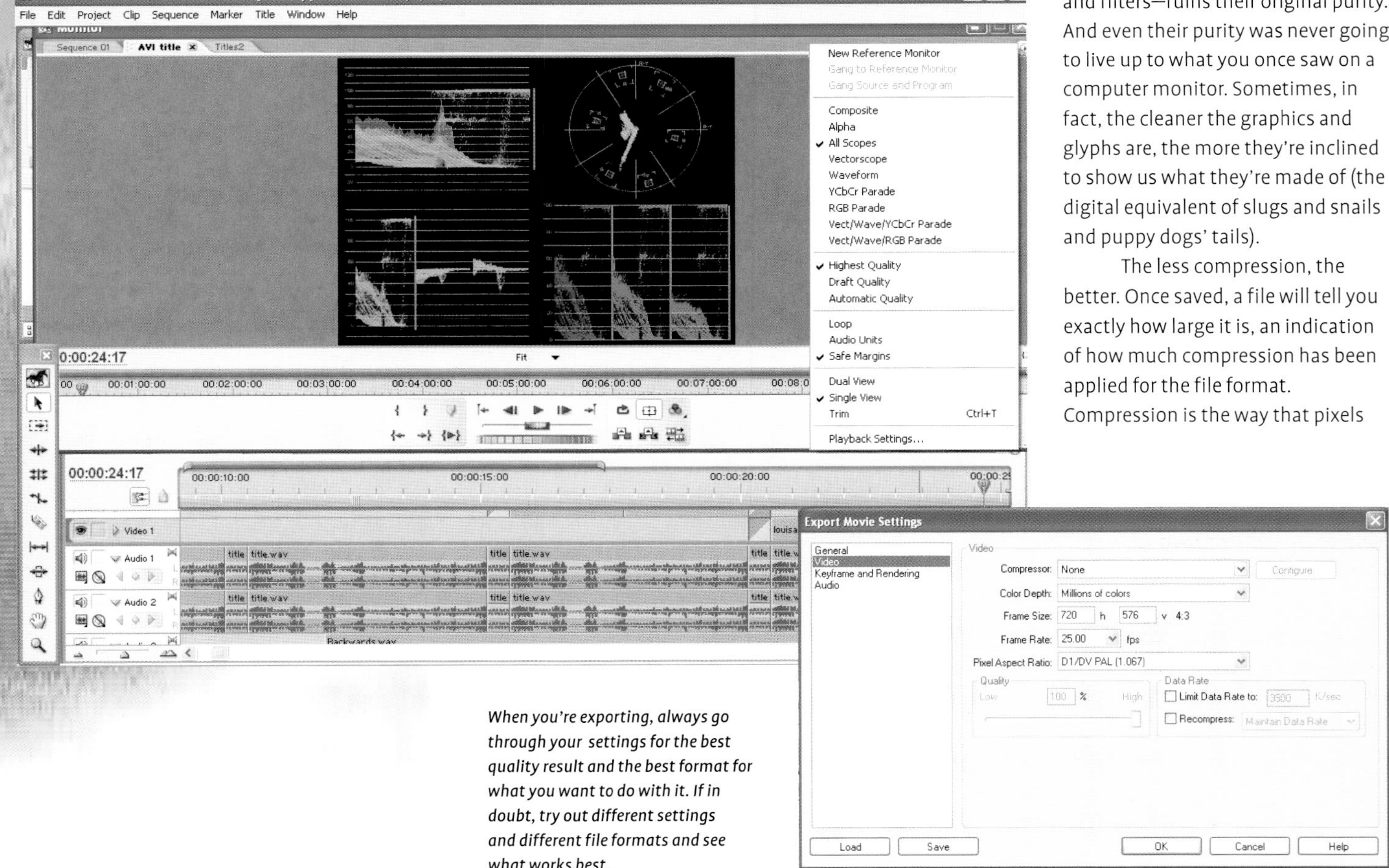

When you're exporting, always go through your settings for the best quality result and the best format for what you want to do with it. If in doubt, try out different settings and different file formats and see what works best.

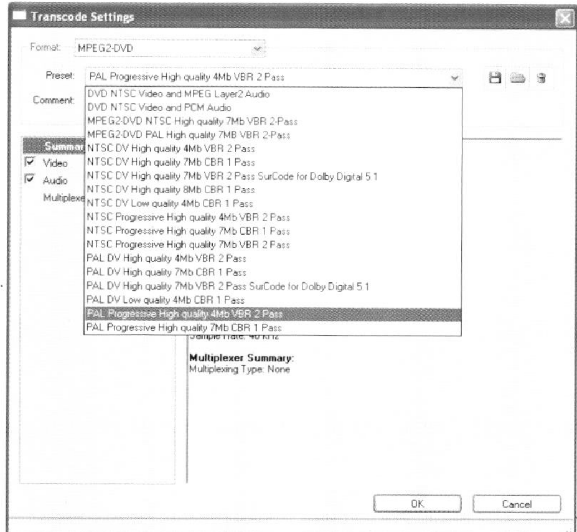

are treated, and different codecs compress using different algorithms. Therefore, depending on the codec, your colors may change, you might find yourself with fewer pixels, or they might be read at lower rates. Premiere Pro's titling is a cut above the rest. It's versatile, flexible—and can be pushed as far as you want. But the final, creative decisions now rest with you, of course.

One thing to remember, though, before you even contemplate putting your work through an encoder, is that all those graphics files and *Title Designer* files churning around with graded, effected, manipulated, transitional video are high maintenance for any hard drive. Premiere Pro is getting better at working in realtime, but make sure you save often and render often.It may just save you from rendering yourself unconscious.

If you're taking it back into Premiere Pro, the Adobe Media Encoder might be a better alternative. Even if you're not, it's loaded with good options for encoding PAL or NTSC MPEG1, MPEG2, Real, AVI, and MOV at constant or variable bitrates. The option for a Progressive Scan output can also make a big difference to the quality of text and graphics, especially for imported Photoshop files or freeze-frames.

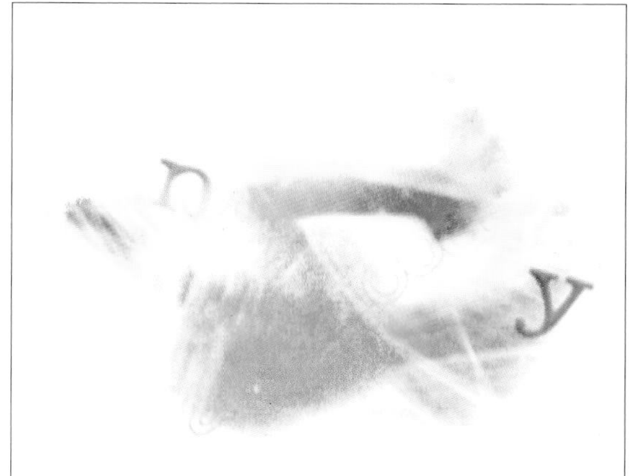

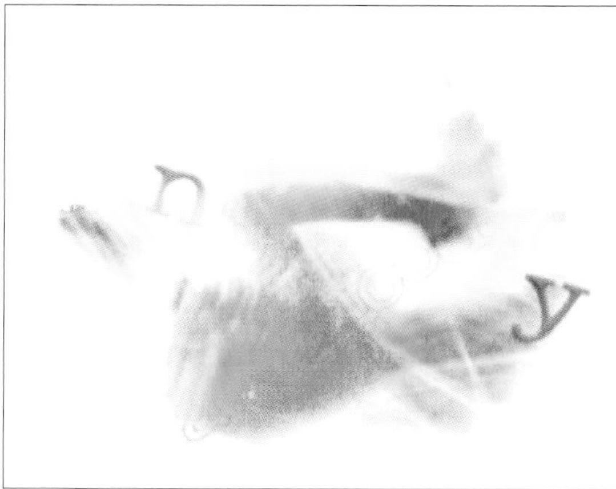

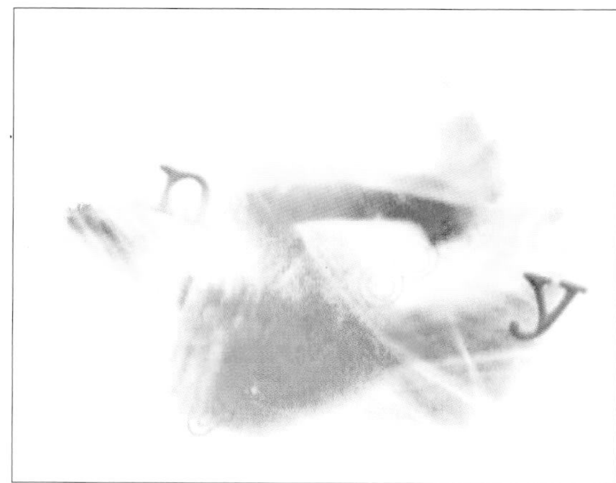

Unfair and subtle, this, but these are exported frames from imported (clockwise from top left) Windows AVI, Quicktime MOV, DVD MPEG-2 and DVD MPEG-2 Progressive Scan files. Respectively, their size is 770,196KB, 341,410KB, 12,279KB, and 12,271KB, giving some indication of how much each is compressed. The AVI, for information, remains uncompressed.

The choice is yours...

glossary

A/B-Roll: A system of video editing where video, taken from two or more sources, is placed on two separate tracks—Video A and Video B—and transitions applied between the two. Premiere Pro does away with this, using multiple tracks that can be grouped and nested on a single timeline, offering more flexibility and control.

Alpha matte: A feature used to define areas of an image that will drop out, appearing transparent when previewed or rendered.

Anchor Point: A control point used in Premiere to control the motion or intensity of an effect in relation to the timeline.

Artefacts: A fault in a still or digital video image (e.g. ugly blocks of color), appearing as a result of limitations in digital processing.

Aspect ratio: The ratio of the width of a picture to its height. This is 4:3 for conventional TV and 16:9 for Widescreen video.

AVI: Audio Video Interleaved. The default file format for captured video files on Windows systems.

Bevel: A chamfered edge applied to an element in an image to give it a simple 3D effect.

Bezier: A method of creating curves from straight lines by adding control points on the line, which can then be dragged in and out to increase or decrease the curvature.

Bin: A virtual "container" used by a video-editing application to store audio and video clips, titles, or stills ready for use on the timeline.

Bitmap: A digital image stored as a grid of pixels, each with its own color and brightness values. When viewed actual pixel size or below, this resembles a continuous tone image, such as a photograph.

Chroma: Chrominance. A technical name for the color component of a video signal.

Codec: An algorithm used to decompress incoming data from a broadcast signal or DVD, and compress data during the export process.

Color Picker: A dialog in an image or video-editing application that enables the user to choose a color from an onscreen palette.

Composite: A video signal combining chrominance and luminance information in a single video stream.

Crawl: A title where text moves sideways from one screen edge to the other (usually right to left).

Cross Fade: An audio transition where audio from one track fades out as audio from another fades in, creating a smooth mix.

CRT: Cathode Ray Tube. The technology behind standard TV sets. A cathode ray tube uses electron guns to project RGB (red, green, and blue) beams of light at a phosphor lining on the inner face of the screen.

De-interlace: Each 'frame' in a video actually contains two 'fields' of alternating vertical lines which are combined together (interlaced) to create the frame. This isn't often noticeable in motion, but if a still image is taken from the video, the lines or a slight blur may become visible. De-interlacing is the process of combining the two fields into a single frame without these effects.

Dissolve: A video transition where the video from one track fades out to be replaced by the video from another track fading in.

DVE (Digital Video Effect): A special effect or transition enabled by digital video processing, often employing complex motion controlled through paths.

ECW (Effects Control Window): A Premiere Pro dialog enabling fine control of the settings and motion of a digital effect.

Edit Line: In a video-editing application, the line on the timeline showing the position of the current frame during playback or editing.

Encode: The process of exporting video to a particular format, usually involving some compression.

Export: The preparation and saving of a clip, image, or finished movie, either for editing in another application, or as a final file for distribution and playback.

Eyedropper: A tool used to sample color values from a clip or image so that it can be duplicated and used in another operation.

Fade: A common transition. In a fade-in the image starts at black, increasing in color until it reaches regular levels. In a fade-out, the image darkens, then fades to black.

Fill: An operation that covers a specific area of the screen or a screen object with color and/or texture.

Font: A complete typeface, consisting of a full range of letter shapes and common punctuation marks, all sharing a common look and style.

Glyph: An individual letter-shape, specific to a particular font.

Hard cut: A cut from one clip to another, without any transition to soften the shift.

HSL: Hue, Saturation, Lightness. A common color model, which defines colors by the Hue (the pure color), the Saturation (the strength of the color varying from a light tint to the full Hue), and the Lightness (or the brightness, ranging from near black to near white).

Kerning: The adjustment of spacing between two characters to improve the look of a piece of text and ensure its readability. The degree of kerning differs between different sets of characters, to take account of the individual letter shapes.

Key: The process of electronically substituting an image or sequence into an area within a video picture. Used, for example, in TV weather broadcasts where a presenter, actually standing in front of a blue or green screen, appears in front of a computer-generated weather map. The overlaid image is keyed to a specified color (Chroma Key) or brightness level (Luma Key).

Keyframe: Used to control motion effects or animation, a keyframe is a point on the timeline where specified changes to an effect or object will take place. The editing application then interpolates how this will effect the frames between keyframes to create a smooth result.

Layer: A feature taken from still image-editing applications, a layer behaves like a transparent acetate sheet to which moving or still video can be assigned. Layers can then be made more or less transparent, deleted, or have their order changed to make compositional changes or montage elements together.

Leading: The space between a line of text and the line below, named after the metal strips that separated them in traditional presses.

Legal Colors: Colors that fit within the standard gamut set by the governing broadcast bodies in a given territory. Computer monitors can display some colors that fall outside these ranges, and particular colors with high luminance values (particularly reds) are forbidden by the major broadcast authorities.

Lower-third: A common form of caption which usually appears in the lower-third of the screen.

Luma: Luminance. The technical name for the brightness component of a video signal.

Matte: An area of the screen designed to mask or reveal video running on another layer in order to create composite images.

MPEG: Motion Picture Expert Group, responsible for the MPEG-1, MPEG-2, MP3, and MPEG-4 formats.

Noise: A digital artefact, which usually takes the form of unwanted speckles of color. Noise can appear if you shoot in dark conditions.

NTSC: National Television Standards Committee. The TV standard for the USA, Canada, Japan, and other countries in South America and the Pacific region. NTSC uses 525 lines made up of two interlaced fields scanning at 29.97 frames per second or 59.94 fields per second.

Opacity: A setting that controls the extent to which a layer in an image or video is solid or transparent.

PAL: Phase Alternation Line. The standard TV display format for the UK, most other European countries (excluding France), Australia, New Zealand, and several African nations. PAL is made up of 625 lines, using 25 frames of two interlaced fields, or 50 fields per second.

Pan: In video, a smooth camera movement where the horizontal angle of the camera changes to show more of the scene or follow a character. In audio, the movement of a particular sound or instrument so that it shifts from left to right (or visa versa) in the stereo field.

Pixel: A single block of color on a computer monitor or TV screen. Pixels on a PC monitor are square. Pixels in a video or TV image are not.

Resolution: A measure of detail in an image, defined by the number of pixels making up the image, and the quantity of those pixels contained in a defined space. The usual measurement is pixels per inch.

RGB: Red, Green, Blue. The additive color model used for TV and computer screens, where all colors are formed from combinations of red, green, and blue light.

Roll: A common form of moving title, most often seen in end-credits, where text scrolls upwards from the bottom of the screen.

Screen-safe: Most TV screens cut off a certain area around the border of the video image during playback. The screen safe (or title-safe) area is the central region of the frame, safe from this involuntary exclusion.

Scrubbing: The action of moving through a video, frame by frame.

SECAM: Sequential Couleur avec Memoire. TV system developed in Russia and adopted by France. It is very similar to PAL 625 but employs a modified system of color encoding.

Telecine: The conversion of film to a TV or video format.

Template: A ready-made project containing all the fundamental elements—often styled for a particular purpose—which can then be tweaked to fit a production.

Timeline: In video editing, the workspace in which audio and video clips can be placed or layered on top of each other in order to assemble the project.

Transition: A visual effect used to transport the viewer from one part of the story to another. The most common transition is a dissolve.

Truetype: A common font standard, used in Windows applications. TrueType fonts should be scalable without losing resolution.

Type Path: A straight or curved line used to position a line of text across the screen. If you move the path, the text will shift to follow it.

White balance: A control used to establish pure white in an image under different lighting conditions, which should enable other colors to be captured correctly.

index

Acknowledgments

Sean Moody, Tech Support
Barrie Dunn, Spiritual Succor
Michelle Horton, Graffix Genius
David and Sarah Fleet, Marital Aid
Barry at the Irish Rover and Lancaster County Prison, NY
Adobe and The Premiere Pro Forum
The NMEC Press Office (RIP)

Thanks to the following for the use of stills in this book:

20th Century Fox Home Entertainment
Anchor Bay Entertainment
Channel 4/American Playhouse/KQED San Francisco/Acorn Media
Columbia TriStar
Dimension Films
Home Box Office Entertainment
Horse Creek Entertainment
Image Entertainment
Momentum Pictures
New Line Cinema
Paramount
Pioneer Entertainment
Touchstone Home Video
Trimark Home Video
TriStar Pictures
Troma Entertainment Inc
Universal
Warner Home Video